Program Evaluation: Patterns and Directions

Edited by Eleanor Chelimsky, U.S. General Accounting Office

Published by The American Society for Public Administration

PUBLIC ADMINISTRATION LIBRARY
Published by the American Society for Public Administration

PAR Classics Series

I. **Professional Public Executives**
    Edited by Chester A. Newland

II. **Perspectives on Budgeting**
    Edited by Allen Schick

III. **Approaches to Organizing**
    Edited by Robert T. Golembiewski

IV. **American Public Administration: Patterns of the Past**
    Edited by James Fesler

V. **Federalism and Intergovernmental Relations**
    Edited by Deil S. Wright and Harvey L. White

VI. **Program Evaluation: Patterns and Directions**
    Edited by Eleanor Chelimsky

Monograph Series

1. **Applying Professional Standards and Ethics in the '80s: A Workbook and Study Guide for Public Administrators**
    Edited by Herman Mertins, Jr. and Patrick J. Hennigan

2. **"The Study of Administration" Revisited**
    James D. Carroll and Alfred M. Zuck

The American Society for Public Administration
1120 G Street, N.W., Suite 500
Washington, D.C. 20005

International Standard Book Number: 0-936678-08-9. Price: $12.95.

Note: The views and opinions expressed by the author are her own and should not be construed to be the policy or position of the General Accounting Office.

Contents

ELEANOR CHELIMSKY

Old Patterns and New Directions in Program Evaluation

The present volume in the *PAR* Classics Series is intended to retrace some of the steps taken by program evaluation over the past few decades and to illustrate those steps through a number of articles selected from among those published by the *Public Administration Review* over a period spanning more than 40 years. It will surprise no one to discover, given the evolution of program evaluation, that the largest number of those articles appeared in *PAR* during the 1970-1984 period. However, the incremental development of the evaluative art—joining a technique here to a method there—has allowed the inclusion of articles from earlier decades, although their authors may not have thought that they were writing about program evaluation.

This essay seeks to relate some of the important milestones traversed by program evaluation, many of which are reflected in the pages of *PAR*. It is written essentially from a federal government viewpoint, although many of the problems and solutions discussed apply to state and local government evaluation as well. The paper looks first at the origins and development of program evaluation (circa 1870 to the present) and next at the emerging consensus in the field on the "rules of the game": that is, the definition, purposes, and currently accepted types of program evaluation. It is, in fact, this latter consensus (on types of program evaluation) that furnished the basis for selecting the *PAR* articles in Part I of this volume. The essay then turns to two major controversies in the field which have marked both the methodological development and use of program evaluation; Part II of this volume reflects those aspects of the controversies which appeared in *PAR*. Finally, consideration is given to the problem of the organization of the evaluation function (Part III of this volume is devoted to *PAR* articles which examined this issue), to the relationship between that organization and the use of evaluation findings, and to the changes in organization that would allow improved use of those findings.

Origins and Development of Program Evaluation

Program evaluation is neither very new nor very revolutionary. It has, in fact, been around for a long time, in one form or another, developing slowly and incrementally under various guises and disguises. Some trace its origins to the Age of Reform in England, where evaluations of educational achievement conducted in the year 1870 brought quite contemporary recommendations for "incentives" to teachers in the form of "payment by results."[1] Others think history's first evaluation took place earlier, when a steward of Nebuchadnezzar's systematically tested the effects of a vegetable diet on the "fairness" and "fatness" of Daniel, Shadrak, Meshak, and Abednego.[2]

Whatever its origins, however, interest in the effects of treatments—or of government programs and policies—is hardly recent. The ability of evaluators to respond reasonably well to that interest, on the other hand, has developed remarkably over the past 20 years or so, as the gradual result of two apparently disparate and independent streams of intellectual inquiry.

One of these streams was the effort, begun during the 1950s, to rationalize the management and resource allocation of defense missions and programs, an effort which eventually grew into the Department of Defense's Planning, Programming, and Budgeting System (PPBS). Only one component of PPBS involved the retrospective activities of program evaluation, however; instead, the main thrust of the effort was on planning, so that the techniques it fostered, such as policy analysis, for example,[3] were essentially tailored by PPBS to delineate likely future effects rather than to identify the actual, observed effects of implemented, existing programs or policies. Developed largely by economists, these analytical techniques—policy analysis, cost-benefit analysis, cost-effectiveness analysis, systems analysis, operations research—all had economics as their core.[4] Among the many economists whose work contributed to this extraordinary burst of new, systematic, quantitative methods for examining public programs and policies, Charles Hitch and Roland McKean are surely two of the most creative and influential.[5]

The other stream, involving such fields as education, public health, or crime and delinquency (rather than defense), antedates the first in that, by the 1950s, large-scale retrospective evaluations were already being commonly performed, using methods of applied social research such as the survey, or computer-assisted statistical analysis.[6] This path of evaluative development, however, was not the achievement of any one discipline but instead received major methodological contributions from a broad array of fields including psychology, sociology, economics, political science, applied statistics, and anthropology. Especially important in the evolution of this stream of evaluative thought during the 15-year period between 1948 and

1963 were the works of Donald Campbell,[7] Lee Cronbach,[8] and Paul Lazarsfeld.[9]

Little by little, over time, the two paths of evaluative inquiry have become less distinct and today it is not uncommon to find a mixture of techniques from both streams used together in a single study.[10] The yield has thus been an increasingly rich repertoire of methods for use in answering different types of questions about policies and programs. This, of course, is not an unusual way for an art or science to mature, and may, in fact, be a very good, if not the best, way. Tocqueville, having held 150 years ago that "the art of administration is undoubtedly a science," pointed out that

> no science can be improved if the discoveries and observations of successive generations are not connected together in the order in which they occur. One man in the short space of his life remarks a fact, another conceives an idea; the former invents a means of execution, the latter reduces a truth to a formula; and mankind gathers the fruits of individual experience on its way and gradually forms the sciences.[11]

Program evaluation has been evolving in just such a fashion, although the timelines involved concern generations rather than lifetimes or long cycles, and although the patterns of evolution have been different for the two evaluative streams.

On the one hand, the applied social research stream of program evaluation seems to have developed with relative steadiness, stimulated first by the Great Society's reform program of the sixties—that is, the "War on Poverty"—with its need to find out what effects its investments were having, and later, by the Nixon and Carter administrations' concern with social program costs, and their consequent efforts to gain improved efficiency through evaluative information.

PPBS, on the other hand, rose quite suddenly to fame and glory. Barely a glimmer on the national consciousness in 1960, its proclaimed success in the Defense Department by 1965 was such that President Johnson ordered its implementation in all agencies of government, despite the fact that "not a single study of this important experiment was undertaken (or at least published) before the decision was made to spread it around the land."[12] But by 1970, only five years later, much of the excitement had faded as analysts came to recognize, often in the pages of *PAR,* the technical prematurity of some of their efforts and the remarkable optimism of some of their expectations. Once again, as with performance budgeting, the assumption had been made that the needed data systems and measures with which to evaluate program outcomes could be quickly and easily developed. With hindsight, of course, and with the knowledge brought by 20 additional years of technical experience, it now seems obvious that the size of the data base and measurement infrastructure needed for something as big as "government-wide PPBS'' made lengthy research and development a prerequisite. As the adventure came to an end, many realized that, in the words of one ardent PPBS proponent, it would take "many years to develop the kinds of output measures we need to understand what we are getting for our money."[13]

The fact that there had been little prior development and testing of measures to represent program outputs was an obstacle to the planning and evaluation of those programs that PPBS could not overcome. Even more, however, the lack of an evaluative information base that could speak to actual experience with existing programs weakened the credibility of estimates for the future made by the various analytical techniques used by PPBS. In effect, measuring future costs and benefits of alternative policies and programs is greatly assisted by knowledge of the current effects of those (or similar) alternatives. But for most programs and policies, the evaluative information needed to support solidly grounded estimates of the future was lacking. Even today, it is still undergoing development in many areas.

With regard to the controversies about PPBS that appeared in the pages of the *Public Administration Review* over the period 1966-1969, it is interesting to note that these *technical* problems with the approach were not grasped until evidence from PPBS implementation had become utterly unmistakable. Instead, the argument had been almost entirely about which kind of rationality was better: political rationality (that is, the assumption that the democratic and pluralistic virtues of incrementalism led to superior decision-making outcomes via "muddling through"[14]) versus scientific rationality (that is, the belief that the outcomes of the muddling through type of decision making could not be declared good, *a priori,* but needed to be investigated empirically, and hence, the incremental system should be replaced by one which, like PPBS, set up a logical system of planning, measurement, analysis of likely impacts, and decision making, followed by evaluation of what had been achieved[15]). Unfortunately for the planning needs of PPBS, however, the placing of evaluation at the tail end of this process meant that its findings would arrive too late to be useful; instead, evaluation results needed to have been available when the planning started. In other words, PPBS opponents and proponents alike came to realize only later that their argument had not dealt sufficiently with a first-order problem: that of feasibility of implementation. In the words of one author, writing in *PAR* in 1969:

> In past writings I argued that program budgeting would run up against severe political difficulties. . . . Now it is clear that for the narrow purpose of predicting why program budgeting would not work, there was no need to mention political problems at all. It would have been sufficient to say that the wholesale introduction of PPBS presented insuperable difficulties of calculation. All the obstacles previously mentioned . . . may be summed up in a single statement: *no one knows how to do program budgeting.*[16]

On the other hand, the slower governmental growth, a tendency toward project or program (rather than system or systems) applications, and infinitely less lofty expectations, allowed the applied social research stream of program evaluation more time to develop an understanding of which initiatives could and could not yet be undertaken, to increase the development of needed support systems such as data bases, and to sharpen its focus on the professional needs of the developing interdisciplinary field. This is not to belittle the considerable growth that did occur, on the contrary, but simply to note a difference in the type of growth from that experienced by PPBS. In fact, over the single decade spanning the late '60s to the late '70s, the federal funds spent on non-defense program evaluation rose from about $20 million to about $180 million. The number of people who could lay reasonable claim to the title of program evaluator went from a handful to several thousands. "The number of studies, the number of evaluation units in government agencies, the number of private research firms, the academic departments having programs in evaluation, the number of professional societies and journals devoted to evaluation, the number of legislatively mandated requirements for evaluation, and the actual use of evaluation findings by legislators [and] managers all increased dramatically during this brief period."[17]

It is important to note that while the problems of PPBS did end in the system's demise, they, nonetheless, were useful to program evaluation in that they confirmed and clarified for many policy-makers and analysts the basic, enduring, governmental need for a program evaluation information base. It was not a startling lesson of the PPBS experience to learn that scientific rationality may be only dubiously achievable in government; many people had already suspected this. What *was* crucial was the discovery that the ordinary "muddling through" of political rationality *also* benefits from sound information—especially empirical information about past program performance—as a regular part of the normal, incremental political process. PPBS had demonstrated both the need for an evaluative information base and the fact that it did not exist. At the same time, the progress being made in applied social research showed that such an information base could be developed—slowly and piecemeal, perhaps, but steadily and cumulatively—over time.

That many policy makers had become aware of this is reflected in the numbers of administrative data bases—whose most important purpose was to allow the monitoring and evaluation of government programs—that were developed in the executive branch over the 1965-1975 period. Title VII of the 1974 Congressional Budget and Impoundment Control Act is another illustration of that awareness, making as it does a very strong statement about the legislative importance and utility of program evaluation, and directing the General Accounting Office to develop its activities in this area.

In summary, two parallel streams of inquiry have contributed to the development of program evaluation as it emerges today. One stream proceeded rather gradually, across the multidisciplinary fields and methods of applied social research. The other, developed mostly by economists, had an explosive growth during the '60s, culminating in the federal development, implementation, and demise of PPBS (1960-1970). Both streams pioneered or used and diffused methods (for example, surveys, case studies, experiments, operations research, longitudinal design, meta-evaluation) which have become part of the everyday language of program evaluation. The controversies about scientific and political rationality which marked the PPBS adventure in the '60s, have been much less salient in recent program evaluation debates, although they may be reflected to some degree in the 1970s arguments about the relative merits of quantitative versus qualitative analysis. In any case, more and more people are now trained in the use of quantitative techniques generally and social science research methods in particular, and the issues which have marked the development of program evaluation over the last 10 years have been in a more Tocquevillean mode. As time passes, consensus has been building in the field in many areas. This is particularly true with regard to the definition, purposes, and accepted types of program evaluation: that is, what might be called the rules of the game.

The Rules of the Game:
Definition, Purposes, and Types of Program Evaluation

Like many scientific endeavors, then, program evaluation has had a long development followed by a formative period during which the rules were always open to debate. Over the 1965-1980 period, in particular, perhaps because of the rapid rise and fall of PPBS, a major issue in the public administration literature had been the definition of program evaluation and how it was related to (or differed from) policy analysis.

Anthony had already noted the prospective character of policy analysis in 1965[18] and Wildavsky in 1969 in the pages of *PAR* (see note 3). Beckman made it official in 1977 when he formally defined policy analysis as "anticipatory," looking "toward decisions which are to be made."[19] This, of course, is significantly different from program evaluation, which in Poland's words, "involves a retrospective examination of program operations. It looks to the past to provide a guide to the future."[20]

That policy analysis is prospective while program evaluation is retrospective has importance essentially because this fact influences the kinds of questions each can address. The emphasis of policy analysis is on *likely* effects (or estimates, or projections); a typical policy analysis question might ask, "What will be the likely effects on hospital use if bed supply is restricted?'' The focus of evaluation, on the other hand, is on *actual* effects (that is, on what has been observed, what has already occurred or is existentially occurring); a typical evaluative question might ask, ''What happened to hospital use after bed supply growth was restricted?''

The grounding of evaluation findings in actual effects not only gives them considerable solidity but also makes them an excellent point of departure for policy analysis calculations. It is also true, however, that this two-step process can be somewhat lengthy. It is therefore necessary, as was learned through PPBS, to begin building the evaluative foundation for policy analysis estimates considerably in advance of the anticipated need for those estimates.

The debate on the question of definition also existed within the program evaluation community itself during this 1965-1980 period, but took a somewhat different form. Here, the question of definition had more to do with developing appropriate techniques and methodologies for answering different kinds of evaluation questions than with distinguishing evaluation from other types of analytical inquiry. This debate soon broadened further to include issues of intent and direction (what are the purposes of program evaluation?), as well as use (who are the clients for evaluation and what are their individual information needs?). With the publication of two sets of evaluation standards, in 1981-1982,[21] some consensus began to emerge in the field, at least with regard to the definition and purposes of program evaluation, if not yet on use or users.

Evaluation Definition, Purposes, and Typical Approaches

How then can program evaluation be defined today? One change that has occurred over the years which is reflected in the recent evaluation standards is that evaluation is no longer confined to the examination of program results or program effectiveness. However, it does generally continue to be viewed as retrospective.[22] Thus, a reasonably well accepted definition might be that program evaluation is the application of systematic research methods to the assessment of program design, implementation, and effectiveness.

The debate about evaluation purposes during the 1965-1980 period involved consideration of the different reasons for which evaluation had been undertaken in the past. These reasons included the congressional need for information on executive branch accountability in the legislative oversight process; the general need for new knowledge about public programs; and the program manager's need for continuous reporting on the status and effects of new or ongoing programs.[23] Today, a typical categorization of purpose might assume that evaluations of government programs serve both general audiences (such as the public or the media) and individual public decision makers with particular information needs *vis-à-vis* those programs. These decision makers may be in the executive or legislative branches of government, they may play management or policy roles, and they may need information from evaluation for three very broad kinds of purposes:

- for *policy formulation*—that is, to assess and/or justify the need for a new program;
- for *policy execution*—that is, to ensure that a program is implemented in the most cost/effective way; and
- for *accountability* in public decision making—that is, to determine the effectiveness of an operating program and the need for its continuation, modification, or termination.

These purposes have specific implications for the kinds of issues evaluations may be asked to address. For example, the purpose of policy formulation, as it applies to new programs, may require information from evaluation that includes:

- information on the problem (or threat) addressed by the program (how big is it? what is its frequency and direction? how is it changing?);
- information on the results of past programs or related efforts that attempted to deal with the problem (or threat) (were those programs feasible? successful? what difficulties did they encounter?); and
- information allowing the selection of one alternative program over another (what are the likely comparative costs and benefits? what kinds of growth records were experienced?).

The evaluative information required for policy execution, as it applies either to new or to existing programs, is quite different from that required for policy formulation. It includes:

- information on program implementation (such as the degree to which the program is operational, how similar it is across sites, whether it conforms to the policies and expectations formulated, how much it costs, how stakeholders feel about it, whether there are major problems of service delivery or of error, fraud and abuse, etc.);
- information on program management (such as the degree of control over expenditures, the qualifications and credentials of personnel, the allocation of resources, the use of program information in decision making, etc.); and
- ongoing information on the current state of the problem or threat addressed by the program (is the problem growing? is it diminishing? is it

diminishing enough so that the program is no longer needed? is it changing in terms of its significant characteristics?).

The purpose of accountability, as it applies to both new and existing programs, requires information from evaluation which again differs markedly from that required for the other two policy purposes. This includes:

- information on program outcomes (what happened as a result of program implementation?);
- information on the degree to which the program made, or is making, a difference (that is, what change in the problem or threat occurred that can be directly attributed to the program?); and
- information on the unexpected (as well as the expected) effects of the programs (e.g., was a program of drug education accompanied by an increase in the use of drugs?).

Not only do these purposes have implications for the kinds of issues evaluations may be asked to address, however, they also have implications for the types of evaluation approaches that are likely to be needed, given those purposes.

Types of Evaluation Approaches

With the close of the 1970s, as noted above, the program evaluation field had matured sufficiently to agree on standards for evaluation practice. In particular, the standards developed by the Evaluation Research Society—addressing program evaluation practice in all topical areas—identified six types of routinely conducted approaches to program evaluation.

(1) *Front-end analysis*

This approach involves evaluative work that is typically done before deciding to move ahead with a new program. As such, it is similar to planning and may thus be prospective in its overall orientation. Typically, front-end analysis primarily addresses policy formulation types of questions, using prior evaluation findings as well as extant data, to estimate likely program feasibility and effects.

(2) *Evaluability assessment*

This approach may be used to answer policy formulation questions by comparing a program's assumptions against its stated objectives, and by asking normative questions about the reasonableness of those assumptions and the likelihood that the projected program activities can fulfill the program's objectives. Evaluability assessment is also used to answer policy execution questions by describing the characteristics of actual program implementation and comparing program objectives with existing program activities. Finally, this approach serves to determine the feasibility and usefulness of performing a later full-scale evaluation of the program's effectiveness; if the latter determination is positive, the approach lays the groundwork for such an evaluation. In that sense, an evaluability assessment may be the first phase of a larger evaluation effort which seeks to answer accountability questions. The focus of evaluability assessment questions may thus be retrospective insofar as accountability or policy execution questions are involved, or prospective, when the questions relate to policy formulation.

(3) *Process evaluation*

This is a form of evaluation that either stands alone or is developed in combination with another type of evaluation. It is always retrospective. As a stand-alone, its purpose is usually to describe and analyze the processes of implemented program activities—management strategies, operations, costs, interactions among clients and practitioners, and so forth—so as to improve them. In combination with another evaluation type (most often an effectiveness evaluation), its purposes may include: (a) helping to determine the design of the effectiveness evaluation or (b) helping to explain its findings. In the first case, the process evaluation will precede the effectiveness evaluation; in the second, the two will be coordinated more or less simultaneously. Thus, the process evaluation addresses policy execution issues, but also helps effectiveness evaluations to answer accountability questions as well.

(4) *Effectiveness or impact evaluation*

Like process evaluation, this evaluation approach is once again retrospective. It seeks to find out how well a program has been working. To do this, it is necessary to be able to show that changes observed are, in fact, the result of the program, rather than that of other factors or forces. This means that the design for this kind of evaluation needs to include a basis for comparison that permits an understanding of what conditions would have been in the absence of the program, or in the presence of alternatives to the program. This, of course, is the quintessential accountability question ("What were the effects of the program?"), but it is also true that effectiveness evaluations are needed for policy execution purposes as well. Findings from effectiveness evaluations of the past also figure prominently in policy formulation efforts, because they provide a sound basis for estimating likely effects of new and similar programs.

(5) *Program and problem monitoring*

This evaluation approach is different from the other five in that it is a continuous, rather than a single-shot process. Its function is to inform on problem characteristics, or to track program or problem progress (long-term or short-term) in several areas (for example, size of or change in the problem addressed by the program, program compliance with policy, changing spread or characteristics of service delivery, etc.). As such, it may address either policy formulation or execution purposes. However, the administrative data systems that develop around the program and problem monitoring effort can also be used to answer accountability types of questions via time-series analysis. The extent to which time-series analysis is possible, however, depends on the quality, completeness, and consistency over time of the data systems involved.

(6) *Meta-evaluation or evaluation synthesis*

This is a form of evaluation that re-analyzes findings from one or a number of existing evaluations to determine what has been learned about a policy or program. Depending on the availability of evaluations and other empirical work, this approach can address many different evaluative questions, including those about the effectiveness of the program and about the extent of existing knowledge in a given program or problem area. As such, meta-evaluation is highly versatile, capable of serving all three types of evaluation purposes: accountability and policy formulation (by informing on what is already known about program effectiveness), and policy execution (by informing on what is unknown and, hence, what the research agenda for program implementation needs to include).

These six approaches, described and classified by the Evaluation Research Society, today constitute the everyday repertoire of program evaluation. As such, they have made a convenient framework here for choosing among *PAR* articles. Part I of this volume thus brings these abstract evaluation types to life by presenting studies exemplifying their approaches that appeared in the pages of *PAR* between 1941 and 1983. In addition, a cumulative reading of the articles in Part I demonstrates the way in which program evaluation has built upon elements from many different forms of research—sample surveys, field experiments, case studies, etc.—and woven them into the fabric of routine evaluation practice in the 1980s.

This is not, of course, to imply either that the path to the current consensus has been without controversy, or that there are no limitations to that consensus. On the contrary, confrontations have been numerous as the field has matured and some of them are still ongoing. Two problem areas, in particular, have been (and continue to be) important preoccupations for evaluation practitioners. These concern the methodological quality and usefulness of the evaluation product. How good is it? Why is it not used more? These questions came to occupy a larger and larger place in the evaluation literature of the 1970s.

Problems with the Technical Quality and Usefulness of Program Evaluation

Methodological Problems

Two types of problems with methodological quality dominated the evaluation field during the 1970-1980 period. The first type had to do with the relative immaturity of the field. An example of this sort of problem might be the great controversy over process evaluation versus effectiveness evaluation (i.e., randomized field experiments) that marked the early '70s. The second type of problem had to do with misapplications of already well established practice. An example here might be the reporting of strong conclusions about program effectiveness based on an inappropriate design or on improperly executed data collection and analysis. Thus, one type of problem was quite complex, having to do with the disciplinary state-of-the-art, along with disagreements in the field about the role of evaluation (should it focus on program improvement or on accountability?) and about what should be considered acceptable as evidence; the other involved the degree of expertise attained by individual evaluators.

A carryover from PPBS had been the idea that, to be useful for policy, the focus of evaluation always had to be directly on the question of program effectiveness. But an early state-of-the-art problem for program evaluation had been precisely the measurement of program effects. In some cases, evaluators found that outcomes could not be clearly determined, or could not be attributed to a particular program. In other cases, it was felt that, whatever its feasibility, outcome evaluation could not bring answers to program improvement types of questions. In still other cases, outcome evaluation was both possible and appropriate, but well-trained evaluators were not available, and establishing the effects of a program with some degree of conclusiveness requires a good deal of skill, training, and experience in the evaluator. In this sense, the two types of methodological problems were intimately related and the controversy over whether to do effectiveness or process evaluation, in fact, illustrated not one but both types of methodological problems.

What then was the nub of that controversy? Traditionally, in social program evaluation, one of the surest ways to derive findings of program effectiveness was to conduct a randomized field experiment. However, this design proved difficult to apply in certain substantive areas (in evaluating health care programs, for example, because of difficulties in measuring health status and, hence, changes in that status, or in anticrime programs, because of difficulties in measuring the crime rate and hence changes in that crime rate, among other problems). In addition, experimental requirements often could not be accommodated within the framework of public program implementation. A classic statement of the dilemma for the program evaluator was given by Marcia Guttentag in 1973:

> The context within which evaluation research is conducted is too different from the classical experimental model. Most of the assumptions of the model cannot be fulfilled. Further, the researcher does not begin with his own hypothesis. He tries to tease hypotheses out of program administrators. They have goals, not hypotheses. Initially, the researcher abstracts those few hypotheses which he considers "researchable" from the program's broad and multifaceted goals. Given the researcher's constraints, the final hypotheses may have little relevance to what is actually going on in the program. In addition, the researcher cannot randomize subjects or treatments. He cannot control the flow of subjects into or out of programs. When he does try to do so, conflicts with program administrators result. Even when a control group is established, true random assignment of subjects to experimental and control groups is rare. The researcher cannot fulfill most of the criteria for validity required by the classical experimental model.[24]

Further, many evaluators felt that even when it had been feasible to implement randomized field experiments, results had been disappointing in that the questions to which answers had been brought often were not core questions (even though they were researchable questions); that when they had been core questions at the start of the program, the experimental design did not have the flexibility to reflect and respond to changes brought to the program's activities or objectives. Thus the question(s) answered at the end of the evaluation—although possibly relevant at its initiation—often finished by retaining only peripheral interest. Finally, many critics felt that the classical model was costly, lengthy in its execution, and uninterpretable, in any prescriptive sense, for policy.[25]

On the other hand, it was (and is) also the case that the experimental design, when feasible to apply, allows both the determination of program effectiveness and a fairly precise assignment of confidence to the findings which is hard to come by with other designs. And it is also true that there have been many opportunities for applying the classical experimental model which were simply not exploited, either because of inadequate skills in the evaluator (e.g., the design was not a familiar one and was therefore avoided, or was instead poorly executed), or because of uncertain program implementation (e.g., a definable program did not exist; that is, money may have been expended, but not on a specific program involving a clear departure from prior practice), or because of inexpert management (e.g., the evaluator was asked aboard too late and there was no time to develop an adequate evaluation design).

Because of these problems with effectiveness evaluation using the experimental model, a counter emphasis on process evaluation was proposed in the early '70s. Weiss and Rein wrote that evaluative research in action programs should be qualitative rather than quantitative, historically rather than experimentally oriented. The research should "identify the forces which shaped the program, the nature of the opposition encountered, the reasons for success or failure, and the program's unanticipated consequences. . . . The issue in the evaluation of broad-aim programs is not, 'Does it work?' but 'What happened?' "[26]

Arguments between proponents of one type of evaluation over another were frequently heard throughout the 1970s. The first two articles in Part II of this volume discuss the views of both sides in this controversy as they appeared in the pages of *PAR*. The papers by Shipman and Boruch, *et al.*, present the elements of opposition which focused—as noted above—on disagreement about the ability of process evaluation to fill the needs of accountability given the evidence it could produce. For one thing, it was not yet clear just how a process evaluation should be designed and conducted. For another, experimentalists were not convinced that process evaluation could "identify the reasons for success or failure" or "the program's unanticipated consequences" since the evidence it could produce was too weak to counter the possibility that the "results" might be simply the luck of the draw (see Boruch, *et al.*). This difference of opinion about what was acceptable as evidence sprang from a deeper difference of view about the role of evaluation, with experimentalists believing that accountability was its sole *raison d'être,* and process advocates feeling that methods to establish accountability had not resulted in useful prescriptions to improve programs.

Most of the other articles in Part II are concerned to some degree with this controversy which strongly marked the first years of the '70s. As the decade came to an end, however, a certain uniformity of evaluation strategy could be seen to emerge. The dividing line between process and effectiveness evaluation began to blur, since most analysts came to recognize that both approaches elicited valuable information *for different purposes.* That is, since all evaluations did not have to ask questions about accountability, the relevant issue became, not which was better as between process and effectiveness evaluation, but rather which method was appropriate, given a specific evaluation purpose (see the discussion of appropriateness in Boruch, *et al.,* Part II of this volume). As a result, many evaluators started to incorporate components of process evaluation in their designs for examining program effectiveness, either to explain their quantitative outcomes more adequately, or to provide a better bias for prescriptive program recommendations. In the same way, fewer studies were designed which seemed to be exclusively number crunching efforts or were restricted to qualitative methods alone. It was at this point (toward the beginning of the 1980s) that the advocates of standards for program evaluation became realistically hopeful of success. And, of course, as noted earlier, those standards now include both effectiveness evaluation and process evaluation as routinely accepted approaches.

In addition to these issues, another one of equal importance—that of the use (or non-use) of evaluation findings—appeared upon the horizon at about the same time. By about 1975, it had begun to be generally admitted that an important measure—perhaps *the* most important measure—of the worth of the evaluative enterprise was the use that managers and policy makers made of evaluators' conclusions and recommendations. That is, program evaluations not only needed to be of high technical quality, they also needed to be useful. Yet, managers and policy makers were expressing some major dissatisfactions with the usefulness of the evaluations they had sponsored and received. Also, as more and more evaluations were being done, it began to be possible to examine retrospectively—in traditional evaluative fashion—the use that had in fact been made of their findings. Thus, the articles in Part II also mirror the greater interest in the use (and users) of evaluation which developed in parallel with concerns for methodological quality.

Problems in the Use of Evaluation

During the '70s, a considerable amount of analytical effort went into the examination of the uses of evaluation (real and potential) and of some of the obstacles to that use. Carol Weiss' article in Part II of this volume looks at ways of defining the many types of use that may occur. Obstacles to use, however, seemed to be almost as varied as types of use. Those most commonly identified fell into three categories that had to do with: (1) misunderstandings about the process by which evaluation findings may be used; (2) the threatening nature of evaluation; and (3) the relevance, timeliness, and manner of presentation of evaluation findings.

(1) *Misunderstandings About Use*

The expectation most typically advanced during the '70s about how evaluation findings would be used by agencies was that the information generated would be fed back into agency decision making at all levels (that is, for example, into policy making, budgeting, program planning, and the management of specific program operations). In reality, however, evaluation findings are only one input into the decision-making process (see the article by Robert Clark—especially his third proverb—in Part II of this volume). Even that single input, however, may be the result of aggregated efforts. The evaluation contribution to decision making—which many researchers have tried in vain to trace—seems to be rather uncertain in process but quite real in outcome, working slowly and cumulatively, over time. As Seeman put it in 1976:

> The way in which evaluation contributes is through the Chinese water torture approach. Each study adds a little bit of information, only a little bit, and after a good many studies you begin to feel it a little more and a little more and your sensitivity to what's happening has heightened a little and in time you come to a point where you say "I can't stand this anymore" but it wasn't that first drop of water that did it. And so you've accumulated a lot of experience from 50 studies, some of which you've done and some of which you've read about that others have done, and you say, "Well, now I do think I have a sense of where I want to go" and somebody says "What led you to that?' The answer is "I don't have the vaguest idea. This study?—well, I do remember that there was a study that told me that 50 percent of the people were moving in this direction," but that's not the study that led you to make up your mind on which way you wanted to go. So in terms of the impact of evaluation on broad program direction and policies it has that kind of cumulative effect, and those who ask which study led to the termination of a particular program just don't understand either decisionmaking or evaluation.[27]

Another misunderstanding about the use of evaluation findings concerned the belief that the need for evaluation is typically synonymous with a need for new knowledge. In fact, decision makers often ask for evaluations not only for knowledge but for a variety of personal, or "position-taking" reasons as well, for example:

- when they are involved with a program they mistrust and want to protect themselves;
- when the program is in an enemy's province (evaluation here can be an assassination instrument);

- when they themselves expect an attack and need to marshal their defense; and
- when the Congress says they *have* to evaluate.

With the evaluation performed and the report published, still another misunderstanding was that the evaluation's findings would quite naturally wind their way through the agency's information channels to the various points within the organization where decisions were made to which those findings were relevant. Unfortunately, and at least in part because of the ad hoc manner in which many agencies' evaluation functions were organized, this did not always happen all by itself. Instead, when evaluation was not part of a continuing loop of program and agency operations, when it was insulated from other agency activities and performed in isolation, its findings were often ignored where they were the most needed: in program planning, implementation, and budget making.

The significance of these gaps between assumptions about use and reality (see the Weiss article in Part II) is that they show to what degree expectations for use had been misleading with regard to the likely character of that use, and exaggerated with regard to its expected size and spread. As a result, over time, the question about the use of evaluation findings became less, Why are they not used? than, What, in fact, is reasonable use?

(2) *The Threatening Nature of Evaluation*

In an article presented in Part III of this volume, Wildavsky points out that "If you don't know how to make an evaluation, it may be a problem for you but not for anyone else. If you do know how to evaluate, it becomes a problem for others." In fact, a major problem in the use of evaluation has been the threat it poses. Why was evaluation seen as a threat? For two reasons at least. First, an evaluation report is public information which, once generated, cannot be kept secret or limited to the private use of a decision maker. Thus, it provides persons other than the responsible decision maker with information which may adversely affect that decision maker. Second, it is a force for change. It seeks ways to improve an existing set of activities, no matter what the purpose of the evaluation. But improvement always involves a change, rather than the status quo, and change can appear threatening. As James Abert has put it:

> The setting of program objectives and the choosing of evaluations are in themselves very emotional undertakings. Program managers generally are not anxious to do it. In fact, trust, confidence, honor, and many of the more noble aspects of life seem to be strongly challenged by evaluation.[28]

Many groups of evaluators, however, have focused efforts on dealing with the threat posed by evaluation. For example, Barkdoll's article in Part II of this volume presents a recently developed Federal Drug Administration for reducing this problem. Evaluation staff at the General Accounting Office have also reported trying to increase the acceptability and use of evaluation findings by involving the decision maker in the process from beginning to end.

> Recommendations for change, particularly major change, should not come as a surprise at the end of an evaluation. . . . The evaluator should not expect that all recommendations will be acted upon. The higher the risk, the less chance that change will take place from the results of one study, no matter how sound. Also, the greater the decision risk, the greater the need to bring the decision-maker and others along with the study.
>
> Researchers or program evaluators need to have more interaction and communication with the decision-maker. If we are to maximize the chances of results implementation, we need to build a greater sense of trust between the decision-maker and the evaluator—trust in his methodology, trust in the validity of his conclusions and the soundness of his recommendations, and perhaps, most important, trust in the evaluator himself.[29]

It does not appear that the threat posed by evaluation will ever be easy to overcome. However, the degree of the problem *for use* is quite different when the decision maker and the program manager are the same person (as in the Abert citation) and where they are different (as in that of the GAO). This has some implications for the organization of the evaluation function (see below).

(3) *Relevance, Timeliness, and Presentation of Evaluation Products*

Some of the loudest complaints by users about evaluation products, especially during the early '70s, had to do with their relevance and timeliness. It was felt, first, that evaluation findings that were relevant to one set of users (those interested in program improvement aspects of policy execution, for example) had limited utility for users requiring, say, accountability kinds of information. Second, sponsors often wondered whether evaluators were pursuing their own research questions or those of the intended users of the findings. As one evaluation sponsor phrased it in 1978,

> The main thing is to have some clear objectives for your program since without them your research efforts will drift toward studies that fascinate individual investigators but may have little relationship to critical social needs. . . . The values and interests of researchers seldom extend to issues related to effective public utilization of their findings.[30]

Finally, the importance of relevance as an issue in the use of evaluation was reinforced by its relationship to timeliness. These two factors, it was argued, interacted in such a way as to result in evaluation findings that could well be methodologically sound but would have become irrelevant with the passage of time. One agency head, speaking in 1976, explained it this way:

> When knowledge *has* been forthcoming, we have not often used it, and I'd say we haven't used it for very good reasons. These reasons don't have to do with caprice or whimsy or individual idiosyncracies, but rather with the way bureaucracies work: the problem is that evaluation studies which take some time tend to get out of sync with the natural flow and needs of the agency. It often happens that by the time an evaluation comes into being—a solid, fine evaluation—the same people may not be there. If they are, their interests may be different. Legislation may have changed in terms of interest in the program. This is why utilization is a major problem for us, and I think we are not alone in this but are rather quite typical of other agencies.[31]

It is true that rational organization of the evaluation function in an agency at least makes it possible to sequence the performance of evaluations with the needs of multiple users in mind. A carefully developed evaluation agenda means that knowledge of important milestones—for example, expiring legislation, upcoming program authorization or reauthorization, budgetary timelines—can influence decisions of *which* evaluations should be done, as well as *when* they need to be started and finished. Put a little bit differently, one way to ensure that evaluation findings will be ignored is to produce a report just after legislation has been passed and budgets approved.

But neither timeliness nor relevance nor rational organization can ensure that evaluation findings will, in fact, be used. Although these are indeed necessary conditions, they are not sufficient conditions, because too many imperatives for use remain outside the control of the evaluator, either in terms of the program's administration (as Horst, *et al.,* point out in Part II of this volume) or in terms of the larger organizational context within which the successful evaluation enterprise must fit (see below, and Part III, especially the Drucker, Siu, and Wildavsky articles).

Some sponsors have, in fact, argued that the importance of timeliness in an evaluation has been much exaggerated since a really good evaluation will always be useful. In the words of one evaluation manager, speaking in 1976:

> I've found in management experience that studies done right are almost always useful; that a decision always seems to be around longer than you think it will be; and that basically, you have to do a study right. Now I'd also add that when I say doing it right, that means that you take a hard look and if 20% of

the information gives you 80% of what you need for decisions, then you don't go to 80% or 100% of the information. You have to make a determination at what point you will get the information needed to make an intelligent decision. Anybody trying for the perfect study or the perfect analysis in the area of public policy is going to be wasting his or her time. On the other hand, those who get panicked into a half-baked analysis will usually rue the day.[32]

While there thus existed some disagreement in the mid-'70s about how to resolve the trade-off between timeliness and excellence, there was no disagreement whatever that evaluators' inattention to the presentation of their findings discouraged their use by policymakers. Almost everyone has deplored evaluation language; the literature of the '70s is full to overflowing with references to evaluator "mumbo-jumbo," pretentiousness, and jargon, all of which were alleged to have made evaluation reports "spooky, unfathomable, tedious to read and complicated to understand."[33]

As a result, evaluators were hard at work, by the end of the '70s, trying (a) to package their products in a form and with a vocabulary more attractive to their audiences, (b) to lower evaluation's threatening profile and increase the incentives for program managers and agency heads to use evaluation findings, and (c) to achieve enough interaction among sponsors, producers, and other audiences for their evaluations to enhance the likelihood that their reports would be used.

In summary, the period between 1970-1980 saw at least two major evaluation debates emerge, the first involving appropriate methodology, the second involving the use of findings. Although neither of these debates has been totally resolved, a great deal more agreement now exists than there was in the early '70s. Evaluators now have a broader and deeper understanding of the policy and program context within which their work is applied. Consensus among them on many issues is reflected in the two sets of published evaluation standards.

The field of evaluation itself has considerably matured. The need for evaluation products is established, thousands of students have been trained in the methods and substances of program evaluation, experience in the field is building, the number of good studies increases steadily, professional societies and standards now exist, and the use of evaluation findings by managers and policy makers in both legislative and executive branches is growing dramatically.

In Stufflebeam's words, it is now possible to study the evaluation field in a comprehensive manner, "by considering its substance (philosophical base, theory, methods, and history), its clients (including social context, needs, and requests for service, sponsors and finances, and audiences and uses of evaluations), its practitioners (special qualifications, nature and extent of practices, and involvements in advancing the field), and [its] formal structures (professional societies, literature, standards, preservice education programs, continuing education, and certification, and licensing).''[34]

Where does that leave program evaluation now? What are its next steps, its new frontiers? It seems reasonable to believe that at least some of the problems of methodology and use summarized above and in the articles of Part II will be improved if not resolved over the next few years as there come to be more and more skilled evaluators, and as users deepen their understanding of what evaluation can and cannot do. Although hurdles of methodology and use are still very real ones today, many current efforts are directed at overcoming them, and continuing progress in the field should sweep many problems along in its path.

On the other hand, the problem of organizing the evaluation function so as to optimize the use of evaluation findings in public management looms very large indeed. Has progress been made, for example, over the last 15 years in developing the infrastructure and evaluative information bases that were missing under PPBS? What is being done today to amass the generalized knowledge needed for judging the effectiveness of executive agency programs? It is in this area of systematic and comprehensive organizational development of the measures, instruments, and data bases needed by program evaluators that some of the biggest challenges of the future are likely to arise.

An Agenda for the Future

Between 1970 and the present, then, both users and evaluators expressed some dissatisfaction with the evaluation product (often in terms of methodological soundness and appropriateness, relevance, timeliness, and presentation). The articles in Part II of this volume specify some of that dissatisfaction, amplifying the kinds of criticisms that were made and the kinds of problems that evaluators confronted, all of which need to be kept in mind as the effort goes forward to improve evaluation use. Certainly today, an important frontier of evaluation still lies in the specific identification of user groups and the proper targeting of evaluation products to meet their needs.

But increasing the use of evaluation necessarily means improving the way evaluation is organized, because organization and use are complementary. "One cannot improve the prospects for utilization without adjusting organization structures and procedures.''[35] A 1972 article by Wildavsky in Part III of this volume helps to make clear why it has been so difficult to organize the successful functioning and use of evaluation in executive branch agencies. The article points out that although "evaluation man" and "organization man" may be in tension with one another and difficult to reconcile, and although a self-evaluating organization *ought* to be possible to create, it is also the case that if such an organization were to come into existence, it would be quite different from other organizations, since it would need to balance (to a degree that other organizations do not):

- evaluation efficacy versus organizational commitment;
- knowledge versus power;
- integrity of evaluation results versus effects on the organization; and
- willingness to be unpopular versus the need for bureaucratic appreciation.

Achieving rationalization of the evaluation function, then, poses some considerable problems. But whatever organizational structure may eventually be preferred for evaluation, it is crucial that that structure should be such as to facilitate, not complicate, the use of evaluation findings. When the numbers of actual and potential evaluation users are considered, along with the varied locations of those users and the differing purposes they may have in requesting evaluations, it becomes clear that a carefully developed organization of the evaluation function is necessary if the appropriate types of evaluations are to be well matched to users' purposes and individual needs.

Consider the typical governmental users of the evaluation product and the policy purposes, discussed earlier in this paper (that is, policy formulation, policy execution, or accountability), that they may want evaluation to serve. At least six user groups can be easily identified in the executive and legislative branches of government. In the executive branch, there are:

- program managers;
- individual agency heads and top agency policymakers; and
- central government budget and policy authorities, such as the Office of Management and Budget (OMB), or the Executive Office of the President.

In the legislative branch, there are:

- the four legislative agencies, that is, the Congressional Research Service (CRS), the General Accounting Office (GAO), the Office of Technology Assessment (OTA), and the Congressional Budget Office (CBO);
- authorization, appropriations, and budget committees; and
- oversight committees.

For what purposes do these users typically sponsor evaluations? What information do they expect evaluation to produce?

In the executive branch, program managers may sponsor evaluations to get information that can help in planning or implementing a new program or in managing and modifying an existing program. Such a manager is thus interested in evaluative information that either serves policy formulation or policy execution purposes and he or she will therefore typically tend to sponsor front-end analysis, process evaluation, evaluability assessment, and program/problem monitoring. The need to answer questions about program effectiveness also exists for the program manager, and the accountability purpose—often imposed by other users (such as OMB or the Congress)—is then served via approaches such as impact or meta-evaluation.

An agency head, on the other hand, will be less interested than a program manager in detailed program information but will nonetheless need some data to determine and/or justify the need for a new program, assess the effectiveness of an operating program, or review the need to continue or modify a program.

With regard to staff from OMB and the Executive Office of the President, these decision makers—in their central budget and policy functions—may also look to evaluation to inform them on the effectiveness of a program or to help in the decision to continue, cut, or otherwise change it.

In the legislative branch, congressional authorization, appropriations, and budget committees use evaluation findings essentially as contributing information to program funding or refunding decisions. Congressional oversight committees rely on evaluation not only to supply findings about agency programs but also to bring information about how agencies are performing their various functions (such as personnel and resource management, for example, or the manner in which an agency has organized itself to conduct evaluation or to ensure internal financial controls). Although all four of these types of congressional committees may use executive agency produced evaluation findings in their negotiation and decision making processes, they also rely on evaluation findings from independent sources such as universities, consulting firms and other groups. They may use those findings directly, through the work of congressional staff, or indirectly, through the proxy of one or another of the four legislative agencies which are heavy users of evaluation products.

CRS, for example, may report findings to congressional sponsors from a wide variety of evaluations in an "issues" paper for legislative use. The GAO, which has a congressional mandate to perform program evaluations, may either report its own findings to the Congress, or analyze evaluation findings from many different sources to inform the Congress, or critique methodological or technical aspects of existing evaluations. OTA may use evaluation findings as a foundation from which to forecast technological impacts, and CBO may use them as part of the empirical base on which to construct the likely outcomes of alternative government policies.

These six different types of evaluation users, then, have some purposes in common and some that are uniquely their own. As a result, there are some areas of evaluative information need that they share and some that are distinct. Only a program manager or the GAO, for example, may require fine-grained information on implementation and operational issues specific to one or two local sites in a large national program. Yet, even though there may not be many audiences for this information, it may be crucial to the needs of those two users. On the other hand, evaluation findings on:

- the effectiveness of a program,
- client satisfaction or frustration with program services,
- the views of program stakeholders,
- trends in the problem(s) addressed by the program, or
- changes in the dimensions or focus of the program

are likely to be helpful to nearly all specific users, and may interest general audiences as well.

The degree of detail needed by users from evaluative information which all of them may want, will differ depending upon the user's particular function and purpose. A member of Congress, for example, may need to be aware only of the major findings of a program evaluation, whereas an agency head—who may be called upon by OMB, the president, or the Congress to defend the program or explain the findings—will require a much more detailed knowledge of the information produced. This means that although the basic information produced by an evaluation may be useful to several different audiences, different versions of that information, presenting different levels of detail, may be needed.

The question of the appropriateness of a particular evaluation to multiple user needs is one that must be considered very carefully. Evaluations are so few in number, and often so costly that the idea of serving several users with the same evaluation is extremely attractive. Yet the article by Hargrove in Part III of this volume shows the difficulties that can arise when a single evaluation is expected to serve both the policy execution information needs of program managers and the accountability needs of agency heads, OMB, and the Congress. Not only does the possibility then exist that no user will be adequately served by the evaluation, but there is also a danger of introducing information distortion inadvertently. Explicit statements by the evaluators about the objectives and limitations of the evaluation are needed to ensure that an evaluation performed, say, for an agency head's information, to learn the opinions of practitioners or stakeholders about a program is not interpreted by a secondary user—the press, for example—as an evaluation of program effectiveness.

In addition, the ability to serve multiple users is further constrained by the need for an evaluation to answer the precise question(s) posed by the sponsor or primary user, and the need for the conclusiveness of the answer(s) given to match that user's particular information need. For example, it is reasonable and necessary to undertake an expensive, large-scale effectiveness evaluation when it is feasible and when the primary user must have the most conclusive information possible. But if an evaluation user's objective is to develop some general information in an area where little currently exists, then less conclusive—and less costly—information may be both appropriate and desirable.

Finally, it is probably important to point out an essential difference in the evaluative information needs of executive branch and legislative branch users. While both branches may want evaluative evidence on, say, the need for a program as part of their policy-formulating role (that is, their planning or authorizing functions), and while they may both want evidence of program efficiency and effectiveness to support their accountability role in the administrative and legislative oversight processes, it is the executive branch which is charged with policy execution and the actual implementation of public programs. As a result, executive branch program managers may often (and quite properly) be virtually the sole users of certain types of detailed evaluative information which supports decision making about program operations.

What do all these complicated patterns of purposes, functions, and evaluation needs of users have to do with the organization of the evaluation function? The answer is clear only when it is understood to what degree the evaluation function in the federal government is currently fragmented. It may be true that this disorganization has been somewhat deliberate, at first reflecting a desire to avoid repeating any PPBS mistakes. Rather than follow the centralized organizational approach adopted by PPBS (centralization here refers to an evaluation unit reporting directly to the top management of an agency, while decentralization refers to a unit reporting to managers at lower levels in the agency), evaluation offices in the early '70s were established "flexibly" within federal agencies: that is, in almost every imaginable mode. Later, the disorganization seemed to reflect less a desire for "creative decentralization" than it did different views about the role of program evaluation and analysis in public management generally. Today organizational arrangements for evaluation include centralized units and decentralized ones; units reporting to the assistant secretary of a department and units reporting to the manager whose program is being evaluated; units prohibited from contact with evaluation sponsors and users, and units colocated with them; units related to (or even integrated with) planning or budget offices and units working in isolation; units benefiting from set-asides to evaluation and units having to compete for funds within the agency.[36]

Although the debate about how the evaluation function should be organized within agencies has been going on for years,[37] it now takes on some urgency with renewed efforts to improve the governmental use of evaluation findings. Part III of this volume includes articles having appeared in *PAR* on the organization of the evaluation or research function, with authors examining different aspects of the problems posed to research groups in government. In this area, one of the most perplexing issues has certainly been that of centralization or decentralization: that is, whether an evaluation unit should be a decentralized part of agency programs, with each program responsible for its own evaluation, or whether the unit should be centralized so as to be independent of the programs to be evaluated. On the one hand, a central unit is efficient, it can develop a critical mass of technical skills, expertise, and people and it is protected from pressures by program managers; however, it often appears threatening and may be held at arm's length or ignored by the very managers it seeks to influence. On the other hand, an evaluation unit that is colocated with a program may capture the confidence of managers, it may learn a great deal more about the program and its problems than a centralized unit will be allowed to learn, and it will certainly reduce the threat to managers that evaluation represents; however, such a dependent unit can easily be prevented from developing, documenting, or publishing any negative findings on the program.[38]

Today, this debate has not yet been resolved to anyone's satisfaction, and the current diversity of the federal evaluation functions, their uncoordinated development, and the recent cancellation without replacement of OMB Circular A-117 (regulating the reporting of evaluation activities) reinforce the already existing impression that the executive branch function is disorganized: that is, both *ad hoc* and unstructured.

But "adhocracy," as an organizational option, has not shown itself in the past to be well suited either to the success of the evaluation function generally, or to the improved use of evaluation findings, in particular. Indeed, many believe that the unstructured evaluation functions of the early '70s virtually guaranteed that various users' needs could not be met. As one evaluation manager saw the problem in 1976:

> You have a federal agency in which the head of the agency decides, either reluctantly or willingly, that an evaluation needs to be done in one of his programs. He summons one of his top people and says either, OMB has told us they want, or the Congress has told us that they want, or I personally want, an evaluation of this program.
>
> The first prominent factor is that there is no evaluation mechanism of any consequence to which he is addressing that question or that task. What exists is buried somewhere in the bowels of the organization. . . . Finally an RFP is issued. However lengthy and wordy that RFP may be, it usually says little more than, "please submit proposals to evaluate this program." In response to that kind of specification, in come a series of proposals from academic

research institutes, commercial research organizations and the like, which range all the way from $25,000 to $2½ million, and all the way from quick and dirty site visits to sophisticated, experimental-design, longitudinal studies.

How those things can be compared and one chosen among them is hard to imagine, but that task gets done. One is chosen. The contract is signed, and work gets underway.

After that the thing is generally lost from view. . . . Some substantial time later, in comes a report. The important thing as far as the evaluation process is concerned is that the report is too late to influence the decisions which gave rise to the need for the procurement of the evaluation in the first place. It is too voluminous to be read by anyone who would be in a position to make those decisions. It's too technically esoteric to be understood by them if it were on time and they were to read it. And there's a good chance it has become irrelevant, policy-wise, to the issues which triggered it at the outset.

The results are that, first, it goes on the shelf where it is unused and uninfluential in policy, program and budget decisions. And second, even worse, when its existence is belatedly and critically recognized, it contributes negatively to the reputation of evaluation.[39]

Thus, if the target to be achieved is a strong, successful evaluation function, if use is an important measure of the value of program evaluation, and if the role of an evaluation unit is to assure the production of evaluative information that can serve both the various policy purposes of evaluation and its different groups of users, then "adhocracy" clearly has critical disadvantages. But how then can the evaluation function be organized? As already noted briefly above, both centralized and decentralized evaluation units possess advantages and disadvantages.

Centralized units have a great deal to recommend them. They can be sensibly structured, they can serve all evaluation purposes and users (although it may not be feasible or appropriate to do so with every evaluation, and although centralized functions have not always succeeded in doing this in the past), they can set agency-wide, sequenced agendas for evaluation and they can be held accountable for their performance. In addition, they present three other quite crucial advantages: the credibility that comes from greater independence (*vis-à-vis* decentralized units); the potential for inter-agency coordination by a higher-level central government unit; and the presence of a substantial group of well trained, highly skilled evaluators that is large enough to ensure the ongoing recruitment of top quality staff, and to allow specialization in the various substantive topics under the agency's jurisdiction. Because of their size and continuity, centralized units also present the advantages of being able (1) to take a comprehensive, systematic approach to evaluation issues and (2) to develop an institutional memory that is both documented and archived (an important goal of evaluative units, given the poorly developed data base of evaluation findings mentioned earlier, and an important goal for any research unit, see the article by Lovvorn and Gilstrap in Part III of this volume). Because of their independence from program managers, centralized units are more likely to conduct effectiveness evaluations serving user accountability needs (see the Hargrove article in Part III). And finally, because of their reporting position in the agency hierarchy, they are closer to the top departmental sponsor of evaluations and are more likely to be successful in promoting the use of the findings.

But centralized units have some problems as well. While they may be independent of the programs being evaluated, it is hard for them to be equally independent of an administrator's ideology or of bureaucratic politics. In addition, central units tend to develop deeply held opinions about program policies, problems and the "right" evaluation questions, and while this may make for stronger evaluations, it may not ensure appropriate ones; in effect, there may be a lack of diversity in the approaches used (e.g., all evaluations do not have to be effectiveness evaluations), and a possibility that important participants (in the implementation of the ultimate evaluation recommendations, for example) may be excluded from debates in which they have legitimate interests. In the Hargrove case study on CETA, for example (see Part III), the author makes clear that the evaluation needs of the program managers were not considered equally, in the central unit deliberations, with the needs of other users. Also, central units are prisoners to some degree of the time/relevance problem discussed earlier. That is, given the high rate of turnover at the executive branch top manager level, with only a two-year average stay in office, and given also the time it takes to conduct complex, multi-phased effectiveness evaluations (depending on the substantive area and issues to be examined, this can range from 18 months to 3-4 years), central units may find it necessary, if only to ensure their survival (see the Wildavsky article, Part III), to conduct more short-term studies and fewer of the effectiveness evaluations which are supposed to constitute a major benefit of centralization.

Decentralized evaluation units bring a quite different set of advantages and disadvantages. When they are well accepted by program managers, decentralized units are in the best position possible to conduct policy execution (program improvement) types of evaluations and to ensure the implementation of the evaluation findings by the program managers. They are more knowledgeable generally about the "nuts and bolts" of programs and the evaluation issues they raise than central units can be. They are the logical locus for evaluation studies of program implementation and operations. Because they are not so closely tied to an administration—being at a lower hierarchical level in the organization—they may be freer politically (if not bureaucratically) to serve wider interests. Finally, the fact that these units perform evaluations and contribute their views to middle- and upper-level management is not only a morale builder among mid-level agency personnel but also allows top management to strengthen policy execution by ensuring that managers and evaluators at the program level have had the opportunity to help formulate—and presumably "buy in"—to those policies.

The disadvantages of decentralization are also multiple. First, the units' lack of independence from program managers unquestionably hurts the credibility of their findings. Second, effectiveness evaluations seem to be less often undertaken by these units than would be desirable. Third, their typically small size makes it difficult for them to attract and retain the most highly skilled evaluators. Fourth, uncoordinated decentralized units can duplicate each others' work or can treat evaluative issues spottily rather than systematically and comprehensively. Fifth, continuity within these small offices is fragile: when one or two key personnel leave, the gap can be unbridgeable. Sixth, it is difficult if not impossible for a decentralized unit to establish the kind of evaluation agenda that is responsive to the needs of an entire agency (see again Hargrove's article on CETA evaluations, in Part III). Finally, program managers are not the only—or even the chief—users of program evaluation. Agency heads, the Congress, and the legislative organizations are equally important consumers of the evaluation product. But there is no assurance that decentralized units can serve these consumers. The problem is that if a lower level group controls the evaluation function in an agency, it may happen that most of the evaluation work done will be dedicated to that group's chief interests, to the exclusion of other interests. In the case of a program manager, as already noted, the chief interest is likely to be in policy execution types of evaluation (such as process evaluations, which do not inform on program effectiveness), rather than in the accountability or policy formulation types of evaluation (such as effectiveness evaluation or meta-evaluation) needed by other users. Indeed, the decentralized evaluation unit has little incentive or capability to ensure support for the different policy purposes of evaluation's multiple users.

What then are the options for organizing the evaluation function in the federal government, if neither centralized nor decentralized units can furnish a perfect solution? At least three options are possible: leaving things as they are; a mixed structure that would be a kind of ecological model maximizing the benefits of both centralized and decentralized units; and a centralized model.

A case can be made for leaving things temporarily as they are, based on two arguments: first, few empirical studies have been done that would allow sensible decisions to be made that flow from strong evidence; and second, settings differ so much across agencies that it is hard to recommend any across-the-board solutions to the problem of rationalizing the evaluation function and the use of evaluation findings (see, for example, the Lovvorn and Gilstrap article in Part III for a type of research/evaluation function that differs notably from the self-evaluating model that has been targeted in this paper). If it is decided to do nothing, however, then a major concurrent commitment needs to be made to do some of the required empirical studies and to examine the appropriateness of different evaluation organization models for different types of agency settings and mission.

A second option could combine centralized and decentralized units in each large agency and add to them a small higher level office in a central agency (e.g., OMB or the Executive Office of the President) to coordinate the units across agencies. This office, however, would need to have a substantive focus as well as a merely coordinating one. In effect, one of the most important reasons why evaluation is needed in government is to develop the kind of cumulative information base that was so saliently lacking for PPBS. Such an information base, however, must be developed *across* the evaluation units that are housed within individual agencies. Hence, it requires a higher level locus. In addition, such a higher level locus is needed for a host of other reasons. Among these, to facilitate communications across evaluation units; to promote a common technical understanding and agreement about the appropriateness and limitations of various methodologies for addressing particular types of questions; to provide for the reasonable development, maintenance, and commonality of administrative data systems that are used for longitudinal analysis; to ensure that all user needs are considered and addressed; to establish government standards of professional practice; and to encourage the continued technical advancement of the field.

The argument for using such an ecological model in the organization of the evaluation function is quite powerful. It would guarantee that evaluative information for all user purposes could be generated within each agency; a critical mass of skills would be assured; politicization of the central unit could be counter-balanced in the decentralized unit and bias in either unit would eventually be controlled because of competition among the units; continuity would be provided even in the smallest units because of the existence of the larger network and the presence of evaluation archives; greater range and diversity of approach and opinion would be available to evaluation users through the differing perspectives of the two types of units; and finally top level agency managers could be certain that the voices of interested program participants had been heard.

This option also calls for a technically competent "honest broker" at the assistant secretary level to mediate conflicts (which are likely to occur quite often), to avoid either major gaps in the evaluation agenda or duplication of studies, to ensure that the ongoing evaluation debate (about what studies to conduct and how to conduct them) is both structured and balanced, and to facilitate the inclusion of all interested parties in that debate.

This option, thus, has some important advantages in that it appears to build on the benefits of both centralized and decentralized functions; to promote healthy competition among the units (competition that could result in higher quality evidence in the evaluations conducted as well as advances in the methodologies and technologies employed); and to correct many of the deficiencies of each of the two types of organizational structure standing alone. However, some serious disadvantages are likely to accrue to this option. These are: highly uncertain feasibility of operation (see the Hargrove article, Part III); increased costs (as compared to other options); lengthy time delays (because of increased participant involvement); and major burdens of conflict resolution pushed up to top management levels.

A final option to consider is the centralized evaluation function. Here there would be central units in each agency along with the higher-level coordinating office referred to earlier (keeping the same functions). Decentralized units would disappear and all program managers would work with the central unit. This centralized model is the one that has been adopted in Canada, where a major effort has been mounted to rationalize the production of evaluations, improve their quality, and increase their usefulness to public policy makers. In 1978, the Canadian Parliament required all agencies of government to establish evaluation units reporting to the deputy minister of each agency.* A higher level unit, the Office of the Comptroller General, was set up in a central executive agency (similar to OMB) to provide the infrastructure, establish the goals, and determine the manner under which the units would operate. Those units are now in place; evaluation frameworks, plans, and research agendas for the agencies are established; and evaluation study findings are coming in regularly. Last September, the first critique of this initiative was published by the Office of the Auditor General of Canada (analogous to the United States' General Accounting Office). The findings are very positive with regard to progress achieved to date in the evaluation units, in the development of the evaluation infrastructure, and in the accomplishment of the task which the Canadian government has set itself: "to make program evaluation an integral part of public sector management."[40]

The advantages and disadvantages of a centralized function have been discussed here earlier, but not in comparison to the mixed model. While some of the disadvantages of a centralized organization would clearly remain—possible politicization, lack of diversity, and uncertainty that relevant voices had been heard—it is also the case that three of the disadvantages of the mixed model would not be present. The feasibility of a centralized organization is quite certain (there is a good deal of experience

---

*A Canadian deputy minister has roles and functions similar to those of an Assistant Secretary in the United States.

in the various federal agencies with the centralized model and some systematic empirical information is now available from Canada); costs would be much lower than for the mixed model; and time delays could be well controlled. It might be advisable to maintain the technically competent honest broker idea at the assistant secretary level, however, because in this way it is possible that at least some of the defects of centralization can be mitigated. It would also be useful to monitor the Canadian experience quite carefully. Despite the differences between parliamentary and presidential forms of government, the results of this experience are likely to be of great interest and value over the next ten years as the issue of improving the applications and usefulness of program evaluation takes on more importance in the United States.

There is, of course, no intention to assert in this paper that no options exist apart from the three discussed above. Rather, many other possibilities for organization can be conceived and, in addition, the three options given are not mutually exclusive: elements of one can be combined with elements of another. Nor is the point here that the only problems facing program evaluation have to do with evaluation use and with the organization of the function. Indeed, there are technical problems, problems of adapting the evaluator's timetable and vocabulary to that of the user, problems of developing interdisciplinary ways of working together in an evaluative framework, problems of evaluator training, preparation, and curricula that have not yet been solved. But the ability to move ahead in all of these areas will depend, in major ways, on the ability to organize the program evaluation function in government. Rationalization of the function—at least within agencies but better still, across agencies—may not be an indispensable condition for progress but it would be of powerful assistance in achieving the purposes of program evaluation: better formulation of policy (i.e., for example, well justified new programs), better policy execution (i.e., programs that work efficiently) and routinely assured accountability (i.e., documentation of program effects). Some kind of systematic organization is needed to develop the kind of information base that can support and justify the initiation of new programs. It is needed to improve the relevance, timeliness, and usefulness of evaluation to all of its audiences. And it is needed to ensure that the ongoing technical advancements of the field are diffused and disseminated widely, so that the performance of program evaluation, the achievement of its purposes, and the appropriateness of its use continue to improve.

Notes

1. George F. Madaus, Michael Scriben, and Daniel L. Stufflebeam, *Evaluation Models: Viewpoints on Educational and Human Services Evaluation* (Kluwer-Nijhoff Publishing Co., Boston, 1983), p. 4.

2. Old Testament, Daniel 1:12-17, cited in David C. Hoaglin, *et al., Data for Decisions* (Abt Books, 1982), p. 7.
3. See the discussion by Aaron Wildavsky in "The Political Economy of Efficiency: Cost-Benefit Analysis, Systems Analysis, and Program Budgeting," *Public Administration Review,* December 1966, pp. 293-302, and by the same author in "Rescuing Policy Analysis from PPBS," *Public Administration Review,* March/April 1969, p. 190.
4. Steven E. Rhoads, "Economists and Policy Analysis," *Public Administration Review,* March/April 1978, p. 114; and E. S. Quade, *Analysis for Public Decisions* (New York: Elsevier, 1975), p. 22.
5. See, for example, Charles J. Hitch and Roland N. McKean, *The Economics of Defense in the Nuclear Age* (The Rand Corporation, March 1960).
6. Peter H. Rossi, Howard E. Freeman, and Sonia R. Wright, *Evaluation: A Systematic Approach* (Sage Publications, 1979), p. 24.
7. For example, Donald T. Campbell, "Factors Relevant to the Validity of Experiments in Social Settings," *Psychological Bulletin,* 1957, pp. 297-312; or "From Description to Experimentation: Interpreting Trends as Quasi-Experiments," in C. W. Harris (Ed.), *Problems in Measuring Change* (University of Wisconsin Press, 1963); or, with Julian C. Stanley, "Experimental and Quasi-Experimental Designs for Research," in N. L. Gage (Ed.), *Handbook of Research on Teaching* (Chicago: Rand McNally, 1963).
8. See especially, Lee J. Cronbach, "Course Improvement Through Evaluation," *Teachers College Record,* 64 (1963), Columbia University, New York; and (with A. L. Edwards), "Experimental Design for Research in Psychotherapy," *Journal of Clinical Psychology,* Vol. 8, January 1952, pp. 51-59.
9. Note the discussions of measurement problems (reliability and validity) and statistical analysis interpretation in Paul F. Lazarsfeld, "Interpretation of Statistical Relations as a Research Operation" in *The Language of Social Research* (Glencoe, Ill.: Free Press, 1955), pp. 115-125; and especially Lazarsfeld's evaluation of voting behavior, using a longitudinal study design, in Paul F. Lazarsfeld, Bernard Berelson, and Hazel Gaudet, *The People's Choice* (New York: Columbia University Press, 1948).
10. See, for example, John F. Holahan's application of cost-benefit techniques to evaluate a rehabilitation program in *A Benefit-Cost Analysis of Project Crossroads* (Washington, D.C.: National Committee for Children and Youth, 1970); or the General Accounting Office's recent use of an applied social research model for evaluating the DOD's joint test and evaluation program (U.S. General Accounting Office: *How Well Do the Military Services Perform Jointly in Combat: DOD's Joint Test and Evaluation Program Provides Few Credible Answers,* PEMD-84-3).
11. Alexis de Tocqueville, citation from 1835 in James W. Fesler, "Programming Research—Linear or Circular?" *Public Administration Review,* 19 (Autumn 1959), p. 285.
12. Aaron Wildavsky, "The Political Economy of Efficiency: Cost-Benefit Analysis, Systems, Analysis, and Program Budgeting," *Public Administration Review,* December 1966, p. 306.
13. William Gorham, cited in Stanley B. Botner, "Four Years of PPBS: An Appraisal," *Public Administration Review,* July/August 1970, p. 425.
14. See, for example, the article by Charles E. Lindblom, "The Science of 'Muddling Through,' " *Public Administration Review,* 19 (Spring 1959), pp. 79-88, and those of Aaron Wildavsky, "The Political Economy of Efficiency: Cost-Benefit Analysis, Systems Analysis, and Program Budgeting," *Public Administration Review,* 26 (December 1966), pp. 292-310; and Frederick C. Mosher, "Limitations and Problems of PPBS in the States," *Public Administration Review,* 29 (March/April 1969), pp. 160-167. See also Aaron Wildavsky, *The Politics of the Budgetary Process* (Little, Brown and Co., 1964).
15. See, for example, Allen Schick, "The Road to PPB: The Stages of Budget Reform," *Public Administration Review,* 26 (December 1966), pp. 243-258; and Bertram M. Gross,

"The New Systems Budgeting," *Public Administration Review,* 29 (March/April 1969), pp. 113-137. See also Yehezkel Dror, *Some Normative Implications of a Systems View of Policymaking,* Rand Corporation, P-3991, December 1968; and Donald T. Campbell, "Reforms as Experiments," *American Psychologist,* Vol. 24, No. 4, April 1969, pp. 402-429. In particular, Professor Campbell noted that we seem to have convinced ourselves that our program decision making is based on program effectiveness when in fact it is not. "So long have we had good intentions in this regard that many may feel we are already at this stage, that we already are continuing or discontinuing programs on the basis of assessed effectiveness. It is a theme of this article that this is not at all so, that most ameliorative programs end up with *no* interpretable evaluation."

16. Aaron Wildavsky, "Rescuing Policy Analysis from PPBS," *Public Administration Review,* 29 (March/April 1969), p. 193.

17. John Evans, "Is Education Evaluation Dying?" paper presented at the 1984 annual meeting of the American Educational Research Association (AERA) in New Orleans as part of Session No. 9.33, "Whither Evaluation—Life, Death, or Reincarnation?"

18. Robert N. Anthony, *Planning and Control Systems: A Framework for Analysis* (Cambridge: Harvard University Press, 1965), p. 16.

19. Norman Beckman, "Policy Analysis in Government: Alternatives to Muddling Through," *Public Administration Review,* 37 (May/June 1977), p. 222.

20. Orville Poland, "Program Evaluation and Administrative Theory," *Public Administration Review,* 34 (July/August 1974), p. 333.

21. Two compatible sets of standards for program evaluation now exist: (a) Joint Committee on Standards for Educational Evaluation, *Standards for Evaluation of Educational Programs, Projects and Materials* (New York: McGraw-Hill, 1981); and (b) Evaluation Research Society Standards Committee, "Evaluation Research Society Standards for Program Evaluation," in *Standards for Evaluation Practice, New Directions for Program Evaluation,* No. 15 (San Francisco: Jossey-Bass, September 1982). The first set applies to educational evaluation only, the second set to evaluation in all topical areas.

22. See, for example, the definition given in the latest edition of Harry P. Hatry, Richard E. Winnie and Donald M. Fisk, *Practical Program Evaluation for State and Local Government* (The Urban Institute, 1981), pp. 4-5: "Program Evaluation, as defined here, focuses on the past performance of ongoing or completed programs; thus it is primarily retrospective."

23. Eleanor Chelimsky, "Differing Perspectives of Evaluation," *New Directions for Program Evaluation,* 2 (Summer 1978), pp. 1-17.

24. Marcia Guttentag, "Special Characteristics of Social Intervention Programs: Evaluation of Social Intervention Programs," *Annals of the New York Academy of Sciences,* Vol. 218, June 22, 1973, p. 6.

25. Eleanor Chelimsky, *Analysis of a Symposium on the Use of Evaluation by Federal Agencies,* Vol. II, MITRE Corporation, July 1977, p. 46.

26. Robert S. Weiss and Martin Rein, "The Evaluation of Broad-Aim Programs: Experimental Design, Its Difficulties and an Alternative," *Administrative Science Quarterly,* March 1970, pp. 103-104.

27. Isadore Seeman, cited in Eleanor Chelimsky, *Analysis of a Symposium on the Use of Evaluation by Federal Agencies,* Vol. II, MITRE Corporation, July 1977, p. 33.

28. James Abert, cited in Eleanor Chelimsky, *Analysis of a Symposium on the Use of Evaluation by Federal Agencies,* Vol. II, MITRE Corporation, July 1977, p. 36.

29. Eleanor Chelimsky, *Analysis of a Symposium on the Use of Evaluation by Federal Agencies,* Vol. II, MITRE Corporation, July 1977, p. 37.

30. Interview with Thomas L. Lalley, in *Appendix to the Proceedings of a Symposium on the Institutionalization of Federal Programs at the Local Level,* by Frank C. Jordan, Jr. (editor Eleanor Chelimsky), MITRE Corporation, May 1979, pp. 788, 792-793.

31. Gerald M. Caplan, cited in Eleanor Chelimsky, *Analysis of a Symposium on the Use of Evaluation by Federal Agencies,* Vol. II, MITRE Corporation, July 1977, p. 35.
32. Alvin Alm, cited in Eleanor Chelimsky, *Analysis of a Symposium on the Use of Evaluation by Federal Agencies,* Vol. II, MITRE Corporation, July 1977, p. 36.
33. William D. Carey, cited in Eleanor Chelimsky, *Analysis of a Symposium on the Use of Evaluation by Federal Agencies,* Vol. II, MITRE Corporation, July 1977, p. 49.
34. Daniel L. Stufflebeam, *Has the Profession of Educational Evaluation Changed With Changing Times?* paper presented at the Meeting of the American Educational Research Association in New Orleans, April 1984, p. 3.
35. Douglas R. Bunker, "Organizing to Link Social Science with Public Policy Making," *Public Administration Review,* 38 (May/June 1978), p. 223.
36. *A Profile of Federal Program Evaluation Activities,* Program Evaluation and Methodology Division Special Study, U.S. General Accounting Office, September 1982.
37. Eleanor Chelimsky, *Analysis of a Symposium on the Use of Evaluation by Federal Agencies,* Vol. II, MITRE Corporation, July 1977, pp. 39-41.
38. Eleanor Chelimsky, "Program Evaluation and Governmental Change," in *Implementing Governmental Change* (Charles E. Gilbert, Ed.), The Annals, American Academy of Political and Social Science, March 1983, p. 110.
39. John Evans, cited in Eleanor Chelimsky, *Analysis of a Symposium on the Use of the Evaluation by Federal Agencies,* Vol. II, MITRE Corporation, July 1977, pp. 39-40.
40. Auditor General of Canada, *Program Evaluation: Report of the Auditor General, 1983,* Chapter 3, Section 3, 27, Ottawa, Ontario.

PART I

Six Approaches to Program Evaluation

The articles from the pages of *PAR* chosen for inclusion in this section are examples of the six types of program evaluation identified by the Evaluation Research Society that are discussed in the introductory essay. They are not, of course, perfect examples of the individual types; indeed, one was written in 1941 before anyone was thinking about evaluation. But they are close enough to give the reader a fairly clear idea of the kind of work that each individual type may demand and of the diversity of approaches represented by the six types under the single rubric: evaluation.

The first article, "Evaluating the Union-Management Relationship in Government" by James L. Perry and Carder W. Hunt (*PAR*, Vol. 38, No. 5, September/October 1978, pages 431-436), is an example of front-end analysis. It is prospective in that it looks toward the development of an evaluation plan or design. It asks a preparatory kind of question: What are the criteria or measures needed for evaluating the union-management relationship in government? This is a question that must be answered before the evaluator can address the cause-and-effect question: Has the union-management relationship in government led to the institutionalization of partisan interests there? This is only one type of front-end analysis, however. Others may ask questions about the status of a problem addressed by a proposed new program (for example, How many illegal aliens enter the United States each year?) or may examine past evaluation findings for similar programs to help set reasonable objectives for the program.

The second article, "The Senior Executive Service: How Can We Tell If It Works?" by Bruce Buchanan (*PAR*, Vol. 41, No. 3, May/June 1981, pages 349-358) is an example of evaluability assessment. Its chief purpose is to determine whether a program, *as implemented,* can be evaluated to establish its effectiveness. In this sense, it is preparatory, but it is also retrospective in that it examines an already operational program, looking at the program's logic (for example, the relationship between program activities and program expectations, see Figure 1 of Mr. Buchanan's article) and operations (especially, their measurability). It asks the preparatory question: Given the complexity and multi-component, broad-aim nature of the Senior Executive Service (SES) program, what standards should be used to answer this question before embarking on a full-scale effectiveness evaluation asking the normative question: Has the SES program accomplished its objectives after five years of operation?

The third article, "Life Histories of Innovations: How New Practices Become Routinized," by Robert K. Yin (*PAR,* Vol. 41, No. 1, January/February 1981, pages 21-28) is an example of process analysis very much like the kind advocated by Weiss and Rein in their famous 1970 paper (*Administrative Science Quarterly,* Vol. 15, No. 1, pages 97-110, see also pages 22-23 of the introductory essay to this volume and the discussion by George Shipman, in the articles of Part II). Although process evaluations may be complementary to outcome (or effectiveness) evaluations and may ask only descriptive questions (for example, How many people are served by the program?), Mr. Yin's paper is a stand-alone evaluation, asking the cause-and-effect question, "What have been the organizational and other factors that have led to the routinization of new practices?" The evaluation strategy adopted for answering this question was the case study: 19 in-depth site analyses were performed, with other evidence collected as well (via telephone) in 90 other sites.

The fourth article, "Controlling Human Factors in an Administrative Experiment," by Herbert A. Simon and William R. Divine (*PAR,* Vol. 1, No. 5, Autumn 1941, pages 485-492) is an example of an effectiveness evaluation, using the experimental design. Although the word evaluation is not used by Messrs. Simon and Divine, and although findings are not given in the paper (it mostly addresses the problems of applying the experimental design in an administrative setting), it shows the kinds of issues that need to be addressed by the evaluator in performing this type of evaluation and furnishes very credible evidence of its feasibility and applicability. It is interesting to note that although the work performed in this evaluation is retrospective (as it is for all experimental evaluations), the question asked was posed prospectively by the authors. In reality, the question answered by the experiment was one of cause-and-effect: What workload or "quota" sizes have led to the most desirable (productive) results in California's State Relief Administration? The performance of the experiment *then* allowed the authors to answer the policy question posed, which was: How large a workload, for most efficient operation, should be assigned to professional workers in the SRA? This is, of course, the opposite of what was attempted in PPBS (see pages 5-7 of the introductory essay), when the effort was made to answer prospective policy questions without first having established the evaluative foundation.

The fifth article, "Federal Merit Pay: A Longitudinal Analysis" by Jone L. Pearce and James L. Perry (*PAR,* Vol. 43, No. 4, July/August 1983, pages 315-325) is another example of an effectiveness evaluation, this time using time-series analysis rather than the experimental design to answer a cause-and-effect question: What were the effects of the implementation of merit pay on managerial motivation in five federal agencies?

Two examples of effectiveness evaluation are given in Part I because of the so very often repeated claim that they cannot be done (see the introductory essay, page 21, citation from M. Guttentag).

The sixth article, "Service Time, Dispatch Time and Demand for Police Services: Helping More by Serving Less," by Michael G. Maxfield (*PAR,* Vol. 42, No. 3, May/June 1982, pages 252-263) is an example of monitoring, using extant (or routinely collected) data. The question asked was descriptive: What have been the problems in San Francisco with respect to police response to citizen requests for service? Extant data were used to monitor police performance so as to determine what the problems were. The findings were then used to answer the policy question, How can those problems be best addressed?

The last article, "Addressing the Believability of Research Results Reported in the Environmental Health Matrix," by Alan G. Urkowitz and Robert E. Laessing (*PAR,* Vol. 42, No. 5, September/October 1982, pages 427-438) is an example of meta-evaluation. It brings together a whole set of already existing research results and examines them in terms of their methodological soundness. Two questions are asked in this paper. The first is both substantive and cause-and-effect: What have been the effects of environmental problems on human health? The second question is preparatory. It asks, How credible are the available research results in making inferences about causality with regard to environmental effects on human health? What gaps, therefore, are present in the existing knowledge on this subject, and what research agenda needs to be established in consequence?

JAMES L. PERRY
CARDER W. HUNT

Evaluating the Union-Management Relationship in Government

Collective bargaining and public employee unionism now pose pre-eminent challenges in government at all levels. Public managers' and legislators' attentions are, at this stage of the development of public sector bargaining, cast around pragmatic concerns such as the legalization of collective bargaining and the administration of day-to-day union-management relations. An area of particular neglect, suggests Newland, is the relationship of collective bargaining to social change, including the accomplishment of general government goals and objectives.[1]

This paper will present a conceptual framework which may be used to evaluate the union-management relationship in government. It will utilize the concepts of organizational effectiveness which have a direct bearing upon union-management relations: absenteeism and turnover, labor productivity, adaptability/flexibility, job satisfaction, commitment, and user satisfaction. Previous evaluative studies of the union-management relationship are first examined in order to demonstrate some of the inadequacies of alternative approaches. The conceptual rationale for using organizational effectiveness as the yardstick against which to evaluate the union-management relationship is explored. We conclude with a discussion of the utility of the newly developed framework for evaluating union-management relationships in government.

The importance of the impact of the union-management relationship on governmental effectiveness cannot be underestimated. Newland argues that "collective bargaining must serve as one of several vehicles for creative change . . . if it is to be compatible with future public interests."[2] A variety of assessments indicate, however, that collective bargaining in government has been an instrument of partisan interests rather than a vehicle for creative change.[3] As long as either public managers pit public employees against citizens or public employee unions pit the public against management, labor-management relations in government will have decidedly negative im-

39

pacts on the parties, the public, and the political system. Methods are needed for re-integrating management, employee, and citizens interests. The evaluative framework we propose highlights the multiplicity of interests that must be balanced through the union-management relationship. It also identifies explicit criteria for which all the parties in public sector bargaining should be held accountable.

Approaches to Evaluating the Union-Management Relationship

Since both "union-management relationships" and "evaluation" have a variety of connotations, it is important to define how we use each of the terms. The union-management relationship is a "continuing institutional relationship between an employer entity and a labor organization concerned with the negotiation and administration of agreements covering joint understandings about wages or salaries, hours of work and other terms and conditions of employment."[4] This definition is broad enough to encompass a variety of governmental forms (e.g., general local governments and special districts) and several types of labor organizations, including employee associations as well as unions. Evaluation "is the notion of judging merit; someone is examining and weighing a phenomenon against some explicit or implicit yardstick."[5] Thus, our objective is to develop a means for judging the merit or quality of the union-management relationship against some explicit criteria.

Some empirical studies have explored bargaining outcomes in local government—for example, wages, hours, and work stoppages—and Dotson has proposed a theory of equity for the public employment relationship.[6] None of these studies has, however, advanced an explicit framework for evaluating the union-management relationship in government. Rather, the implicit perspectives which public administrators presently use to evaluate the quality of union-management relations rely heavily upon experience in the industrial sector. This transfer is not surprising given the private sector's relatively long experience with collective bargaining. The approaches of those private sector studies discussed below are indicataive of the perspectives which public administration has thus far relied upon to evaluate union-management relations.

Early studies of the union-management relationship in industry placed primary emphasis on its immediate dysfunctions—strikes and lockouts.[7] The relationship was evaluated in terms of the ability of the two parties to resolve conflicts of interest without resort to economic warfare. These studies were primarily descriptive in nature, largely limited to a narrow concern with strikes, and were based upon a number of uncritical assumptions about the elements that contribute to satisfactory labor relations.

Later studies distinguished between the *outcomes* of the union-management relationship (economic warfare, industrial peace, strikes, etc.) and the *process* by which such outcomes were achieved. Whyte evaluated the union-management relationship in terms of four basic concepts: interactions among the participants; symbols (words or objects that symbolize relations); activities of the participants; and sentiments (the way people feel about themselves and others).[8] Derber, Chalmers, and Stagner developed a framework based upon three primary dimensions: union influence (the scope and depth of union participation); attitudes (i.e., the attitudes of both management and the union); and pressure (e.g., contract pressure, grievance pressure).[9] The common thread which ran through these studies was an emphasis on the individual perspectives of the parties; the relationship was evaluated by the way in which it was independently perceived by the union and by management.

These evaluative frameworks embody several common themes. One theme is the emphasis on conflict (competition) and cooperation (harmony) and the assumption that healthy labor relations are somehow the result of maximizing the latter and minimizing the former. Deutsch and others suggest, however, that the negative connotations of conflict are unrealistically simplistic:

> It has been long recognized that conflict is not inherently pathological or destructive. Its very pervasiveness suggests that it has many positive functions. It prevents stagnation, it stimulates interest and curiosity, it is a medium through which problems can be aired and solutions arrived at; it is the root of personal and social change.[10]

A strong case may be built for the argument that union-management conflict in government, and particularly the strike, has indeed served some positive functions. The use of the strike by public employees has frequently highlighted inequities in public employment, occasionally expanded important issues to the attention of the public, and recently catalyzed public backlash against employee benefits considered by some as too generous.

A second theme of these evaluative studies is that, while they generally distinguish between process and outcome, their emphasis is almost exclusively on process considerations. Little direct attention is accorded probably the most significant outcome of the union-management relationship—the extent to which the parties achieve their separate goals and take into account the goals of others. The almost exclusive emphasis on process leaves one to infer that, if union-management interactions appear to be accommodative, then some reasonable resolution of conflicts of interest must have been achieved.

The validity of the assumptions underlying this inference, however, is questionable within the institutional context of government. Studies of industrial collective bargaining employ a closed system perspective, relying upon assumptions about a competitive market setting and a bilateral relationship in order to evaluate the union-management relationship as an isolated entity. The quality of union-management interaction suffices as an evaluative criterion since it is assumed to be directly related to profitability and mutual survival; as long as the two parties survive it can be assumed that the interests of third parties are being served.

Assumptions about market competition and bilateralism are highly suspect in governmental contexts. Monopoly and multilateralism appear more appropriate for characterizing the context of public sector bargaining. Stanley writes of the differing contexts: "The private employer must stay in business and sell his goods and services in order to pay his employees. . . . Governments, on the other hand, have to stay in business, and their payrolls are met from taxes or fees imposed on the public."[11] The collective bargaining process in government also frequently involves a multiplicity of parties and interests.[12] The complexity of resolving conflicting employee, management, *and* citizen interests highlights the inadequacies of evaluating union-management relationships in government simply on the basis of whether they are predominately conflictual, accommodative, or cooperative.

The shortcomings of these private sector frameworks, in their own right and as models for the public sector, do not mean that alternative frameworks or criteria are unavailable for evaluating the union-management relationship in government. Harbison and Coleman suggest, for example, the "extent to which such relations promote the attainment of the commonly held goals of a free society, broadly defined as economic progress and equality, the enhancement of the freedom, dignity, and worth of the individual, and the strengthening of democratic political institutions."[13] Derber, et al., note that "results which might also be worth analyzing include productivity or efficiency, labor turnover, absenteeism."[14]

These alternatives imply that, in addition to evaluating the union-management relationship in terms of the process of interaction, it would also be constructive to judge the quality of the union-management relationship by the extent to which the groups achieve their separate goals and take into account the goals of relevant others. This broadens the scope of evaluation to include the impact of the relationship on the delivery of goods and services to the public. It can also lead the way to the definition of explicit standards of reasonableness, an objective to which a process approach contributes little. The following section presents the conceptual foundation of a framework for evaluating the union-management relationship in government.

Organizational Effectiveness as the Basis for Evaluation

The literature on organizational effectiveness reflects a common belief that organizations differ in the extent to which they achieve their goals and meet the demands placed upon them. Researchers have, however, disagreed over the crucial question: Effectiveness of what? In response to this question, two principal schools of thought emerge from research on organizational effectiveness: the goal approach and the systems approach.[15]

The goal approach to organizational effectiveness assumes that the organization has a limited and definable number of goals. The degree to which such goals are achieved becomes the degree to which that organization is "effective." Measures are developed to assess how well various goals are being met, and evaluation of the relative success of the organization vis-a-vis goals achievement follows quite naturally. The major criticism of the goal model is that goals are only abstractions which have little or no meaning in organizational decision-making.

This, in fact, is precisely the argument advanced by proponents of the systems view—that complex and dynamic organizations are subject to a variety of goals which are too numerous and too elusive to submit to definition. Schein puts the systems view succinctly when he writes:

> Acknowledging that every system has multiple functions, and that it exists within an environment that provides unpredictable inputs, a system's effectiveness can be defined as its capacity to survive, adapt, maintain itself, and grow, regardless of the particular functions it fulfills.[16]

Thus the systems view is primarily concerned with successful performance of various types of activities regardless of the goals the organization pursues.

Neither of these perspectives is adequate by itself as a conceptual basis for evaluating the union-management relationship in government. The goal approach, even when organizational goals can be specified, is unable to provide a satisfactory means for assessing the extent to which the parties take into account the goals of others. On the other hand, the systems approach tends to ignore the need to measure the programmatic accomplishments of government organizations vis-a-vis the union-management relationship.

Mohr and Warren offer some ideas useful for integrating the two approaches described above. Discussing the organizational goal concept, Mohr distinguishes between transitive and reflexive goals:

> A transitive goal is one whose referent is outside of or in the environment of the organization in question. A transitive goal is thus an intended impact of the organization upon its environment. . . . We may identify as the general

reflexive goal of an organization that inducements will be sufficient to evoke adequate contributions from all members of the organizational coalition.[17]

Warren suggests that an organization's sphere of activity can be defined "in terms of an organization's access to necessary resources," including 'not only those resources needed for task performance . . . but also those needed for maintenance of the organization itself."[18] Cross-classifying Mohr's distinction between transitive and reflexive goals with Warren's distinction between task accomplishment and system maintenance serves to identify four components of organizational effectiveness. These four components are displayed in Table 1. This conceptualization defines organizational effectiveness not only in terms of the conventional notion of environmental impact, but also in terms of intermediate process goals such as efficiency and employee satisfaction. The effectiveness of a governmental unit is therefore the extent to which, among other things, it uses resources efficiently, it accomplishes programmatic objectives, and it satisfies the aspirations of its employees. Since this notion of organizational effectiveness reflects the interests of management, organized employees, and citizens, it provides an appropriate conceptual basis from which to evaluate the union-management relationship.

The Evaluative Criteria

Although measures of the four components of effectiveness can be used as yardsticks for evaluation, factors other than the union-management relationship independently influence the effectiveness of government organizations (e.g., the competence of management and the aggressiveness with which the government organization interacts with its environment). The effectiveness criteria must therefore be limited to concepts associated with the impacts of the interactions and decisions which occur under the um-

TABLE 1
Components of Organizational Effectiveness

	Task Performance	System Maintenance
Transitive	Achieving intended environmental impacts	Acquiring environmental resources needed for maintenance of the governmental organization
Reflexive	Optimizing resource utilization and goal-directed activity	Maintaining or enhancing inducements/contributions ratios

brella of the union-management relationship.[19] We employ two rules for selecting specific criteria:

1. That the set of measures used reflect all four of the components of organizational effectiveness.
2. That each measure have the potential to be significantly influenced by union-management interaction or by decisions covered under the collective agreement.

Using these criteria we have selected six concepts for evaluating the union-management relationship: absenteeism and turnover, labor productivity, adaptability/flexibility, job satisfaction, commitment, and user satisfaction. As a group these concepts have high face validity for measuring the extent to which the parties achieve their goals and take into account the goals of relevant others. Each of the six concepts is discussed briefly below.

Absenteeism and Turnover

Absenteeism represents the failure of organizational members to report for scheduled work. Turnover (separation) is the amount of change in organizational personnel. Absenteeism and turnover are likely to be related to a number of factors that vary with the quality of union-management decision-making: pay and promotions, supervisory relations, job content, and job autonomy and responsibility.[20] The levels of absenteeism and turnover, in turn, influence the cost and quality of the services an organization provides. Macy and Mirvis demonstrate the significant costs associated with absenteeism and turnover because of the need to adapt manning requirements and to recruit and train new employees.[21] Seashore, Indik and Georgopoulos indicate that absenteeism is important to the delivery of services, particularly those which operate under a highly coordinated, daily schedule such as refuse collection and urban mass transit, where any kind of absence may severely disrupt the work process.[22]

Labor Productivity

Labor productivity represents the efficiency of human inputs in the production and delivery of goods and services. It is likely to be influenced significantly by wage, benefit, and working condition decisions arrived at in collective bargaining negotiations and by the attitudes of members of both organizations developed through their continuous interaction. Since labor productivity is a ratio of labor costs to outputs, it provides an alternative to evaluating the union-management relationship merely in terms of absolute wage levels.

Adaptability/Flexibility

Adaptability refers to an organization's ability to solve problems and to react to changes in its environment. It reflects an organization's readiness to tackle unusual problems, initiate improvements in work methods and operations, and try out new ideas and suggestions. As a criterion for judging the quality of the union-management relationship, it measures the extent to which collaborative decision-making among the parties actually occurs.[23]

Job Satisfaction

Job satisfaction refers to an individual's affective orientation to his or her work role.[24] It is a function of job characteristics such as pay, working conditions, interpersonal relations, responsibility, and recognition. The extent to which union-management decision making and interaction fulfills the goals of individual union members is likely to be reflected in an employee's job satisfaction. The level of job satisfaction is likely to be influenced both by the quality of negotiated settlements and by the ongoing actions of union and management in administering the collective agreement.

Commitment

Campbell defines commitment as "the strength of the predisposition of an individual to engage in goal-directed action or activity on the job."[25] Individual commitment to organizational goals is likely to be influenced by both the adequacy of employee representation by their bargaining agent and the fairness with which employees perceive they are treated by management. Katzell and Yankelovitch indicate that the degree of individual commitment to organizational goals is also strongly associated with several of the other criterion measures suggested here, particularly productivity and job satisfaction.[26]

User Satisfaction

User satisfaction is an evaluative criterion grounded in the perceptions of the recipients of the organization's goods and services. The quality of user evaluations is likely to reflect user assessments of the cost and quality of goods or services, the scope and responsiveness of the services provided, and user reaction to contacts with organizational members. User evaluations are likely to vary with the quality of the union-management relationship because of its effect on the community of services, the cost or quality of services, and the ability of the governmental unit to respond to public needs and demands.

Utility of the Evaluative Framework

These concepts have a variety of uses as a tool for evaluating the union-management relationship in government. First, the six concepts discussed above could be used as a means for comparing similar governmental organizations or organizational subunits. The use of a uniform evaluative framework would facilitate identification of factors conducive to constructive union-management relationships in government. More importantly, it would focus evaluation of the union-management relationship in government on its consequences for governmental performance rather than on the partisan evaluations of unions, management, legislators, or the public. Second, measures of each of the concepts can be used to continuously monitor the effects of the union-management decision-making and to refocus negotiations on the solution of joint problems rather than the attainment of partisan interests. Third, since unit costs can be attached to measures such as labor productivity, turnover, and absenteeism, incentive plans could be developed from these measures which would make rewards contingent upon appropriate changes in the effectiveness indices. Finally, a less tangible benefit of such an evaluative framework might be its influence on the perspectives of the parties and outside observers. The public interest would be served if the parties involved in public sector union-management relations developed standards of reasonableness and used them in pursuing creative change through collective bargaining.

Notes

1. Chester A. Newland, "Public Personnel Administration: Legalistic Reforms vs. Effectiveness, Efficiency, and Economy," *Public Administration Review,* Vol. 36, No. 5 (September/October, 1976), pp. 529-537 at p. 532.
2. Chester A. Newland, "Collective Bargaining and Public Administration: Systems for Changing and the Search for Reasonableness," in *Collective Bargaining and Public Administration,* Chester Newland and Joseph Domirtz (eds.) (Chicago: Public Personnel Association, Public Employee Relations Library, No. 34, 1971), p. i.
3. See, among others, Felix A. Nigro, "The Implications for Public Administration," *Public Administration Review,* Vol. 32, No. 2 (March/April, 1972); Lee C. Shaw and R. Theodore Clark, Jr., "The Practical Differences Between Public and Private Sector Collective Bargaining," *UCLA Law Review,* Vol. 19 (1972), pp. 867-886; and Raymond D. Horton, "Arbitration, Arbitrators, and the Public Intrest," *Industrial and Labor Relations Review,* Vol. 28, No. 4 (July, 1975), pp. 497-507.
4. Harold W. Davey, *Contemporary Collective Bargaining,* 3rd edition (Englewood Cliffs, N.J.: Prentice-Hall, 1972), p. 19.
5. Carol Weiss, *Evaluation Research* (Englewood Cliffs, N.J.: Prentice-Hall, 1972).
6. For examples of studies focusing on public sector bargaining outcomes see Ronald G. Ehrenberg, "Municipal Government Structures, Unionization, and the Wages of Fire Fighters," *Industrial and Labor Relations Review,* Vol. 27, No. 1 (October, 1973), pp. 36-48; Paul Gerhart, "Determinants of Bargaining Outcomes in Local Government

Labor Negotiations," *Industrial and Labor Relations Review,* Vol. 29, No. 3 (April, 1976), pp. 331-351; and James L. Perry and Leslie J. Berkes, "Predicting Local Government Strike Activity: An Exploratory Analysis," *Western Political Quarterly,* December 1977. Dotson's essay is worth reconsideration today as the basis of a normative theory of public employment. See Arch Dotson, "A General Theory of Public Employment," *Public Administration Review,* Vol. 16 (Summer, 1956), pp. 197-211.

7. Indicative of these studies are R. Lester and E. Robie, *Constructive Labor Relations: Experience in Four Firms* (Princeton, N.J.: Princeton University Industrial Relations Section, Report No. 75, 1948) and C. Golden and V. Parker (eds.), *Causes of Industrial Peace Under Collective Bargaining* (New York: Harper & Brothers, 1955).

8. William F. Whyte, *Pattern for Industrial Peace* (New York: Harper and Row, 1951).

9. Milton Derber, W. Ellison Chalmers, and Ross Stagner, *The Local Union-Management Relationship* (Urbana, Ill.: Institute of Labor and Industrial Relations, University of Illinois, 1960).

10. Morton Deutsch, "Conflicts: Productive and Destructive," *Journal of Social Issues,* Vol. 29 (1969), pp. 7-41. For additional discussions of the positive functions of conflict see Louis A. Coser, *Continuities in the Study of Social Conflict* (New York: The Free Press, 1957), and Richard Walton and Robert McKersie, *A Behavioral Theory of Labor Negotiations* (New York: McGraw-Hill, 1965).

11. David T. Stanley, *Managing Local Government Under Union Pressure* (Washington, D.C.: The Brookings Institution, 1972), p. 19.

12. For discussions of multilateralism in public sector bargaining see Hervey A. Juris and Peter Feuille, *Police Unionism: Power and Impact in Public Sector Bargaining* (Lexington, Mass.: D.C. Heath, 1973), and Thomas A. Kochan, "A Theory of Multilateral Collective Bargaining in City Governments," *Industrial and Labor Relations Review,* Vol. 27, No. 4 (July, 1974), pp. 525-542.

13. Frederic Harbison and J. R. Coleman, *Goals and Strategy in Collective Bargaining* (New York: Harper & Row, 1951), p. 9.

14. Milton Derber, W. Ellison Chalmers, and Ross Stagner, "Environmental Variables and Union-Management Accommodation," *Industrial and Labor Relations Review,* Vol. 11, No. 3 (April, 1958), pp. 413-428 at p. 420.

15. For a review of the effectiveness literature see John P. Campbell, et al., *The Measurement of Organizational Effectiveness: A Review of Relevant Research and Opinion* (San Diego, Calif.: Navy Personnel Research and Development Center, 1974).

16. Edgar H. Schein, *Organizational Psychology,* 2nd edition (Englewood Cliffs, N.J.: Prentice-Hall, 1970), p. 118.

17. Lawrence B. Mohr, "The Concept of Organizational Goal," *American Political Science Review,* Vol. 67, No. 2 (June, 1973), pp. 470-481 at pp. 475-476.

18. Roland L. Warren, "The Concerting of Decisions as a Variable in Organizational Interaction," in *Interorganizational Decision Making,* Matthew Tuite, Roger Chisolm and Michael Radnor (eds.) (Chicago: Aldine, 1972), pp. 19-32 at p. 22.

19. Even careful selection of measures is no guarantee that other intervening factors will not influence the criteria. It is not necessary, however, to define a complex model of all causal relationships in order to conduct an evaluation. Hatry, et al., suggest that other influences on the criteria should be considered in the normal course of identifying the positive and negative impacts of a specific program or set of activities. See Harry Hatry, Richard Winnie, and Donald M. Fisk, *Practical Program Evaluation for State and Local Government Officials* (Washington, D.C.: The Urban Institute, 1973).

20. For a discussion of factors associated with absenteeism and turnover see Lyman W. Porter and Richard M. Steers, "Organizational, Work, and Personal Factors in Employee Turnover and Absenteeism," *Psychological Bulletin,* Vol. 80 (1973), pp. 151-176.

21. Barry A. Macy and Philip M. Mirvis, "A Methodology for Assessment of Quality of Work Life and Organizational Effectiveness in Behavioral-Economic Terms," *Administrative Science Quarterly,* Vol. 21, No. 2 (June, 1976), pp. 212-226.
22. Stanley Seashore, B. Ineik, and B. Georopoulos, "Relationships Among Criteria of Job Performance," *Journal of Applied Psychology,* Vol. 44 (1960), pp. 195-202.
23. We view adaptability as an integral part of what Walton and McKersie term integrative bargaining or joint problem-solving. See Walton and McKersie, *op. cit.*
24. See Edward E. Lawler, III, *Motivation in Work Organizations* (Monterey, Calif.: Brooks/Cole Publishing Co., 1973).
25. Campbell, et al., *op. cit.,* p. 80.
26. Raymond A. Katzell and Daniel Yankelovitch, *Work, Productivity and Job Satisfaction: An Evaluation of Policy-Related Research.* Final report to the National Science Foundation, No. SSH 73-07939, 1975.

1978 (290-294)

BRUCE BUCHANAN

The Senior Executive Service:
How We Can Tell If It Works

As this is written, the Senior Executive Service (SES) is still in the early stages of infancy. Federal agencies are struggling, under the watchful eyes of the Office of Personnel Management, the General Accounting Office, congressional committees, the Office of Management and Budget, the press, and a host of evaluation researchers, to install the new machinery and procedures mandated under Title IV of the Civil Service Reform Act of 1978 (CSRA).

Few government ventures have attracted as much evaluation research attention as has civil service reform. In November 1979, the central management agencies of the federal government convened a conference on public management research, which sought to encourage special attention to CSRA.[1] Sponsored and unsponsored evaluation studies are being launched by scholars at universities around the nation. OPM has awarded at least three contracts to conduct "organizational assessments" aimed at clarifying the consequences of the reform. Federal departments and agencies like DHHS and NASA have extensive "in-house" evaluations under way. A variety of articles has already probed the theoretical strengths and weaknesses of the SES and other aspects of CSRA.[2] Moreover, survey research into the reactions of senior executives to the SES program has begun to appear, highlighting a wary skepticism within the ranks.[3]

Despite this early flurry of research attention, the important questions— questions whose answers will decide the ultimate fate of this large-scale experiment in public management—are just beginning to come into focus. Precisely what is the SES intended to accomplish? What are the principal threats to its success and survival? How realistic are the expectations of those policy makers and institutions—OPM, GAO, OMB and the Congress —whose judgments will be decisive? If things go wrong, what will be the likely causes? Most importantly, however, as the public management research community marshalls its resources for the task of evaluation, what shall be the criteria for success? If we view the SES as a "program"[4] that must prove itself (Section 415 of Title IV provides for a congressional "sunset" review after five years have elapsed), how good is "good enough"?

Purposes and Data Sources

This article is offered as a preliminary attempt to develop workable criteria for evaluating the Senior Executive Service. The analysis is based, in part, on documentary research (discussed below) and, in part, on some 69 interviews with policy makers, personnel specialists and SES members conducted in Washington, D.C., between August 1979 and August 1980. The 24 "policy makers" were affiliated with the White House Domestic Policy Staff, OPM, OMB, GAO, and congressional committees. Each of these people either helped to design the SES or aided in the effort to win legislative approval for CSRA. The 10 personnel specialists were responsible for the implementation and management of the SES system within the Departments of Health and Human Services,[5] Energy, Housing and Urban Development, Transportation, Agriculture, and Treasury.

Since the great diversity of the executive branch made a truly "representative" sample of SES interviews prohibitively large and expensive, a strategy of concentrating most of the SES interviews (29 or 35) within a single department—HHS—was followed. This made it possible to obtain a comprehensive exposure to, and appreciation for, the impact of SES on one reasonably typical administrative setting. A measure of protection against the threat to external validity posed by a potentially unrepresentative sample was afforded by carefully cross-checking HHS results against the responses of six additional senior executives in the Departments of Labor, HUD and Treasury. One other "validity check" was obtained by asking the 10 personnel specialists in each of the six departments mentioned above to examine a summary of the SES interview results. Since these personnel specialists were in regular contact with the SES contingents in their respective departments, they were able to comment upon the extent to which the findings reported here reflected the consensus among the senior executives with whom they were acquainted. Minor variations were noted, but the consensus was that the generalizations drawn later in this article were supported by the attitudes of the executives in their departments. These precautions increase confidence that the generalizations offered here are supported by the experience of a significant proportion of the executive branch. No claim of pure statistical "representativeness" can be supported, however, nor is such a claim made.

SES: Objectives and Program Design

Meaningful evaluation of any program requires prior clarification of program aims and performance standards. Yet, such an exercise is all the more essential in connection with the SES, if only because bureaucracy and its imputed failings are such symbolic, value-laden issues for much of the general public. Such public sentiment virtually guarantees close congressional scrutiny of SES performance. Such sentiment might—in the absence of carefully crafted and widely discussed evaluative standards—predispose the Congress to overreact to isolated instances of highly publicized abuse or failure, or to erect unrealistic standards for use in reaching final judgments about SES or other aspects of CSRA.

A related problem revealed by the interviews is the existence of multiple perspectives concerning the purposes of SES. Some see it as little more than a personnel system; a collection of practices and procedures allowing a more rational tracking and distribution of human resources. Others view SES as a management control device similar in potential to PPB or MBO. Still others see SES as an elite cadre, membership in which might instill pride and enthusiasm in public service. Each of these visions is partially accurate. The differences in emphasis are likely to produce variations in ''bottom line'' performance expectations without some effort to clarify purposes and build consensus on standards.

Evaluation must begin, then, with a clear vision of the *raison d'etre* of the SES, and with clarification of the hypothesized linkages between the components of the SES program and the various objectives those components are intended to achieve. Figure 1 schematizes an effort to grasp the logical relationships in this network. Although no official effort to identify these relationships was available, it was possible to infer logical interconnections from a review of such authoritative sources as the final staff report,[6] the legislation,[7] congressional testimony[8] and the interviews with 24 ''policy makers'' who helped design the SES.

The Senior Executive Service in its entirety is an extremely complex, intricate, and multifaceted system of elaborate procedural relationships among various new administrative entities embedded in multiple institutions at several hierarchical levels. To capture all this in a flow chart would require many pages of diagrams. Figure 1 necessarily omits much of this detail. Still, the figure captures the essential thinking behind the program and embodies its intended effects under ''ideal'' conditions.

Thus, the ultimate objectives—depicted at the extreme right of Figure 1— are logical responses to the moral and management failures of Watergate and Great Society program implementation: to increase the effectiveness of program performance and to increase public confidence in and satisfaction with the integrity and the competence of federal program administration.

FIGURE 1

Senior Executive Service Program Design Logic

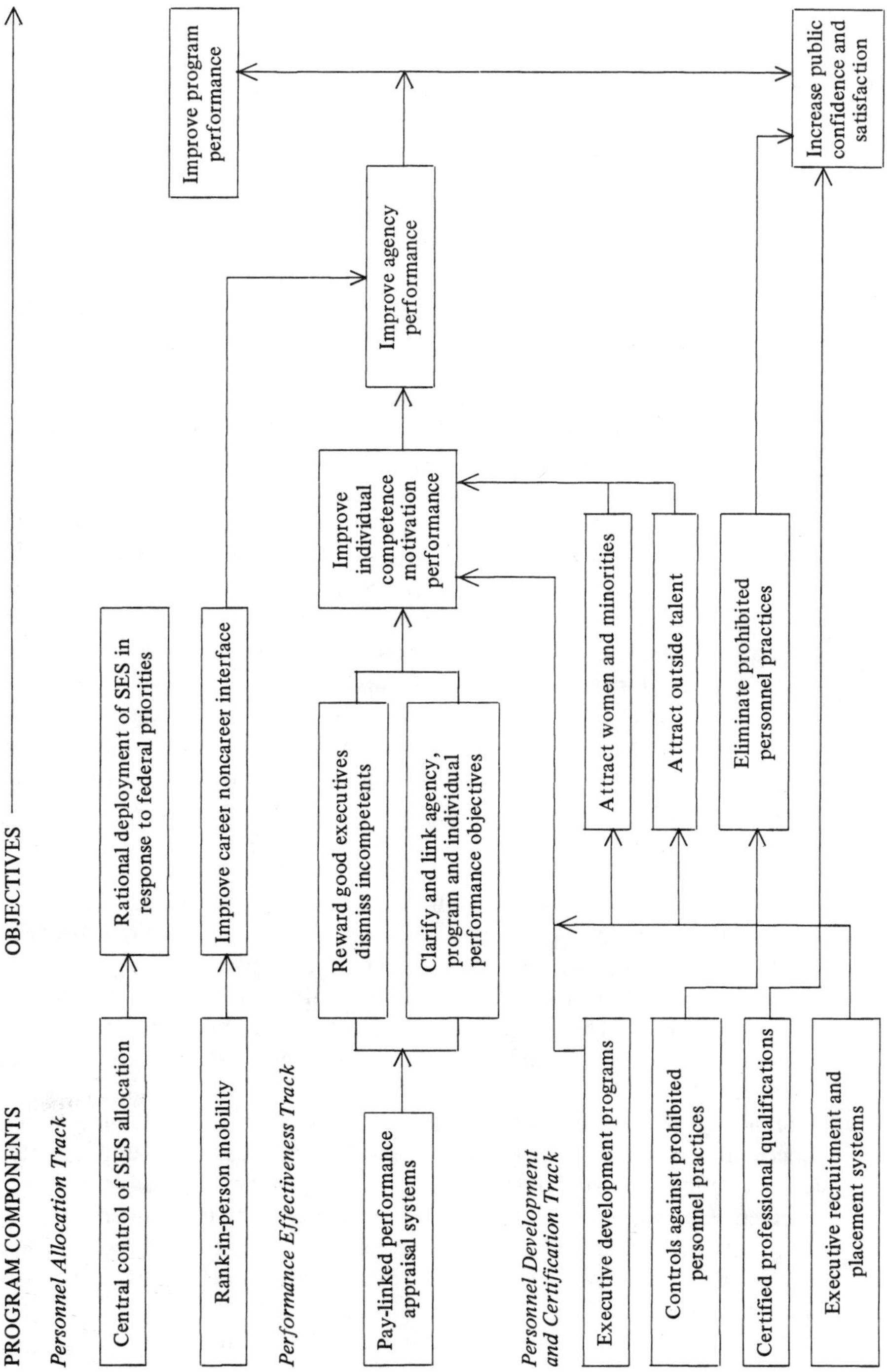

As indicated, the program components are clustered into three major "tracks," shown at the left of Figure 1: Personnel Allocation, Performance Effectiveness, and Personnel Development and Certification. Each track is presumed to make an independent contribution to improved agency and program effectiveness, and to interact with and supplement the others in pursuit of the same end. The program designers expect that demonstrated increases in program effectiveness, coupled with strict controls on political tampering, and formal certification of the professional competence of senior executives, will eventually produce a new increase in public confidence in federal management, and greater public satisfaction with the delivery of federal services.

The logical assumptions can be gleaned by reading Figure 1 in an "if . . . then" manner. Beginning with the performance effectiveness track—justifiably considered the "heart and soul" of the SES program—we can note that *if* senior executives are required to develop performance appraisal plans, evaluation against which shall form the basis of all personnel actions, *then* grounds for rewarding good executives and dismissing incompetents will exist, as will the incentives needed to impel individuals to clarify their performance objectives and to identify their contributions to agency and program objectives. In time, knowledge that excellent performance is rewarded should increase the performance motivation of senior executives, and performance-based feedback should enable them to increase their competence and sharpen performance effectiveness. The eventual result of these dynamics, if they are sufficiently refined and entrenched, is improved agency and program performance in the long run. This process is supplemented by the rational deployment of talent and by the executive training and certification activities embedded in tracks one and three. Thus, *if* there is centralized deployment of SES personnel within the departments, and *if* there is rank-in-person mobility, *then* the formerly rigid distinctions between political, non-career positions and career posts need no longer inhibit the most rational deployment of management talent in response to evolving federal priorities. The people best suited to given tasks are now made available to sharpen their effectiveness via the performance appraisal process.

Similarly, *if* there are executive development programs, recruitment and placement systems, certified professional qualifications, and controls against favoritism and mistreatment, *then* it becomes possible to bring talented persons, representing a cross-section of society (women, minorities, *and* Anglos), to the level of experience and professional competence necessary for entry into the SES. Newcomers are thus delivered into the performance appraisal process in a position to profit from and respond to the performance feedback and effectiveness training it can provide. The assumption that increased program effectiveness, coupled with controls against political abuse, and certified professional qualifications will combine to produce increased public confidence and satisfaction, was mentioned earlier.

Problems

Figure 1 depicts the consequences of SES if—as is highly unlikely—the components of the program shape results just as the designers intended. In an ideal world, the ultimate objectives would serve as the logical criteria against which the performance of the SES would be evaluated. In fact, however, the early indications are that unanticipated forces are working to disturb the ideal relationships depicted in the figure. Various problems and pitfalls have emerged to threaten—on a government-wide basis—the ultimate success of the SES. If workable criteria are to be developed for evaluating the Senior Executive Service, it will be necessary to identify these problems and take them into account. This should point toward a realistic sense of what can be expected of SES as a program.

Skepticism among SES Membership

Top federal executives have opposed earlier efforts to install SES-like personnel procedures because they invariably reduce individual autonomy.[9] Involuntary transfers and reassignments, *de facto* demotions, and pay increase denials take place with or without the consent of the executive, and with significant reductions in appeal rights under SES. Other bases of opposition are suggested by the results of survey research. For example, the Federal Executive League, in a survey of supergraders conducted before the birth of SES, found a significant fear of political abuse (e.g., partisan or personal favoritism supplanting merit as the basis for personnel actions) among their sample. Lynn and Vaden, in a survey of 1,207 GS 15-18 managers, found little enthusiasm for SES or other aspects of the 1978 reform act. Interviews conducted for this study tended to support these findings, but also uncovered additional specific sources of disillusionment. Perhaps the most significant threat to membership support for SES was the congressional action to alter SES bonus provisions in the summer of 1980. Acting angrily in response to NASA's decision to award bonuses to the maximum allowable percentage of its senior executives (50 percent), a Senate-House conference committee reduced to 25 percent the proportion of SES executives eligible for bonuses. In addition, a paycap freezing the salaries of all top government executives was imposed. Next, OPM Director Alan Campbell, acting to shore up political support for the beleaguered bonus system, issued a directive to agencies limiting bonus awards to a maximum of 20 percent of their career SES personnel; in effect, "going the Congress one better" in hopes of demonstrating good faith.

These actions bred anger and resentment, and added a negative cast to the more neutral skepticism apparent in the interviews conducted in the fall of 1979 and the spring of 1980. Summer 1980 interviewees often characterized these events as "a breach of faith," suggesting that while they were expected to take initiatives and risks under SES, the Congress and OPM were free to view the bonus system—perhaps the major *quid pro quo* SES incentive—as optional, whenever it was politically convenient to do so.

Another factor frequently mentioned by interviewees as inhibiting unqualified enthusiasm for SES was the then-approaching 1980 presidential election. Many executives felt that a change of administrations was likely, and were suspicious that a new administration might use SES provisions to "clean house" in political terms. While acknowledging that a Republican administration had as much to gain from a healthy and effective SES as a Democratic administration, and, thus, might make no effort to apply purely partisan values to its operation, a majority of interviewees still insisted that a major test for the SES must be its ability to weather changes in administrations without wholesale political manipulation. Until this test is passed, they argued, it is only rational to adopt a "wait and see" attitude.

A third source of tentativeness in the attitudes of executives toward SES was anxiety and uncertainty about the operation of the performance appraisal process within their agencies. Most departments were not scheduled to complete the first official performance appraisal cycle until late 1980. In the summer of 1980, many executives were uncertain whether the process could be objective and equitable, and in any case whether the outcomes would be cheerfully accepted by those who were judged harshly or excluded from bonuses.

Together with some lingering resentment over President Carter's "Bash the Bureaucrat" campaign for the CSRA legislation, and scattered concern about the "unmeasurability" of executive success, the three factors just reviewed fueled a significant amount of skepticism about the long-term prospects of the Senior Executive Service among those interviewed for this article. Why, then, did as many as 97 percent of eligible supergrade personnel opt to be "grandfathered" into the SES in July of 1979? Because it was, and is, "the only game in town" according to a majority of our interviewees, and not because of any sense of unqualified endorsement. Clearly, the long-term success of the SES depends heavily on positive, supportive attitudes within the ranks. The apparent absence of such support in the early going is a significant, though potentially reversible, threat to success.

Problems with Measuring Performance Effectiveness

The presence of this problem varies with the susceptibility of department and agency objectives to quantification. Still, our interviewees at all levels—policy makers, personnel specialists, and senior executives—expressed concern with the ability of the mandated performance appraisal plans to account adequately for the intuitive, subjective, and ambiguous aspects of "good" managerial performance. A related concern is the seeming inability of any performance appraisal plan to deal adequately with the unpredictables of political life: congressional action and electoral change; or with such intangible yet critical skills as interpersonal competence, or political sensitivity.

The performance planning and appraisal process also creates opportunities for various inequities to take root and further erode the support for SES among its membership. One such opportunity concerns the "good faith" with which performance objectives are set by individual executives. Interview results suggested that SESers are watching each other closely for signs of manipulation; for example, the setting of too easily attainable work goals in the hopes of inflating chances for salary raises and bonuses. Should such manipulation become commonplace, perceptions of inequity would threaten executive support for the performance evaluation process.

A related and complicating factor concerns the means for comparing the difficulty of individual SES jobs, and the ambitiousness of the objectives set within such jobs, as equitable bases for distributing rewards and promotions. In many departments and agencies around the government, no formal mechanism exists for making such judgments; they are left to the subjective interpretations of superiors and performance review boards. Since such factors are likely to figure importantly in judgments of the quality of individual performance, the absence of objective and uniform means of classifying and comparing position difficulty and work plan ambition may invite invidious comparisons and contribute to perceptions of inequity. Any of the difficulties mentioned, if they assume government-wide proportions, could erode the confidence of senior executives in the performance planning and appraisal process and subvert its operation.

Problematic Linkages Between Individual and Program Objectives

Title IV of the 1978 reform act requires "that compensation, retention and tenure (be) contingent on managerial success, which is measured on the basis of individual *and* organizational performance" (emphasis mine). Later in Title IV, subchapter 11 requires that "written appraisals of performance (be) based on the individual *and* organizational performance requirements established for the rating period involved" (emphasis mine).

Thus, the act clearly intends that the performance of organizational programs be improved, and envisions that performance appraisal plans be one mechanism by which this consequence is secured. The early indications are, however, that this linkage is by no means a certainty.

More than one of the interviewed executives pointed out that linkage is not automatic; that there is no *necessary* connection between measures of individual effectiveness on the one hand and of program effectiveness on the other. If the sum of improved individual performances is to result in improved program performance, then explicit and concerted efforts to build these linkages will be required. Departments and agencies must require that program objectives be incorporated into the work plans of senior executives. Defining, measuring, and linking these objectives is stubborn and difficult work. There are signs that this work is not yet receiving the attention it deserves.

One such sign is the relative indifference to the linkage question that characterized the reactions of policy makers, personnel specialists, and senior executives interviewed for this study. Another is the results of survey research conducted by the Office of Personnel Management *before* the implementation of CSRA. Of some 14,000 federal employees surveyed, only 25 percent said they found their performance ratings helpful in determining their contributions to the organization.[10] None of this is definitive, and two of the six departments contacted did report efforts to build linkage into the performance planning process. Should linkage fail to become a preoccupation of SESers and their supervisors on a government-wide basis, however, the ability of the SES to bring about improved program performance will be compromised.

Missing Program Components

The point here is that the designers of the SES program may have failed to include components whose presence later proves to have been necessary to achieve the ultimate objectives. In such a case, eventual failure is predestined by a design flaw or omission. For example, a cornerstone of the reform is decentralized authority over personnel actions. The undisputed premise is that agency control over its own staff is a precondition to improved program performance. Yet, as a few interviewees noted, there is no corresponding provision for agency control over financial resources. Transferring or reprogramming public monies is a touchy business, requiring at least informal congressional approval.[11] Financial resources, then, are considerably less flexible than human resources. Since flexibility in both areas is arguably required to produce performance results, the lack of financial flexibility could well offset the performance benefits of increased control over personnel. The end result might be little demonstrable improvement in performance, even though agencies had successfully implemented all aspects of the SES program. At the very least, this limitation suggests that expectations for program achievement should be tempered by the facts of financial and other limitations beyond the control of the executive.

Another example of a "missing component" derives from the fact that the financial incentives and penalties applied to GS 13 to 15 managers are not applied to those below these grades. CSRA does contain statutory requirements for performance standards and appraisal at the lower levels, but the absence of comparable financial incentives could work against improvements in program performance. Again, the result may be less improvement in program performance, not because of poor implementation or malfeasance, but because the SES program is not supported by provisions arguably necessary for a reasonable chance of success.

A related omission of potential import is the lack of equivalence between the incentives provided SES members, as compared with those available to GS 13-15s, the "merit pay" group. Whereas SESers have the opportunity to earn bonuses that represent genuine additions to their incomes, GS 13-15 people must earn merit pay from the "comparability pay" fund that used to be distributed automatically. In effect, they perceive that they are now expected to perform exceptionally in order to "earn back" what used to be theirs as a matter of course. Some resentment toward these and other SES advantages among GS 13-15s was noted by personnel specialists among the interviewees for this study. These perceptions of inequity might eventually be allayed by the fact that senior executives must sacrifice job security for their greater financial incentives (they can be demoted and reassigned for inadequate performance), should this CSRA provision be meaningfully implemented. But as matters stand now, inequivalent incentives may threaten effective working relationships between SES and merit pay personnel, and dilute the motivation of those compensated at the lower rate.

One additional "missing component" deserves mention: any direct provision for upgrading public confidence in and satisfaction with federal program performance. As Figure 1 implies, the designers' assumption seems to be that controls against political abuse, certified professional qualifications, and any improvements in program performance resulting from SES will somehow automatically become known to the general public. In fact, it seems quite possible that performance could improve, and the other components operate quite successfully without any of this becoming common public knowledge. The upshot is that explicit efforts to influence public opinion on these matters might be necessary if this objective is to be seriously pursued.

Uneven SES Implementation

This potential problem derives from the fact that federal agencies vary in terms of their expertise in and experience with such SES-type procedures and performance appraisal and executive development. Agencies also differ in terms of their enthusiasm for SES and the zeal with which they are implementing its provisions. Such natural distinctions will inevitably produce a variety of outcomes at evaluation time. This raises the question of whether blanket, "across-the-board" judgments of the success or failure of SES are appropriate, or even possible in any objective, fair-minded sense. It also suggests that evaluators should guard against overreaction to *any* single agency's experience with SES, be it dramatic success or spectacular failure. From a personnel system whose major provisions include unprecedented grants of autonomy to agencies, uneven consequences are to be expected, and should not by themselves provoke adverse judgments among evaluators.

Public Sector Problems

These include possible conundrums that would spring from inconsistencies between features of the SES system and characteristics unique to the public sector. For example, the successful operation of the "pay for performance" and bonus provisions of SES require that funds be appropriated in a timely fashion by the Congress. Should Congress delay appropriations, as it is wont to do, effective operation of these provisions would simply cease, arresting momentum and eroding support for SES among its membership.

Another example concerns the difficulties of operating an effective performance appraisal process in the "goldfish bowl" atmosphere of the public sector. Industrial experience with performance appraisal procedures involving negotiation of performance objectives and supervisor judgment of subordinate competence suggests that these are sensitive matters for subordinates, and that the process works best when conducted with some measure of discretion, or even privacy.[12] Because of the relentless pressure to scrutinize and publicize these processes in the public sector—pressure spawned by the understandable desire to prevent manipulation or abuse—the possibility exists that scrutiny will reduce the appraisal process to perfunctory or ceremonial proportions in order to protect the sensitivities of those being evaluated. Difficult judgments about performance effectiveness might either be driven underground and left undocumented, or eliminated altogether. Either outcome would be inconsistent with the intent of the SES program.

As a final example, note the inconsistency between the efficiency dynamic implicit in performance appraisal processes, and the maximization dynamic encouraged by the federal budget process. Should a senior executive seek to attain the maximum program impact for each dollar, thus keeping the budget down, or should he adopt the traditional bureaucratic posture of asking for more than he needs, in order to protect his agency's stakes at appropriations time?[13] These impulses will surely collide. If history is any guide, the maximization dynamic will prevail, neutralizing any increase in cost-effectiveness that might have resulted from the work planning and objective-setting features of SES.

Attributing Changes to SES

The last of the problems to be mentioned concerns research design and "quasi-experimental" controls, critical factors in any evaluation research effort. The problem here is not with the program *per se*. Rather, it has to do with whether or not any changes in the dependent variables (in this case, program performance and public satisfaction) can be clearly and unarguably attributed to the independent variables, the SES program components (Figure 1). Officials interviewed in the agencies charged with formal evaluation of CSRA—GAO and OPM—express considerable skepticism on this point. In fact, anyone who studies this problem closely must conclude that, from the standpoint of strict experimental design, such attributions will prove to be extremely difficult if not impossible.

The reason is that the rival hypotheses are numerous and not readily susceptible to the kind of controls necessary to eliminate them as plausible explanations for observed changes in the dependent variables.[14] How, for example, could it be certain that any measured increases in effectiveness resulted from SES and not from a breakthrough in program technology or from the impact of numerous other government-wide efforts to improve government effectiveness, like the President's Management Intern Program, or OPM's Office of Productivity programs? Similarly, changes in public confidence might as readily be the result of a tax cut or some widely publicized government success or failure, as of the long-term impact of the SES.

The point, then, is that it will be very hard to tell, in any rigorous or precisely certain way, just exactly what the impact of SES is on program performance or public attitudes. It will be necessary to rely on a careful review of alternative explanations for any changes, and, finally, on informed judgment, in assaying effects of SES.

Problem Implications

Where does this litany of difficulties leave us? One inescapable conclusion is that it would be unreasonable to hold the SES program accountable for its ultimate aims at the end of the short five years that legislation allows for the program to prove itself. Even without the seven major problem areas just reviewed, the massive, government-wide effort needed merely to create, install, and fine-tune the administrative machinery and procedures —ERBs, PRBs, performance appraisal plans, recruitment systems, executive development programs—will more than exhaust the first five years. Obviously, then, the formal objectives will be inadequate as short-run, and possibly even long-run criteria for success. We must place the SES into a broader context and identify more realistic standards, standards which reflect the political realities and the organizational and human limitations just reviewed.

Another important conclusion is that the problems reviewed pose serious threats to the ultimate success of SES regardless of how much time Congress allows. One major reason for this is that the majority of the problems are not susceptible to "final" solutions. They will stay "solved" only in the context of sustained and difficult efforts to keep them under control on a government-wide basis. Thus, without ongoing surveillance, senior executive support for SES may decline, linkages between individual and agency objectives might dissolve, performance measures may become arbitrary or otherwise insensitive to the actual performance of executives, and excessive publicity might undermine the performance appraisal process. The problems raised by missing program components could presumably be solved simply by adding the missing components. Even in this case, however, success cannot be assured, for it depends on the creation of a fragile, unpredictable political coalition able to get supplementary legislation through Congress.

The Senior Executive Service, thus, emerges as a program whose complexity and reliance on the diligent good-faith efforts of literally thousands of people render it uniquely vulnerable and perhaps perpetually fragile. In these terms, SES is a program in trouble before it is even "out of the gate."

Does all this mean that SES should be abandoned, or hopes for it revised drastically downward? Certainly not. Despite the difficulties, SES represents a theoretically sound and unprecedentedly comprehensive effort to improve the functioning of the federal government. It is based on the best thinking that could be marshalled, and the final product is as true to that thinking as the political process is ever likely to allow. It is clearly a step in the right direction, and deserves adequate time—perhaps as much as a generation—to establish and prove itself. It also deserves the opportunity to be adjusted and refined on the basis of experience.

The question thus emerges: how—in an evaluation-conscious government —can a flawed but promising program demonstrate its promise and avoid consumption by its flaws in the short run? Put another way, if we cannot expect attainment of the ultimate objectives within five or even 10 years, what *can* we expect? How might we clearly and objectively distinguish between "good enough" and "not good enough" within the too-short five-year "deadline" the Congress has imposed on the SES?

How We Can Tell If It Works

It would appear that there are four major indicators that will tell us whether or not SES is "on track" after five years, with real prospects for reaching its ultimate aims. These are: (a) successful installation and evidence of smooth operation of SES administrative machinery; (b) evidence of positive, supportive attitudes among the membership toward SES; (c) evidence of substantial, government-wide preoccupation with clarifying the linking individual, agency, and program performance objectives; and (d) clear indication that the SES can pass the "political" test posed by periodic changes in presidents and their policies. Let us consider why each in turn deserves to be considered an "acid test," and why each tells us important things about the health and long-term prospects of the SES program.

SES as a System of Personnel Procedures

First and most obviously, the machinery must be installed, debugged, made to complete several cycles, and accepted by those involved within five years. As noted earlier, this will not be easily accomplished. Consider, for example, the sheer size and scope of the machinery involved, and the effort required to install a completely new personnel system throughout the upper reaches of the executive branch.

Each department must create and refine executive development programs, special record-keeping systems, systematic recruitment mechanisms, and manpower planning procedures. Executive resource boards (ERBs) with broad responsibilities for planning and reviewing the qualifications of prospective executives must be constituted and made to operate smoothly. Performance review boards (PRBs) intended to monitor the equity and quality of the performance appraisal process must also be successfully established. Most important, if only because of its pervasiveness, is the performance appraisal process itself.

This entails literally thousands of diadic negotiation processes between superiors and subordinates across the bureaucracy. The change from the *status quo* to the new, MBO-like work plans is proving to be a dramatic one in many cases. As George S. Odiorne has warned, setting performance objectives is often as much a political process as it is an exercise in rational planning.[15] These negotiations threaten to disturb the *status quo,* disrupt longstanding comfortable routines, and introduce unpredictable changes in the professional, political, and personal relationships of top federal executives. Little wonder, then, that there is resistance and an element of unpredictability. Because of the potential for disruption, it should be apparent that expecting established, fully operational performance appraisal plans for all 8,000-plus senior executives, in addition to the other machinery, is not an indulgent, too-easily-met evaluative standard. Indeed, it is an open question whether these things can be accomplished in the allotted time. How can we "measure" whether the machinery and the procedures are, in fact, functioning smoothly and well? Questionnaire surveys of SES member attitudes toward, and experience with, the performance appraisal process and the supporting administrative machinery, interviews with members of PRBs and ERBs, on-site observations of the functioning of executive development programs, ERBs and PRBs—all are among the data collection methods already planned by evaluation researchers. The major question to be answered by these means is whether SES machinery and processes are operated with care and thoroughness and taken seriously by participants (success), or operated perfunctorily and viewed indifferently or negatively (failure).

SES as a Career Development and Motivation System

As we noted, the early indications are that skepticism tinged with cynicism dominate the attitudes of the supergraders who were "grandfathered" into the SES in July 1979. Many interviewed executives felt threatened by various aspects of SES that were discussed earlier. Others looked upon SES as just another "top-down" panacea, which, like PPB or ZBB, will fade into obscurity after a brief flurry. Very few executives interviewed for this project expressed much identification with the SES, or were impressed at the prospect of membership in an "elite cadre" of topflight public managers. If such attitudes take root and come to be representative of the government-wide membership by the fifth-year review, it may well be an indication of program failure. For this reason, SES members' general sense of identification with the SES, and their specific attitudes toward its various components should be monitored *via* questionnaires and interviews, administered and conducted annually at a minimum, as a key index of the health and prospects of the service. Indifferent or unsupportive attitudes would make it unarguably clear that SES had not succeeded in establishing itself as a career-development and motivation system in the minds of its membership—something it must do if its ultimate objectives are ever to be realized. Some explanation will be necessary to make this point.

Those who view SES as primarily a device for tightening overhead control of executive performance may overlook its potential for nurturing long-term psycyhological attachments on the part of its membership to agency and departmental missions, and to the SES itself as an embodiment of the ideal of top-flight professional public management.

Why are enduring psychological attachments—like commitment, identification or loyalty—important? Because of the well-founded presumption that those who feel committed to an ideal, e.g., excellence in public management, are much more likely to display intense motivation and exemplary performance in seeking to implement various expressions of the ideal, e.g., departmental or agency missions and programs, than those who do not feel this way. Public career services like the forest service, foreign service, and the Marine Corps have long recognized the value of special feelings of *esprit,* and have been cultivating organizational commitment for generations.

How are attitudes like organizational commitment instilled? Research shows that they result from such career experiences as the sense of sharing in noble and worthy enterprises with valued colleagues, the feeling that one has personally made important contributions to the success of one's agency, the belief that one's value to the agency is acknowledged and respected, and the belief that one's skill, competence, and efficacy are increasing with organizational experience. People who work in organizations that provide need-gratifying experiences like these report a growing sense of attachment, or commitment, to such settings.[16]

The point is that SES contains certain "person-centered" processes which —if properly conceived and implemented—can provide an orchestrated career development experience capable of instilling commitment to SES ideals. For example, a performance appraisal process that the executive viewed not solely as a device for extracting his efforts, but also as a feedback mechanism aimed at helping him develop his talents, sharpen his skills, increase his own value, and recognizing his accomplishments, could encourage the growth of commitment. SES also contains provisions for "mentor" relationships and individual development plans (IPDs) for individual managers. Mentors and managers could design IDPs which supplemented the performance appraisal process by creating a forum for long-term career planning that is independent of the current work assignment. The SES program also provides for sabbaticals, which allow time and resources for personnel development external to the work setting.

By such means SES could, in theory, unleash the motivation and tap the enthusiasm of its membership to an extent that made attainment of the ultimate objectives depicted in Figure 1 possible. This will not happen without an earnest good-faith effort by all concerned to launch SES and to make it work for both individuals and agencies. This is precisely what is threatened most by the early indications of apathy and hostility.

SES as a Device for Coordinating Governmental Effectiveness

Why should this be an "acid test" of the SES? First because linkage—secured by requiring senior executives to incorporate program objectives into their formal work plans as performance appraisal criteria—is the means by which the efforts of key people can be focused, guided, and coordinated so as to bring about program results at the aggregate level. Second, because the early indications suggest linkage has not achieved the status of a widespread preoccupation—something it must do if program performance is to be positively affected by SES.

Why has the linkage question not achieved the center-stage prominence it deserves? Partly because most early attention has focused on the pragmatic problem of learning how to operate a performance appraisal process. For many this entails a fundamental reorientation and, at least, a short-term preoccupation with procedures and mechanics that drives out concern for more subtle issues like linkage.

There are more serious obstacles as well. One derives from the fear of entrapment by "unmeetable" performance expectations. Senior executives understandably seek to keep their work responsibilities within manageable limits. A manager pressed to accept responsibility for the success or failure of a program will first ask whether he has sufficient power and resources to bring about program success. Since federal executives usually do have less control over financial and human resources than their private sector counterparts, there will be resistance on these grounds.

These problems are compounded by the fact that the nature of many federal agencies' objectives is such that linkages between individual tasks and program outcomes will rarely be clear and unequivocal. In soft, hard-to-measure program areas like health or welfare, program outcome data gathered in field settings close to program target groups may bear little obvious relationship to executive behavior at the Washington headquarters, or even the nearest regional office. Of course, the linkages do exist, can eventually be discerned, and ultimately even be measured, but this requires painstaking effort and involves a long-term process of gradual refinement. As some interviewed executives argued, there are few real incentives to undertake such an arduous task.

Such difficulties make clear that the linkage of individual, agency, and program goals is far from a foregone conclusion. Despite its central importance, linkage has yet to become a major issue, and this is a danger signal. Evaluation researchers should follow the linkage question closely, although it will not be an easy task. The results of this study suggest that the efforts to "measure" linkage will be the most costly, demanding, and difficult part of the evaluation research agenda, requiring extensive familiarity with the people, programs, and cultures of the agencies under investigation; in effect, in-depth case studies. If the SES program goal of increased agency effectiveness is ever to be more than a lofty "dead letter," linkage must become a government-wide preoccupation. For this reason linkage belongs among the four "bottom line" criteria recommended here.

SES as a Means of Reconciling Professionalism with Political Responsiveness

The relationship between the career civil service and the elected and appointed political leadership is a complex subject whose intricacies cannot be fully explored in the space available here.[17] Still, whether or not the SES facilitates this relationship, as it is in part intended to do (Figure 1, "improve career-noncareer interface"), must be considered an important test of its success.

In addition to streamlining outmoded structures and practices, the SES is intended to make it easier to reconcile the conflicts between the need for bureaucratic responsiveness to political direction on the one hand, and on the other the need for nonpartisan, professional management and technical competence that can maintain policy continuity and stability in government operations as administrations change.[18] In addition to the provisions aimed at enhancing competence and professionalism, SES embodies such safeguards against political abuse as the 120-day moratorium on involuntary reassignments following changes in supervisory personnel, and limitation on non-career (i.e., "political") appointments. On balance, however, these appear to be outweighed by the greatly strengthened personnel powers SES makes available to the political leadership; notably performance appraisal, bonuses, and demotions, all of which can be expected to increase the responsiveness of senior executives to their political superiors.

This imbalance invites abuse, and thus requires continuing scrutiny of the career-noncareer interface. Given this requirement, how can it be determined whether SES operates to reconcile professionalism with political responsiveness? Evaluation criteria in this area will necessarily evolve and mature with experience, but it is possible here to note certain standards that are likely to remain important. One such standard is the collective judgment of the senior executives themselves that the balance is being successfully maintained. A small percentage of this group can be expected to view all influence attempts as illegitimate, but majority questionnaire and interview responses to the following kinds of questions can serve as a barometer of the status of the career-noncareer relationship: do senior executives feel free to vigorously advocate worthy views at odds with the political commitments of superiors, or do they suppress such views because they have learned that outspokenness can lead to covert political reprisal? Do SESers feel that bonuses and other rewards go to the truly competent, or primarily to the politically loyal? Do they report that incoming administrations use the 120-day moratorium to acquaint themselves with the talents of SES careerists in the departments, with a view toward retaining those qualified, or do they signal their intention to "clean house" in political terms, merely biding their time for the required 120 days?

Other relevant evidence is more demographic in nature. For example, how many career senior executives who are known to be sympathetic to the opposing party does the political leadership retain in important positions because of professional or managerial competence? How widely does the number of successful Merit Systems Protection Board appeals based on political abuse vary across administrations? Many additional questions of this sort can and should be posed, and reasonable people may differ concerning the kinds of answers that should be interpreted as "successes" or "failures." But this is work that must be done, and the political test must be "passed" anew with each change in administrations.

Conclusion

Like most attempts to convert sound theory into workable practice, the Senior Executive Service has encountered a variety of problems that have infused the early implementation process with uncertainty. I have argued that these difficulties require a hard-nosed appraisal of what—short of its ultimate objectives—can reasonably be expected of the SES as a program, and have suggested four criteria against which progress might usefully be gauged.

This review of difficulties should not be taken to imply that the survival of the Senior Executive Service is in jeopardy. Those who think it is should remember that whatever the Congress does, or whoever wins any particular presidential election, some kind of high level personnel system for the federal government must and will remain in place. Whatever it is called, it will most likely resemble the SES in important particulars, if only because no significantly better approach has yet been designed. These realities place a limit on how badly the SES can "fail."

The more pressing danger is that the momentum and enthusiasm generated at the legislative stage will continue to erode through the middle and later stages of implementation. This will mean that we will have failed to take maximum advantage of an historic opportunity to upgrade simultaneously the effectiveness of the higher civil service, the status of public management as a profession, and the responsiveness of the bureaucracy to the president. Continued resentment, indifference, and perfunctory compliance on the part of those involved with the SES would be measurable signs of this kind of failure.

Reversing these trends requires the ability to keep the faculties of effort and enthusiasm alive despite the inevitable disruptions and characteristic unsupportiveness of the political environment. This is no easy task, but it is justifiably considered one of the central problems, if not a defining characteristic, of public management.

Notes

1. *Public Management Research Conference,* sponsored by the General Accounting Office, the General Services Administration, the Office of Management and Budget, and the Office of Personnel Management, convened at the Brookings Institution, Washington, D.C., November 19-20, 1979.
2. See, for example, the articles by Rosen, Howard and Thayer on various aspects of SES and CSRA in *Public Administration Review* (July/August 1978), pp. 301-304. Also relevant is S. D. Foster, "The 1978 Civil Service Reform Act: Post-Mortem or Rebirth," *Public Administration Review* (January/February 1970), pp. 78-85; and J. R. Dempsey, "Carter Reorganization: A Midterm Appraisal," *Public Administration Review* (January/February 1979), pp. 64-77. For "deep background" on the history and origins of the SES concept, see "Perspectives on the Senior Executive Service: A Literature Review," unpublished manuscript, *CONSAD Research Corporation,* October 1979.
3. N. B. Lynn and R. E. Vaden, "Bureaucratic Response to Civil Service Reform," *Public Administration Review* (July/August 1979), pp. 333-342.
4. This perspective on SES derives from R. E. Schmidt, J. W. Scanlon, and J. W. Bell, *Evaluability Assessment: Making Public Programs Work Better,* Washington: The Urban Institute Contract Report 1217-50-01 (October 1978).
5. Department of Health and Human Services, formerly Health, Education and Welfare. Senior executives were interviewed in connection with an evaluability assessment of the SES conducted by DHHS's Office of Evaluation and Technical Analysis to which the author served as a consultant.
6. The President's Reorganization Project, *Personnel Management Project,* Final Staff Report, Volume 1 (December 1977).
7. *The Civil Service Reform Act of 1978,* Public Law, 95-454 (October 13, 1978).
8. *Legislative History of the Civil Service Reform Act of 1978,* Committee on Post Office and Civil Service, House of Representatives, Volumes 1 and 2 (March 27, 1979).
9. For discussions of earlier SES-like proposals, including the "Senior Civil Service" of the Second Hoover Commission (1955), the "Career Executive Service" proposal of the Eisenhower Administration (1948), and President Nixon's 1971 proposals for a "Federal Executive Service," see H. Emmerich, *Federal Organization and Administrative Manage-*
9. *For discussions of earlier SES-like proposals, including the "Senior Civil Service" of the Second Hoover Commission (1955), the "Career Executive Service" proposal of the Eisenhower Administration (1948), and President Nixon's 1971 proposal for a "Federal Executive Service," see H. Emmerich, Federal Organization and Administrative Management* (University: University of Alabama Press, 1971) and J. W. Fesler, *Public Administration: Theory and Practice* (Englewood Cliffs: Prentice-Hall, 1980).
10. Office of Personnel Management, "1979 Federal Employee Attitude Survey: Preliminary Findings," News Release (November 9, 1979).
11. L. Fisher, *The Constitution Between Friends* (New York: St. Martin's Press, 1978).
12. See, for example, D. D. McConkey, "MBO—Twenty Years Later, Where Do We Stand," *Business Horizons* (August 1973), pp. 25-35.

13. A. Wildavsky, *The Politics of the Budgetary Process,* 3rd Edition (Boston: Little Brown, 1979).
14. Cf., T. D. Cook and D. T. Campbell, *Quasi-Experimentation: Design and Analysis Issues for Field Settings* (Chicago: Rand McNally, 1979).
15. G. S. Odiorne, "The Politics of Implementing MBO," *Business Horizons* (June 1974), pp. 13-21.
16. For a discussion of the commitment development process, see B. Buchanan, "Building Organization Commitment: The Socialization of Managers in Work Organizations," *Administrative Science Quarterly* (December 1974), pp. 533-546. For a discussion of differences in managerial commitment between business and government organizations, see B. Buchanan, "Public Managers, Business Executives and Organization Commitment," *Public Administration Review* (July/August 1974).
17. Cf., H. Heclo, *A Government of Strangers: Executive Politics in Washington* (Washington, D.C.: The Brookings Institution, 1977).
18. For a timely discussion of these issues that includes attention to the role of the SES in a revised Executive Office of the President, see, *A Presidency for the 1980s: A Report on Presidential Management* by a panel of the National Academy of Public Administration (November 1980).

1981 (349-358)

ROBERT K. YIN

Life Histories of Innovations: How New Practices Become Routinized

The Life History Approach

A fire department in a southern city initiated a new paramedic service in 1973. Four years later, the service was so pervasive that the department avoided citywide budget cuts, and the "innovation" was considered a routine part of the department's operations. Innovations like this one continually emerge in urban bureaucracies. Little is known, however, about how such practices become routinized—i.e., how they become part of "standard practice." Instead, most previous research has focused on earlier steps in the innovation process, such as adoption (Rogers, 1962; and Warner, 1974) or implementation (Berman and McLaughlin, 1978). Yet, to develop a full theory of organizational innovation (Becker and Whisler, 1967; Clark and Guba, 1965; and Rowe and Boise, 1974) requires an understanding of the routinization process. In addition, policy initiatives must account for the long-term consequences of innovation and must deal with routinization. This is true whether a municipal service practice is based on new technology (e.g., Lambright and Flynn, 1977) or on organizational changes such as municipal decentralization (e.g., Yin and Yates, 1975).

The routinization process was studied by examining the *life histories* of six types of innovations, to assure a variety of settings and bureaucratic practices:[1]

Type of Innovation	Urban Service
Computer-assisted instruction (CAI)	Education
Police computer systems	Police
Mobile intensive care units (paramedics)	Fire
Closed circuit television systems (CCTV)	Education
Breath testing for driver safety	Police
Jet-Axe	Fire

The life histories were developed through case studies on the use of these innovations at 19 sites,[2] but corroborating evidence was also collected with telephone interviews at 90 other sites (see Tables 1 and 2). The sample of case studies covered many years, with the innovation often having been adopted over 10 to 15 years ago. In other words, a deliberate choice made in the study design was to identify and select a sample of "old" innovations, and then to trace life histories in a post hoc or historical manner.[3]

In contrast to previous studies of organizational change, which have relied heavily on attitudinal changes (e.g., Berman and McLaughlin, 1978; and Hage and Aiken, 1970), the life histories were analyzed in terms of the achievement of actual organizational events. Ten such events were conceptualized as either *passages* (transitions from one organizational state to another) or *cycles* (survival over periodic organizational events), not unlike the approach used to study human adult development (Sheehy, 1976). The ten events covered the procedural, budget, personnel, and other resources needed to sustain any organizational practice over time:

1. *Equipment turnover* (cycle): Have procedures been established for purchasing/leading the new generations of equipment needed to update the innovation?
2. Transition to support by *local funds* (passage): Is the practice supported by "hard" (local) money?
3. Establishment of appropriate *organizational status* (passage): Is the new practice located in the correct organizational unit?

TABLE 1
Nineteen Case-Study Sites, by Innovation

Innovation/City	1970 Population (thousands)	Innovation/City	1970 Population (thousands)
CAI		*CCTV*	
Dallas, Tex.	844	Omaha, Nebr.	347
Oakland, Calif.	362	Portland, Oreg.	380
San Diego, Calif.	697	Rochester, N.Y.	296
Tampa, Fla.	278		
		Breath Testing	
Police Computer		Akron, Ohio	275
Boston, Mass.	641	Cincinnati, Ohio	451
Indianapolis, Ind.	746	Memphis, Tenn.	624
Miami, Fla.	335		
Nashville, Tenn.	448	*Jet-Axe*	
		Omaha, Nebr.	347
MJCU		Rochester, N.Y.	296
Birmingham, Ala.	301		
Dallas, Tex.	844		
Denver, Colo.	516		

TABLE 2
Ninety Telephone Interview Sites, by Innovation

Innovation/City	1970 Population (thousands)	Innovation/City	1970 Population (thousands)
CAI		*MICU*	
Atlanta, Ga.	497	Baltimore, Md.	906
Baltimore, Md.	906	Cincinnati, Ohio	451
Birmingham, Ala.	301	Gary, Ind.	175
Denver, Colo.	516	Jacksonville, Fla.	529
Fort Worth, Tex.	393	Kansas City, Kans.	507
Honolulu, Hawaii	325	Madison, Wis.	172
Kansas City, Mo.	507	Memphis, Tenn.	624
Louisville, Ky.	362	Phoenix, Ariz.	582
Newark, N.J.	382	Portland, Oreg.	380
New Orleans, La.	593	St. Paul, Minn.	310
Phoenix, Ariz.	582	Salt Lake City, Utah	176
Rochester, N.Y.	296	Seattle, Wash.	531
St. Louis, Mo.	622	Toledo, Ohio	383
Toledo, Ohio	383	Tucson, Ariz.	263
Tucson, Ariz.	263	Warren, Mich.	179
Wichita, Kans.	277		
		CCTV	
Police Computer		Anaheim, Calif.	166
Baltimore, Md.	906	Atlanta, Ga.	497
Birmingham, Ala.	301	Fresno, Calif.	166
Buffalo, N.Y.	463	Honolulu, Hawaii	325
Denver, Colo.	516	Indianapolis, Ind.	746
Kansas City, Mo.	507	Milwaukee, Wis.	717
Long Beach, Calif.	359	Phoenix, Ariz.	582
Louisville, Ky.	362	St. Louis, Mo.	622
Oakland, Calif.	359	Salt Lake City, Utah	176
St. Louis, Mo.	622	San Jose, Calif.	447
San Diego, Calif.	697	Santa Ana, Calif.	156
Seattle, Wash.	531	Seattle, Wash.	531
Tucson, Ariz.	263	Springfield, Mass.	164
Washington, D.C.	757	Tucson, Ariz.	263
		Jet-Axe	
Breath Testing		Charlotte, N.C.	241
Atlanta, Ga.	497	Cincinnati, Ohio	451
Austin, Tex.	252	El Paso, Tex.	322
Baltimore, Md.	906	Honolulu, Hawaii	325
Dallas, Tex.	844	Jacksonville, Fla.	529
Indianapolis, Ind.	746	Kansas City, Mo.	507
Jacksonville, Fla.	529	Louisville, Ky.	362
Jersey City, N.J.	260	Minneapolis, Minn.	434
Kansas City, Mo.	507	St. Paul, Minn.	310
Minneapolis, Minn.	434	St. Petersburg, Fla.	216
New Orleans, La.	593	Salt Lake City, Utah	176
Oklahoma City, Okla.	368	San Francisco, Calif.	716
St. Louis, Mo.	622	Santa Ana, Calif.	156
San Diego, Calif.	697	Tucson, Ariz.	263
Seattle, Wash.	531	Worcester, Mass.	177
Tampa, Fla.	278		
Tucson, Ariz.	263		

4. Establishment of stable arrangement for *supply and maintenance* (passage): Can supplies and repairs be obtained according to regular agency procedures?

5. Establishment of *personnel classifications or certification* (passage): Can the personnel system hire the new specialists that may be needed to carry out the new practice?

6. Changes in *organizational governance* (passage): Has the new practice become part of the agency's formal regulations, the governing local ordinance, or a new bond issue that may define the "standard" equipment to be purchased?

7. Internalization of *training* program (passage): Does the regular training academy or inservice training program provide the necessary courses to cover the new skills needed by practitioners?

8. *Promotion of personnel* acquainted with the innovation (cycle): Have persons familiar with the new practice now been promoted into positions of greater responsibility and power, from which they can support the practice even further?

9. *Turnover in key personnel* (cycle): Has the new practice, after an appropriate period of time, continued even after the original personnel have changed?

10. Attainment of *widespread use* (cycle): Is the new practice applied, on an agency-wide basis, to all functions for which it is relevant?

Further research may suggest additions to this list. The main characteristic of the passages or cycles, however, is that they represent organizational, and not attitudinal events. Thus, they provide objective measures of routinization; the more passages or cycles achieved during a life history, the more routinized a practice may be considered to be.

The Incidence of Routinization

The study found that routinization may follow a series of stages: an improvisation stage, an expansion stage, and a disappearance stage ("disappearance" means that the innovative practice continues, but is no longer regarded as new). The improvisation stage primarily called for the daily operation of the new practice, even if on a limited basis and with ad hoc procedures. During the latter two stages, the achievement of the ten passages and cycles served as the operational criteria for routinization. These stages emerged after a chronological analysis of each life history. Table 3 shows four illustrative life histories, two involving mobile intensive care units and two involving computer-assisted instruction.[4] Within each pair, the examples show a highly and poorly routinized case, even though many of the factors during initial adoption may have appeared similar. The life histories highlight the occurrence of specific passages and cycles (the numbers in parentheses in the table refer to the ten passages or cycles defined earlier).

The life histories showed that what was most important was the basic occurrence of passages and cycles, and not necessarily their chronological sequence. Moreover, the point at which a practice became "routinized" could not be defined in any absolute sense. Thus, for subsequent analysis of the data, three degrees of routinization were distinguished—innovations that had become marginally, moderately, and highly routinized. These three degrees of routinization simply reflected the number (0-3; 4-6; and 7-10) of the ten passages and cycles that had been achieved by any given innovation.

On balance, it was found that a good proportion of the innovations had attained the status of being "highly routinized." Eight out of 19 case studies (42.1 percent) and 31 out of 90 telephone sites (34.4 percent) fell into this category; conversely, 21.1 percent of the case studies and only 20.0 percent of the telephone sites fell into the opposite category of "marginal" routinization. These results were notable in two respects. First, they indicated that many innovations in these two samples had lasted and become a virtual part of standard practice. This was particularly true for the use of breath testing, mobile intensive care units, and police computer systems. Such encouraging results mean that local agencies can innovate and may not be the bastions of "resistance to change" that they have been typically construed to be.[5]

Second, the proportion of highly routinized innovations was much higher than that found in a study of federal innovations in education (Berman and McLaughlin, 1978; and McLaughlin and Berman, 1975). That study found that none of the innovations had lasted much beyond the period of initial federal funding, thereby leaving a much more pessimistic view of bureaucratic change. The apparent discrepancy in findings may have two rather simple explanations: The present study focused on *technological* innovations, whose hardware components were easier to trace than the organizational innovations that marked the Berman and McLaughlin study; and the present study also sampled from innovations that had not necessarily been initially supported by federal funds (in fact, about half of the innovations in the case studies had been locally initiated and supported). From the localist perspective, then, many innovations can be and have been adopted, implemented, and routinized. These may, however, simply not be the innovations included on the agendas of federal agencies.

An initial question that followed the assembling of these routinization scores was whether there was a simple relationship between routinization and the chronological age of the innovation. The older innovations might have been the more routinized ones, and this alone might have accounted

TABLE 3

Chronologies of Four Illustrative Life Histories

Improvisation Stage	Expansion Stage	Disappearance Stage	Current Status
City A: Mobile Intensive Care Units (Highly Routinized)			
Advisory MICU committee formed (1968) by city ordinance	Training continues at university (76 certified paramedics, more being trained, although all units fully staffed)	Second generation of Lifepaks being installed	Fire department: about 600 persons
Large federal MICU grant not funded (1969)	Three more vehicles purchased	Civil service classification being sought for MICU coordinator	City population: about 300,000
MICU initiated with DHEW funds; one vehicle; local funds support after first year, as well as purchase of two more vehicles (1, 2, 3)	Civil service classifications established for paramedics (5)	Full-time MICU coordinator established and new incumbent appointed; creates standard procedures bulletins (4, 9)	About six active and one reserve MICU units cover entire city
Head of MICU committee (outside fire department) initiates training and coordinates with state	Fire department changes name to include "Rescue Service" (6)	Fire officers begin large-scale citizen training program in cardio-pulmonary resuscitation	No transport service, which is still private
Fire department chief and deputy chief are strong supporters, select exemplary trainees (1973-1974)	Paramedic assignment part of fire department promotion ladder, involves small additional pay (8)	MICU helps fire department avert across-the-board budget cuts (1976)	MICU responds to about half of all fire department calls
	State MICU regulations incorporate fire department's experience (1975)		Head of MICU committee is still same incumbent
City B: Mobile Intensive Care Units (Poorly Routinized)			
General Hospital begins own MICU system (1973)	Fire department continues to consider MICU training for own personnel (1977-		Fire department: about 950 persons
Fire department is asked by General Hospital to initiate MICU to one outlying community: all training (14 officers) and equipment covered by federal funds and administered by General Hospital; paramedics receive extra pay, covered by fire department funds			City population: about 520,000
Only low number of calls for this unit			No MICU units currently in operation under fire department

Table 3 (continued)

Improvisation Stage	Expansion Stage	Disappearance Stage	Current Status
General Hospital withdraws training, certification, and support after one year; fire department service ends General Hospital, and not state, plays certification role (1975-1976)			

City C: Computer-Assisted Instruction (Highly Routinized)

Improvisation Stage	Expansion Stage	Disappearance Stage	Current Status
NSF grant for CAI; ten terminals and computer time purchased from private company; data processing director coordinates (3) First court-ordered school desegregation helps CAI First generation CAI computer (Burroughs 5500) acquired on lease-purchase with local funds (was second generation for administrative application); 18 CAI terminals purchased with external funds in relation to desegregation (2, 4) First CAI coordinator appointed First round of in-service training for CAI (1968-1973)	New comptroller hired (had been data processing director) (8) Second generation CAI computer (Burroughs 6700) acquired on lease-purchase with local funds; more terminals (1) Two other CAI computers (Hewlett-Packard and PDP) purchased with external funds; additional applications and terminals New CAI coordinator hired (9) First mathematics CAI supervisor appointed (5) State certifies advanced computer mathematics courses (6) Second court-ordered school desegregation: impact on CAI operation? (1974-1976)	CAI coordinator's position shifted to curriculum department (1977-	District: about 140,000 students City population: about 844,000 About 110 on-line CAI terminals; time oversubscribed (10) Drill-and-practice, problem-solving applications Considering CAI-oriented mathematics textbooks Competition with administrative application for computer time Adoption and use still at teacher's discretion In-service training not yet formalized

Table 3 (continued)

City D: Computer-Assisted Instruction (Poorly Routinized)

Improvisation Stage	Expansion Stage	Disappearance Stage	Current Status
Six high schools purchase programmable calculators on local funds	Two new data processing directors hired in quick succession		District: about 65,000 students
State grant to 3 elementary schools for 15 terminals; plagued by breakdowns and only operates for 6 months	In-service training offered sporadically by data processing directors		City population: about 360,000
First generation CAI computer (Honeywell 6025) purchased with local funds (was third generation for administrative application); 13 terminals used to replace programmable calculators (2, 4)	Several individual CAI projects with external funds begin and end at individual teacher's initiative (1973-		About 13 terminals (same since 1971); time undersubscribed
Trial with computer payroll application is unsuccessful (1962-1972)			Main CAI application is computer programming
			No strong top administrative or practitioner support for CAI

for the pattern of scores. To examine this proposition, the data were arrayed along two dimensions: the median age of all the innovations versus the degree of routinization (see Table 4). For the case studies, the age of innovations made no difference in predicting the degree of routinization; for the telephone interviews, there was even a slight tendency in the opposite direction—i.e., the younger innovations tended to be more routinized. In sum, the degree of routinization was not related to the chronological age of the innovation. Similar analyses showed that the degree of routinization was also unrelated to the type of innovation or the location or size of the city involved.

The Conditions that Lead to Routinization

In contrast to these initial analyses, other probes suggested that the important conditions for routinization were *internal* to the specific local agency. The conditions are summarized in Figure 1 and described below, based on both the case study and telephone results.

The initial conditions involve the role of an innovator (or innovator-team), who must develop agency support for the innovation and establish the appropriate skills and resources for operating it. Among the other important initial conditions, some group of agency practitioners must be trained to use the innovation as frequently as possible. Thus, a breath-testing practice need not, at first, be applied on an agency-wide basis. For a test period, the equipment can be used in a single precinct alone, as long as the full range of breath-testing activities—including use of the results in court cases—is carried out repetitively.

Routinization is now likely to proceed further if the innovation becomes part of a core agency practice. One way of defining a core practice is if the innovation displaces an old practice. Under this definition, the new practice

TABLE 4
Age of Innovation by Degree of Routinization

Source of Evidence	Degree of Routinization		
	Marginal	Moderate	High
Case Studies (n = 19)			
Above median age[a]	2	3	4
Below median age	2	4	4
Telephone Interviews (n = 82)[b]			
Above median age[a]	12	20	13
Below median age	5	17	15

[a]Median defined independently for each type of innovation.
[b]No information on age for eight cases.

FIGURE 1

Complete Life History of a Local Service Innovation

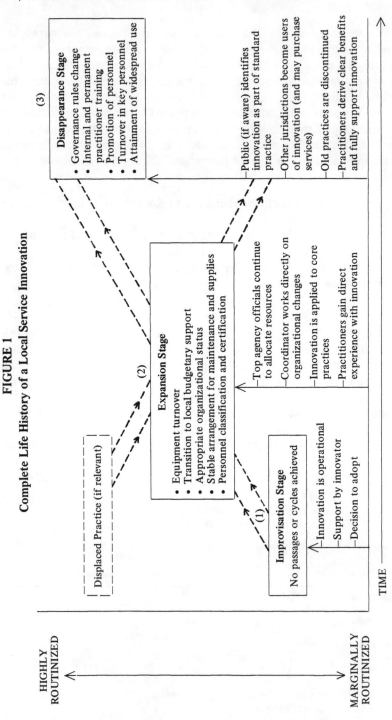

can be routinized more effectively if the capability for carrying out the old practice is systematically removed after the new practice has been installed (e.g., breath-testing procedures replace the more traditional urinalysis procedures). This dual tactic is often forgotten by those supporting an innovation, who rightly focus on installing new practices but who negligently fail to attend to the policies needed to terminate the old practices. In contrast, if a practice is totally new to an agency and does not logically displace an old practice, a core function may still emerge if the agency mandate is formally expanded.[6] For instance, one "fire" department actually changed its name, as a result of the addition of a paramedic service, to become known as a "fire and rescue" service. Subsequent budget cutbacks, applied to all municipal agencies, were averted by this agency because of its expanded functions.

Throughout its early life history, an innovation must also gain increased support from agency practitioners. This support will result in part if the innovation does cover a core practice. However, the innovation must also operate effectively. A distinctive finding of the study was that the "effectiveness" of the innovation usually had to be proven in practitioner terms— e.g., convenience, reduced physical effort, additional sense of safety on the job, or elimination of distasteful tasks—which are different from the criteria typically used by external evaluators. Thus, for some innovations, external evaluators will not always predict correctly whether there have been service payoffs. A good example is in the use of computer-assisted instruction, where the narrow evaluation objective would assume some type of savings in educational manpower. Instead, the successful cases showed that instructional time increased, because teachers and students were so pleased that they attacked new types of math problems—and designed new courses in computer math.

Finally, an important internal condition is the specific support of top agency administrators. These administrators are usually an essential part of the key decisions about an innovation—e.g., whether to adopt and try it in the first place, whether to make staff available through some ad hoc arrangement (e.g., overtime or special hours), or whether to make budgetary funds available each year. Without administrative support, most innovations will fail to become routinized (the main exceptions are innovations that may initially be adopted by individual practitioners at no cost to an agency). In the case of the jet-axe, for instance, the use of the new equipment was frequently supervised directly by the fire chief, who could use his discretionary powers to take such action. The administrators also appear to respond to bureaucratic incentives. If an innovation permits an expanded agency budget, for instance, the administrator may have a strong incentive for routinizing the innovation. Police computer systems were especially relevant in this regard, however, more research needs to be done about the bureaucratic incentive system of top administrators, especially given the confluence of actors—e.g., union representatives, staff from the municipal executive's office, and local legislators—involved in determining agency policies (Yin, 1977).

In contrast to all these internal conditions, external financial and technical assistance, in the form of federal grants and awards, were consistently found to be unrelated to the degree of routinization. This did not mean, however, that local agencies could as easily innovate without such external assistance. Rather, the lack of relationships was due to the inability to distinguish between two very different conditions—where local officials actively pursue external assistance, and where such assistance is the result of initiatives by a federal granting agency or other external agent. External assistance may in fact be very important to routinization if such assistance follows local initiatives and matches local needs and agendas.

Future Implications

These findings are in basic agreement with those of another recent study (Lambright and Flynn, 1977; and Lambright, 1979). That study examined innovations in two cities and focused on political rather than administrative conditions, but nevertheless agreed on the importance of internal conditions. Thus, if these results are confirmed by further research, federal and local officials will soon be able to assess and influence routinization.[7] For federal agencies, the support of local innovations must include an explicit awareness of the routinization process. Policy direction could even be incorporated into initial solicitations (e.g., Weidman, 1977). For local agencies, officials should work actively to get specific passages and cycles accomplished, should routinization be desired. In summary, several strategies were found to be effective in promoting routinization:

- At the outset, it was important to get the new practice operating on a daily basis, even if this was done by limiting its scope. An important condition during this improvisation stage was for the coordinator to be able to make his/her own repairs to keep the new equipment in use.
- The new practice had to have concrete benefits for service practitioners— e.g., convenience, reduced physical effort, greater potential for promotions, and additional sense of safety on the job. These types of benefits were not necessarily the same as those covered by external evaluators.
- If the new practice displaced an old one, specific steps needed to be taken to eliminate the old way of doing business—e.g., by eliminating the forms and procedures associated with the old way.
- The new practice had to be ultimately expanded to its fullest logical extent, or else it continued to be regarded as a "special project," which

precluded it from becoming a standard practice. This expansion was facilitated by having the practice incorporated into the "orders of the day" (police and fire) or into local ordinances governing the agency's operations as a whole.

- The time lags for achieving the various passages and cycles were different, so that it was important to get an early start on certain activities— e.g., establishing the personnel classifications for any new job skills that may be required by the new practice—to ensure later routinization.

Notes

1. For separate descriptions of these six types of innovations, see Bukoski and Korotkin (1975), Colton (1974), Page (1975), Wigren (1976), Mason and Dubowski (1976), and Frohman et al. (1972), respectively.
2. The case studies were based on an innovative methodology, whereby a *chain of evidence* from field observations to conclusions was established (see Yin, 1979). Basically, the methodology involved the tabulation of key events in each life history.
3. Although organizational memories may be difficult to tap, this procedure avoided the even greater uncertainties that can follow the tracing of "new" innovations forward in time (Kimberly, 1976). To our knowledge, the notion of life histories of innovations first received brief mention in Tansik and Radnor (1971).
4. See Yin (1979) for the full set of life histories that was collected from the 19 case studies.
5. Similar conclusions are found in Feller et al. (1976).
6. Thus, those supporting the innovation must work for changes in an agency's rules of governance, as reflected in a city ordinance, a bond issue's definition of the "standard" practices that may be financed, or even a perpetual shift reflected in a new agency name or reviews of the agency's budget.
7. For a discussion of the policy issues concerning organizational innovation, see Roessner (1979).

References

Becker, Selwyn, and Thomas L. Whisler, "The Innovative Organization: A Selective View of Current Theory and Research," *Journal of Business* 40 (October 1967): 462-469.

Berman, Paul, and Milbrey McLaughlin, *Federal Programs Supporting Educational Change,* Vol. 8. Santa Monica, Calif.: The Rand Corporation, R-1589/8-HEW, 1978.

Bukowski, William J., and Arthur L. Korotkin, *Computing Activities in Secondary Education,* Washington, D.C.: American Institutes for Research, September 1975.

Clark, David, and Egon Guba, "An Examination of Potential Change Roles in Education," paper presented at Seminar on Innovation in Planning School Curricula, Airlie House, Warrenton, Va., October 1965.

Colton, Kent, "Computers and the Police: Police Departments and the New Information Technology," *Urban Data Service* 6 (November 1974): 1-19.

Feller, Irwin, Donald C. Menzel, and Lee Ann Koazk, *Diffusion of Innovations in Municipal Governments,* University Park, Pa.: Institute for Research on Human Resources, Pennsylvania State University, June 1976.

Frohman, Alan, et al. *Factors Affecting Innovation in the Fire Services,* Cambridge, Mass.: Pugh-Roberts Associates, March 1972.

Hage, Jerald, and Michael Aiken, *Social Change in Complex Organizations,* New York: Random House, 1970.

Kimberly, John R., "Issues in the Design of Longitudinal Organizational Research," *Sociological Methods and Research* (February 1976): 321-347.

Lambright, W. Henry, *Technology Transfer to Cities: Processes of Choice at the Local Level,* Boulder, Colo.: Westview Press, 1979.

Lambright, W. Henry, and Paul J. Flynn, "Bureaucratic Politics and Technological Change in Local Government," *Journal of Urban Analysis* 4 (1977): 93-118.

Mason, M. F., and K. M. Dubowski, "Breath-Alcohol Analysis: Uses, Methods, and Some Forensic Problems—Review and Opinion," *Journal of Forensic Sciences* 21 (January 1976): 9-41.

McLaughlin, Milbrey, and Paul Berman, *Macro and Micro Implementation,* Santa Monica, Calif.: The Rand Corporation, P-5431, May 1975.

Page, James O., *Emergency Medical Services for Fire Departments,* Boston: National Fire Protection Association, 1975.

Roessner, J. David, "Federal Technology Policy: Innovation and Problem Solving in State and Local Governments," *Policy Analysis* 5 (Spring 1979): 182-200.

Rogers, Everett M. *Diffusion of Innovations,* New York: The Free Press, 1962, p. 306.

Rowe, Lloyd A., and William B. Boise, "Organizational Innovation: Current Research and Evolving Concepts," *Public Administration Review* 34 (May-June 1974): 284-293.

Sheehy, Gail, *Passages: Predictable Crises of Adult Life,* New York: E. P. Dutton, 1976.

Tansik, David A., and Michael Radnor, "An Organization Theory Perspective on the Development of New Organizational Functions," *Public Administration Review* 31 (November-December 1971): 644-652.

Warner, Kenneth E., "The Need for Some Innovative Concepts of Innovation," *Policy Sciences* 5 (December 1974): 433-451.

Weidman, Donald R., "Writing a Better RFP: Ten Hints for Obtaining More Successful Evaluation Studies," *Public Administration Review* 37 (November/December 1977): 714-717.

Wigren, Harold E., et al. *A Survey of Instructional Closed-Circuit Television 1967.* Washington, D.C.: National Education Association, 1967.

Yin, Robert K. *Changing Urban Bureaucracies,* Lexington: Lexington Books, 1979.

———, "Production Efficiency vs. Bureaucratic Self-Interest: Two Innovative Processes?" *Policy Sciences* 8 (December 1977): 381-399.

Yin, Robert K., and Douglas Yates, *Street-Level Governments,* Lexington: Lexington Books, 1975.

1981 (21-28)

HERBERT A. SIMON
WILLIAM R. DIVINE

Controlling Human Factors in an Administrative Experiment

In industrial research the experimental method has several times been successfully used to determine the manner in which production varies when conditions of work are altered, but experimentation has not proved easy in this field. Human beings, unlike the inert materials of the physics laboratory, cannot easily be subjected to the rigorous controls which are necessary for a successful experiment.

These difficulties of human control have no doubt discouraged the application of the experimental method to problems of public administration. In the past few years, however, a number of experiments have been conducted in the public welfare field which indicate that, under favorable circumstances and with careful planning, the administrator can obtain by this method valuable information to assist him in his task of management.

The most recent of these experiments—conducted in the California State Relief Administration—affords many illustrations of the difficulties encountered in handling the human and psychological problems of such a study as well as the methods which may be used to overcome these difficulties. A brief description of this experiment may encourage others engaged in administration and administrative research to utilize experimental techniques for testing and administrative principles and procedures, and may assist them in handling some of the problems to be faced in any such experimentation.

The study was conducted by the Bureau of Public Administration of the University of California in cooperation with the California State Relief Administration. It was undertaken to determine how many social workers were needed by the State Relief Administration for the most effective operation of the agency's program. The study sought to discover how large a work load, for most efficient operation, should be assigned to the professional workers engaged in each of the agency's two principal operations, that is: (1) how many new applications for relief should be handled by each "intake" worker, and (2) how many active cases should be handled by each "carrier" worker.

The customary procedures of the State Relief Administration may be briefly outlined as follows.

1. A needy unemployed person, applying for aid, is interviewed in a district office of the S.R.A. by a *qualifier*.

2. If the applicant is tentatively accepted by the qualifier, collateral inquiries are made, and a visit is paid to his home by a *field intake worker*. If the applicant is found eligible, he is certified for relief.

3. After the applicant is accepted, his case is referred to a *carrier worker* who is expected to re-investigate the case at intervals in order to determine whether he is still eligible for relief.

In order to determine the work quotas which would produce the most desirable results, quotas of different sizes were actually tested in practice under comparable conditions. Each step in the S.R.A. procedure was studied; that is, to test the office interview, different qualifiers were assigned applications at the rates of 50, 75, 100, and 125 per week, respectively, and the operating results observed. Different field intake workers were assigned applications at the rates of 8, 12, and 16 per week, respectively. Similarly, carrier workers were assigned loads of 60, 100, and 150 active cases, respectively.

Identifying the Variables

One of the first tasks in planning the S.R.A. experiment was to identify the variables which might be expected to influence the results of operation under the different experimental quotas. Until these variables could be identified and, in large part, controlled, successful experimentation was impossible.[1] The principal factors which it was thought might influence results were the following.

A. *Factors affecting the comparability of work units.* The volume of work handled by each social worker was measured in terms of "applications" and "cases." Obviously, these are not entirely homogeneous units, since the cases handled might be of varying degrees of complexity. If two workers were to be compared, it was essential that they be assigned cases of the same average degree of complexity.

B. *Factors affecting the output per worker.* The number of work units completed by each worker and the quality of the work done would depend upon a number of personal and organizational factors.

1. *Pace of workers.* Over short periods of time, workers might markedly increase or reduce their work pace or the number of hours worked per day. The purpose of the experiment was not to achieve a "speed-up" or "slow-down" but to study changes in production at a normal work pace.

2. *Procedures and work methods.* Most of the variables which have been studied in industrial experiments have fallen in this category. The typical time-and-motion study seeks to determine the time required to produce a given result under different methods of work.

3. *Ability, training, and experience of workers.* Any comparison of procedures must be between workers of comparable ability. Professional attitudes and quality of supervision proved to be of great importance.

4. *Workers' attitudes and aims.* The morale in the agency or organizational units, the aims and motives which guide the workers would affect performance. Especially important would be the attitude of the workers toward the experimental study, and their expectations as to what effect the findings of the study would have upon the work of the agency and upon their own jobs.

5. *Environmental influences on workers' behavior.* Certain environmental conditions which affect workers' attitudes required special consideration. The workers' security and insecurity in their positions, the agency's political situation, domestic or social conditions in workers' homes would all affect performance.

6. *General working conditions.* Some of the earliest administrative experiments dealt with fatigue and its relation to hours of work, lighting, other physical facilities, and so forth. Not so much importance is attached to these physical variables as was once the case, but they must nevertheless be considered significant.

Methods of Controlling Variables

Many of these human variables did not present any particular difficulty since they could be eliminated by proper design of the experiment. Differences in the complexity of cases were minimized by assigning them at random to the workers handling the different quotas. The same procedures and work methods were employed throughout the experiment. Workers were assigned at random to the different experimental quotas so that there would be no significant differences in ability. General working conditions in the agency and other environmental circumstances presumably influenced workers under all quotas alike.

The variables which gave particular trouble were the control of work pace and the attitudes of the workers toward the experimental study. Special steps had to be taken to deal with these factors.

Since the willing cooperation of each worker was essential to the experiment, it was felt that control could be achieved only through a complete understanding of the workers' attitudes and the motives lying behind those attitudes. A worker performing his job in the agency would be influenced by a very complex hierarchy of motives comprising his expectations for personal reward from the job, his notions as to the purpose of his work and its place in the general scheme of the organization, his attitudes toward the organization's goals, and his attitudes toward fellow employees.

This entire structure of motives would determine the manner in which the worker did his job. When he realized that he was being subjected to an experimental situation, that situation might mean something very different to him—in terms of his own hierarchy of motives—from the normal working situation. A worker who is the subject of a time-and-motion study will be acutely conscious of the possible consequences of the study for the security of his job, his working conditions, the contents of his pay envelope, and the efficiency of the enterprise. All these considerations will influence his reaction to the study, and that reaction may be entirely different from his reaction to his regular work.

In the S.R.A. study, a conscious effort was made to understand the workers' reactions to the experimental situation and to modify those reactions so as to approximate, as closely as possible, normal working attitudes. It was recognized that "normal" attitudes would certainly not be achieved merely because the workers knew that management or the experimenters wished to carry out a study. The proper reactions could be assured only by helping the worker see the true implications of the study in terms of his own aims and purposes. Three principal techniques were employed to bring about this understanding.

1. *Demonstrating the consistency of the experiment with the workers's broader motives.* To the worker, the experiment might seem inconsistent with the objectives he was trying to attain in his daily job. The cooperation of such a worker could be obtained only by interpreting the study in terms of his more fundamental values and by showing him that these broader values would be benefited by a temporary sacrifice of some of his immediate objectives and attitudes. In this way his attention might be detached from the narrower frame of reference—the conditioned reflexes, so to speak—forced on him by his regular daily schedule of work.

2. *Showing the worker the implications of his behavior for the attainment of his own objectives.* In many cases, noncooperation resulted from a misunderstanding by the worker of how his own behavior would affect the realization of his objectives. While the first technique sought to modify behavior by calling attention to different and broader objectives, this second technique accepted existing objectives but encouraged the worker to revaluate the appropriateness of his behavior toward those objectives. The first dealt with "ends," the second with "means."

3. *Avoiding any unfortunate consequences of the experiment for the individual worker.* The experiment was designed so that it would not threaten the job security, earnings or opportunities for promotion of the worker.

This description will serve to indicate, in a highly simplified form, the general approach and technique. Where the reaction or attitude desired in the experiment conflicted with the known aims and values of the worker, the experimental situation was redefined for him so as (1) to direct his attention to objectives which were broader than those in conflict with the study and (2) to change his expectation of unfavorable outcomes. The ideal was so to present the situation to the worker that he would want to react in the manner required for the successful conduct of the experiment.

Specific Problems of Control

A major problem in the actual conduct of the experiment centered around the question of work pace. The workers were instructed to work at a normal pace and to make such adjustments in the quality and thoroughness of their work as would be necessary to enable them to complete the required number of work units. Since all factors except the size of work quotas were held constant, presumably a comparison of the different groups would reflect the extent to which the size of quota affected the quality of the work. For a clear understanding of the experiment it must be emphasized that its purpose was to detect changes in quality of work resulting from changes in the number of work units handled, and that it was intended that there should be no change in work pace.

The Problem of a Speed-up

One of the greatest obstacles to the maintenance of normal operating conditions in the experimental units was the tendency of workers with the higher quotas to increase their efforts in an attempt to do work of the same quality that would be expected with a quota only one-half or one-third as great. As has been pointed out, for validity an experiment must test the various quotas under ordinary conditions in the agency, which would mean that the workers would exert no more or no less effort than usual. Clearly, if workers with higher quotas exerted special effort during the experimental period, a picture of what would occur during normal operations in the agency would not be obtained. The question of whether the pace at which workers normally operated should be raised or lowered was beyond the province of the experiment.

In spite of the fact that the importance of maintaining a normal rate of work was emphasized in both oral and written instructions to the workers participating in the experiment, observations revealed that workers with the higher quotas were working harder than usual. Evidence of inability to make the adjustment necessary to handle at their usual pace the increased volume of work was brought out in interviews with the workers. In one extreme case the nervous reaction of a worker attempting to maintain the highest standard of performance was such that it seemed best to remove him from the experiment because of possible consequences for his health. An analysis of the situation indicated that there were four principal factors that tended to produce abnormal effort on the part of workers with the higher quotas.

1. Each social worker was dealing with human beings, and it was his natural reaction to have more concern for the concrete problems of an individual client than for an abstract notion of an experiment. A social worker is attracted to that profession largely by the opportunities it affords to alleviate distress; the natural sympathies of the worker, crystallized by the customs and traditions of the social work profession, tend so to dominate his action that concern for the welfare of the relief recipient will outweigh formal instructions "not to work too hard." Therefore, when a worker's quota is doubled or tripled, it is natural for him to continue to exert every possible effort to aid the client and hence to work at a pace that could not be maintained over an extended period.

2. A second factor was the desire of workers to maintain the standards that were customary in the social work profession. An employee's attachment to his own particular job leads in turn to a "conditioned" reaction pattern centering around his trade or profession. When he has time and sufficient information to make a carefully reasoned decision, that decision will reflect values and objectives derived from his attachment to his profession; when there are not the time and data for a rational decision, a worker will tend to react in terms of the "accepted" standards of performance of his profession. The workers participating in this experiment were accustomed to a particular standard of work that was considered satisfactory by the social work profession. Since their loyalties tended to adhere to that profession, there was a strong reluctance to alter the quality of performance if it would conflict with their notion of established professional standards.

3. Similarly, the attachment of workers to the agency, their organizational unit, and their supervisor led to the formation of reaction patterns consistent with previous agency policy. The influence of supervision was an especially important factor in the maintenance of standards of work. In one of the districts of the S.R.A. experiment, for example, the district supervisor was a particularly effective leader and had earned the unqualified respect and trust of all employees in the office. Because of the loyalty of the staff, this supervisor had been able over a period of time to raise the standard of work in the district to a high level. The workers in this district were proud of its reputation for excellent work and were not easily persuaded to relax their standards for the sake of an experiment.

4. There were several personal factors which also conflicted with the necessity that workers with high quotas lower the standard of their work. Such an adjustment was difficult to reconcile with the worker's desire for

advancement, and perhaps appeared to him a denial of his opportunity to demonstrate his ability to his superiors. The most pressing personal conflict was fear or sense of insecurity of the workers. In addition to a hesitancy to relax quality of performance for fear of being branded inefficient, there was the more definite possibility that any work performed during the experiment might be turned against the individual worker when there was some future occasion for evaluating his work.

Preventing a Speed-up

In attempting to overcome the influence of the factors mentioned above so that workers would maintain a normal pace during the experiment, several steps were taken.

In order to influence the workers to diminish the amount of attention given to each client when more clients were assigned to them (item 1 above), an attempt was made to appeal to the motive of concern for *clients* in the plural. It was pointed out that it would be to the best interest of the clients if the workers were able to make the necessary adjustments in their work, for the experiment was providing a scientific test designed to determine the most efficient quotas. Similarly, in attempting to neutralize the hesitancy of workers to adjust work standards because of conflict with professional (item2) or agency (item 3) standards, the appeal was made that the welfare of the social work profession and of the agency would be promoted by the experiment, and that the workers would be doing the greatest good for their profession and agency by making the adjustments in their work that were required in the experiment.

In dealing with the workers' fear and insecurity (item 4), every attempt was made to assure them that no evaluations of their work would be made during the period of the experiment, and that no work performed during the experiment would be held against them at any time in the future. This assurance was at first given orally to the workers, but when they expressed a fear that this agreement might not be understood by future officials in the agency, an administrative order was prepared and distributed which gave written protection to the workers. As an added assurance, workers were permitted to enter at the end of the dictation for every case record a note that the work was done during an experiment. Although these precautions may seem exaggerated, they were necessary to remove any doubts from the workers' minds that work performed during the experiment would not be charged against them professionally.

These steps had a considerable effect in overcoming the hesitancy of workers with high quotas to lower the standard of their work in order to meet the quotas assigned to them. However, the most effective means of control consisted in appealing to a conflicting motive in such a way as partially to counterbalance the tendency to increase work pace. The motive employed was that of the personal—and perhaps selfish—interest of the workers in the results of the experiment. The majority of the workers participating in the experiment hoped that the study would establish the superiority of lower work quotas, for they felt that the lower quotas would enable them to provide better service to recipients of relief and would involve more favorable working conditions for themselves. It was pointed out to them that the workers with higher quotas were introducing a bias in favor of those quotas by working harder than were workers at lower quotas. When the workers and supervisors in the experimental districts realized this, there was a noticeable change in their reactions and attitudes and the work pace returned to normal. The final action spring which induced the workers to adjust their work to a normal pace was the realization that it was to their best interest and the best interest of their clients and the agency to resume their usual rate of work.

This device, while a powerful one, was likewise dangerous. If the workers were too clearly aware of the effect which a changed work pace would have upon the results of the experiment, there would be a strong impulse to manipulate those results. Manipulation of this sort is perhaps the most serious difficulty that faces a time-and-motion expert who is seeking to set standard times for operations in an industrial plant. In the S.R.A. study, this danger was mitigated by the strong complex of motives operating in the opposite direction. As a result, the motives making for a high work pace tended to counterbalance the motives making for a low work pace, and something like the normal pace resulted. Observation of the workers after the adjustment had taken place indicated that this balance had been substantially achieved. If there was any departure from a normal pace it was upward rather than downward for the workers with a high quota.

Need for Training Workers

An entirely distinct factor that proved an obstacle to the maintenance of normal operating conditions in the experimental units was that the workers with the lowest quotas found difficulty in adjusting the standard of their work upward so as to make full use of their time. Because they had become conditioned to a certain level of performance, workers who were assigned low quotas during the experiment tended to maintain only that level of work, whereas they might be expected to increase the amount and quality of attention given to each case when their quotas were reduced. This problem arose largely because the workers were accustomed to certain procedures for handling each case and found it difficult to interrupt their routine by introducing additional services. In some instances the workers were at a loss as to what to do with the extra unit time per case which their lower quotas allowed. In these instances, supervision was necessary to point out extra duties that should be performed by the workers.

A more effective remedy for this situation would have been to precede the experiment with a period of in-service training designed to stimulate the workers by pointing out avenues into which extra efforts could be directed.

General Environmental Factors

Many of the psychological factors that enter into an administrative experiment affect equally all of the experimental units. This is especially true if all of the units are located in the same building or office. In the S.R.A. study variations in performance caused by such factors as the type of equipment used, office space, light, heating, ventilation, or the weather, were minimized because all of the experimental groups were operating under the same conditions.

Similarly, many intangible psychological factors presumably applied with equal force to all of the experimental units. However, bearing in mind the experiment's task of simulating actual working conditions and predicting performance under those conditions, it is not permissible to ignore these variables. Although such factors may be equalized, unless they are equalized at a level that will approximate actual operating conditions, there is no assurance that the results of the experiment will apply under normal conditions.

For example, there are such factors as morale and the sincerity and interest of workers participating in an administrative experiment. Clearly the reliability of an experiment in administration is greatly dependent upon the interest and cooperation of the workers themselves, for without their active support valid results are impossible to obtain.

The average worker in any shop or office is too much concerned with the pressure of his own job and the duties it entails to become vitally interested in an experiment that is being imposed upon him. Yet since an experiment is dealing with a normal cross section of workers, it is necessary to "sell" the workers on the experiment being conducted in order to prevent their lapsing into a state of hostility and noncooperation toward it. To this end, workers in the S.R.A. experiment were given a series of talks to explain the purposes and importance of the experiment in which they were participating. It was found that they were particularly receptive to an explanation of the significance of the study given by an individual outside the agency whose prestige and reputation were very high with them. Undoubtedly these explanations and discussions of the methods, purposes, and significance of the experiment stimulated the workers and brought out a degree of cooperation that could not otherwise have been expected.

During the actual conduct of the experiment there were several occasions when conditions in the agency outside the control of the experiment were in a turmoil, and the uncertainty about the future had a noticeable effect upon morale throughout the agency. With rumors of impending dismissals and reorganizations running rampant, workers were not able to work normally and their fears and anxieties led to carelessness and indifference toward their work and the experiment. In this situation meetings of the experimental workers were called, and they were assured both orally and in writing that because of the importance of the experiment there would be no changes in their office until the conclusion of the study. The result of these assurances was heartening, for as the workers realized that the experiment was saving them at least temporarily from the upheavals that other offices were experiencing, their attitude became extremely favorable toward it and they made every effort to give the fullest cooperation to those directing it.

Value of Experimentation

The S.R.A. study demonstrates again, as experiments in the private management field have previously demonstrated, that the experimental method can be a powerful research tool in administration. To be sure, the administrative experiment involves difficulties which are not found in the natural sciences. But if the difficulties are greater, so also is the need. Within the realm of the administrative sciences lie the gravest problems which face us today—the problems of human organization. No tool can be neglected which has proved its value in studying these problems.

Aside from its contribution to administrative theory, the administrative experiments can be justified in terms of dollars-and-cents results. The S.R.A. experiment, for instance, cost the agency about $15,000. The saving which it was estimated would result from adoption of the recommendations of the study was more than $80,000 per month. Even the partial adoption which the agency found possible within the statutory financial limitations under which it was operating undoubtedly repaid the cost of the study several times over each month.

Notes

1. The authors derived much assistance in locating these factors from reports of earlier administrative experiments in the private management field. The pioneer studies of psychological factors in work-situations are discussed in Elton Mayo, *The Human Problems of an Industrial Civilization* (Macmillan Company, 1933).

1940 (485-492)

JONE L. PEARCE
JAMES L. PERRY

Federal Merit Pay:
A Longitudinal Analysis

Pay for performance has long been a goal of federal personnel policy, but in practice few civil servants have been denied their periodic salary increases, regardless of their performance.[1] Merit pay, as mandated by the Civil Service Reform Act of 1978 (CSRA), bases the compensatiaon of grades 13-15 supervisors and management officials on their rated performance.

Merit pay has probably been the most complex of the CSRA's provisions for two reasons. First, the various payout mechanisms had to be established. Such questions as the appropriate size of pay pools and whether managers at the various grades/steps should receive identical salary increases for identical performance ratings had to be determined before payouts could be made. The difficulties of arriving at satisfactory solutions to these problems are reflected in the timing of OPM's comprehensive merit pay guidelines, released in draft in February 1981,[2] two and one-half years after the passage of CSRA, and in the last-minute General Accounting Office (GAO) intervention to alter the payout formula.[3]

Second, merit pay was implemented concurrently with the new objectives-based performance appraisal system on which merit payouts would be based. This new performance appraisal system is significantly different from the trait-based systems used to rate most federal managers prior to the change. Now the elements, or components, of each job need to be specified and objective indicators of relative performance on each element must be developed. Ratings on these individualized "contracts" are then combined for each manager so that the performance of all the managers in a pay pool can be rated for merit pay purposes. Although there were objections to tying pay to a new, untested, performance appraisal system,[4] virtually every agency in the federal government was required by the pressures of statutory deadlines to implement concurrently the new performance appraisal and merit pay systems for managers.

95

This paper assesses the effectiveness of the new merit pay system after the initial government-wide payout in October 1981. Applying a longitudinal research design to the motivational premises on which merit pay is based, we evaluate the early reactions of employees to merit pay. We conclude with a discussion of some of the important contingencies affecting the motivational effectiveness of merit pay.

The Theory Behind Merit Pay

The merit pay provisions of CSRA are based on a widely accepted perspective on motivation drawn from Vroom's expectancy theory.[5] In its simplified form, the theory posits that if individuals expect to receive a valued reward for high performance, they are more likely to strive for this level of performance than if there were no "pay off." Federal merit pay is expected to increase effort and, therefore, performance by changing the probability that performance will lead to the outcome (salary increase) that is assumed to be positively valued by most managers. Therefore, the merit pay initiatives of CSRA are expected to result in higher overall managerial performance since many, if not all, federal managers will see more benefit in striving for high performance under this program than under the previous compensation system.

Although few would argue with the general proposition that pay-for-performance should increase performance, Deci[6] has criticized motivation systems that rely on externally mediated rewards, i.e., rewards such as money administered by someone other than the individual. He argues that the results of his laboratory experiments indicate that managers who are working on intrinsically interesting jobs will lose interest in them or that extrinsic rewards will motivate behavior at the expense of intrinsic motivation. Others, however, have argued that Deci's results do not appear to support his work motivation conclusions, and they provide evidence to support the traditional theory that rewards are additive, with those actions that lead to the greatest rewards most likely to be repeated.[7]

Unlike Deci, most behavioral scientists believe in the merit pay principle and attribute the frequent failures of merit pay to inadequacies in its implementation. In his classic review of pay research, Meyer[8] concluded that merit pay systems fail because managers actually make relatively small salary discriminations between subordinates. Furthermore, Meyer argued that the results of merit pay decisions are likely to be a threat to most managers' self-esteem. For example, he found that 90 percent of the managers at General Electric rated themselves as above average. "The effects of the actual pay increases on motivation are likely to be more negative than positive. The majority of the people feel discriminated against because, obviously, management does not recognize their true worth."[9]

Other implementation difficulties, such as lack of trust between supervisors and subordinates[10] and conflicting reward schedules,[11] have been blamed for the failures of merit pay for managers in private sector firms.

The performance ratings on which payments are based have also been recognized as important factors in implementation. Each of the leading compensation texts takes pains to demonstrate the importance of accurate performance measurement as a basis for merit pay.[12] Latham[13] has argued that goal-setting approaches to managerial jobs work less well than for more routine blue-collar or clerical jobs because managerial jobs are more complex, with more need to adapt to changing priorities, and so more difficult to measure objectively.

Although we possess some research evidence about the application of merit pay systems in the private sector, there is generally no comparable data for the federal sector. Two exceptions are Rainey's study of incentives in business and government and a recent comptroller general's report on merit pay in the U.S. Postal Service.[14] In a comparison of perceptions of incentives in business and government (involving state and federal middle managers), Rainey argued that it may be more useful for public organizations to stress improvements of career development and performance valuation and measurement than of managerial discretion over pay decisions. He concluded that managerial discretion over pay would create as many problems as it solved.

The comptroller general study concluded that the Postal Service program, initiated in 1972, could be improved because appraisals have not always been accurate and the allocation of merit increases has detracted from the recognition given high performers. Previous evaluations of CSRA merit pay systems, especially those based on the eight agencies which implemented merit pay before the statutory deadline of October 1, 1981, have focused on characteristics of the payouts[15] or implementation process,[16] but not on merit pay as a motivational program.

The present study reports evidence on managerial motivation before and after implementation of merit pay in five federal agencies. Since the purpose of merit pay is to change managerial motivation, we will want to know whether or not it makes a difference in the motivation of a wide cross-section of federal managers. Using the motivational model on which merit pay is based to direct our inquiry, we seek answers to three questions:

- Do federal managers value pay increases?
- Are federal managers likely to expect effort to lead to high rated performance under the objectives-based appraisal systems?
- Are federal managers more likely to expect good performance to lead to increased pay under merit pay than under the previous time-in-grade compensation program?

Methods

Research Design

The study used a time-series design, involving repeated measurements of employee attitudes at fixed intervals, to assess the results of the merit pay intervention. Agencies were required to implement the new, objectives-based appraisal systems no later than October 1, 1980 and to award pay according to the results of these appraisals beginning in October 1981. Surveys were conducted at four points to correspond with significant stages in the implementation process:

June 1980—The first pre-treatment survey preceded the implementation of the appraisal systems that would be used to evaluate performance for purposes of allocating merit pay awards (pre-performance appraisal).

December 1980—The second survey was conducted after introduction of the new performance appraisal systems in October 1980 (post-performance appraisal).

June 1981—The third survey was taken near the end of the appraisal period, by which time appraisal feedback and merit pay "dry runs" had been conducted (pre-merit pay award).

December 1981—The fourth survey was conducted after merit pay awards were made in October 1981 (post-merit pay award).

By tracking employee reaction to performance appraisal and merit pay from the pretest in June 1980 to the post-test in December 1981, we could identify whether the interventions were having the anticipated effects on employees. In terms of the motivational model underlying merit pay, we expected to find that pay was a valued reward throughout the period, that effort would be perceived as leading to high rated performance after introduction of the new, objectives-based appraisal system, and that good performance would be perceived as being rewarded with increased pay after the merit pay awards.

Research sites and sample. The research sites consisted of organizational subunits in five diverse agencies of the federal government, representing civilian and defense agencies and technical and non-technical missions: the Transportation and Public Utilities Service (TPUS) of the General Services Administration, Washington, D.C., the Naval Ship Weapon Systems Engineering Station (NSWSES) in Port Hueneme, California; NASA-Ames Research Center, Moffett Field, California; 21 Social Security Administration (SSA) offices in the Southern California area; both the National and California State offices of the Department of Agriculture Farmers Home Administration (FmHA) and Soil Conservation Service (SCS); and the California office of the Agricultural Stabilization and Conservation Service (ASCS).[17]

Federal Employee Survey (FES). Two forms of this instrument were developed, one for employees GS-13 (or equivalent) and above and a second for GS-12 (or equivalent) and below. The present study reports data only from grade 13 to 15 managers and supervisors. The instruments were pretested on a group of 30 federal employees from two different agencies prior to field administration. The final versions of the surveys required from 30 to 45 minutes to complete. Employees were notified by personal letter about the date, time, and location of the questionnaire administration.[18]

Semi-structured interviews. Interviews were conducted with a stratified, random sample of employees, managers, and union representatives during each quarterly site visit. The format of the interview included structured and open-ended questions. The interviews included questions about major CSRA initiatives as well as potentially significant issues that arose during the course of the study (e.g., the hiring freeze, the presidential transition). These interviews were used primarily to aid in the interpretation of the FES results.

Archival data. As a supplement to the employee attitude and interview data, archival data were collected on organizational performance and other agency activities. Among the documents obtained were collective bargaining agreements, annual budget/expenditure reports, and, when possible, work volume, labor productivity, unit costs, and quality indicators.

Value of Pay as a Reward

Managerial positions offer many rewards—salary, challenging work, promotions, status, and the satisfaction of making a contribution to a community or to national defense are just a few examples. If these other rewards are more important than pay to federal managers, they are not contingent on high performance, we might expect merit pay to have little resultant effect on performance motivation.

In Table 1, we see how merit pay managers rated the various rewards available to them during each of the four periods studied. In all four periods, "challenging work responsibilities" and "retirement benefits" were ranked first and second, respectively. In June 1980 (before performance appraisals for merit pay were introduced) and December 1981 (after the first merit pay awards), merit pay managers ranked these rewards, together with "friendliness of the people you work with" and "location," as more important than their pay as reasons for remaining in their positions. Unlike pay, the other four are geared to maintaining an employee's membership and are not awarded only to high performers. Retirement

TABLE 1

Merit Pay Managers' Reports of the Importance of Organizational Rewards

Questionnaire Item[a]	Mean Response				T-test Probability[b]			
	June 1980	Dec. 1980	June 1981	Dec. 1981	June 1980-Dec. 1980	Dec. 1980-June 1981	June 1981-Dec. 1981	June 1980-Dec. 1981
	N=153	N=186	N=184	N=135				
How important are each of the following factors in your decision to remain in your present position?								
pay	3.82 (5)c	3.82 (4)	3.84 (3)	3.69 (5)	.472	.381	.043**	.081*
challenging work responsibilities	4.54 (1)	4.37 (1)	4.31 (1)	4.31* (1)	.005***	.199	.480	.001***
friendliness of the people you work with	3.95 (3)	3.87 (3)	3.76 (5)	3.87 (3)	.141	.095	.107	.151
fringe benefits	3.55 (8)	3.49 (8)	3.49 (8)	3.48 (8)	.266	.475	.454	.235
promotional opportunities	3.71 (6)	3.58 (7)	3.56 (7)	3.55 (7)	.133	.426	.475	.107
job security	3.61 (7)	3.72 (6)	3.58 (6)	3.65 (6)	.145	.077*	.236	.350
opportunity for public service	3.18 (9)	3.11 (9)	3.01 (9)	3.15 (9)	.280	.191	.117	.418
retirement benefits	4.05 (2)	4.00 (2)	3.92 (2)	3.98 (2)	.314	.205	.268	.270
location	3.86 (4)	3.80 (5)	3.78 (4)	3.84 (4)	.310	.439	.335	.421

[a] Responses are on a Likert-type scale of 1-5 with 1 = not at all to 5 = a great deal.
[b] The figures reported indicate the probability that the difference between the means of the two samples cannot be due to chance alone. The closer the t-test probability is to 1.0, the more likely the difference between the means could have occurred by chance. The closer the probability is to 0, the less likely the difference occurred by chance. One-tailed tests were used and the pooled variance estimate probability is reported.
c Rank order of item for time period specified.

*Probability ≤ .10.
**Probability ≤ .05.
***Probability ≤ .01.

benefits, for instance, are not contingent on outstanding performance, only satisfactory performance and tenure.

Manager perceptions of the different rewards fluctuated during the 18-month period. The importance of two rewards, friendliness of co-workers and job security, declined significantly between December 1980 and June 1981. The results for these rewards are probably a reflection of actions taken by the Reagan administration to freeze hiring and to reduce the size of the federal work force beginning in early 1981. The decline in the importance of challenging work responsibilities, which initially occurred in December 1980 and has remained at the lower level since then, probably represents the uncertainty and changes in direction which the managers of federal programs have experienced since the November 1980 presidential election.[19] The change in the importance of pay coincides with President Reagan's decision to limit comparability increases in October 1981 to 4.8 percent, rather than 15.1 percent, which would have provided full comparability with similar private sector jobs.

None of the fluctuations above appears to be the result of merit pay, *per se,* but of concurrent environmental events. In fact, although the importance of pay declined significantly between June 1981 and December 1981, employees continued to express general agreement with the pay-for-performance concept, as reflected in the results in Figure 1. After the introduction of merit pay, their reported willingness to work harder in return for contingent pay increased appreciably. Thus, it appears that while the importance of pay may have declined, it remained sufficiently valued to motivate increased effort.

Effect of Effort on Rated Performance

Since merit pay is contingent upon rated performance, merit pay's efficacy depends on whether or not federal managers in our agencies expect effort to lead to highly rated performance under the objectives-based appraisal systems. Figure 2 presents managers' assessments of the extent to which effort led to high rated performance between June 1980 and December 1981. Over this period, managers became *less* likely to agree that their new "appraisal process is effective" or "helps me to improve my job performance." In contrast, they are more certain of the standards used to evaluate their performance and find it less difficult to document differences in performance among managers. These managers have a clearer understanding of the criteria on which they will be judged, but apparently feel these criteria are not the best ones to promote improved performance or agency effectiveness.

This finding has important implications for merit pay. The merit pay program itself is expected to increase the subjective probability that per-

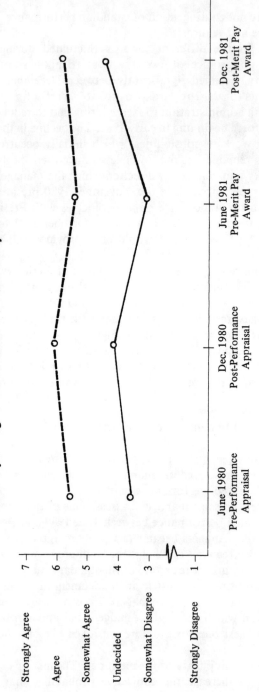

FIGURE 1
Merit Pay Managers' Beliefs About the Value of Pay as a Reward

FIGURE 1 (continued)

Questionnaire Item	Mean Response				T-test Probability[a]			
	June 1980 N=154	Dec. 1980 N=177	June 1981 N=183	Dec. 1981 N=133	June 1980-Dec. 1980	Dec. 1980-June 1981	June 1980-Dec. 1981	June 1980-Dec. 1981
– – – – I personally want to see better performers get larger financial rewards.	5.79	5.90	5.87	5.95	.179	.382	.240	.125
_____ I would probably work harder on my job performance if I thought I would then receive a cash reward or unscheduled pay increase.	3.97	4.15	3.92	4.47	.178	.110	.003***	.007***

[a]The figures reported indicate the probability that the difference between the means of the two samples cannot be due to chance alone. The closer the t-test probability is to 1.0, the more likely the difference between the means could have occurred by chance. The closer the probability is to 0, the less likely the difference occurred by chance. One-tailed tests were used and the pooled variance estimate probability is reported.

***Probability ≤.01.

FIGURE 2

Merit Pay Managers' Beliefs About the Effect of Effort on Objectives-Based Appraisals

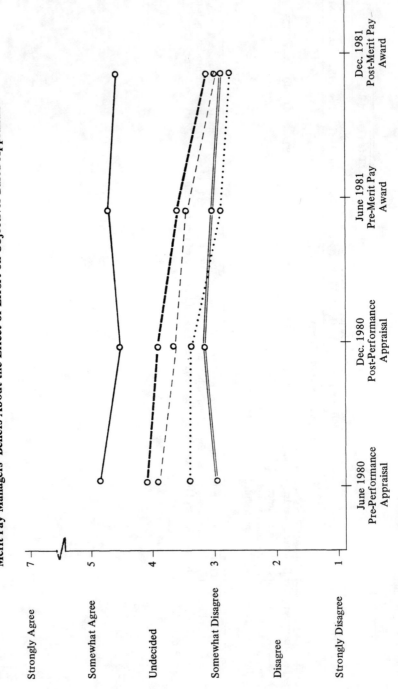

FIGURE 2 (continued)

Questionnaire Item	Mean Response				T-test Probability[a]			
	June 1980	Dec. 1980	June 1981	Dec. 1981	June 1980-Dec. 1980	Dec. 1980-June 1981	June 1981-Dec. 1981	June 1980-Dec. 1981
	N=154	N=185	N=185	N=136				
- - - - All in all, I feel that the current performance appraisal process is effective.	4.23	4.04	3.69	3.31	.151	.013**	.019**	.001***
. . . . . I am *not* sure what standards have been used to evaluate my performance.	3.51	3.49	3.06	2.99	.463	.005***	.355	.006***
‾‾‾‾ I have no control over the factors on which my performance is judged.	3.10	3.21	3.08	3.00	.253	.195	.337	.307
‾‾‾‾ It is difficult to document the actual performance differences among managers and supervisors.	4.95	4.58	4.69	4.65	.013**	.241	.411	.053*
‾‾‾‾ Overall, the current performance appraisal process helps me to improve my job performance.	3.99	3.87	3.80	3.57	.253	.330	.111	.018**

[a]The figures reported indicate the probability that the difference between the means of the two samples cannot be due to chance alone. The closer the t-test probability is to 1.0, the more likely the difference between the means could have occurred by chance. The closer the probability is to 0, the less likely the difference occurred by chance. One-tailed tests were used, and the pooled variance estimate probability is reported unless otherwise noted.

*Probability $\leqslant$ .10.
**Probability $\leqslant$ .05.
***Probability $\leqslant$ .01.

formance will lead to a valued outcome, yet if the objectives-based performance appraisal system implemented concurrently with merit pay results in a *reduced* expectation that effort will lead to increased rated performance, overall motivation will remain the same or be reduced.

Pay-Performance Contingency

In this section, we want to examine whether federal managers are more likely to expect good performance to lead to increased pay under merit pay than under the previous "time-in-grade" compensation program. We can trace the expectations of managers from June 1980 to December 1981 when all managers had received their ratings and payouts.

Managers' beliefs concerning the extent of the contingency of their pay on high performance under the previous compensation system and under merit pay appear in Figure 3. Managers are less likely to perceive that high performance will lead to increased pay in December 1981 than in June 1980. They feel that supervisors and managers are not paid in proportion to their contributions and merit pay does not encourage them to perform well. During their first merit pay appraisal period and after the first payouts, managers seemed *less* likely to expect more pay for higher performance than they did under the previous compensation program.

With the responses of all managers taken as a whole, the results indicate that merit pay managers do not expect their pay to be based on their performance to any greater extent under merit pay than under the previous "time-in-grade" system. These managers may believe that merit pay awards will be made but that they will be contingent not on "performance" or "contribution to the organization," but on some other measure. Merit pay increases will, after all, be based on a "substitute" for actual performance —a performance appraisal rating derived from the new, objectives-based performance appraisal system. It is possible that managers who have had no experience with this type of performance appraisal prior to the introduction of merit pay do not trust it to record genuine "high performance" and these suspicions tend to increase after these managers are rated.

It might be useful to see if those who do not trust their current performance appraisal system are also the ones who believe pay is not contingent on high performance and, in addition, do not favor the present merit pay practices. That is, do those who do not believe that their performance is accurately measured also feel that merit pay is not contingent on good performance? Table 2 shows substantial support for this explanation: those who feel most confident that their appraisal process is effective are also most likely to feel that good performance will be rewarded, and to favor merit pay. Those reporting greater distrust of performance appraisal —that it is ineffective, unfair, and subjective, and that appraisals do not

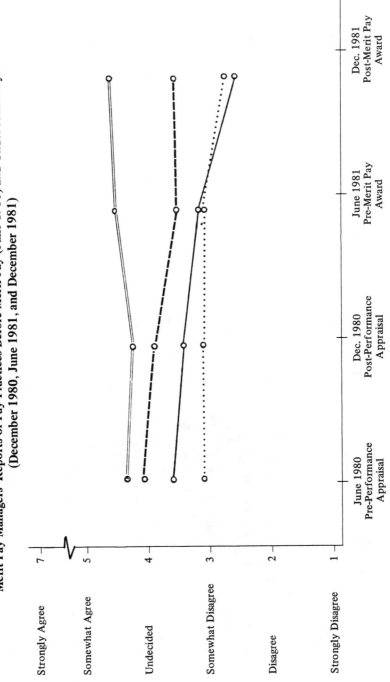

FIGURE 3

Merit Pay Managers' Reports of Pay Practices Before Merit Pay (June 1980) and Under Merit Pay (December 1980, June 1981, and December 1981)

FIGURE 3 (continued)

Questionnaire Item[a]	Mean Response				T-test Probability[a]			
	June 1980	Dec. 1980	June 1981	Dec. 1981	June 1980-Dec. 1980	Dec. 1980-June 1981	June 1981-Dec. 1981	June 1980-Dec. 1981
	N=152	N=176	N=182	N=134				
- - - - If I perform especially well on my present job it is likely I would get a cash award or unscheduled pay increase.	4.05	3.90	3.67	3.63	.203	.098*	.410	.019**
. . . . . . Supervisors and managers are paid in proportion to their contribution to the organization.	3.15	3.15	3.11	2.81	.491	.390	.034**	.033**
____ Under the present system, financial rewards are seldom related to manager or supervisor performance.	4.37	4.26	4.40	4.47	.268	.188	.361	.298
____ All in all, current merit pay provisions encourage me to perform my job well.	3.52	3.47	3.18	2.75	.409	.053*	.014**	.001***

[a]The figures reported indicate the probability that the difference between the means of the two samples cannot be due to chance alone. The closer the t-test probability is to 1.0, the more likely the difference between the means could have occurred by chance. The closer the probability is to 0, the less likely the difference occurred by chance. One-tailed tests were used, and the pooled variance estimate probability is reported unless otherwise noted.

*Probability ≤ .10.
**Probability ≤ .05.
***Probability ≤ .01.

TABLE 2
Correlations Between Confidence in Performance Appraisal and Contingency of Pay on Performance Among Merit Pay Managers in December 1981

	Trust of Appraisal			
	All in all, I feel that the current appraisal process is effective.	The standards used to evaluate my performance have been fair and objective.	It is difficult to document the actual performance differences among managers and supervisors.	Overall, the current performance appraisal process helps me to improve my job performance.
Pay is contingent on performance				
If I perform especially well on my present job it is likely I would get a cash award or unscheduled pay increase.	.31***	.38***	-.18**	.21***
Supervisors and managers are paid in proportion to their contribution to the organization.	.17*	.29***	-.12*	.17**
All in all, current merit pay provisions encourage me to perform my job well.	.50***	.31***	-.01	.57***
Favor Merit Pay				
All in all, I am strongly in favor of the merit pay provisions of the Civil Service Reform Act.	.47***	.32***	-.04	.51***

*Probability ≤ .10.
**Probability ≤ .05.
***Probability ≤ .01.

help them to improve their performance—also tend to report that pay is not contingent on good performance. Only one indicator of distrust of appraisals—reported difficulty of documenting managerial performance—was unrelated to expectations of contingent pay and attitudes toward merit pay. These findings have important implications, indicating that acceptance of merit pay depends on accurate appraisals, as perceived by those being rated.[20] Without performance ratings that are perceived to reflect true performance, merit pay will not motivate good performance but only a quest for "high ratings."

Discussion

These results indicate that a diverse sample of federal managers do not appear to be more highly motivated under merit pay than under the previous time-in-grade compensation policies. Although these findings represent the reaction to the initial year of merit pay only, and may change with the passage of time, they serve to identify two types of contingencies that influence the prospect for developing a successful merit pay system. The first set of contingencies involves the motivational theory itself, e.g., the value of rewards and their linkage to performance. The second set of contingencies revolves around environmental support, e.g., congressional appropriation of funds.

Using the motivational model on which the merit pay program was based, we have identified a major weakness in the current approach. It is not that federal managers do not value pay as a reward, since they report that it is among the handful of important reasons for remaining in their current positions. Where the present merit pay program fails as a motivational program is in the methods used to measure performance. These managers report that effort is *less* likely to lead to a good performance rating, and therefore these managers believe that merit pay does not encourage them to perform their jobs well or contribute to their agencies' effectiveness.

Qualitative evidence from Social Security Administration (SSA) field offices indicates the disruptions that can occur when merit pay is tied to an insufficiently-developed performance appraisal system. Setting specific standards of performance for merit pay managers in local claims offices has had a large impact on the managers' behavior. There is clear evidence that the setting of these specific standards has focused managerial actions on their attainment; managers work hard to obtain good ratings on those standards that are measured. Yet not all of those acctions could be considered "good management." Each manager and supervisor interviewed related stories of "gaming" the statistical measures of performance. "Gaming" is another form of goal displacement, i.e., when the goal is no longer "effective management" but "a good score on the statistics." Most of

SSA's performance statistics can be "manipulated" with no direct harm (or benefit) to a claimant. For example, for the processing-time statistics, one can simply fill out an application but not let the claimant sign it until the earnaings records and proofs are received. Therefore, the two weeks it takes someone to obtain a birth or marriage certificate are not counted in processing time statistics, and the claimant experiences no delay in payment, but the manager receives a better performance rating.

Our results indicate that problems reside not only with the appraisals themselves, but with their linkage to pay. The CSRA requirement that the funds budgeted for merit pay not exceed the cost of the previous system places significant constraints on both the size of rewards and the margin for error in performance appraisals. The first constraint diminishes the probable value of a reward to an employee by setting an upper limit on the potential salary gain associated with outstanding performance. And since a fixed, rather than a variable, merit pay budget heightens the significance of allocational errors (for example, unnecessarily large payments to poorer performers)—because one employee's gain is another employee's loss—it becomes more difficult to create expectations that rewards will be contingent on performance. In a nutshell, if all managers and supervisors receive relatively uniform performance appraisals, the reward differentials among managers will be trivial and merit pay will have negligible motivational effects. Similarly, if performance appraisals are normally distributed across the ratings range, but are perceived as arbitrary or inappropriate measures of performance, merit pay will be of little motivational consequence. The linkage between merit pay and performance appraisals—specifically their accuracy and fairness—is, then, also critical for the effectiveness of merit pay.

It is the role of the merit-pay-pool manager to "manage the linkage between the performance appraisal and the merit pay determination" so that they "must be involved in both the performance appraisal and the merit pay process."[21] Raters are expected to change ratings only as necessary "based on specific information concerning the employee's performance, or on the manager's personal knowledge of and/or judgment about such performance."[22] Unfortunately, there is no assurance that the exercise of such managerial discretion will not be arbitrary and, more important, that employees will share a poor manager's perception even when changes are arguably appropriate. As reported by the GAO in September 1981, some managements have changed performance appraisal ratings without sufficient or legal justification.[23]

Pool management at the research sites varied considerably along a continuum from passive to active control of the ratings distribution.[24] In some cases, for example, the Transportation and Public Utilities Service of the General Services Administration, the performance ratings of merit-pay-pool members were not altered before the monetary distribution was cal-culated. In contrast, at SSA, raters were asked to change the ratings that the pool managers felt were out of line.

The modification of appraisal ratings to achieve agency merit pay goals may have a number of undesirable consequences that are consistent with the results reported here. A manager who requests changes in ratings (or per-sonally changes them) can be viewed as manipulative by those in the pool, and this may result in dissatisfaction with the appraisal used to compute pay awards. Changing a rating may not only create immediate dissatisfaction, but it may undercut the perceived validity of the entire performance ap-praisal system. A less problematic management strategy for dealing with in-adequacies in performance ratings might involve devoting more effort to the early stages of the appraisal process. At the Navy site, for instance, an audit of performance appraisals by the management of one pool concluded that objectives were rarely related to position descriptions and that measurement standards were unclear, especially for "above target" ratings. Under these circumstances, any modification of ratings would clearly ap-pear arbitrary and improvement of the validity and objectivity of appraisals would be a better management strategy.

If the motivational theory underlying merit pay is correct, and if con-tingencies like those above can be overcome,[25] the success of merit pay hinges on yet other contingencies within the policy environment. For in-stance, the system still needs to overcome the effects of policy implementa-tion failures like the September 1981 comptroller general decision. The comptroller general determined that the Office of Personnel Management formula for calculation of merit pay was not in conformance with CSRA, requiring immediate corrective action. The result was that subsequent pay-outs, which assured full comparability, provided only small merit pay dif-ferentials between managers.

While this particular breakdown in interagency communications may be a one-time occurrence, there are other apparent environmental contingencies. The pay cap on federal managerial salaries is among the other threats to the potential success of merit pay. A legitimate question confronting policy-makers is whether these types of environmental contingencies can be "managed" in such an uncertain political context. The answer at this stage is "No," and there is considerable opinion that such contingencies cannot be overcome because they are a permanent part of the political en-vironment.[26]

Conclusions

Why has the new merit pay system encountered so many difficulties? There seem to be several reasons. First, the new performance appraisal system was not adequately pretested. The fact that pay was tied to an "unknown" performance appraisal system exacerbated the implementation problems. There are bound to be problems—for example, unanticipated effects of certain measures and difficulty in developing accurate measures for certain job elements—in any new performance appraisal system. All of these problems create stress for those who are being evaluated. Yet under "normal" circumstances, most managers can assume that their own supervisors will be aware of these temporary imperfections and will not withhold salient rewards because of them. Under merit pay, this supervisor flexibility was either removed or made so administratively cumbersome (as in the SSA example) that the effort was simply not worth the heavy investment. Furthermore, the reward tied to this untried appraisal system was a very visible and a very salient one; and this "merit pay spotlight," focusing on the new appraisal system, led to heightened anxiety over its apparent imperfections. Under these circumstances, implementation of both merit pay and objectives-based performance appraisal were more stressful and prone to failure than if performance appraisal had been fully implemented prior to attaching merit pay to it.

Second, there is an inherent contradiction in the guidance that calls for accurate appraisals based on consultation with the ratee along with "managed" ratings to ensure against payout inequities. Performance appraisal ratings must be accurate representations of a manager's performance, and they must also be managed by pay pool managers and personnel specialists to maintain equity across pay polls, with a sufficient dispersion of ratings within a poor to ensure that the size of the increase received by the "best" managers is large enough to motivate their effort. This represents a significant contradiction in the merit pay system. If the ratings are accurate, why should they be manipulated? Will this not make them less accurate? In fact, this contradiction seems to be based on several assumptions: that all pay pools contain the same proportion of high/average/low performers; that managerial performance is naturally distributed in a manner that allows high performers to receive increases two to four times greater than low performers; and, finally, that the only reason actual ratings do not reflect this is that raters either willfully, or through ignorance, distort their ratings. These assumptions seem tenuous at best and deserve to be more openly debated.

Finally, merit pay, a traditional motivational technique in the private sector, has encountered difficulties that are peculiar to its public sector context. It is doubtful that any merit pay system in the private sector has had to function in the face of an inherently ambiguous performance environment, tight budgetary restraints, freedom of information about individuals' salaries, diffuse authority for implementation, a major managerial succession, and significant changes in organizational goals. Yet, these types of factors are continuing features of the public sector context for merit pay. Although merit pay is desirable in principle, its effectiveness may be severely constrained or negated within the environment of the federal sector.[27] This issue also deserves further scrutiny and debate.

This analysis suggests several policy implications. Although merit pay is still in its "fair trial stage," steps might be taken now to increase the probability that its operation will at some point coincide with the intent of its designers. The validity of performance appraisals will need to be improved, and supervisory training in standards development and appraisal feedback increased. Only when the performance appraisal systems become accepted indicators of actual performance will a motivating link betwen performance and pay be possible. Greater support will have to be generated from Congress and OMB to assure adequate funding for federal compensation programs. The analysis also indicates that any effort to extend merit pay to lower level professional and administrative employees, as recommended by the President's Reorganization Project,[28] would be premature. There is no indication that the merit pay experiment at grades 13-15 has been sufficiently successful to warrant the coverage of employees in grades 1-12. This choice should probably be deferred until there is evidence affirming the original decision to bring merit pay to the federal service.

Notes

1. See President's Panel on Federal Compensation, *Report to the President* (Washington, D.C.: U.S. Government Printing Office, December 1975).
2. See U.S. Office of Personnel Management, *Merit Pay Systems Design* (Washington, D.C.: U.S. Office of Personnel Management, February 1981).
3. Comptroller General of the United States, *Office of Personnel Management's Implementation of Merit Pay (Decision B-203022)* (Washington, D.C.: U.S. General Accounting Office, September 1981).
4. U.S. General Accounting Office, *Federal Merit Pay: Important Concerns Need Attention* (Washington, D.C.: U.S. General Accounting Office, March 1981).
5. Victor H. Vroom, *Work and Motivation* (New York: John Wiley, 1964).
6. Edward L. Deci, "The Effect of Contingent and Noncontingent Rewards and Controls on Intrinsic Motivation," *Organizational Behavior and Human Performance* 8 (1972), pp. 217-229.
7. Bobby J. Calder and Barry J. Staw, "The Interaction of Intrinsic and Extrinsic Motivation," *Journal of Personality and Social Psychology* 31 (1975), pp. 599-605.
8. Herbert H. Meyer, "The Pay for Performance Dilemma," *Organizational Dynamics* 3 (1975), pp. 39-50.
9. *Ibid.*
10. Edward E. Lawler, III, *Pay and Organizational Effectiveness* (New York: McGraw-Hill, 1971).
11. W. Clay Hamner, "How to Ruin Motivation With Pay," *Compensation Review* 3 (1975).
12. Thomas A. Mahoney, *Compensation and Reward Perspectives* (Homewood, Ill.: Irwin, 1979); Alan N. Nash and Stephen J. Carroll, *The Management of Compensation*

(Monterey: Brooks-Cole, 1975); Thomas H. Pattern, *Pay: Employee Compensation and Incentive Plans* (New York: Free Press, 1977).

13. See G. P. Latham, "A Review of Research on the Application of Goal Setting in Organizations," *Academy of Management Journal* 18 (1975), pp. 824-845.

14. See Hal G. Rainey, "Perceptions of Incentives in Business and Government: Implications for Civil Service Reform," *Public Administration Review* 39 (September/October 1979), 440-448; Comptroller General of the United States, *Postal Service Merit Program Should Provide More Incentive for Improving Performance* (Washington, D.C.: U.S. General Accounting Office, November 24, 1980).

15. See, for example, Steve Rappold, "The Merit Pay Payout: CAB's Experience the First Year," *Management* 2 (Spring 1981), pp. 10-11; Efstathia A. Siegel, "Eight Agencies Link Pay to Performance: Will Merit Pay Work?" *Management* 2 (Spring 1981), pp. 15-17.

16. Betty Jane Narver and Sharon Wells, *Implementation of Merit Pay: Experiences in Two Federal Agencies* (University of Washington: Institute for Public Policy and Management, March 1981).

17. Within each of these organizations, two random samples of managers were selected. One sample was designated a permanent panel and was asked to participate in each administration of the survey. The second random sample was drawn from a cross-section of employees who were replaced at each administration of the survey. The two samples were selected so that responses from members of the cross-sectional sample could be compared with those of the panelists in order to detect any repeated-measurement bias among the panelists.

    No bias was found and thus the panel and cross-section have been combined for this study. Data from the SSA field offices were not used in the statistical analyses for this paper. SSA employees began the performance appraisal process one year prior to the other agencies, and at the last moment (September 1980) merit payouts were not made pending system review. Therefore, SSA did not conform to the time frame for introduction of the performance appraisal and merit pay systems required by the time-series design.

18. A test-retest administration of the June 1980 FES was conducted to determine the reliabilities of the questionnaire items. The two administrations of the survey occurred at a site not involved in the evaluation—the Internal Revenue Service, Los Angeles. The surveys were administered at a two-week interval under conditions similar to those used in the five evaluation sites. The final number of usable questionnaires totaled 66, with 28 GS-13 and above respondents. The appropriate statistic for assessing retest reliability is the Pearson product moment correlation coefficient. The mean coefficient for the items appearing on both employee and managerial questionnaires was .61 and the mean coefficient for items appearing only on the managerial questionnaire was .55.

19. It is noteworthy that this decline in the perceived importance of challenging work responsibilities, though not attributable to CSRA, runs counter to established trends in the general workforce during the 1970s. See Raymond A. Katzell, "Changing Attitudes Toward Work" in *Work in America: The Decade Ahead,* Clark Kerr and Jerome M. Rosow (eds.) (New York: Van Nostrand Reinhold, 1979).

20. Additional support for this argument is provided in Lloyd G. Nigro, "Attitudes of Federal Employees Toward Performance Appraisal and Merit Pay: Implications for CSRA Implementation," *Public Administration Review* 41 (January/February 1981), pp. 84-86.

21. U.S. Office of Personnel Management, *Merit Pay System Design* (Washington, D.C.: U.S. Office of Personnel Management, October 1981), p. 79.

22. *Ibid.,* p. 80.

23. U.S. General Accounting Office, *Serious Problems Need to be Corrected Before Federal*

Merit Pay Goes Into Effect (FPCD-81-73) (Washington, D.C.: U.S. General Accounting Office, September 1981).

24. For a more detailed discussion of some of the issues involved in merit-pay-pool management, see James L. Perry, Carla Hanzlik and Jone L. Pearce, "Merit-Pay-Pool Management and Merit Pay Effectiveness," *Review of Public Personnel Administration* 3 (Fall 1982).

25. W. Clay Hamner, "How to Ruin Motivation with Pay"; Carol J. Loomis, "The Madness of Executive Compensation," *Fortune* (July 12, 1982), pp. 42-52.

26. See Robert W. Hartman and Arnold R. Weber (eds.), *The Rewards of Public Service: Compensating Top Federal Officials* (Washington, D.C.: The Brookings Institution, 1980).

27. For a general discussion of the efficacy of different motivational techniques, including monetary incentives, in the public sector, see James L. Perry and Lyman W. Porter, "Factors Affecting the Context for Motivation in Public Organizations," *Academy of Management Review* 7 (January 1982), pp. 89-98.

28. The President's Reorganization Project, *Personnel Management Project,* Volume 1, Final Staff Report (December 1977), p. 161.

1983 (315-325)

MICHAEL G. MAXFIELD

Service Time, Dispatch Time, and Demand for Police Services: Helping More by Serving Less

Introduction:
Police Services and the Management of the Patrol Function

The management of police patrol operations is a complex endeavor. On the one hand police are the principal public agency responsible for implementing crime control policy, while on the other hand they respond to the multitude of other problems which befall urban residents. Police are trained in the use of deadly force and other instruments of violence, but they are most commonly confronted with mundane, non-threatening problems. One of the dilemmas facing police administrators is how to balance the critical and non-critical demands for police service. Most would place threats to life and limb, whether the result of crime or accidental misfortune, in the former category, while relegating what turns out to be the majority of police duties to the non-critical category. Included among this latter group are verbal disputes among neighbors or relatives (although either of these may erupt into violent attacks), uncivil behavior in the form of homeless derelicts or teenagers occupying their street corner turf, and such criminal events as burglaries discovered by householders returning from an extended vacation. The variety of events which precipitate the mobilization of police includes some incidents which clearly require a rapid police response, others which may be resolved as well, if not better, without police intervention, and, what is probably the largest group, those incidents in which it is unclear whether action by the police is either necessary or desirable.

Given this task environment, it is safe to say only that law enforcement agencies must be flexible enough to expect the proverbial unexpected. Not only are police unsure what their next encounter with clients on the street will produce, they are also uncertain about when they will be mobilized and where they will be sent. The vast majority of mobilizations are reactive, in which police respond to calls for assistance from urban residents.[1] A relatively small number of police encounters with citizens are the result of officer-initiated activity. Operations researchers analyzing the police patrol function have shown that incoming calls from citizens follow a Poisson process,[2] so that it is difficult to predict exactly when and where different demand levels will emerge. The volume of requests for police services displays some periodicity with respect to the time of day, but the nix of different types of demands for police intervention adds to the uncertainty of law enforcement.

These kinds of uncertainties create problems for managers charged with the responsibility to administer patrol operations and to control the disbursement of input resources into the police function. They must balance the provision of a timely response in those situations where there are threats to life or property against the need to conserve resources. Yet, they must also recognize that police must often be dispatched where the need for such a response is not altogether clear. This is further complicated by the fact that decisions about the necessity of a mobile response are difficult to make without actually sending a unit to investigate, and because the reasons why a police response is unwarranted may be difficult to communicate to distressed citizens who feel that such a response is of the utmost importance. For these reasons police departments have generally not restricted access to the service of patrol units. Recent research on the kinds of problems people bring to the attention of police indicates that police do in fact restrict the deployment of patrol officers in some cases, but the decision rule seems to be: When in doubt, send a unit to investigate.[3]

This policy creates different kinds of problems for managers of patrol operations in that the volume of requests for service may easily outstrip the capacity of police to respond to calls. Furthermore, some researchers have suggested that readiness to respond to all manner of requests for service may, in turn, increase the number of such requests.[4] Related to this is the fact that police are the last or only recourse for assistance, information, or support in the personal crises of numerous urban residents. Cumming, *et al.,* describe the supportive function police provide for many disaffected individuals.[5] Police also act as information brokers for a surprising number of callers as reported by Antunes and Scott.[6] Finally, the police themselves actively promote their services and, through the use of 911 systems, make it easier for citizens to contact them. Even public telephones announce that no dimes are required to call the police, prompting calls from no small number of dimeless information seekers and pranksters.[7]

This paper addresses these problems by presenting an analysis of calls for police services in San Francisco. The analysis focuses on the management of the volume and variety of incoming calls for service, and of the workload which this volume imposes on patrol operations in the field. Problems in dispatching operations are examined, and alternative solutions to managing the workload are discussed. Indicators of patrol operations which are readily collected and archived are used to analyze the volume of calls for service, the internal processing time for dispatching patrol units, the amount of time patrol officers spend investigating different types of calls, and inter-district dispatching created by imbalances in the volume of demand and the availability of patrol resources.

Service Time, Dispatch Time—Two Critical Input Resources

Personnel costs are foremost among law enforcement agencies, and the patrol division consumes the largest share of salaries in police departments.[8] Accordingly, the expenditure of police personnel hours in responding to citizen calls for service is the most valued input into the production of police services. The principal service police provide is the time of their personnel. This means that decisions about which incidents warrant a police response are necessary to control the disbursement of this valued input. These decisions are potentially very important, since failure to dispatch a patrol unit in situations where there are threats to persons or property may result in serious injury. Furthermore, a sizeable proportion of arrests are made at the scene of an incident shortly after it has occurred.[9] For these reasons, the policy of most police departments is to dispatch a mobile patrol unit when requested by citizens calling the police.

The speed of response to calls for service is another valued characteristic of police patrol operations. All other things being equal, a rapid response represents a greater expenditure of police resources than does a more deliberate response. Recent research by the Kansas City, Missouri Police Department has questioned the long-held assumption that the key to capturing suspects lies in a speedy response to all citizen calls for service.[10] Nevertheless, a fast response is generally valued over a slower one, by police and victims if not by criminals.

Two important input resources that police provide their clients are, therefore, access to the services of police officers, and the celerity with which that access is granted. The availability of these resources to citizens in need of police services is affected in general by two factors: the level of demand for police services, and the internal procedures by which calls for service are processed.

The effect of demand levels on the availability of police personnel inputs is straightforward. Given some finite capacity to respond to citizen calls for assistance, police can spend less time handling individual incidents as the number of such requests increases. Constraints in the face of high demand are, in part, externally imposed by the citizens to call police. As demand increases, decisions concerning which incidents warrant a mobile response become more important, and the limited availability of patrol units renders the time spent by officers investigating individual incidents more valuable.

The processing of citizen calls for police service can be both a cause of the restricted availability of input resources in high demand periods, and an adaptive strategy for dealing with excess demand. If access to police services in the form of dispatching a patrol unit in response to citizen calls is not controlled, then limited availability of patrol units in high demand periods becomes more likely. Similarly, if demand increases, and access to services is not restricted, it becomes more likely that the speed of police response to citizen calls will be reduced. This simply recognizes that as the capacity of the police response system becomes taxed or saturated, and patrol units are less readily available to be dispatched, delays in the initial response to citizen calls will increase.

The relationship between the level of demand for police services and the capacity of a police department to respond to such demand is an important issue in the management of police resources. These issues present problems in the short- and long-term distribution of police resources in time and space, and in adapting to periods of high demand for police services. The general concerns of police managers and administrators are to provide the most effective use of available resources. Accordingly, adapting the capacity of patrol resources to meet varying levels of demand for services is a critical management problem.

In situations where demand for police services outstrips the capacity of the department to respond to citizen calls for services, there are several adaptive strategies, not necessarily mutually exclusive, which may be employed to manage the excess workload. These include: (1) "stacking" calls for service, or placing them in a queue awaiting the availability of a patrol unit; (2) reducing the amount of time patrol units spend servicing individual calls in high demand periods; (3) assigning priorities to incoming calls; and (4) inter-jurisdictional dispatching, or assigning units to calls which occur outside their area of formal responsibility. In addition, there are two long-range responses to excess demand: increasing the size of the patrol force, and reallocation of existing personnel resources. With the exception of increasing personnel levels, which is a policy not routinely under the control of police administrators, I will briefly discuss each of these adaptive responses. After examining the distribution of demand for services in San Francisco, I will discuss some of the problems associated with implementing these policies in that city.

Managing the Volume of Calls for Police Service

Stacking calls for service in high demand periods is not so much an overt adaptive strategy as it is a reaction to excess demand in the absence of other policies. When the rate of incoming calls for service outstrips the capacity of the patrol force to respond to them, calls are placed in a queue and assigned to patrol units as they become available. The pure application of this strategy is that as demand grows, so does the queue. Stacking is generally dysfunctional in the absence of any specified criteria for screening calls to be placed in a queue. One obvious consequence of this policy is increasingly lengthy dispatch times for those calls which are stacked.

Another tactic for reducing the pressure of high demand on the patrol function can be to reduce per-incident service time. By reducing the amount of time spent investigating individual incidents police may respond to more calls. Tien, *et al.,* equate this response with the general queuing theory axiom that clerks will work faster when there are more clients waiting to be served.[11] Their analysis shows further that reductions in service time per incident are greater than would be predicted for a given increase in demand. Police tend to reduce the amount of time per incident faster than the number of incidents increases, thus producing a slight decline in overall workload as demand grows. This is similar to the load-shedding behavior described by Maxfield, *et al.,* in which police "unfound" a larger proportion of criminal incidents in areas exhibiting high demand for police services.[12]

Virtually all large metropolitan police departments assign priorities to incoming calls for service. These are based on the seriousness of the incident, whether or not there is any personal injury, and the likelihood of capturing an offender. Incoming calls for service which do not meet these criteria are assigned lower priorities for dispatch, and may be stacked as demand levels increase. Dispatchers seek to assign patrol units immediately to high priority calls regardless of demand levels.

The fourth type of adaptive response is inter-jurisdictional dispatching of patrol units, or sending officers deployed in one police beat or district to respond to an incident which occurred in another area. Assigning patrol units to specific geographical areas in cities has been used as a management device since the origins of urban police,[13] although innovations in the technology of communications have reduced the need for decentralized and district-specific policing in large cities. In theory, patrol officers are held accountable for crime and other problems which occur in their assigned areas. They will also develop a detailed knowledge of their patrol beat which will aid in detecting suspicious acts, and enable them to develop closer relationships with the residents and merchants in the area they serve. Inter-jurisdictional dispatching, however, is a common phenomenon in most large cities. Bottoms[14] reports that in a seven-day sample of calls for service in Chicago, 13 percent were answered by a car assigned to a district other than that in which the incident occurred, and only 23 percent of calls were handled by the beat car assigned to the area of the incident. Gay, *et al.,* concur, saying that police beats have come to be almost exclusively administrative rather than operational units.[15]

manage the patrol workload reflect political and organizational constraints, and to some degree load-shedding by patrol officers. I will first describe the specific characteristics of patrol dispatch operations in San Francisco. My analysis of calls for service and responses to demand focuses on three points: (1) patterns of variation in the volume of requests for different services; (2) the relationship between volume of demand and service time—the amount of time police spend in handling different types of calls; and (3) the effects of variations in demand and service time on the delay between the time a call is received and a patrol unit is dispatched. Following this analysis, I will describe how management problems in the San Francisco Department at the time of this study constrained the ability of the patrol function to adapt to periods of high demand for services.

Police Dispatch Operations in San Francisco

Figure 1 shows a time line which depicts the police response process from the time a call is received by a telephone complaint clerk until the time a patrol unit completes its investigation of the incident. The first stage in the response process is when a complaint clerk answers the telephone, receiving a call from a citizen. This is labeled t_1 in Figure 1. In San Francisco most complaint clerks are civilian police department employees, predominantly women. A few sworn police officers who are recovering from illness or injury are also assigned to the centralized communications facility on a temporary basis. The complaint clerk records preliminary information—location, type of incident, number of people involved, whether or not there is a personal injury—on a call-received (CR) slip. The complaint clerk also records what time the call was received and assigns one of three priority designations to the call based upon the seriousness of the incident, the presence of injuries, and whether or not the incident is described as "in progress."

The CR slip is then forwarded to radio dispatchers, who are located in the same room, *via* a conveyor belt; that is t_2 in Figure 1. During the time the data examined here were collected, there were three dispatchers, each having responsibility for three police districts. The same personnel rotate assignments as complaint clerks and dispatchers. Dispatchers assign calls to specific patrol units and record the time of dispatch on the CR slip, labeled t_2 in Figure 1. The time interval between t_1 and t_3 represents internal dispatch processing time, the interval between when a call was received and when a car was dispatched to handle the incident. This interval defines *dispatch time*. The interval between t_3 and t_4 represents travel time, from the time a patrol unit accepts the dispatch until it arrives on the scene. Although police radio a dispatcher indicating that they have arrived on the scene, this information is not recorded on the data available here. The point at which the patrol unit radios back to the dispatcher that it has completed the call is t_5. The interval between t_3 and t_5 represents *service time,* the amount of time a patrol unit spends on a call for service. This may include time spent preparing reports, booking suspects, searching for lost juveniles, and so forth.

This information is recorded on CR slips for every call which generates a dispatch. The data used in the analysis reported below were collected by the police department for a six-week period in 1977 (May through June 10) for use in an internal patrol allocation study. Only calls from private citizens were collected. This excludes officer-initiated activity, both on-view incidents detected by police on patrol, and incidents in which a citizen flagged down an officer on the street. Certain types of incidents are, therefore, not represented, crimes of vice and traffic citations being the most frequent. The data included here do represent the vast majority of citizen-initiated calls for service, and as such document the patrol response function in San Francisco during this six-week period.

These are the two indicators of the value of police input resources consumed by citizens' calls for service. Dispatch time expresses the delay between the time a call was received by telephone operators and the time a patrol unit was sent by radio dispatchers. Service time expresses the commitment of police personnel resources to individual incidents. Dispatch time depends on how quickly a dispatcher can assign a patrol unit to respond to an incident. This is, in turn, affected first by the priority designation assigned by complaint clerks, and second by the availability of patrol units to assign to the call. As we will see below, the most common cause of dispatch delay is the volume of calls for service. Dispatch delay may also be related to service time. Lengthy service time can produce a bottleneck in the police response function which exacerbates delays in dispatch time during high demand periods.

FIGURE 1
Sequence of Events in the Police Response Process

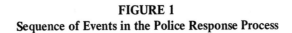

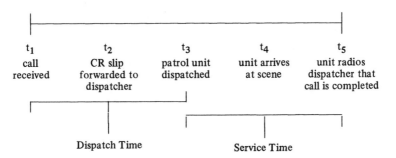

t_1	t_2	t_3	t_4	t_5
call received	CR slip forwarded to dispatcher	patrol unit dispatched	unit arrives at scene	unit radios dispatcher that call is completed

Dispatch Time   Service Time

TABLE 1
Mean Dispatch Time for Ten Types of Calls for Service (in minutes)

	Number of Calls	Percent of Total	Mean Dispatch Time	Standard Deviation	Coefficient of Variation
Meet Complainant	4,902	20	20.2	26.1	1.3
Alarm	2,804	12	2.9	3.2	1.1
Burglary	2,199	9	18.1	25.8	1.4
Family Fight	1,896	8	12.7	20.2	1.6
Disturbance	1,803	7	24.2	29.6	1.2
Helpless Person	1,636	7	14.7	23.6	1.6
Suspicious Circumstances	1,106	5	7.5	14.3	1.9
Vehicle Theft	1,026	4	19.6	25.2	1.3
Assault	945	4	10.2	18.3	1.8
Robbery	580	2	4.4	9.2	2.1
Other	5,353	22			
Total	24,250	100			

Patterns of Demand, Service Time, and Dispatch Time

Table 1 shows the breakdown of calls for service in San Francisco for ten of the most common categories of incidents. These calls reflect the interpretation of problems articulated by citizens to complaint clerks, those individuals whom Antunes and Scott refer to as the gatekeepers of the police response function.[17] The first column shows the number of incidents in each category during the six-week period, and column 2 shows these as a percent of total calls for service. The third and fourth columns contain the mean dispatch time, in minutes, and the standard deviation for each of these categories. The last column shows the coefficient of variation, which expresses the ratio of the standard deviation to mean dispatch time.

The second category in Table 1 contains those incidents in which police have been alerted of an audible alarm sounding somewhere. This group includes about 12 percent of all calls for service. Robbery and assault are the most common violent crimes, accounting for about 2 and 4 percent respectively, of all calls for service during this period. The most common criminal incidents brought to the attention of police in San Francisco are burglary and auto theft. About 9 percent of calls for service reported burglaries, while vehicle theft made up about 4 percent of calls.

The balance of the categories shown in Table 1 contain incidents which were not initially classified as potential criminal incidents by complaint clerks. The disturbance category, accounting for about 7 percent of calls, includes complaints about noisy parties, juvenile disturbances, and the like. Persons in need are allegedly senile or insane persons, drunks, and people reported to be passed out in public places. These individuals accounted for about 7 percent of calls for service. Suspicious circumstances include reports of prowlers, suspicious individuals, and persons who appear to be breaking into a building or tampering with an automobile; these were about 4 percent of all calls. Family fights were more common, accounting for 8 percent of incidents which produced a dispatch. By far the largest category is "meet complaint." These are incidents in which the complaint clerk is unable to extract further information about the nature of the problem from the caller, calls in which the complainant's message is garbled or otherwise unintelligible, and calls which are simply too complicated for dispatchers to explain to patrol officers over the radio. Meet-complainant calls were about 20 percent of calls for service.

Two characteristics of the figures for dispatch time in Table 1 stand out. First, some of the dispatch times are quite lengthy, up to an average of 24 minutes between the time a call is received and a unit dispatched in response to incidents classified as disturbances. Secondly, there is considerable variation in dispatch times within incident categories, as evidenced by the standard deviations and coefficients of variation. The standard deviation of dispatch time for robbery is twice the mean of this category, indicating that there are sharp differences in the speed with which units are dispatched in response to these incidents. The longest delays in dispatch time are for disturbances and meet complainant calls among the non-criminal incidents, and for burglaries and vehicle theft among the calls initially coded as criminal incidents.

We, therefore, find that there is considerable delay, in internal processing time, in dispatching patrol units to respond to many calls for service in San Francisco. Incidents which are potentially serious, such as robberies, assaults, and family fights, and those in which it appears that police had been notified of an incident in progress, such as alarms and suspicious circumstances, generate the most rapid response, but even the dispach times for these incidents are not particularly prompt.

Part of the explanation for these rather lengthy dispatch times lies in the range of variation about the mean shown in Table 1. Dispatch times as measured here are affected by the availability of patrol units for dispatch, and this is, in turn, partially dependent on the rate of incoming calls for service. The large variations about some of the means indicate that there are some periods when the response to calls for service is fairly prompt, and other times when there are long delays in dispatching patrol units. This illustrates the problem of "stacked" calls for service in San Francisco.

The relationship between demand levels and dispatch time is shown in Figure 2 which aggregates the number of calls for service and mean dispatch time into one-hour intervals according to when calls were received by complaint clerks (t_1 shown in Figure 1). In this figure two scales are shown on the vertical axis. The scale ranging from zero to 40 measures mean dispatch time (in minutes), while the scale from 1:00 a.m. to 12:00 a.m. expresses the total volume of calls in each hour. By comparing these indicators in one-hour intervals we can assess the extent to which dispatch time decays as the volume of demand increases.

The number of calls for service reaches its maximum value between the hours of 5:00 and 6:00 p.m. The rate of calls fluctuates at a generally high level until the interval between 11:00 p.m. and midnight, after which there is a steady decline in volume until 6:00 a.m. This distribution of the volume of calls over a 24-hour period is very similar to that for the hourly distribution of crime in a midwestern city presented in Gay, et al.[18] This general pattern appears to be a typical distribution over a 24-hour period.

Mean dispatch time generally increases beginning at 6:00 a.m. throughout the day, with particularly high values between 2:00 and 4:00 in the afternoon, and from 10:00 to 11:00 at night. Dispatch time and the volume of

FIGURE 2
Dispatch Time and Volume of Calls by Hour

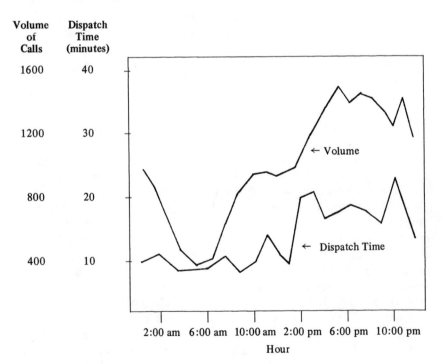

calls for service are strongly related, with a Pearson product moment correlation of .78, treating the 24 one-hour intervals as cases. This shows that high levels of demand do produce increased delays in the processing of calls, and result in some stacking. In high demand periods there is a steady deterioration in the speed with which units are dispatched, with an average delay of more than 20 minutes for three hours of the day.

As noted above, this can be a dysfunctional adaptive response to high volume situations, but delayed time through queuing calls is obviously a reaction to high demand in San Francisco. In contrast, in Figure 3 we do not see any systematic pattern of reduction in service time as an adaptive response to increased volume of calls for service. In this figure, the vertical scale ranging from zero to 50 expresses service time in minutes. Peak service times, between an average of 43 and 52 minutes per incident, occur from

FIGURE 3
Service Time and Volume of Calls by Hour

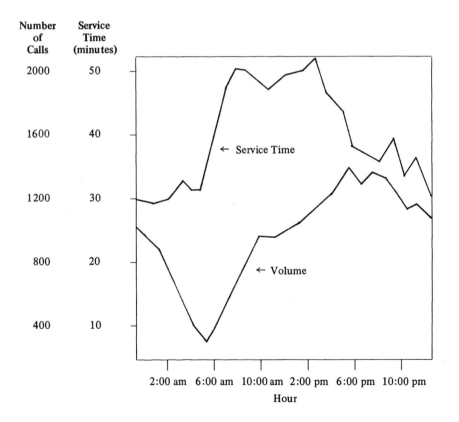

7:00 a.m. to 3:00 p.m. This is a period of steady increase in the volume of calls for service, and includes that interval when delay in dispatching is greatest. There is no overall relationship between demand and service time; Pearson's r equals -.01.

This suggests that lengthy dispatch times are in part caused by the absence of reduction of service time in times of peak demand. Calls are stacked because dispatchers are unable to assign calls to a patrol unit. Because police do not adopt the load-shedding strategy of reducing per-incident service time, there are more lengthy delays in the dispatch queue. Police actions in the field are not always responsive to shifts in demand levels.

The assignment of dispatch priorities to incoming calls does appear to be effective in reducing dispatch delay. Table 2 shows the number of calls for service in each of the three priority categories, and the mean dispatch time for the incidents in each group. Calls of the highest priority were about 26 percent of all calls generating a dispatch in the six-week period examined here, with mean dispatch delays of 3.2 minutes. Mean dispatch times for high priority incidents remained relatively low throughout the 24-hour intervals, ranging from a low of 2.1 minutes between 8:00 and 9:00 a.m. to a high of 4.1 minutes between 7:00 and 8:00 p.m. In contrast, the mean dispatch times for priorities 2 and 3 were 17.1 and 23.3, respectively. Incidents coded as priority 2 are to be held for ten minutes awaiting the availability of a patrol unit in the same district. The lowest priority incidents may be held indefinitely while police deal with other calls.

In high demand situations, calls may be assigned to available patrol units based in different districts. Figure 4 shows that the number of cross-district dispatches closely follows changes in the volume of calls for service, until the increase in out-of-district dispatches between 10:00 p.m. and 1:00 a.m., a period in which the volume of calls declines. The correlation between these two indicators is .79, indicating that cross-district dispatching is a common response to high levels of demand for patrol services.

TABLE 2
Mean Dispatch Time by Priority of Call

Priority Designation	Mean Dispatch Time (in minutes)	Standard Deviation	Coefficient of Variation
Highest	3.2	4.1	1.28
Intermediate	17.1	24.4	1.43
Lowest	23.3	28.4	1.22

FIGURE 4
Inter-District Dispatches and Volume of Calls by Hour

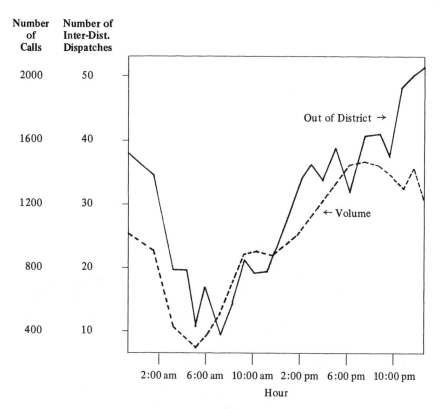

Managing the Workload: Some Problems, Some Suggestions

Two characteristics of dispatch operations in San Francisco contribute to the patterns displayed in Figures 2 and 3. Dispatchers, as described above, are responsible for assigning incoming calls for service to patrol units. Their general responsibilities include monitoring the status of patrol units—location, and whether or not the unit is handling a call. The first problem concerns the use of civilian dispatchers which dates to 1972. Prior to that time only sworn officers were used as complaint clerks and dispatchers. Although it has reduced the cost of dispatch operations, the deputy chief of Support Services Bureau in the department during the time of this study thought the shift to civilian employees created some difficulty in the assignment of patrol units to calls for service.[19] He reported that officers sometimes tried to refuse a call, asking dispatchers to assign it to another unit. Such requests are more frequent with civilian dispatchers, and are more commonly granted. Although there are no available data which directly address this problem, it obviously can produce more lengthy delays in dispatching patrol units.

The second point relates both to dispatch time and service time. In the communications room there is no visual display which enables dispatchers to monitor the location or status of units assigned to their radio frequencies. Instead, dispatchers place a CR slip in an "active" slot corresponding to the patrol unit to which they have assigned the call. In addition to the active bins, there are filing slots for stacked calls awaiting the availability of a patrol unit, and a bin for those calls which have been completed. Dispatchers do not have any automated or readily visible device for monitoring the status of calls waiting, or the status of patrol units in service. The speed with which waiting calls are assigned depends on the dispatchers' ability to keep track of how long they have been in the "hold" slot. Similarly, dispatchers cannot easily monitor how long patrol units have been servicing individual calls unless they check the recorded times on CR slips. This exacerbates a problem which has been recognized by supervisors in the communications section. Patrol officers will remain "in service" after completing the call to which they have been dispatched, and take additional time to enjoy a break or cup of coffee without being interrupted by another assignment. These difficulties are compounded in high demand situations, and the incentives for officers to delay reporting their availability for subsequent assignments are greater when they expect another call immediately. This obviously compounds the problem of delay in dispatching units in high demand periods, contributing to the problem of stacked calls.

Inter-district dispatching is a generally undesirable solution to the problem of high demand. This is because of the increased travel time involved in cross-district dispatching, both to the scene of the incident, and back as the unit returns to its assigned district and beat. Because of variation in the levels of demand and availability of patrol units, the smaller patrol beat has largely become a record-keeping artifact and an administrative rather than operational unit.[20] But the patrol division is organized and administered by districts, and although the nine districts in San Francisco are more than are needed from an operations efficiency standpoint, regular cross-district dispatching of patrol units is not a feasible solution given the present configuration of districts.

The principal reason why cross-district dispatching is so common in this city is unequal levels of demand for services across police districts. As described above, a reallocation of patrol resources along revised district boundaries is one possible long-range solution to the sharply unequal demand for services, and inter-district dispatching of patrol units. There are, however, internal and external obstacles to such reallocation in San Francisco. The external obstacles focus on neighborhood identification with district police stations. An earlier study of police facilities in San Francisco recognized this problem:

> Although much of the police service is provided from the patrol car rather than the district station, the presence of district station buildings symbolizes the availability of police service and tends to provide psychological assurance to neighborhoods of continued police concern and commitment to community safety.[21]

Some years ago the temporary closing of two district stations generating the lowest volume of calls for service was intensely opposed by the interest groups which characterize local politics in the Bay Area. Not only were the two districts reopened, but the city charter was amended to make any future changes in police district boundaries subject to resolution by the county board of supervisors. Furthermore, a temporary shift from at-large to district election of the county board of supervisors increased the identification of supervisors with "their" police district, prompting some calls for the creation of two additional police districts so that the 11 supervisorial districts would correspond with police districts.[22] At-large election of supervisors was reinstated in November, 1979. Internal opposition to redeployment comes from the city's police officers association, which has opposed the deputy chief of field operations' proposed policy of shifting police officers from one district to another. Whatever adjustments in personnel are made among existing districts usually result from the assignment of new police officers, or requests for transfers from experienced officers.

Apart from these political constraints on the reallocation of patrol forces there remains the problem of how to deal with short-term imbalances in demand and the availability of patrol units. As noted earlier, most allocation models assume the distribution of incoming calls follows a Poisson process in which some proportion of hours will result in a saturated patrol force. The size of this proportion depends upon the absolute numbers of patrol units which are deployed, which is in turn dependent on the availability of resources and the tolerance of officials for idle capacity during those times when the rate of incoming calls is lower. In an atmosphere of growing resource scarcity in the public sector, most administrators will tolerate some level of saturation of the patrol response system as a trade-off in conserving resources. This simply means that unless decision makers have unlimited resources to devote to police patrolling, they must be willing to tolerate some excess demand regardless of how sophisticated a patrol allocation model is used. Thus, there are practical as well as political reasons why long-term reallocation of patrol resources cannot solve the problems identified here.

TABLE 3
Mean Service Time (in minutes)

	Mean Service Time	Standard Deviation	Coefficient of Variation
Alarm	17.1	21.9	1.28
Robbery	43.1	44.1	1.02
Assault	47.9	49.7	1.04
Disturbance	26.1	29.0	1.11
Family Fight	33.7	35.5	1.05
Burglary	51.5	38.7	0.75
Person in Need	39.4	39.8	1.01
Vehicle Theft	46.4	35.3	0.76
Meet Complainant	44.4	38.1	0.86
Suspicious Circumstances	27.9	33.3	1.19

Some of these problems may be addressed through reduction of service time. While we have seen that this is not routinely employed to alleviate high demand for services in San Francisco it is, nevertheless, a possible means to increase the availability of patrol units. That there is room for reduction of service time can be seen in Table 3 which displays mean service time for the ten incident categories presented earlier. This table shows that the types of calls which place the greatest stresses on the police response function in terms of time expended in investigation are burglaries, assaults, and vehicle thefts. As argued above, the commitment of manhours to investigate different types of incidents represents a significant expenditure of police resources. The Kansas City Response Time Study[23] has shown that most burglaries and auto thefts are discovered hours, or even days, after they have occurred. A prompt response to calls about these crimes is unlikely to produce an arrest on the scene. Furthermore, the study of the investigative function by Greenwood, et al., has shown that follow-up investigation of these incidents is seldom productive.[24] Skogan and Antunes support these findings by showing that in incidents such as burglaries, where victims can provide little information about suspected offenders, arrests are infrequent.[25]

If the efforts of patrolmen in investigating burglaries are not likely to be productive, then a potentially valuable first step towards conserving police resources may lie in further limiting the police response to these delayed-discovery crimes, especially since they consume large numbers of patrol manhours. Police may respond to a larger number of incidents more quickly by reducing the amount of time they spend investigating individual incidents. We have seen, however, that under the current dispatching system it is difficult for dispatchers to monitor the activities of patrolmen who sometimes remain "in service" in the parking lot of a coffee shop for some minutes after completing investigations of incidents. Therefore, either general guidelines from administrators, or a system which makes it easier for dispatchers to monitor the length of time police spend investigating service calls is a prerequisite for increasing the availability of patrol units through reducing service time for certain types of incidents. Lighted display systems which inform dispatchers of the status and reported location of patrol units, and which display information on calls for service awaiting dispatch can make it easier to monitor service time and expedite the assignment of calls to patrol units.

Finally, recent research on the police response system has focused on the use of referrals and deferred response in handling calls for service.[26] Gay, *et al.*, describe four types of deferred response:[27] telephone reports, mail-in reports, referral to district station, and referral to another public or a private agency. Telephone reports can include a variety of incidents and types of dispositions. Complaint clerks may resolve some incidents by simply talking with callers and listening to their problems. Some types of internal referrals also fall into this category. Complaint clerks may record information about delayed-discovery crimes such as burglary and submit a form to the investigative division, thus bypassing the costly and often unproductive action by patrol officers. Mail-in reports may also be used for certain types of discovery crimes. In these types of incidents complaint clerks send callers a questionnaire instead of a patrol car. Victims complete the form which is then submitted to the investigative division for follow-up. Mail-in reports have been used for some types of incidents in San Francisco for at least the past 11 years. For some types of incidents callers may be asked to visit the district station with jurisdiction in their neighborhood and report the incident to station personnel. Callers with domestic problems, people complaining about disputes with neighbors, landlord/tenant disputes, homeowners troubled by stray dogs, and many other complainants may be served as well, if not better, by other public agencies, or perhaps private groups.

The use of referrals and telephone reports is described in detail by Scott and Moore.[28] Such referrals are possible because a substantial number of citizen calls to police are either requests for information or complaints about problems which relate only peripherally to even the broadest conception of the police mission. Similarly, the large number of calls classified simply as "meet complainant" suggests that there is a substantial number of incidents which are eligible for more careful screening. Antunes and Scott describe how complaint clerks may reduce their workload by adopting the simple decision rule to send a patrol unit unless they are certain that such a response is not warranted.[29] This can be a costly decision rule, as evidenced by the often lengthy delays in the dispatch queue. More judicious screening of incoming calls by complaint clerks can reduce the number of calls which are stacked at dispatch consoles.

Summary and Conclusion

This paper has described various approaches to the more effective management of police patrol operations in light of recent research on the effectiveness of patrol and on the need for speedy response to calls for service. Problems with "stacked" calls for service in San Francisco are related to several characteristics of patrol operations. Imbalances in the demand for police services and the availability of patrol units to handle the calls is the most proximate cause of queues at dispatch stations. While some excess demand for services is to be expected, long delays are endemic for certain types of calls in San Francisco. Extended service time for certain incidents contributes to backlogs at the dispatch station, and there is no consistent reduction in the amount of time officers spend servicing calls during periods of highest demand. Dispatchers are restricted in their ability to monitor service time by the equipment in the communications section, and in some cases by the intransigence of patrol officers. As a result, internal delays in processing calls for service grow longer.

These problems are not restricted to the San Francisco Police Department. The varied nature and unpredictable volume of citizen calls for assistance reduce the capacity of police to respond to all incoming service calls. Accordingly, possible approaches to alleviating the excess demand on patrol operations in San Francisco and other cities are to reduce the types of calls to which patrol units are dispatched, and to reduce the amount of time they spend investigating certain types of calls. All urban police departments may use these strategies. They refer not so much to the actions of police on the street, as to the actions of complaint clerks and dispatchers who act as gatekeepers for the patrol force. More judicious screening of certain types of calls by complaint clerks, increased use of referrals and deferred response, and more aggressive monitoring of patrol units in the field by dispatchers may increase the productivity of patrol officers. These are management policies which increase information about and control over officers on the street.

Finally, this paper has shown how information on dispatch and patrol operations which is routinely collected may be utilized for more effective management of the patrol response. While the San Francisco Police Department did not routinely keypunch and analyze these data at this writing, CR slips in this city and in most others are easily transformed into a machine-readable format to facilitate analysis of dispatch time, service time, the volume of out of district dispatches, and other indicators of dispatch and patrol operations. Unlike complex patrol allocations models which can be of limited effectiveness in reducing patrol backlog, analysis of the volume of calls for service and their disposition may be easily undertaken with a minimum of equipment and technical assistance, and can provide valuable information for police patrol managers.

Notes

1. Albert J. Reiss, Jr., *The Police and the Public* (New Haven: Yale University Press, 1971).
2. The Poisson distribution is a mathematical expression in queuing theory which describes the frequency of random events. For example, if, over time, a police district receives two service calls per hour, according to a Poisson distribution the calls will occur as follows:

14%	no calls
27% of hours	1 call
27% of hours	2 calls
18% of hours	3 calls
9% of hours	4 calls
4% of hours	5 calls
1% of hours	6 or more calls

   For specific applications of queuing theory to the rate and frequency of calls for police service see: Richard C. Larson, *Urban Police Patrol Analysis* (Cambridge: MIT Press, 1972).
3. George E. Antunes and Eric J. Scott, "Calling the Cops: Police Telephone Operators and Citizen Calls for Service," *Journal of Criminal Justice,* Vol. 9, pp. 165-180.
4. William G. Gay, T. H. Schell, and Stephen Schack, *Prescriptive Package: Improving Patrol Productivity, Volume I, Routine Patrol,* National Institute of Law Enforcement and Criminal Justice (Washington: Government Printing Office, 1977).
5. Elaine Cumming, Ian Cumming, and Laura Edell, "Policeman as Philosopher, Guide, and Friend," *Social Problems,* Vol. 12, pp. 276-286.
6. Antunes and Scott, *op. cit.*
7. *Chicago Sun Times,* "Pranksters and Lost Dogs Tie Up 911 Line," January 5, 1978.
8. Michael T. Farmer, *Survey of Police Operational and Administrative Practices* (Washington: Police Executive Research Forum, 1978).
9. Brian Forst, Judith Lucianovic, and Sarah J. Cox, *What Happens After Arrest?* (Washington: Institute for Law and Social Research, 1977).
10. Kansas City, Missouri Police Department, *Response Time Analysis: Executive Summary* (Kansas City, Mo.: Board of Police Commissioners, 1977).
11. James M. Tien, James W. Simon, and Richard C. Larson, *An Alternative Approach in Police Patrol: The Wilmington Split-Force Experiment* (Cambridge, Mass.: Public Systems Evaluation, Inc., 1977).
12. Michael G. Maxfield, Dan A. Lewis, and Ron Szoc, "Producing Verified Crimes: Verified Crime Reports as Measures of Police Output," *Social Science Quarterly,* Vol. 61, pp. 221-236, 1980.
13. The closest to a standard police administration text is: O. W. Wilson and Roy C. McLaren, *Police Administration,* 4th edition (New York: McGraw-Hill, 1977). The administrative use of patrol beats is described in a very readable history of urban police in the U.S.: Robert M. Fogelson, *Big City Police* (Cambridge: Harvard University Press, 1977).
14. Albert M. Bottoms, *Allocations of Resources in the Chicago Police Department*

(Chicago: Operations Research Task Force, Chicago Police Department, 1972).

15. Gay, *et al., op. cit.*

16. Robert L. Sohn and Robert D. Kennedy, *Patrol Force Allocation for Law Enforcement —An Introductory Planning Guide,* National Criminal Justice Information and Statistics Service (Washington: Government Printing Office, 1978). Nelson B. Heller, William W. Stenzel, Allen D. Gill, and Richard A. Kolde, *Field Evaluation of the Hypercube System: Final Report* (St. Louis: Institute for Public Program Analysis, 1977). Jan M. Chaiken and Peter Dormont, *Patrol Car Allocation Model: User's Manual* (Santa Monica, Calif.: Rand Corporation, 1975). Larson, *op. cit.*

17. Antunes and Scott, *op. cit.*

18. Gay, *et al., op. cit.,* p. 35.

19. Personal interview, August 1978.

20. Michael G. Maxfield, *Discretion and the Delivery of Police Services,* unpublished Ph.D. dissertation, Department of Political Science, Northwestern University, 1979. Gay, *et al., op. cit.*

21. San Francisco Department of City Planning, "Police Facilities: Community Facilities Element of the Comprehensive Plan of San Francisco," unpublished document, 1974, p. 10.

22. Maxfield, *op. cit.*

23. Kansas City Police Department, *op. cit.*

24. Peter W. Greenwood and Joan Petersilia, *The Criminal Investigation Process: Volume I: Summary and Policy Implications* (Santa Monica, Calif.: Rand Corporation, 1975).

25. Wesley G. Skogan and George E. Antunes, "Information, Apprehension, and Deterrence: Exploring the Limits of Police Productivity," *Journal of Criminal Justice,* Vol. 7, pp. 217-241, 1979.

26. Raymond Sumrall, Jane Roberts, and Michael Farmer, *Differential Police Response Strategies Study* (Washington: Police Executive Research Forum, 1980).

27. Gay, *et al., op. cit.*

28. Eric J. Scott and Analee Moore, "Patterns of Police-Referral Agency Interaction," National Institute of Justice (Washington: Government Printing Office, 1981).

29. Antunes and Scott, *op. cit.*

1982 (252-263)

ALAN G. URKOWITZ
ROBERT E. LAESSIG

Assessing the Believability of Research Results Reported in the Environmental Health Matrix

Many public management functions are based on a knowledge of causal relationships and associations which can be provided by research. Setting objectives, assigning priorities, and developing program plans all involve an understanding (or at least a guess) about the effects of certain actions on desired outcomes. Even program evaluation can be viewed as a research effort to identify, among other things, whether a program had an effect and the magnitude of that effect. Information regarding cause-and-effect relationships and associations is a key ingredient in most public management functions. This paper describes a procedure which responds to the needs of environmental and health planners for specific forms of environmental health information. In particular, the procedure provides a tool which can help administrators and others evaluate and use the scientific information dealing with the health effects of environmental exposures. The procedure generates a quantitative measure of the credibility or believability of research results that link environmental factors to human health. The information is expressed in quantitative form for maximum utility in the planning process.[1]

The procedure first classifies research studies about environmental health relationships by the type of evidence they provide, and then assesses the believability of each study and the totality of study results. The assessment produces a study rating for each research study; the study rating is determined by accumulating points on attributes of effective research design. All of the results for a particular environmental health relationship are summarized into a measure called a believability index.

The believability index can be used in two extensions of the procedures. In the first extension, the indices help to resolve situations of conflicting or variable results from different studies of the same environmental health relationship. The second extension involves the setting of priorities for environmental health problems. There is a triad of factors that must be con-

137

sidered in measuring the size of an environmental health problem: (1) the size or importance of the health problem, (2) the size or importance of the environmental problem, and (3) the strength of the association between the environmental cause and the health effect. Measures of each of the elements of the triad can be combined to produce an environmental health problem measure. A believability index can serve as a measure of the third factor, the environmental health link. The outlines of these extensions are presented in this paper.

Background

The effect of the environment on human health has long been recognized under the rubric of public health. Traditionally, administrative concern in public health has focused on the prevention of communicable diseases by means of advances in immunology and public and private sanitation.[2] The more recent development of the concept of environmental health has incorporated social, economic, nutritional, and chemical exposure factors within its view of the human environment.[3] Within this context, a major task has been to link specific environmental factors with specific health effects.[4]

The direct inclusion of environmental health considerations in appropriate public plans and actions has been hindered, however, by the absence of a concise and understandable way of identifying and summarizing the vast amount of information about suspected and known causal links between environmental hazards and health effects.[5] Planners would derive considerable benefit from a technique for evaluating how well the existing body of evidence establishes the credibility of suspected relationships. This paper describes a procedure for summarizing such information into a useful format for planning purposes.

Making Inferences About Causality—A Critical Factor

The most common use of causal research for public policy and decision making is to evaluate pilot programs and full government programs.[6] In this context the evidence of causality comes from a limited number of studies and the evidence is used more to evaluate public policy which has already been made, than to make decisions about future policy.

In the recent controversy over whether saccharin is a carcinogen, Darby and Gohagan made significant contributions to using environmental health research in the formulation of public policy.[7] In their papers they reviewed the evidence of all the saccharin studies in order to assess the overall meaning of the entire body of results. Most importantly, they used criteria which were developed from knowledge of the assumptions and shortcomings inherent in the statistical methods which are commonly used to analyze the results of most laboratory experiments. As a result of their analyses, they were able to assess how well the link between saccharin and cancer had been established (*viz.*, not well at all).

In general, however, very little attention has been paid to developing techniques for reviewing a body of research and evaluating its contribution to knowledge about causality. Most discussions of research methods and causality in the health and social sciences are written for the researcher, intending to help find the design that will maximize a study's ability to identify correctly a causal sequence.[8] For experienced researchers, Campbell and Fiske show a matrix method for assessing a body of research if the results are expressed as correlation coefficients.[9] Simon and Suchman pay some rigorous attention to the problem of judging plausibility, or believability, but the former deals with theories and the latter with the results of evaluative research studies.[10] For management users of research, who are not experts in research methods and statistics and who do not need detailed evaluation criteria, more qualitative treatments of understanding and assessing research results are provided by Davitz and Davitz, and Katzer, Cook and Crouch.[11]

For decision makers in the area of environmental health, these assessments are made difficult because there are several forms of research results, and it is not yet clear how to reconcile and integrate all of them into the planning process. For example, laboratory experiments on animals are difficult to extrapolate to the human population,[12] and such extrapolations are by their very nature controversial. Epidemiological research, on the other hand, seems more immediately useful to public planners and decision makers because the results deal directly with human populations. In order to use compatible research, the procedure presented in this paper pertains only to research on humans (epidemiological and clinical research).

Susser presents a comprehensive, though qualitative, discussion of strategies for assessing research rigor and making causal inferences from a body of epidemiological research, including a way to "judge the accumulated data by a number of defined criteria."[13] Susser lists the following criteria for evaluating how well causal relations are determined:

1. Correct temporal sequence of variables.
2. Consistency of association on replication.
3. A strength of association between dependent and independent variables which involves measurement of covariation and the degree of change attributable to independent variables (e.g., by correlation and multiple regression analysis).
4. Enough specificity of association that the separate causes of individual effects can be identified.
5. Coherent explanation—whether the relationships found are consistent (coherent) or inconsistent (incoherent) with existing theory.[14]

A qualitative assessment of one research study about one or a small number of environmental health relationships, based on the qualities of effective research procedure described above, could be produced by experts. With time, the body of research could be assessed using criteria such as Susser's, and a qualitative judgment made of how well the causal relationship(s) have been determined. Sophisticated and qualitative assessment of each research study may not be practical, however, under budgetary and priority constraints, even at the national level. Furthermore, planners and administrators cannot be expected to possess the required capabilities to perform such an assessment, namely: (1) expertise in field and experimental research methods, (2) "substantive knowledge of the diseases under study,"[15] (3) time to do the assessment, or (4) sufficient resources to purchase sufficient experts' time to do the assessment.

A Structure for the Assessment of Causal Evidence

A method has been proposed for summarizing existing knowledge regarding environmental health links into a relatively simple matrix format, called the Environmental Health Matrix.[16] In that matrix format, the columns of the matrix represent environmental exposure factors and the rows represent health conditions. Each column-row intersection, a cell, represents a potential link between environment and health, and provides information reflecting research evidence for that link. The matrix concept has been tested; it facilitated the manipulation of information into varied formats which met immediate needs of health planners in the state of Pennsylvania.[17]

One of the needs of the health planners was to assess how well existing environmental health research had identified and established the causal links between specific diseases and specific, identifiable conditions in the environment. Such an assessment required the review and evaluation of a body of environmental health research for each cell of the Environmental Health Matrix. Of course, not all potential links, as represented by cells of the matrix, had human research evidence available. The final matrix had 28 rows (health effects) and 110 columns (environmental conditions). Of the roughly 3,000 cells, research evidence was found for slightly more than 200.

Two questions of Pennsylvania environmental health planners were: (1) What does the evidence mean? and (2) How much reliance can be placed on the results of the research? The first question led to the development of the concept of identifying the "nature of the evidence." The second question led to the development of the concept of "believability."

Believability does not refer to the findings of any one research study, but rather to the credibility of a set of research results. A low degree of believability, as the term is used here, does not imply that research findings are wrong, or that the research was conducted improperly, but that the findings do not convincingly support the indicated relationship. The concept of believability is a global measure of how well a body of evidence has established the existence of a link between an environmental cause and a health effect. The basis for believability arises out of the discussion in the preceding section, as does the need for a formal, inexpensive assessment procedure.

A Formal Assessment of Believability

This paper presents two new techniques that can be used (1) to assess the degree of believability of a body of environmental health field research and (2) to include such assessments in the Environmental Health Matrix for use by planners. The two phases of the procedure are described below.

The procedure is both needed and practical, considering the scope of the relevant applications and the amount of information that must be consolidated for such applications. The procedure is designed to be used by anyone familiar with research methods; theoretically, that includes the public planners and decision makers themselves. As a practical matter, the decision makers will probably confine their activities to interpretation and use of the information produced, leaving others to produce the information. The algorithmic nature of the procedure, and the assumptions behind it, however, are easily understood; also, the output of the procedure is quantitative, and is designed to fit into the structure of the Environmental Health Matrix. For all these reasons, communication and understanding between the users and producers of the information should be at a maximum.

Phase I—Initial Screening

The first part of the procedure consists of a "nature of evidence" grading scale that is used to classify each environmental health research study according to an approximation of its contribution to an understanding of the causality of an environmental factor on a health condition. Guidelines based on statistical criteria are used to permit the rapid classification of environmental research studies. The procedure has been tested by graduate students who were relatively unfamiliar with research methods. Using the initial screening procedure, they were able to classify hundreds of environmental research studies in a short period of time.

Phase I of the procedure is shown in Figure 1. Phase I is an initial screening which uses statistical significance to place each study into one of four nature of evidence categories prior to further assessment:

(1) Positive Evidence—statistically significant results (at the p ≤ .15 level) for a harmful effect.
(2) Inconclusive—data analyzed but results not statistically significant.
(3) Suspected—no data analyzed, or not enough data presented to determine significance of results.

FIGURE 1
Procedure for Classifying Research Studies by Nature of Evidence
(Phase I–Initial Screening)

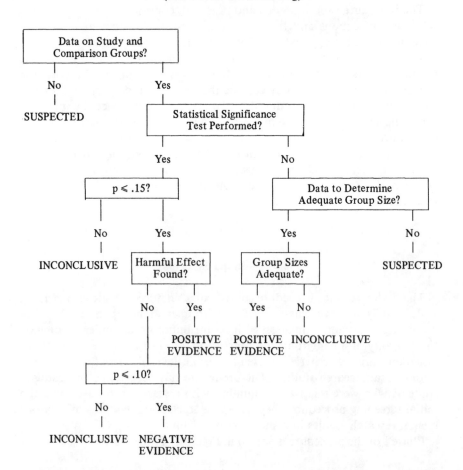

TABLE 1

Procedure for Classifying Studies that Did Not Test for Statistical Significance

1. For studies that did not test for significance, calculate:

   d = Absolute value (study group proportion − control group proportion)

   $$s = \frac{\text{control group proportion} \times (1 - \text{control group proportion})}{\text{control group size}}$$

   $$\Delta = \frac{d}{s}$$

2. Look up value of Δ in Table 2 and obtain the value of n.

3. If sample group size and control group size are greater than or equal to n, study is POSITIVE EVIDENCE.

4. If either of the groups has an inadequate size, classify that study as INCONCLUSIVE.

(4) Negative Evidence—statistically significant results (at $p \leqslant .10$) showing a beneficial effect.

Figure 1 shows the screening procedure, which is described and explained in more detail in Appendix A. Any study can be processed by this procedure, but a study must show enough data to identify the size of the study and comparison groups, and the proportion of each group which showed the health effect for it to be classified as other than suspected evidence. With that data, statistical significance can be estimated using the steps in Tables 1 and 2 and the study can be assessed for believability in Phase II.

Phase II—Believability Assessment

As noted in any description of research methods, statistically significant results are not proof of a relationship, and a lack of significance does not prove lack of a relationship.[18] Planners need to go beyond the statistical evidence which is indicated by the Phase I screening. The details of the evidence, and the collective information provided by all studies on the same topic must also be considered.

As mentioned earlier, the assessment of the rigor and believability of causal evidence, if done subjectively, requires time and expertise which are generally not available to planners. The believability assessment which is described below overcomes most of these limitations.

All studies not classified as suspected are assessed for believability within each Phase II category of evidence. The procedure in Phase II assigns point values to various aspects of the conduct of field research in environmental health as shown in Table 3. Points are assigned to the following attributes: study group used, control group used, assurance of non-exposure in the control group, and the study type. The closer the study conforms to a concept of the "best" research design, the more points it gets on each attribute. The point values are subjectively derived to reflect the order of ability of various research circumstances and designs to produce useful results for environmental health planning. For example, the use of study-specific control groups gets more points than using comparison groups from different populations; a longitudinal cohort study gets more points than a narrow time-frame, cross-sectional study. The rationale for the assigned point values and sources used in developing them are given in Appendix B.

Study results which do not present comparative data are classified as suspected. Without comparative data on study and control groups, the statistical significance of the results cannot be determined and a believability assessment, which assesses comparison groups and study groups, cannot be performed.

Using this point system (Table 3), a study can receive a maximum of 21 points and a minimum of three. A study's point total, divided by 21, gives the study rating. The minimum point total a study can have is three, so the lowest possible study rating is 3/21, or .143 while the highest study rating is 21/21, or 1.0. A category index is the average of the study ratings of all of

TABLE 2

The Number of Subjects Required in Each of Two Groups for a Two-Tailed test with $a = \beta = .15$ for Various Values of Δ

$$n = \frac{2}{\Delta^2} (2.04)^2$$

Δ	n	Δ	n
.10	866	.60	24
.15	385	.65	20
.20	216	.70	17
.25	138	.75	15
.30	95	.80	13
.35	70	.85	12
.40	54	.90	10
.45	42	.95	9
.50	34	1.00	9
.55	28		

TABLE 3
Believability Assessment Procedure (Phase II)

For each study in each category of evidence in a cell, assign:	Points

1. *Comparison group point values.*

   Comparison group which was not drawn from the same population as study group:

Crude rates from another area	1
Crude rates from a larger area which contains the area of study	2
Crude rates from a similar geographic area (urban, rural)	2
Add *2 points* if age-sex-race adjusted rates were used	
Add *1 point* if any other adjusted rates were used	

   Study-Specific Control Group (drawn from same population as study group):

Randomly chosen from assumed unexposed members of population	4
Chosen to match study group on age-sex-race characteristics	6

2. *Assurance of non-exposure in comparison group.*

No assurance	0
Some assurance (e.g., comparison group has lower exposure by media studied, but other media not accounted for)	1
Fair assurance (e.g., occupational exposures or other media accounted for)	2
Good assurance (comparison group could not come into contact with substance at such a concentrated dose as study group)	3

3. *Study group point values.*

Study group is non-random sample of exposed population	1
Study group is represented by crude rates of assumed exposed population	2
Study group is random sample of exposed population	4
Study group is represented by adjusted rates of assumed exposed population	5
Study group is entire population	6

4. *Study type point values.*

Cross-sectional, short-time period	1
Cross-sectional, longer time period covered	2
Cross-sectional, retrospective—period may approach latency period	3
Longitudinal—study group composition changes	4
Longitudinal—cohort study	6

5. Divide point total by 21 (maximum possible points) to produce the *study rating.*

Average the study ratings to produce a *category index.*

the studies in each nature of evidence category, excluding suspected. The category indexes can also range from .143 to 1.0.

The particular range from .143 to 1.0 obviously depends on the point values assigned to the individual attributes of research design identified in Table 3. These point values and the subsequent study rating represent *relative* rigor or believability of research results rather than an absolute measure of believability. The development of a more refined and universally justified or accepted point system is left to further research. In the meantime, useful information can be derived even from this system.

Also, it is important to note that a low study rating does not imply that the design or conduct of a study is poor. The conduct of the study can be considered to be as good as possible given the field conditions that were faced, but if the study rating is low, it is reasonable to conclude that the study does not contribute strongly to a conviction of causality in the environmental health relationship that was studied.

In summary, then, every study in each of the nature of evidence categories from Phase I screening (except for the suspected category), is rated according to this point system. The mean study rating of all studies in each nature of evidence category of a particular environmental health relationship is called the category index of believability. Thus, for every environmental health relationship for which there is human research evidence, all of the study results are first identified by a nature of evidence category (positive evidence, inconclusive evidence, etc.), the studies within each category are then assessed for believability, and a believability index is then calculated for each category.

An Example of a Believability Assessment

The research project which developed the Environmental Health Matrix attempted to find the environmental correlates of leading causes of death in Pennsylvania—cancer, respiratory diseases, cardiovascular diseases, and physical injuries.[19] After expanding those general disease categories for specific sites and conditions, 28 diseases were studied. Literature searches conducted by graduate students found over 110 environmental correlates, producing a matrix of approximately 200 non-empty cells.

A representative block of the matrix is shown in Figure 2. The first three rows list three diseases: gastrointestinal, bladder, and skin cancer; for these diseases all the potential causes identified in the literature search are shown on the columns. This block cannot truly stand alone, however, because some of the causes have been studied for other effects. For example, airborne asbestos (the fourth and eighth columns) has also been associated with lung cancer, as shown by the entries in the last row of Figure 2. Yet lung cancer has been associated with other causes,[20] so additional columns

FIGURE 2

Selected Block from the Environmental Health Matrix

	Community Environment — Unspecified — Vinyl Chloride	Community Environment — Unspecified — Arsenic and Sunlight	Community Environment — Air — UV Light	Community Environment — Air — Asbestos	Community Environment — Water — Asbestos	Community Environment — Water — Nitrates	Community Environment — Water — Arsenic	Occupational Environment — Air — Asbestos	Occupational Environment — Air — Polynuclear Hydrocarbons	Occupational Environment — Unspecified — Vinyl Chloride
G.I. Cancer	PE-1 i = .429				PE-1 i = .476 I-3 i = .476	PE-1 i = .381		PE-1 i = .428	PE-2 i = .667	PE-1 i = .286
Bladder Cancer									PE-2 i = .452 S-1	
Skin Cancer		S-1	PE-1 i = .571 S-1				PE-1 i = .381 I-1 i = .286		PE-2 i = .381 I-1 i = .238 S-3	
Lung Cancer				PE-1 i = .381				PE-1 i = .238		

KEY: Capital letters identify the evidence category from Phase I–Initial Screening (Figure 1):

PE = Positive Evidence
I = Inconclusive
S = Suspected
NE = Negative Evidence

Numbers following capital letters indicate number of studies found in that evidence category.
i = category index of believability; average of study ratings from Phase II–Believability Assessent (Table 2).

TABLE 4
Comparative Results of Two Believability Assessments
(Points assigned to each study on each attribute)

Cell and Study	Step 1 Comparison Group	Step 2 Assurance of Non-exposure	Step 3 Study Group	Step 4 Study Type	Step 5 Study Rating
A.1	2	1	4	3	.476
A.2	1	2	4	2	.428
A.3	1	1	4	2	.381
Category Believability Index (mean) i = .428					
B.1	4	3	4	1	.571
B.2	6	3	4	1	.667
B.3	4	1	4	1	.476
Category Believability Index (mean) i = .571					

Cell A refers to the Gastrointestinal Cancer-Asbestos (Occupational Air) cell of the Matrix in Figure 2 (the eighth column).

Cell B refers to a cell from the complete Environmental Health Matrix (Pulmonary Dysfunction-Polyurethane Gas), which is not shown in Figure 2.

would be involved; those columns (causes) would almost certainly be linked to other rows (effects), *et cetera.* Planning for environmental health must somehow be responsive to that complex web of relationships. The believability assessment helps to manage that complexity.

Table 4 contains the results of a believability assessment of two individual cells from the complete Environmental Health Matrix. Cell A is from Figure 2, containing three studies of the possibility of airborne asbestos causing gastrointestinal cancer. Cell B contains three clinical studies of the effect of polyurethane gas on pulmonary dysfunction, with the subjects themselves used as controls before the gas was administered. (Cell B is from the Environmental Health Matrix, but the details are not included in this paper.) All of the studies were rated as showing positive evidence after Phase I screening.

Table 4 contains the results of the Phase II believability assessment for the cells. Shown are the believability attributes of each study and the points given on each attribute. An examination of the table demonstrates the need for the Phase II believability assessment. Each of the six studies presented in Table 4 showed positive evidence, but the variation on the believability point scores is such that individual study ratings range from .381 to .667. The studies from Cell B were all clinical studies, which are easier to control, and which provide more believable information for environmental health planning. Cell B has an average believability rating (category index) of .571, compared to the index of .428 of Cell A; thus, the conclusion is that, overall, planners can place more reliance on the *possibility* that polyurethane gas causes pulmonary dysfunction (cell B) than the possibility that asbestos causes gastrointestinal cancer (cell A).

Problem Size and the Measure of Believability, or Believability in Context

An examination of the results shown in Table 4 places believability and even strength of association in the proper perspective. Even though the link between polyurethane gas and pulmonary dysfunction is more believable than the asbestos-gastrointestinal cancer link, believability must be put into context with the other two elements of the triad of factors that determines the size or importance of an environmental health problem. In particular, the size of the health problem and of the environmental problem must be considered as well. For example, as a health problem, gastrointestinal cancer is a chronic disease, expensive to treat, and often fatal. Pulmonary dysfunction, on the other hand, is an acute effect of unknown significance.

As an environmental problem, asbestos is ubiquitous in the community and occupational environments, while polyurethane exposure is more limited. Consequently, from a public planning viewpoint, it is likely that health and environmental planners would rate the asbestos-gastrointestinal cancer problem as larger and of a higher priority than the polyurethane-pulmonary dysfunction problem, despite the higher believability index of the latter link.

The measure of believability is an intermediate step in meeting the planners' need to make hundreds of such judgments and decisions. In addition to believability, planners need indicators of the size and importance of each health problem and also of the size of the associated environmental problems.[21] The health indicators could include the physical or economic severity of the health effect and the number of people affected; environmental indicators are less well developed, but they could include the amount of the substance present in the environment, the dose received by the populace, or the amount produced and potentially present in the environment.[22]

What Is the Proper Measure of Believability for a Complete Cell of the Matrix?

Neither cell assessed in Table 4 contained anything but positive evidence. Most cells in the matrix do not present such a clear picture of the evidence. Of the 13 cells with entries in Figure 2, six have inconclusive and/or suspected evidence, which does not support a conclusion for a harmful effect.

Additionally, five of the seven cells with positive evidence cells have only one study in them.

Such weakening of the positive evidence opens the question of the proper way to measure believability. Using a criterion of extreme caution with regard to human health, the positive evidence index only would be used as a believability measure, implying that the non-supportive studies failed to discover the harmful effect.

Perhaps a more objective approach would be to compare the positive evidence to the inconclusive evidence. Inconclusive evidence, which indicates that there is no relationship, may be identifying no effect, or it may be indicating that there is an association too weak to be identified in every study.[23] If that were the case, then such inconclusive evidence should be allowed to compensate for positive evidence and lower the measure of believability, because the "real" association would be correspondingly weaker.[24] For example, some ratio of positive to inconclusive evidence might be developed—a ratio of the indices or a ratio of the point totals—as a believability balance ratio. The development of this concept is left to further research.

Conclusion

A procedure has been presented which responds to the needs of environmental and health planners for specific forms of environmental health information. Quantitative study ratings are derived from qualitative discussions of effective techniques in causal research. The procedure represents one way of translating those subjective assessment values into a useful quantitative form.

Essential to the effective use of the Environmental Health Matrix is a method for identifying or measuring health and environmental problems.[25] Regardless of how the health and environmental problems are measured, and whether individual or composite indicators are used, however, the size of the environmental health problem depends on three things: the environmental problem size (the cause), the health problem size (the effect), and the believability of the research establishing the association. Those three quantities, suitably combined, produce a quantitative measure of the environmental health problem which is represented by one cell of the matrix.

The quantitative techniques for measuring the size and priority of environmental health problems need to be developed further. In addition, alternative methods for measuring believability might be developed, and the variations which they cause in the final measures of problem size and priority could be studied. It remains for future research to determine whether the environmental health problem measures are sensitive to different ways of measuring believability. In the meantime, however, it is important to recognize the need for such a believability assessment as part of the environmental health planning process. The procedure presented in this paper attempts a preliminary step toward meeting this need.

Appendix A.
Phase I—The Screening Procedure

This appendix describes the procedure by which the research studies are initially classified into one of four categories of evidence. All studies can be classified, but those classified as suspected cannot be assessed for believability in Phase II.

Figure 1 describes the screening procedure in which any study that suggests an environmental health relationship, but which does *not* show comparative data on study and control groups is classified as *suspected*. Any study which shows comparative data but does not show an effect at a level of significance of $p \leqslant .15$ is considered to be *inconclusive*. Studies with evidence less than that level of significance which show harmful effects are *positive evidence*. The .15 level was chosen because in a situation as uncertain as environmental health research, it may be better to err on the side of caution. Positive evidence therefore recognizes statistical results at a higher probability of being due to chance alone than would be appropriate in many other contexts. Significant ($p \leqslant .10$) studies which showed *no harmful* effects or which showed healthful effects are considered to be *negative evidence*.

Of course, if planners were to consider only results which were reported in statistical form, other types of useful information would be excluded by default. For example, many environmental health studies do not present results using statistical measures of relationships, but in the form of comparisons of rates (e.g., differences, ratios).[26] Therefore, additional steps are included in the screening phase of the proposed procedure. These steps provide a method for taking research results reported in the form of rates of occurrence and determining whether the results are based on an adequate sample size and whether the conclusions are adequately protected against Type I and Type II errors. In other words, this part of the procedure approximates the level of significance which would have been achieved if a statistical test had been performed; studies which do not show significant results are classified as *inconclusive*.

The additional steps are shown on the right side of Figure 1 and are described in Table 1. They are adapted from a method suggested by Edwards for determining whether a sample size is adequate.[27] The procedure is based on a two-tailed test, which has the most power for avoiding Type I and Type II errors simultaneously.

The original procedure described by Edwards dealt with the group means of continuous variables, which are distributed normally. Epidemiological data usually deal with dichotomous variables (each subject has or does not have the condition in question); group means are thus the proportion of subjects with the condition and they are distributed hypergeometrically. Edwards' procedure has been adapted by taking the difference of group proportions rather than of group means, and computing the standard deviation(s) in the control group or population as:[28]

$$s = \sqrt{\frac{pq}{n}}$$

where

  p = proportion in control group with the condition
  q = proportion in control group without the condition (1 - p)
  n = control group size

With those adaptations, the difference between sample group and comparison group proportions (d) can be expressed as a fraction of the standard deviation(s) of the control group or population distribution (see Step 1 in Table 1). The smaller the fraction (d/s), the larger must be the sample and comparison group sizes for adequate assurance of protection against Type I and Type II errors. Table 2 shows selected values of Δ (d/s) and the corresponding group sizes (n) necessary for the probability of a Type I error (α) and the probability of a Type II error (β) both to be equal to 0.15.

The only requirement for processing by this procedure is that a study show enough data to identify the size of the study and comparison groups and the proportion of each group which showed the health effect (see Table 1). If those values cannot be determined, the study is classified as *suspected.*

Appendix B.
The Rationale for Phase II—The Believability Assessment

The believability assessment proposed in this paper is an adaptation of existing information and discussions regarding the evaluation of field research. For example, Susser, as discussed in the section entitled *Making Inferences About Causality—A Critical Factor,* provides some basic information. Neither Susser, nor anyone else writing about research methods, however, is foolhardy enough to do more than indicate that some designs are better than others for some purposes. In preparing the procedures described in this paper, however, the authors have risked being foolhardy enough to specify, quantitatively, how good various designs are for the limited purposes and specific needs of environmental health planners.

The points that can be assisted on the various attributes range from 1 to 6, except for Assurance of Non-exposure in the Comparison Group, which has a low value of 0 and a high of 3. The highest point value is assigned to the "best" method for design or conduct of a health research study, the lowest value to the "worst" method. The specific methods which receive the "best," "worst" and intermediate point values are obviously arbitrarily and subjectively chosen, but the relative value of the methods can be identified by relating them and the relative point values they receive to Susser's criteria for effective causal research in the health sciences.

An examination of Table 3 will show that the scales of values in the various steps relate to Susser's criteria. In step 1 of Table 3 a comparison group from the same population as the study group is worth more than other comparison groups. Within those two categories, age-sex-race matching is preferred. These orderings contribute to the specificity of association (Susser's Criterion 4) which is important for identifying individual effects. Closely matched control groups also aid coherence of explanation (Criterion 5) by reducing doubt raised by other, unstudied causes or rival hypotheses.

In the study group itself (Step 3), random samples are better than non-random samples, which have unknown biases, and the whole population is better than a sample for increasing specificity of association (Criterion 4). In much epidemiological research, population rates, available from a system for collecting vital statistics, are used as total population measures. The more detailed these rates are (e.g., age-sex-race adjustment), the higher the value assigned to either the study or control group attribute. Larger and more representative groups can contribute to measuring strength of association (Criterion 3) by increasing the specificity of causal models and by providing data for parameter estimation; thus population rates have higher values than sample group rates.

The points assigned to various research design attributes have been determined subjectively and do not represent any universally accepted valuation of research design attributes. Nevertheless they do represent a starting point for *relative* weighting of relevant attributes of different study designs. Further research is obviously needed to refine these and any alternative point value systems and to establish their relative validity for assessing believability of research results. The rationale behind the ranges of point values in Table 3 has been presented in order to provide a starting point for such further research, discussion, and testing.

Criterion 2, consistency of association on replication, stands as the foundation of the paradigm used by physical scientists for identifying causal relationships.[29] Social and health scientists also attach great importance to replication, but the complexity and stochastic nature of social systems often make two non-experimental studies of the same phenomenon noncomparable. That situation creates the need for additional criteria and a judgmental rule of thumb that replication is achieved when *other researchers* find compatible results. It is reasonable to assess one researcher's findings, self-replicated three times, as less believable than three different researchers finding the same relationship.

That would seem to imply that the assessment of study designs should not include all the studies on the same topic from one researcher or a recognizable group of researchers. (An earlier version of this method did include that restriction.) Such a restriction would be prudent if strength of association were somehow being measured. In that case, too many strong findings from one researcher would dominate the measure, resulting in an artificially higher value than independently conducted, replicative studies would justify. The procedure outlined in the text assesses believability, however, not strength of association. Furthermore, the procedure averages the study ratings, so that while one researcher's findings may dominate a category index, the index will reflect the quality of the study designs, not the findings of the studies. Studies with weaker designs, even though they may have high measures of association, receive lower study ratings and thus produce a lower believability index.

It is assumed that through researcher integrity and the review process, multiple reports of the same study will not get into the literature. Yet much health research is conducted on cohorts, such as the Framingham heart study.[30] By their nature, those studies must be reported several times in the literature, and would exert perhaps disproportionate influence on their category indexes. A troublesome dilemma is that such longitudinal cohort studies have the highest valued design.

Some cohort studies would not reach the assessment stage because they are not comparative in nature, and do not have control groups. Such studies would be classified as Suspected, and would not be assessed for believability. Thus the procedure screens out some cohort studies, but expertise and time are required to screen the rest. It is expected, however, that not enough validity would be lost by performing the believability assessment for all studies that pass screening to make it worth conducting separate subjective assessments of all longitudinal cohort studies to determine which of them should be included or excluded from use in the matrix.

Notes

1. Government Studies and Systems, Inc., *A Taxonomy of the Health System Appropriate in Plan Development,* Department of Health, Education and Welfare Contract No. HRA-230-76-0105 (1976). Institute of Medicine, *Health Planning in the United States: Issues in Guideline Development* (Washington, D.C.: National Academy of Sciences (IOM Pub. 80-01, 1980).

2. J. J. Hanlon, *Public Health: Administration and Practice,* sixth edition (St. Louis: C.V. Mosby Co., 1974).
3. P. W. Purdom (ed.), *Environment and Health,* second edition (New York: Academic Press, 1980).
4. National Institute of Environmental Health Services, *Human Health and the Environment: Some Research Needs* (Washington, D.C.: U.S. Government Printing Office, 1977).
5. National Committee on Vital and Health Statistics, *Statistics Needed for Determining the Effect of the Environment on Health,* U.S. Department of Health, Education and Welfare, Pub. No. (HRA) 7-1457 (Washington, D.C.: Government Printing Office, July 1977). E. J. Calabrese, *Pollutants and High Risk Groups: The Biological Basis of Increased Human Susceptibility* (New York: Wiley-Interscience, 1978).
6. Carol J. Weiss, "The Many Meanings of Research Utilization," *Public Administration Review,* Vol. 39, No. 5 (Sept./Oct. 1979), pp. 426-431.
7. William P. Darby, "An Example of Decision-Making on Environmental Carcinogens: The Delaney Clause," *Journal of Environmental Systems,* Vol. 9, No. 2 (1979), pp. 109-121. John Kenneth Gohagan, *Quantitative Analyis for Public Policy* (New York: McGraw-Hill, 1980).
8. D. T. Campbell and J. C. Stanley, *Experimental and Quasi-Experimental Designs for Research* (Chicago: Rand-McNally, 1963). H. M. Blalock, Jr., *Causal Inferences in Non-Experimental Research* (Chapel Hill: University of North Carolina Press, 1964). P. J. Runkel and J. E. McGrath, *Research on Human Behavior: A Systematic Guide to Method* (New York: Holt, Rinehart and Winston, Inc., 1972).
9. D. T. Campbell and D. W. Fiske, "Convergent and Discriminant Validation by the Multitrait-Multimethod Matrix," *Psychological Bulletin,* Vol. 56 (1959), pp. 81-105.
10. E. A. Suchman, *Evaluating Research: Principles and Practice in Public Service and Social Action Programs* (New York: Russell Sage, 1967). H. A. Simon, "On Judging the Plausibility of Theories," *Logic, Methodology and Philosophy of Sciences III,* van Rootselar and Staal (eds.) (Amsterdam: North Holland Publishing Co., 1968), pp. 439-458.
11. J. Katzer, K. H. Cook and W. W. Crouch, *Evaluating Information: A Guide for Users of Social Science Research* (Reading, Mass.: Addison-Wesley, 1978). J. R. Davitz and L. L. Davitz, *Evaluating Research Proposals in the Behavioral Sciences* (New York: Teachers College Press, Columbia University, 1977).
12. National Research Council, *Drinking Water and Health* (Washington, D.C.: National Academy of Sciences, 1977).
13. M. Susser, *Causal Thinking in the Health Sciences: Concepts and Strategies of Epidemiology* (New York: Oxford University Press, 1973), p. 72.
14. *Ibid.,* p. 142.
15. *Ibid.,* p. 74.
16. R. E. Laessig and Alan G. Urkowitz, "The Environmental-Health Matrix: Information Use in Planning," *American Journal of Public Health,* Vol. 72, No. 4 (1982), pp. 373-375.
17. Robert E. Laessig and Alan G. Urkowitz, Environmental-Health Planning Matrix for Pennsylvania: Final Report (Philadelphia: Drexel University, developed under contracts 581315 and 581316 for the Pennsylvania Department of Health, Office of Planning and Development, April 1979).
18. R. E. Winch and D. T. Campbell, "Proof? No. Evidence? Yes. The Significance of Tests of Significance," *American Sociologist,* Vol. 4, No. 2 (1969), pp. 140-143.
19. Pennsylvania Department of Health, Bureau of Health Planning, *The Pennsylvania Preliminary State Health Plan,* 1979-83 (1979).
20. L. B. Lave and E. P. Seskin, *Air Pollution and Human Health* (Baltimore: Published for Resources for the Future by Johns Hopkins University Press, 1977).

21. P. W. Purdom, R. E. Laessig, and A. Hebb, *Health Planning Related to Environmental Factors: Volume I, Preliminary Technical Guidelines.* Report prepared under Department of Health, Education and Welfare Contract HRA 230-76-0247 (Philadelphia, Pa.: Drexel University, 1978).

22. W. A. Thomas (ed.), *Indicators of Environmental Quality* (New York: Plenum, 1972). S. L. Brown, B. R. Holt and E. E. McCaleb, *System for Rapid Ranking of Environmental Pollutants* (Menlo Park, Calif.: Stanford Research Institute, 1976).

23. P. E. Meehl, "Theory-testing in Psychology and Physics: A Methodological Paradox," *Philosophy of Science,* Vol. 37 (1967), pp. 103-115.

24. Positive Evidence and Negative Evidence are contradictory—they show beneficial and harmful health effects, respectively. At present no cells show both types of evidence, so at this time we have not tried to develop a formal procedure which resolves such a situation.

25. Rand Corporation, *Algorithms for Health Planners* (Santa Monica, Calif.: Rand Corp., 1975). Health Planning Research Services, Inc., *A Guide to Priority Setting Methods* (Fort Washington, Pa.: Health Planning Research Service, Inc., 1977). P. W. Purdom, R. E. Laessig and A. Hebb, *Health Planning Related to Environmental Factors,* Vols. II-V. Report prepared under Department of Health, Education and Welfare Contract HRA 230-76-0247 (Philadelphia: Drexel University, 1978).

26. J. S. Mausner and A. K. Bahn, *Epidemiology: An Introductory Test* (Philadelphia: W.B. Saunders, 1974).

27. Allen L. Edwards, *Statistical Methods, second edition* (New York: Holt, Rinehart and Winston, Inc., 1967), pp. 226-242.

28. W. A. Spurr and C. P. Bonini, *Statistical Analysis for Business Decisions* (Homewood, Ill.: Richard D. Irwin, Inc., 1973), pp. 240-241.

29. T. S. Kuhn, *The Structure of Scientific Revolutions, second edition* (Chicago: University of Chicago Press, 1970).

30. S. G. Haynes, S. Levine, N. Scotch, et al., "The Relationship of Psychosocial Factors to Coronary Heart Disease in the Framingham Study I. Methods and Risk Factors," *American Journal of Epidemiology,* Vol. 107 (1978), pp. 362-383. S. G. Haynes, M. Feinlieb, W. B. Kannel, et al., "The Relationship of Psychosocial Factors to Coronary Heart Disease in the Framingham Study II. Prevalence of Coronary Heart Disease," *American Journal of Epidemiology,* Vol. 107 (1978), pp. 384-402. S. G. Haynes, M. Feinlieb, W. B. Kannel, et al., "The Relationship of Psychosocial Factors to Coronary Heart Disease in the Framingham Study III. Eight Year Incidence of Coronary Heart Disease," *American Journal of Epidemiology,* Vol. III (1980). S. G. Haynes and M. Feinlieb, "Women, Work and Coronary Heart Disease: Prospective Findings from the Framingham Heart Study," *American Journal of Public Health,* Vol. 70 (1980), pp. 133-141.

1982 (427-438)

Problems with the Technical Quality and Usefulness of Program Evaluation

Seven articles that appeared in *PAR* between 1971 and 1980 clearly reflect two themes discussed in the introductory essay: (1) the controversy about the experimental design and its application to social program evaluation; and (2) the problem of ensuring evaluation's usefulness and being able to measure that use. These articles, which form Part II of this volume, are different from those selected for Part I in that, with one exception, all are written from the specific perspective of program evaluation. (The exception is the article by Carol Weiss, which speaks to the larger topic of research utilization rather than addressing program evaluation alone.)

The first article, "The Evaluation of Social Innovation" by George H. Shipman (*PAR*, Vol. 31, No. 2, March/April 1971, pages 198-200), which appeared in the same *PAR* issue with an editorial by Orville F. Poland entitled "Why Does Public Administration Ignore Evaluation?," focuses on two important points: the difficulty of performing program evaluation and the applicability of the experimental design to the often "exploratory" and "opportunistic" managerial context in which public programs develop and operate. The article by Robert Weiss and Martin Rein, referred to in the introductory essay, is reviewed at length, as is a rejonder by Donald Campbell. From the viewpoint of this volume's discussion, three points may be of interest. First, it is clear that the issue of use and users of evaluation had not yet come to the fore in 1970-1971. Weiss and Rein seem to assume that the program administrator is the only user of evaluation findings. (For example, while it may be true that "conclusions reached after the termination of the program" would be irrelevant to the program's managers, they might be relevant indeed to the Congress, especially in the case of a pilot or demonstration program.) Second, the "alternative methodology" offered by Weiss and Rein posits that case studies could provide a basis for generalization to a larger class, yet a major methodological problem with case studies is precisely their generalizability to a larger population or universe. Further, as noted in the introductory essay, it is uncertain how process evaluations would address accountability types of questions. (That is, the assumption that the program administrator is the only user here leads to a second assumption: that the description of what is happening in the program is more important than knowledge about program effectiveness. Yet this is true only for users who do not present accountability questions.) Finally, the idea of using evaluation to affect policy formulation types of questions was not yet on the horizon (see the introductory essay). Instead, while the unfortunate fact that "innovations are too often justified by over-promising their efficacy" was recognized, it was dealt with by the uncertainly realistic expedient of cautioning evaluation sponsors to accept willingly the "dangerous risk" of a "no-effect result." Today, the suggestion would probably be to assure appropriate justification for new initiatives through front-end evaluation performed by independent evaluators.

The second article is "Randomized Experiments for Evaluating and Planning Local Programs: A Summary on Appropriateness and Feasibility," by Robert F. Boruch, David Rindshopf, Patricia S. Anderson, Imat R. Amidjaya, and Douglas M. Jansson (*PAR,* Vol. 39, No. 1, January/February 1979, pages 36-40). This paper accomplishes three purposes: it reexamines—nine years after the Weiss and Rein article—the feasibility of using randomized field experiments; it assesses the results of using certain other types of evaluation designs to establish effectiveness ("the evaluation designs, even when implemented well, yielded data which did not support the idea that a program worked or did not work"); and it presents the important concept of appropriateness in evaluation design, discussing such factors as the question posed (is it, in fact, required that program effects be estimated?), maturity of the program (is it too early to look for effects?), specification of the program (is the program well enough described and understood or is a preliminary process evaluation required?), competence of personnel (are the technical demands of a randomized field experiment beyond the training of available evaluation staff?), and resources (is there time and money sufficient to perform the evaluation properly?).

The third article, "Program Management and the Federal Evaluator" by Pamela Horst, Joe N. Nay, John W. Scanlon, and Joseph S. Wholey (*PAR,* Vol. 34, No. 4, July/August 1974, pages 300-308) is a response to some of the problems various observers had found with program evaluations, both in terms of their methodologies and of the use made of their findings. The authors ask the utilization question, "why have those in charge of programs and those who evaluate them not been able to join their efforts in a way that leads more frequently to significant improvements in program performance?" They discuss six charges that were often levelled at program evaluation's door by its many critics in the early seventies, and restate those charges as symptoms of three underlying problems: (1) lack of program definition; (2) lack of clear logic with regard to program objectives, program design, and program activities; and (3) lack of sound program management. They then point out that those problems are not the responsibility of the evaluator, but of the program's administration. This article, thus, represents not only some early attention to problems of evaluation use (that is, one use only: improvement in program performance), but also a focus on the evaluation *milieu* and some program management imperatives governing the ability to perform evaluations.

The fourth article, "Writing a Better RFP: Ten Hints for Obtaining More Successful Evaluation Studies" by Donald R. Weidman (*PAR,* Vol. 37, No. 6, November/December 1977, pages 714-717) continues with the effort to increase the usefulness of evaluations performed, as in the preceding article, but instead of invoking the entire programmatic milieu, concentrates exclusively on one particular node in the evaluation procurement process: the request-for-procurement (RFP). In effect, the RFP is a crucial point at which the usefulness of an evaluation can easily be precluded through organizational inattention (see the remarks of John Evans on this subject in the introductory essay).

The fifth article is "The Proverbs of Evaluation: Perspectives from CSA's Experience" by Robert F. Clark (*PAR,* Vol. 39, No. 6, November/December 1979, pages 562-566). This paper synthesizes some of the points made by the preceding articles in Part II within the real-world context of a specific federal agency. In particular, the author reiterates the problems found in applying the experimental design (see Shipman and Boruch, *et al.*) and points to the issue of the appropriateness of any evaluation design with regard to the question posed, the "situational" context of the program and the schedule of user decisions for which information is required (see Boruch, *et al.* and Horst, *et al.*). The paper recommends multiple methods and measures, and then goes on to question two other aspects of the conventional wisdom in evaluation: the expected benefits accruing to evaluation use from the greatest possible participation of program managers in the evaluation, and the belief that the only proper use for evaluation findings is to affect "specific and discrete" (i.e., measurable) program decisions.

The sixth article, "The Many Meanings of Research Utilization" by Carol H. Weiss (*PAR,* Vol. 39, No. 5, September/October 1979, pages 426-431), is devoted exclusively to the issue of use and makes the important point that at least seven models of use need to be examined in addressing the question of whether or not a particular study has made a contribution to public policy. Although the paper speaks to social science research rather than to program evaluation, the models of use described appear to hold as well for the latter as for the former. In particular, the author makes the point that the problem-solving or decision model (the same one evoked by Clark in the preceding article) involves expectations that are "wildly optimistic." In Weiss' words, "It probably takes an extraordinary concatenation of circumstances for research to influence policy decisions directly: a well defined decision situation, a set of policy actors who have responsibility and jurisdiction for making that decision, an issue whose resolution depends at least to some extent on *information,* identification of the requisite informational need, research that provides the information in terms that match the circumstances within which choices will be made, research findings that are clear-cut, unambiguous, firmly supported, and powerful, that reach decision-makers at the time they are wrestling with the issues, that are comprehensible and understood, and that do not run counter to strong political interests." The author thus sees the direct policy decision based on evaluation findings as either a fairly rare event or one which pertains to "low-level, narrow-gauge" decisions, and thinks that the way in which research findings are most frequently used in the policy arena is through what she calls the Enlightenment Model (similar to the "Chinese torture" idea discussed earlier; see the remarks of Seeman cited in the introductory essay to this volume).

The seventh and last article in Part II of this volume is "Type III Evaluation: Consultation and Consensus" by Gerald L. Barkdoll (*PAR,* Vol. 40, No. 2, March/April 1980, pages 174-179). It undertakes consideration of the organizational agency context within which both evaluations and programs must fit. Just as many management problems have been mistakenly perceived as evaluation problems (Horst, *et al.*), just as decision use has been mistakenly perceived as the only "good" use of evaluation findings (Weiss) so this article points out that some organizational adaptation of evaluation must take place if it is to work well. The author finds it unreasonable to expect program managers to tolerate "the humiliation of publicly exposed faults, flaws, and shortfalls" without some reaction such as "stonewalling" or "aggressive counter-attacks" (perhaps involving the validity of the criteria used, the appropriateness of the measurement techniques applied, or the credibility, professionalism, and motives of the evaluators). As a result, agency management needs to consider the organization of its evaluation function in such a way as to reverse the threats and disincentives to program managers implied by evaluations of their program. The author then describes the solution found by the Federal Drug Administration: an evaluation process characterized by "cooperation," "openness," "trust" and "timeliness," as well as by a "consensus-building" (rather than authoritarian) type of management along with a highly-skilled evaluation staff.

GEORGE A. SHIPMAN

The Evaluation of Social Innovation

The evaluation of operating programs is never an easy or a simple task. Probably no other aspect of the administrative discipline is so open to irrelevant criteria, loose and unreliable methodology, and subjective judgments. A familiar tendency is to observe the style of operations. If they conform to some set of conventions deemed pertinent, if managerial methods meet the appraisers' expectations, and if reasonable prudence is judged to control the use of resources, the verdict of a sound operation is rendered. The outcomes of the program are rarely tested, sometimes because they are intangible and illusive, but often because of confidence that a sound operation inevitably produces the intended product.

But rigorous, disciplined evaluation requires that the impact of the program be identified and measured against the objectives sought. The unanticipated consequences are equally in point. Then, in the framework of the objective, the input of resources, the process of action, and the consequences realized, both intended and unanticipated, the question of effectiveness can be brought closer to disciplined judgment.

The difficulties of program appraisal are compounded, of course, when the program is a broad-aim, broad-impact undertaking. Into this class fall such efforts as the stimulation of social change, the prevention of crime and delinquency, and various aspects of the poverty and model cities planning programs. The characteristic intent of such undertakings is to generate social products which are intermediate in the sense that they interact with each other and stimulate the civic and social interactions that are counted upon in turn to bring about the changed circumstances the program seeks. All this relies upon a complex and problematical chain of causation, to say nothing of the constraints, contingencies, and exogenous influences conditioning the task environment. The open-endedness of program evaluation is readily apparent in the case of broad-aim programs. A reasonable, if less apparent, estimate is that evaluation is equally elusive in the case of the more familiar and traditional types of public services.

Robert S. Weiss and Martin Rein draw attention to the complexities of evaluating broad-aim programs in their article, "The Evaluation of Broad-Aim Programs: Experimental Design, Its Difficulties and an Alternative," and Donald T. Campbell follows with a commentary, "Considering the Case Against Experimental Evaluations of Social Innovations," both in the March 1970 issue of the *Administrative Science Quarterly* (Volume 15, Number 1, pp. 97, 110). Weiss and Rein point out that the preferred design for research-based program evaluation is an experimental one. Selected aspects of the situation are chosen for observation and analysis. Measurement is applied before and after the application of the program. Differences are recorded and observed changes, to the extent they can be attributed to the program, are evaluated in terms of the program's objectives. Two situations may be observed concurrently, one in which the program is operating, and another, the control, in which it is not. Differences between the two are analyzed to arrive at conclusions about the program's impact. The authors argue that the difficulties in the use of experimental designs are so serious as to make their use in program evaluation highly questionable. To demonstrate, they use a case study of a situation in which the experimental design was attempted.

The case is one in which an evaluation study was to be undertaken along with the operation of a broad-aim program seeking to bring about changes in community institutions. The research task encountered understandable difficulties in developing evaluation criteria, in selecting focal points for analysis, in the selection of a control situation, in the identification of pertinent data, and with related research problems. The efforts progressed, but were detached from current operations of the program. The aim was objective evaluation at a future stage of accrued change influence, not an interim appraisal of the current experience of the ongoing activities.

The program administrators correctly regarded the evaluation project as having little to contribute to the solution of current problems and difficulties. They needed and wanted concurrent evaluation and counsel. Conclusions reached after the termination of the program were, for them, irrelevant. But the design of the evaluation analysis was not susceptible to interim or progress readings. Neither were the specific effects of various activities identifiable where total impact was the point of observation. Thus, the evaluation effort came to be regarded as a low-priority concern. The key members of the research staff left the project. The evaluation effort was essentially a failure.

The authors regard this experience as typical. In this instance, the evaluation project was responsible to the program administrators, and there were inevitable frictions. In instances where an external agency has been used, problems of cost, administrative irrelevance, and difficulty of interpretation have been encountered.

The major difficulties are in the nature of the experimental design. Satisfactory criteria are difficult to come by. Broad-aim programs are characterized by only partially formulated objectives, which are also relatively non-specific. The desired outcomes are understood in terms of broad and comprehensive changes, but the specific evidence of these changes are uncertain. The program has to be exploratory and, indeed, opportunistic. Operational measures, at least at the present state of knowledge, are not applicable. Moreover, the situation is not controlled. Comparisons cannot exclude exogenous factors, and there are too few replications of such studies to provide a useful sampling of a random character. Action programs differ; each is an adaptation to the needs, the constraints, and the capabilities of the individual community. These variations tend to elude experimental evaluation. The design has limited information capabilities. Where no results are observed, the reasons for the apparent outcome are obscured by the absence of data. Where positive results occur, the tendency is to follow them at the expense of negative results. But the reasons for the positive results are not within the scope of the data.

Weiss and Rein offer an alternative methodology for evaluating broad-aim programs, one built around process-oriented qualitative research, historical analysis, and case studies. The purpose would be to develop a nearly complete description of the community systems before the intervention, the nature of the intervention, and the new or changed systems resulting. The case studies would provide a basis for generalization to a larger class. The authors note that such research must have a conceptual framework. Systems theory, the unfolding of events, and the interaction of political forces are potential frameworks, and can be used in a mutually complementary way. Alternative possibilities are functional analysis and pattern analysis. These can be applied separately, or assimilated into other frameworks. Possibilities are suggested for keeping data within manageable proportions by the limitation of samples and the analysis of qualitative data so as to arrive at the desired level of generalization. The difficulties are recognized of information reporting, of the disclosure of individual roles and behaviors to the actors' disadvantage, of bias and coloring, and of inadvertent emotional involvement. Even so, the outcomes, intended and unintended, of program efforts can be observed. Appraisals from alternative perspectives are possible. Weiss and Rein urge that, altogether, the qualitative approach permits the analyst to use careful, balanced empirical work as a basis for disciplined appraisal.

Donald Campbell's comments recognize points of substantial agreement, but disagree with the view of the experimental method and the proposed alternative methodology. He reformulates four of Weiss and Rein's points in terms of alternative implementations of an experimental approach. The first has to do with criteria and the use of operating definitions. While conceding the weakness of using singular criteria, he holds that this practice is not intrinsic to the experimental method. The method should also include a rigorous attention to unintended consequences. Multiple measures and perspectives, he emphasizes, are entirely compatible with experimental evaluation. Also, multiple sources of data are possible. Experimental analysis is not limited to survey research data, but extends to a variety of archival records which can yield information for before-and-after analyses and fine-grained time series. The second point, on the question of control groups, argues that some gains in interpretation result from using less-than-perfect control groups, particularly where rival hypotheses are posed for testing in an effort to isolate the unique influence of the intervention program. Campbell agrees that some remedial programs cannot be evaluated in any meaningful way, and that some evaluations are not worth undertaking. It appears that he would prefer not to evaluate some broad-aim interventions at all, rather than to rely upon a strictly qualitative test, such as Weiss and Rein propose.

He recognizes, for his third point, that the probability of no-effect outcomes discourages the use of evaluation analysis. Innovations are too often justified by over-promising their efficacy; a no-effect result is a dangerous risk for the reformers and administrators committed to the intervention. Willingness is needed on the part of the public and legislators to face the possibility of no-effect outcomes as a normal characteristic of exploratory problem solving. Because one plausible effort did not work, it does not follow that the administrators were incompetent or that alternative interventions will also be ineffective. In his fourth point, he agrees that a failure to consider the characteristics of the intervention process seriously limits the interpretation of the significance of outcomes. But the study of process itself requires an experimental design, so that meaning can be applied to the data obtained.

These comments no more than skim the content of the two articles. They merit close and analytical reading. The significance of their central concern cannot be avoided. Major socioeconomic problems call for disciplined intervention, even though causation is speculative and remedial steps are problematical. The challenge to administrators is to shoulder the task of search-and-discover experiments at intervention, meticulously designed and subjected to hard-headed, highly disciplined evaluation. This is the path to realistic problem solving in a society that looks to its governments as the ultimate recourse for relief from its burdens, and for the fulfillment of its aspirations. Reliable, searching program evaluation is a concern at the frontier of the administrative discipline.   —*George A. Shipman*

ROBERT F. BORUCH
DAVID RINDSKOPF
PATRICIA S. ANDERSON
IMAT R. AMIDJAYA
DOUGLAS M. JANSSON

Randomized Experiments for Evaluating and Planning Local Programs: A Summary on Appropriateness and Feasibility [1]

Consider the following scenario. An idea for day care and homemaker services for the elderly is developed, primarily as an alternative to long-term hospital care. The program's purpose is to help to stabilize the costs of caring for the chronically ill, but without degrading their health status. The question then posed is: Does the day care program work in the field, and if so, what are its relative costs and benefits?

To answer the question fairly, it is not unreasonable to install the program at one or more sites and to conduct field tests at each. Moreover, we might test the program within a site using a *randomized field experiment:* half of an eligible target group is assigned to the new program and half is assigned, at least temporarily, to a control condition in which clients receive normal services. The main purpose of the randomized assignment here is to guarantee that the program participants are equivalent to nonparticipants in the long run, and, consequently, that comparison of the two groups will be as fair and as unequivocal as possible.

This paper summarizes some of the authors' research findings on the feasibility of randomized tests for planning and evaluating *local* programs. The summary is brief; the observations made here are documented relentlessly in other reports.[2]

Brief Justificatiaon for Randomized Tests

The simplest justification for assigning people randomly to alternative programs is tied to the idea that estimates of a program's costs and effects ought to be as fair and as unequivocal as possible. By unequivocal, it is meant that any post-program difference in health status between two groups will be clearly attributable to the differences in the effects of programs *rather* than to pre-existing differences between participants and nonparticipants, or to natural differences between their growth or deterioration rates, and so on. Other evaluation designs will usually yield more ambiguous evidence.

Reliance on randomized tests appears to have grown over the past five years for a variety of reasons. The most important is that evaluation of many new programs of the 1960s and early 1970s—in law enforcement, education, health services, welfare reform, and other areas—have been ambiguous, at best, and misleading, at worst. The evaluation designs, even when implemented well, yielded data which did not support the idea that a program worked or did not work. In the most invidious cases, weak programs have been found erroneously to have negative effects and programs which actually have had moderate positive effects have erroneously been found weak. Randomized experiments are a reasonable strategy for avoiding some, but not all, of the interpretive problems encountered in these early studies.[3]

Though they are useful in principle, randomized experiments will not always be appropriate or feasible in practice. Any evaluation is difficult; and the requirement for randomization, as a guarantor of better estimation of program effects, can make the process of evaluation more difficult by generating managerial, ethical, or other problems. The difficulties may be trivial, as they have been in many cases. If substantial, the difficulty must be balanced against the interpretability and usefulness of results based on alternative designs which are easier to implement. The remainder of this paper summarizes the feasibility and appropriateness of experiments for local use: within a hospital, school, or other institution; within a country, region or state; and so on.

Feasibility of Randomized Tests

It is reasonable to exploit three criteria in gauging the feasibility of randomized field tests. The first is general precedent: Have field experiments for planning been conducted locally and with some success? The second concerns specific precedent: Can one carry out a pilot test prior to a major experimental field test to gauge feasibility? The final criterion pertains to situational constraints: Can the special requirement of randomized assignment be met easily with conventional or new strategies?

General Precedent as Evidence of Feasibility

Although randomized field tests are considered exceptional, they have been conducted much more frequently than is generally recognized.[4] In *local court systems,* randomized tests have been set up to establish: how well bail requirements work in the Manhattan Bail Bond Experiment; whether pre-trial hearings actually reduce trial costs and complexity; and the effects of increased legal counsel for juvenile offenders in two major cities. Tests of *police-related practices* are far less frequent but they can be dramatic: the Police Foundation's Kansas City Patrol Experiment assayed costs and effectiveness of alternative patrol strategies; and the Los Angeles Sheriff's Office served as the auspices for comparing military and collegial training regimens for police cadets. Randomized tests of *education programs* include tests of Sesame Street, the Electric Company, and other shows produced by Children's Television Workshop. They include a large number of experiments, often supported by the National Institute of Education, within school districts and within school programs or program components for disadvantaged preschoolers and adolescents, and for teachers with training needs. In *health services,* the National Center for Health Services Research has provided support for local field experiments on day-care and homemaker services for the elderly and chronically ill, comparisons of the quality of care offered by physicians and nurse practitioners, comparisons of alternatives to visiting nurse programs, and assessments of alternative methods of providing information about emergency medical services to those in need of medical care. A state school of pharmacy has run excellent field tests on ways to encourage people to adhere to their drug regimens: conventional prescription and doctor's advice were compared to the use of specially developed pill dispensers.

Inventing more effective *prison and parole programs* and delinquency control strategies is difficult enough without having to cope with the consequences of poor evaluation design. It is for this reason that a variety of new programs in this sector are being tested using randomized experiments. New income subsidy arrangements for parolees and work release programs are compared, for instance, to no-program (control) conditions to determine if they influence costs and recidivism rates. The assessment of new programs for youthful status offenders, undertaken by Vancouver's Health and Welfare Planning Council, programs for ex-addicts developed by Chicago's Safer Foundation, and others build on a small, high quality tradition of experimental tests in the juvenile sector initiated by the California Youth Authority.

Judging from precedent then, simplistic claims that it is impossible to assign individuals randomly to programs for the sake of fair estimates of program effects are simply unwarranted. That randomized field experiments, just like any other mode of evaluation may *fail* to be implemented for legitimate reasons is also clear.[5] However, most of the tests listed in the bibliography cited in footnote 4 have been implemented well.

Evidence for feasibility based on precedent is persuasive only in the crudest sense. It implies that what has been done already can probably be done again; but this is imperfect evidence. Simply because other researchers have mounted good randomized experiments does not mean that an experiment can be mounted successfully or should be mounted in a situation at hand.

Pilot Tests and Preliminary Tests as a Demonstration of Feasibility

Pilot tests can yield more direct evidence on the feasibility of randomized experiments. A small experiment is mounted prior to the main field experiment to anticipate problems in the field and to resolve them. The problems may bear not only on the random assignment process, but also on reliability of measures, integrity of the program, and other elements of the evaluation plan.

The point is that the evaluation design must often be field tested, just as programs themselves are. The test is important not only for randomized experiments, but also for quasi-experimental designs which are likely to yield more equivocal results. In the absence of good precedent, and without the opportunity for pilot study, it is reasonable to use a variety of general criteria for appraising feasibility of a randomized test. These are considered next.

Randomization as a Constraint on Feasibility

Whether randomized experiments are possible depends partly on how well they can be justified, and on how well the process of randomized assignment can be executed. We discuss justification first, then make some observations on the problems of execution and assuring sufficiently large groups for credible evidence.

Rationale, Rhetoric and Design of Experiment. As has been noted, a fundamental rationale for randomized tests is based on the need for less equivocal information about effectiveness of a program, its components, or its variations. Relative costs and effects are a basic criterion for the executive who must decide how to allocate scarce resources, and that concern may also be politically advantageous. Randomized tests carry the promise of better estimates of each. The emphasis on lowering equivocality is more scientific. It represents an attempt to move some of the arguments about social programs from the political into the scientific arena. It also reflects the evaluator's ethical obligation to program clients: to obtain the least equivocal estimate of program costs and effects.

It can reasonably be expected that other arguments will be more sensible to other groups with an interest in a program. Moreover, those arguments can be used to design experiments which are both easier to implement and more informative. Randomized assignment has been justified on moral grounds, for example, and a variety of arguments falling under this rubric have been persuasive. Equity is a fundamental notion; where there is an oversupply of eligible recipients for a scarce resource, randomized assignment to the resource is fair. Vancouver's crisis intervention program for youthful status offenders affords equal opportunity to eligible recipients, and, since not all can be accommodated, they are randomly assigned. In fact, experts such as Cook and Campbell, argue that randomized experiments are most likely to be carried out successfully when the boon (real or imagined) is in short supply and the demand for the boon is high.[6] This rationale dovetails neatly with a normal managerial constraint: new programs cannot be emplaced all at once but must often be introduced gradually. Experiments can then be designed to capitalize on the staged introduction.

More often than not, objections to randomized assignment on ethical grounds focus on the deprivation or risks which are thought to be sustained by members of the control group. Clearly, if the program is known to be effective, then argument against an experimental test of the program against a no-program condition needs to be heard.[7] Rejecting the use of a "no program" comparison group does not, however, preclude randomized experiments which get at the relative benefits or costs of different levels of service, especially where it is not clear that a larger investment actually results in people being better off. Nor does it preclude comparing two alternative programs or program components dedicated to the same end.

Similarly, it will, at times, be politically unacceptable to assign individuals randomly to control conditions. The ethical, moral, and economic justification may be quite irrelevant. In such instances, it is often possible to ameliorate difficulties by comparing program variations against one another, rather than comparing a novel program to an existing one or to no program at all. "No program" may, after all, be an unacceptable political option in any event, and perhaps, the most we can do is to choose the invented variation which works best for the investment.

Finally, law related interests in scientific enterprise invariably trail the products of that enterprise. Court decisions on the matter exist, for example, but they are scarce. In *Aguayo v. Richardson*[8] and in *California Welfare Rights Organization v. Richardson,*[9] the use of randomized experiments in assessing new welfare reform programs was challenged and the challenges were dismissed by the courts. Legislation with explicit reference to experiments is far more common than court decisions, and is far more characteristic of federal than state law. Some of the pertinent statutes have been listed by the U.S. General Accounting Office and the Library of Congress, and the more recent federal laws may serve as models for state legislation.[10] Within executive agencies, there is some agreement that randomized tests can yield remarkably persuasive evidence for program planning, judging from Caplan's surveys of policy makers and legislative staff.[11] That interest is also evident occasionally among staff in some state agencies, such as Virginia's Joint Legislature Audit and Review Commission and the Washington State Governor's Office of Management and Budget.

Executing Randomization. Any criteria used to assign people to a service or material treatment can, of course, be corrupted. Some school district evaluations of their Title I reading programs were flawed because students who did not need the program, judging by their reading test scores, got it. Elsewhere, schools ineligible for Title I funds got them. So, too, can the randomized assignment be degraded and it is clear that loss of control can be easy. Judges who initially agreed to assign offenders randomly to alternative rehabilitation programs, for example, have sometimes failed to do so.[12] In Weaver's evaluation of approaches to Parent Effectiveness Training, the randomization was delegated to a screening staff who simply failed to follow instructions,[13] and so, conscientious control over randomization is imperative. Anticipating exceptions is also essential. There must be some way of accommodating friends and relatives if nepotism is a strong tradition. So long as they can be identified by the evaluator, beneficiaries can be excluded from the final data analysis. Individuals may also remove themselves from the group to which they have been randomly assigned, for a variety of reasons. Consequently, monitoring systems and devices for minimizing dropouts are ordinarily used to enhance the likelihood of a successful experiment.

Randomized Assignment and Size of the Group. Evaluating any demonstration project may be difficult because the program itself does not attract a sufficiently large number of participants. This can be a nettlesome problem in local experiments, where the target group may not be particularly large to begin with. If the number of individuals assigned to each program variation is small, *any* evaluation, randomized or not, will be less reliable. Moderate program effects will be swamped by normal variation in human behavior if the sample is small. To the extent that the groups are large, the experiment will be more likely to show effects when they exist.

Prediction and control of throughput then influence feasibility. In many cases, clients enter programs sequentially, and randomizing at the point of entry until group size is sufficiently large is a natural strategy. The tactic is often feasible in alcoholism treatment experiments, for example.[14] Batch processing is also pertinent. Individuals who turn up sequentially are grouped periodically and then assigned to programs.[15]

Collaborative multi-site experiments are a sound vehicle for generating larger samples and more reliable statements about the average size of a program's effect. Community mental health centers, outreach programs, school districts, and training centers seem to be no less capable of collaboration than research hospitals which have often used collaborative trials successfully to assay drug effectiveness.

Whether the sample size in an experiment is adequate can be determined by a competent statistician or methodologist based on information about the expected size of a program's effect, and the probable quality of program implementation and of observations made on program recipients.[16]

Appropriateness

Appropriateness is a precondition for feasibility, determined partly by the answers to more fundamental questions: Is estimating the effects of a program, rather than some other type of evaluation, warranted? Will methods other than randomized experiment yield good estimates of effect? Are resources, especially manpower, sufficient? All concern both local and national evaluations, randomized or not.

Estimating Effects. Considering the idea of estimating program effects, it is clear that some evaluations, including some experiments, have been mounted prematurely. As a consequence, these experiments have failed to provide much useful information. If the goals of a program or policy are overblown, for example, it is far more reasonable to determine what the objectives and operations are at the delivery level than to estimate effects immediately. Furthermore, a fair evaluation must be based on actual goals as well as on the advertised ones. In some instances, not much is known about the program itself and a process evaluation is then also warranted. Sometimes, despite political rhetoric, the target group and their needs are not well specified. That makes needs assessment surveys a legitimate, perhaps essential, pre-evaluation step.[17]

More generally, the main concern lies in determining the manner in which a program may be evaluated. In elementary form, this concern implies a simple question: Do we know enough, about the program, its target group, and its operations, to make estimates of program effects meaningful? An elaborate answer may require examining the "evaluability" of a program to establish what we think we know, and what characteristics of a program can be tested for effects. This concern does not imply that one should rely any less on an understanding of program effects than on process assessments or opinion surveys. It behooves the evaluator and program administrator to recognize that if the only methods for understanding programs were the latter, medical practitioners would still be using thalidomide, laetrile, and orgone boxes.

Alternative Methods of Estimating Effects. The little data that does exist on direct *costs* of randomized experiments and good quasi-experiments suggest that price differences are not appreciable.[18] However, it would be irresponsible to assume merely that costs are similar, just as it would be irresponsible to assume that alternative methods cannot be found to yield results as unequivocal as those stemming from an experiment. A notable difference in cost/equivocality ratio may justify the alternatives.

It is clear that many alternatives to randomized experiments often yield misleading estimates. The best illustrations stem from research in which randomized experiments and nonrandomized tests are run in parallel. Estimates from the randomized tests are compared to estimates from, for example, a before-after design or a time series analysis.

The results lend further evidence for the contention that the estimates based on nonrandomized experimental designs will normally differ from those based on the randomized tests.[19] That there are exceptions where the results are the same, is also clear. The problem, however, is that one often cannot know in advance whether this will be true. The state of the art is well-developed enough to anticipate chronic threats to validity of analysis in nonrandomized experiments, but not sufficiently well-developed to predict them accurately and to accommodate them.

Data stemming from alternative evaluation designs are usually, but not always, more difficult to interpret than data from randomized tests. The problem stems from the fact that in comparing groups, e.g., program recipients to nonrecipients, there will *normally* be a variety of competing explanations for a difference. A few such explanations are obvious: selection differences—creaming—will produce natural differences between groups and those may be mislabelled as being attributable to the program. Many competing explanations are more subtle: regression, covariance, and matching techniques, designed to produce equivalent groups after assignment to program exists, provide no formal guarantee of the long-run equivalence of the groups and, hence, no formal guarantee of fair comparison. It is often a matter of faith that all pertinent matching variables have been used and all those used are free from measurement error. To understand better how competing explanations bias estimates of program effect, Cook and Campbell have produced a formidable list of threats to validity in analysis of quasi-experiments.[20] More importantly, they order those designs on a continuum of the ambiguity in the results produced by each design, for some are subject to fewer threats to validity or competing explanation, than others. Earlier versions of their taxonomy have been used to good advantage in manpower evaluations, programmatic research on education programs, assessments of quality in evaluations of recent social service programs, and elsewhere.[21] It is adaptable to local settings, especially since the approach assumes a thorough familiarity with the setting, program recipients, and program operations.

Finally, a randomized test can be flawed seriously enough to yield no less ambiguous information than is provided by an alternative evaluation design. To the extent that an experiment induces artificial competition between program variations, Hawthorne effects, and the like, the experiment's results will be more difficult to interpret. Those problems can be accommodated in some settings, but not in others. The Cook and Campbell listings can be helpful here as in understanding results of a quasi-experiment.

Resources. Any high quality evaluation requires competent staff, and that is true for experiments as well as other evaluation designs. A small staff of good caliber people can produce fine evaluations—witness Earle's evaluation of police training programs and Kelling's work with staff on the Kansas City patrol experiments.[22] However, even competent managers confronted by the relatively novel technical demands of program evaluation can fail dismally. To facilitate access to technical support and better exploitation of local personnel, a variety of approaches is possible. Scioli's paper in this Symposium deals with a number of them. The old saw about reading the instructions when everything else fails is pertinent here too. There are a variety of good monographs which deal with managerial, institutional, and statistical problems in social experiments. Some of these texts are cited in footnotes 2, 6, 7, and 18. Finally, cooperative trials, in which the resources of several institutions or communities are pooled to sustain high quality technical support, are often a reasonable strategy. Community wide cooperation of this sort is often well organized in service programs (e.g., fire control). It is still a novel approach to the improved exploitation of local experts and resources for conducting evaluations and should be tried more frequently.

Notes

1. This paper is based on research supported by the National Institute of Education (NIE-C-74-0115).
2. See R. F. Boruch, P. S. Anderson, D. Rindskopf, I. R. Amidjaya, and D. Jansson, "Randomized Experiments for Evaluating and Planning Local Programs: Appropriateness and Feasibility," Research Report (Evanston, Ill.: Northwestern University, Psychology Department, 1977), and H. W. Riecken, R. F. Boruch, D. T. Campbell, N. Caplan, T. K. Glennan, J. Pratt, A. Rees, and W. Williams, *Social Experiments: A Method for Planning and Evaluating Social Programs* (New York: Academic, 1974).
3. T. C. Chalmers, J. B. Block, and S. Lee, "Controlled Studies in Clinical Cancer Research," *New England Journal of Medicine,* Vol. 287 (1972), pp. 75-78; E. W. Stromsdorfer, *Review and Synthesis of Cost Effectiveness Studies of Vocational and Technical Education* (Columbus, Ohio: ERIC Clearinghouse on Vocational & Technical Education, 1972); M. L. Wargo, P. L. Campeau, and G. K. Tallmadge, *Further Examination of Exemplary Programs for Educating Disadvantaged Children* (Palo Alto: American Institute of Research, 1971); R. F. Boruch, "On Common Contentions about Randomized Field Experiments," in G. V. Glass (ed.), *Evaluation Studies Review Annual* (Beverly Hills, Calif.: Sage, 1976), pp. 158-194; and H. S. Havens, "Statement before the Senate Com-

mittee on Human Resources, on Expenditures, Problems, and Prospects of Management and Utilization of Program Evaluation" (Washington, D.C.: U.S. General Accounting Office, Program Analysis Division, October 6, 1977).

4. R. F. Boruch, A. J. McSweeney, and E. J. Soderstrom, "Bibliography: Randomized Field Experiments for Program Development and Evaluation," *Evaluation Quarterly* (1978, in press).

5. See L. L. Roos, N. P. Roos, and B. McKinley, "Implementing Randomization," *Policy Analysis,* Vol. 3, No. 4 (1977), pp. 547-559, for a thoughtful analysis of a randomized test on extended medical care in Canada.

6. See P. S. Anderson, A. Schneider, and C. Cleary, *The Vancouver, Washington Crisis Intervention Program: Experimental Tests* (Vancouver, Wash.: Health & Welfare Planning Council, 1977) and T. D. Cook and D. T. Campbell, "The Design and Conduct of Quasi-experiments and True Experiments in Field Settings," in M. D. Dunnette (ed.), *Handbook of Industrial and Organizational Psychology* (Chicago: Rand-McNally, 1976), pp. 223-325.

7. See J. P. Gilbert, B. McPeek, and F. Mosteller, "Progress in Surgery and Anesthesia: Benefits and Risks of Innovative Therapy," in J. P. Bunker, B. A. Barnes, and F. Mosteller (eds.), *Costs, Risks, and Benefits of Surgery* (New York: Oxford University Press, 1977) for an interesting examination of available data on the likelihood of an innovative program's being successful and the implications for arguments about the ethical propriety of experiments.

8. See M. J. Breger, "Legal Aspects of Social Research," paper presented at the Symposium on Ethical Issues in Social Research, University of Minnesota, Minneapolis, April 1976, in general, and *Aguoyo v. Richardson,,* 352 F. Supp. 452 (S.D.N.Y.), in particular.

9. See again Breger, "Legal Aspects of Social Research" for a general legal analysis and *California Welfare Rights Organization v. Richardson,* 348 F. Supp. 491 (N.D. Cal. 1972) for particulars.

10. See, for example, U.S. General Accounting Office, *Program Evaluation: Legislative Language and a User's Guide to Selected Sources* (Washington, D.C.: U.S. General Accounting Office, 1973).

11. See N. Caplan, "Social Research and National Policy: What Gets Used, by Whom, for What Purpose, and with What Effects?" in S. S. Nagel (ed.), *Policy Studies Review Annual,* Vol. 1 (Beverly Hills, Calif.: Sage, 1977), pp. 68-78.

12. See R. F. Conner, "Selecting Control Groups: An Analysis of the Randomization Process in Twelve Social Reform Programs," *Evaluation Quarterly,* Vol. 1, No. 2 (1977), pp. 195-244.

13. D. Weaver, "Evaluation of Methods in Parent Effectiveness Training," Research report, Northwestern University Psychology Department, Evanston, 1975.

14. See again Anderson, *et al., Crisis Intervention.*

15. T. J. Cook, "The Safer Foundation Tests of a Program for Ex-addicts," unpublished memo, Research Triangle Institute, Durham, North Carolina, 1976.

16. See again Riecken, *et al., Social Experiments,* and Bunker, *et al., Costs, Risks, and Benefits of Surgery.*

17. See P. Kotler, *Marketing for Nonprofit Organizations* (Englewood Cliffs, N.J.: Prentice-Hall, 1975).

18. See footnote 2, *supra.*

19. See footnote 3, *supra.*

20. See footnote 6, *supra.*

21. See, for example, E. Hardin, "On the Choice of Control Groups," in M. E. Borus (ed.), *Evaluating the Impact of Manpower Programs* (Lexington, Mass.: D.C. Heath, 1972), pp. 41-59; and H. E. Freeman and I. N. Bernstein, *Academic and Entrepreneurial*

Research: The Consequences of Diversity in Federal Evaluation Studies (New York: Sage, 1975).

22. G. L. Kelling, "Development of Staff for Evaluations," in L. Sechrest (ed.), *Proceedings of a Conference on Emergency Medical Services* (Washington, D.C.: U.S. Government Printing Office, 1977).

1979 (36-40)

PAMELA HORST
JOE N. NAY
JOHN W. SCANLON
JOSEPH S. WHOLEY

Program Management and the Federal Evaluator

In 1969, The Urban Institute completed an extensive study of federal evaluation and concluded that, "the most impressive finding about the evaluation of social programs in the federal government is that substantial work in this field is almost non-existent."[1] A limited resurvey of the field in 1972 revealed a quite different picture: funds committed to evaluation had mushroomed, many studies had been completed, and the use of large-scale social experimentation was increasing.[2]

This growth in evaluation has contributed information—often imperfect, sometimes incorrect—to today's arguments about the direction, method, and purpose of social programs. Without evaluation, many arguments would have remained at the level of polemic. There is no question that the presence of program evaluation has heightened the consciousness of federal program managers and policy makers to the fact that they may, from time to time, have to respond to queries about the effectiveness of their programs.

While evaluation has firmly established itself since 1969 in both the budget and the administrative rhetoric of the federal government, there is little evidence to show that evaluation generally leads to more effective social policies or programs. On the contrary, the experience to date strongly suggests that social programs have not been as effective as expected and have not improved in performance following evaluation. This situation can be phrased as a critical management problem which we see confronting governmental agencies:

> Why have those in charge of programs and those who evaluate them not been able to join their efforts in a way that leads more frequently to significant improvements in program performance?

Having been able both to observe and to participate in the development of federal program evaluation, we have chosen here to raise three proposi-

176

tions about the root causes of the above problem. If these causes are the crucial ones and if we can come to understand their true impact, federal program management and evaluation stand on the edge of a period of increasing success. If not, and the causes of these weaknesses continue to be ignored, then evaluation, program management, the programs themselves, and those the programs are intended to serve will all continue to suffer.

This paper elaborates on why the three root causes, when they exist, block further improvement of many programs. The idea of a "preassessment" of program evaluability is introduced as one tool for improving both program management and program evaluation. We begin with a discussion of the conventional treatment of evaluation problems and then present an alternative diagnosis and prescription. Although much of the material presented is addressed to federal managers and federal evaluators, we believe the problems and solutions discussed also hold for state and local government.

Apparent Causes of Evaluation Problems—and an Alternative Statement

Most reviews made to determine what causes programs and their evaluations to be ineffective include one or more of the following conclusions:[3]

- Evaluations are not planned to support decision making.
- The timing, format, and precision of evaluation studies are not geared to user needs.
- Evaluation findings are not adequately communicated to decision makers.
- Different evaluations of the same program are not comparable.
- Evaluation fails to provide an accumulating, increasingly accurate body of evidence.
- Evaluation studies often address unanswerable questions and produce inconclusive results.

The first three apparent causes deal with aspects of evaluation use. They occur at the interface between the producers of evaluations and the prospective users of evaluation.

The second three apparent causes deal with the methods used by the evaluators in assessing the interventions of the programs in society. They occur at the interface between the producers of evaluation and the program as it exists. They concern flaws in making measurements and comparisons and in drawing conclusions.

Our experience to date in studying the management problem—namely, the lack of significant improvement in program performance—and in watching various agencies attack the apparent causes of the problem has led us to conclude that these six statements largely refer to symptoms, rather than causes. We believe that the causes of the problem may more properly be described by one or more of the following three propositions concerning the program itself:

- *Lack of Definition:* The problem addressed, the program intervention being made, the expected direct outcome of that intervention, or the expected impact on the overall society or on the problem addressed are not sufficiently well defined to be measurable.
- *Lack of Clear Logic:* The logic of assumptions linking expenditure of resources, the implementation of a program intervention, the immediate outcome to be caused by that intervention, and the resulting impact are not specified or understood clearly enough to permit testing them.

When one or more of these three propositions is true, both the problem (lack of significant improvement in program performance) and the six apparent causes listed earlier can easily occur. In cases where the first two propositions hold, an enormous range of possibilities will present themselves as to which measurements and comparisons to make—with no criteria for making sound choices. In cases where the last proposition holds, even exceptionally high quality evaluation is not likely to be used well, if used at all. If a program suffers from one or more of these three flaws, there is a very low probability that the evaluation information useful to program improvement can be produced. Thus the program may be "unevaluable" until the flaws are corrected.

A statement that the quality and value of evaluation are strongly affected by the degree to which these three conditions exist is not a startling finding. What has not been realized or acknowledged in the past, however, is that these three factors are not the responsibility of the evaluator. While the conventional apparent causes relate to how the evaluator does his job, these latter three propositions describe an organizational environment over which the evaluator typically has little control. Evaluators, more than any other group in an agency, will appear unable to complete their work successfully when these conditions exist, regardless of how they deal with the apparent causes.

Why the Apparent Causes Are Suspect

In the past few years, we have conducted a number of federal program evaluations and helped to develop evaluation planning systems for several federal agencies. In the course of our work, we have observed many attempts to treat the six apparent causes directly by improving the use and methodology of evaluation. These attempts include policy review and dissemination panels, letting contracts for methodology development, high level reviews of evaluation plans, task forces to select better questions for evaluation, better systems for collecting data, requiring program offices to submit advance descriptions of how evaluation findings will be used, and the tightening of contract selection and monitoring procedures to increase contractor responsiveness to agency needs. In some cases, the "solution" was reorganization: centralizing previously decentralized evaluation units. Since revenue sharing, talk of decentralizing a previously centralized evaluation office has gained popularity. In this case, the headquarters office would no longer be responsible for conducting national program evaluation, but instead would go into the business of building local evaluation capability.

As these proposed solutions were implemented, however, we have continued to talk with and work with participants in the process from the assistant secretary level, through the program level, and on down to the recipients of services. We find that the management problem—that is, the lack of significant improvement of program performance—continues to exist and the same apparent causes continue to be cited, whether there are high or low quality evaluation efforts. Improvements in programs and in delivery of effective services remain far below the levels desired or expected. If the root causes of the problem lay within the evaluation process, we believe that these correctives would be showing some degree of success. Consequently this experience led us to search for alternative explanations and, finally, to the consideration of the three conditions stated above as root causes of the problem.

The Source of the Problem

The significance of the proposed causes can best be understood by contrasting the nature of the intervention that the social programs of today attempt to make in the society at large with the principal types of program interventions attempted in the past. Many older, classical government activities involved program interventions whose nature was clearly defined and agreed upon and which were described in detail in a body of law or regulation (e.g., Social Security). The implementation of such activities was largely an act of administration of the laws and regulations. Evaluation of success or failure of the act of implementation was primarily a matter of assessing compliance with the guiding laws and regulations. Discretion was at a minimum (at least over the short term). Arguments might take place about whether *goals* were adequate, but the *details of the program intervention* were determined in advance.

In contrast, many new missions that the federal government has been called upon to undertake (e.g., lowering hard core unemployment) involve problems in which the proper program intervention mechanism is not well understood, or defined, or in some cases even known. Since in these cases no one knows exactly what detailed program intervention will be of value, greater management discretion is allowed and exercised. While in some cases research may be undertaken or experiments may be made to increase understanding, more typically a purportedly successful type of program intervention is simply put into place and an agency or bureau is charged with making it into a successful operation. In this case, evaluation is expected to report to those in charge of a program on whether the use of discretion in choosing specific program intervention techniques was successful and perhaps to suggest modifications or alternatives.

The newer program areas are characterized by uncertainty and discretion: uncertainty as to the nature of the problem and what constitutes effective strategies of intervention, and discretion in how the problem and the intervention are defined and how the intervention is implemented. These conditions make sound and rapid evaluation all the more important to effective management. Consider, however, how today's program environments can disable evaluation through three factors: lack of definition, lack of a clear logic, and lack of management.

Lack of Definition

Examination of program legislation, regulations, policy manuals, plans, and budget to determine what a program intervention is can be very deceptive. What at first seems clear often evaporates when the test of measurability is applied. The language used turns out to be ambiguous precisely where it would have to be specific in order for evaluation to be useful. Three common forms of inadequate language are: the vaporous wish, local project packaging, and how-to-do-it rule making.

The vaporous wish is the eloquent but elusive language of goals put forward for most federal programs. Exactly what are the "unemployability," "alienation," "dependency," and "community tensions" some programs desire to reduce? How would one know when a program crossed the line, successfully converting "poor quality of life" into "adequate quality of life"? Would anyone recognize "improved mental health," "improved local capability," or "revitalized institutions"? The problems addressed by social programs are almost never stated so that institutions, people, or the relevant socioeconomic conditions could be classified according to the degree to which they are afflicted with a problem. It is very hard to propose a solution to a problem that is ill-defined or undefined. How much harder it is to evaluate the success of that proposed solution.

Next, there is the project packaging language which purports to describe the intervention activity to be planted in the field and the expected outcome for those directly served by that activity. As any experienced site visitor will attest, this language is often so annoyingly imprecise that it is difficult to tell what parts of a local operation are under discussion and even harder to distinguish compliance or assess performance. For example, project characteristics prescribed in various program guidelines include: "coordinative mechanism," "integrated services," a "range of modalities," "extended career ladders," "accessibility of services," "continuity of care," "multidisciplinary teams," "outreach capability," etc. Projects should produce "upgraded job skills," "increased cultural enrichment," "increased personal autonomy," "improved family cohesion," etc. Rarely are useful measures or norms for these activities and outcomes provided.

How-to-do-it rule making is the third kind of language that is commonly found. Here the terms are very concrete and specific. We find guidance on factors like the qualifications of project directors, the contents of affiliation agreements with other local agencies, reporting relationships, the use of consultants, and accounting practices. This guidance appears to be definite and all inclusive. Closer examination shows that it usually tells how to run the part of a project which does not deal directly with the intervention into society. Guidance for the part of the project which actually produces effects in society is not provided.

When these three forms of language predominate, the intervention activities in the field may be diverse indeed. Our experiences examining field operations indicate that program packaging is generally skin deep and that very different project activities and definitions of outcome often parade under the same assumed program names. An examination of 20 projects in the same program will often reveal 20 very different program intervention designs, different in activity and purpose. This means that the program activity and objective, as implemented in the field, cannot be defined on a common base of measurable terms. It is often difficult to find any consensus among federal level policy makers as to what the definitional base should be. This lack of a common framework can disable management and evaluation efforts alike.

It is becoming clearer that many federal social programs are simply envelopes for a large federal investment in a problem area. A program may be deceptive in the sense that it has enough content to allow it to be described in the media, lobbied into existence, and established as a federal effort—and yet the program interventions are not spelled out in any detail. Many program administrators over the last decade have essentially received a program envelope with only vaporous wishes and money inside. Although more detailed definition may not have been necessary in order to spend the money, much more detailed definition is needed to evaluate the process and outcome.

If it is decided that certain programs should be further defined, who in an agency should be responsible for the tasks? It should not be left to the auditors or to the evaluators or to the information system people, because the choice of specific measurable definitions is not merely a technical task. The definition of what is to be measured in a program is central to policy making and program management. If there are many different ways to measure the problem a social program purports to influence, this often means that there are many different problems. For many programs, no one has yet exercised the prerogative of selecting which specific set of social ills the program is trying to cure or the methods of cure. Legislation or regulations rarely make this choice, and the choice has policy implications since it further specifies program intent and intervention. One of the major factors in shaping and directing a program is carefully selecting what the program is going to do. The failure to define measurable interventions, outcomes, and impact for a program is a major policy making defect. Those in charge of the agency and the program, rather than the evaluators, should have primary responsibility for program definitions.

Lack of a Clear Logic of Testable Assumptions

Even if the policy makers or program managers have provided measurable definitions, there still may not be unanimity within a federal social program about design or logic. As a result, different evaluation efforts are often based on *different* assumptions linking program intervention with immediate outcome and ultimate program impact. The measures and data collection instruments used are those that seem most reasonable to the evaluator. In this context it is easy to understand why evaluation findings are often noncomparable. When there is no carefully determined framework to guide the program, there is, of course, no such framework for evaluation studies. Nor is there a framework for systematically accumulating knowledge of program performance. In fact, it becomes unclear what program performance means.

Program assumptions might be as simple as that "the transfer of money to school districts will raise the reading level of disadvantaged students" or that "the training of the unemployed will lower unemployment." Often the board program charters from the Congress referred to earlier have caused clusters of competing assumptions to grow up in many social programs. One set of assumptions may be used for arguments with friends, for instance, and another for argument with enemies. This may be good politics, but it makes for difficult evaluation design, since evaluation design should relate to the information needed to validate, refute, or modify a set of operating assumptions.

Without an adequate description of the assumptions governing the intervention of a program into society, it is more likely that evaluators will be asked to address unanswerable questions far removed from the actual activities taking place. To take a quite reasonable example, a program office might insist on funding an evaluation to assess the relative effectiveness of different drug treatment modalities. The evaluator may then find that these modalities do not represent pure, mutually exclusive approaches which are replicated in multiple local settings. He is likely to find, on the contrary, that a "halfway house" or a "therapeutic community" in one locale bears no resemblance in operating assumptions to others which go by the same name. After spending a lot of money, time, and effort, the evaluator will be forced to tell the agency what types of programs are really out there, rather than how successful they are, and also that the only way to test the effectiveness of alternative assumptions of treatment is to implement a program-level experiment, or introduce planned and enforced variations into the program design. Those in charge of the program may feel that the evaluator has once again failed to answer their questions. There are many examples of evaluations being mounted to answer questions which bear no relationship to the program activity actually taking place in the field. This counterproductive practice results from the failure of the agency to describe carefully the program assumptions so that they can be implemented and tested.

Summing up, even when the intervention, expected outcome, and impact are defined in measurable terms, the more subtle questions of the logic linking (a) program expenditures to production of the intervention, (b) intervention to outcome, and (c) outcome to impact on the problem must still be considered. The use of the word "logic" here is not meant to imply that the linking assumptions are loose or tight, valid or invalid, defensible or stupid. All that is implied is that a program in reality is based on an interrelated set of assumptions about what is believed to happen (and sometimes why) when money is spent and the intervention made. The absence of statements of these assumptions might be expected to cause a problem for both program managers and evaluators. The evaluators often notice the absence first, however, because they must design tests of these assumptions. Tests cannot be designed for people who are unable to, or refuse to, state their assumptions.

Once again (as with measurable definitions) the statement of the logic of testable assumptions is a policy question, not one that should be decided by the evaluators. Evaluators should test the assumptions about what works. Those in charge should make the initial assumptions underlying the funding and operation of the program.

Lack of Management

To get at the significance of lack of management, it is important to realize that evaluation is useful only if it is, in fact, a tool of management. A manager has a variety of tools to employ that include direction of his line management, planning, budgeting, audit and financial control, administration (for that part of his activity that can be clearly defined and where a law or set of rules is used to guide program implementation), policy analysis, and evaluation. Evaluation is needed principally in support of policy analysis and management discretion. Evaluation performs the same function for management that audit and control do for budgeting and that compliance checks do for administration.

One way of understanding the role of evaluation as a management tool is to explore how a "textbook manager" might use evaluation in attempts to improve program performance and then to contrast that with the way evaluation more frequently is used.

Evaluators and the "textbook manager" cooperate very well. When the policy decisions about program design are to be made, the evaluator asks the manager to specify the measurable definitions, the assumptions of the program linking these definitions, what kind of performance data would cause the manager to act, and the kinds of action the manager has the authority and willingness to implement. Armed with this guidance, the evaluator estimates the level of error associated with collecting the evidence, estimates the ranges of possible findings, and bounds the cost of the proposed evaluation. The evaluator is then equipped to provide a service not commonly rendered at present. He can advise management on the cost and feasibility of procuring evaluation evidence, and the manager can weigh these factors against the potential value of evidence for improving program performance. When the evaluation is finally commissioned, the evaluator has a clear basis for judging the best level of aggregation, precision, and delivery schedule because he has a user for the proposed evaluation. Many market surveys and internal evaluations are conducted this way in industry. When this kind of rational planning occurs, one does not generate evaluation studies in search of users and uses.

The utility of social program evaluation depends at least in part upon defining the decision context as well as the program design. The "textbook manager" has already defined his program in measurable terms and has indicated what it purports to accomplish. If evaluation is to contribute to program improvement, there must be at least a few decision areas where the manager will rely on program performance feedback (measures of impact, outcome, intervention activities), as well as on political pressures, popular approaches, or his own hunches and beliefs. Else why buy evaluation at all? The "textbook manager" knows in advance and can specify what level of evidence will prompt him to act at all, or cause him to select among alternative actions. Further, he has the authority to act.

Return with us now to reality, where the typical government administrators live. These administrators participate in continual agency debate over program issues, but the debates proceed in a language which means different things to different people. The debates are not centered on a measurable set of program descriptions nor are the assumptions guiding the program intervention made clear enough to be testable. In fact, most of the people in this world will go to great lengths to keep these two things ambiguous in order to expand their area for maneuver. The administrator is a decision maker—he does take action. As in "textbook" management, many of his actions are based on guesses about what is needed, shifting academic opinions and political support, and the demands of a set of higher level policy makers subject to continual turnover. Unlike the "textbook" management, however, the typical government administrator does not establish and test assumptions linking intervention activities to program performance. Typical government administration might be called "pseudo-management," because all its management activity takes place in a process that is not linked to actual program results. In its own terms, such "pseudo-management" is good if its activities remain acceptable to an ever-changing cast of characters at the policy level.

Evaluators and pseudo-managers operate independently of one another. There is no basis for communication between them. The pseudo-manager has no real use for evaluation and the evaluator can provide few, if any, services to assist in pseudo-management. In fact, sound evaluation results may present a clear and present danger to the pseudo-manager. In this environment, the evaluator can expect his work to have minimal impact. The problem for the evaluator is to distinguish pseudo-management from textbook management. On the surface it appears to us that pseudo-management predominates in social agencies; the potential for textbook management is yet unknown.

Our emphasis on identifying actual users of evaluation and on prespecifying the decision context and uses of evaluation information may seem excessive. Yet the desired use of evaluation information determines not only how much it is worth but also the form and accuracy that it must have. And if those in charge of a program have no use for information about that program, then there is no real way to design an adequate evaluation for them. What this might mean may be demonstrated by an example.

Assume that a federal drug treatment program for heroin abusers defines outcome success in the following terms: the client reveals absence of heroin use six months after discharge from treatment, as tested by three randomly spaced urinalyses during the follow-up period and one urinalysis at the end of the six months. Those in charge of the program say that they require information about this outcome to assist in decisions about the following: allocation of technical assistance among drug treatment projects, reallocation of funds among projects, and assignment of headquarters staff to study problems associated with achieving a desirable outcome level. But suppose those in charge are challenged to specify in advance how decisions might vary with the range of possible evaluation findings. For example, will a task force convene for program redesign if national program cure rates average 5 percent, 15 percent, or 50 percent? Will technical assistance be given to projects whose average cure rate falls below 5 percent? Is there technical assistance to give? Can projects be closed down? Will a stated national objective of a 30 percent cure rate be adjusted downward, if the actual average cure rate found is 15 percent? This type of dialogue would permit the evaluator to assess the potential value of evaluation information by identifying plausible and practical uses for it and also permit the evaluator to assess the specific type and accuracy of the information required.

The level of validity and reliability required in measurable data should be an important factor used in analyzing the method of collection, the cost of data collection, and the methods and cost of data analysis before data collection efforts ever begin. The "conclusiveness" of data only takes on meaning in relation to particular actions the data may suggest. But as we saw earlier, if everything is left ambiguous, no one will know what level of evaluation findings would or should prompt action and therefore what level of validity and reliability are required in the evaluation data. This means that, in our example, drug program evaluations which show cure rates of 2 percent, 5 percent, 20 percent, 50 percent, and 75 percent could all be dismissed by the pseudo-managers as "inconclusive" for decision making.

When a single individual does not have the authority to take or to elaborate on the kinds of action mentioned above, those individuals whose consensus is required must be found and consulted. The point is that management of a program is a policy matter. Evaluation cannot prescribe management actions. Rather, the needs of management should define evaluations.

The Consequences of Evaluating When These Conditions Exist

Why should the evaluator worry about the soft, unmeasurable underbelly of social program goals, objectives, and activity; about the obscure logic of program assumptions; or about whether there is a management vacuum? If our analysis is correct, weaknesses in these areas can disable an evaluation effort while making the failure appear to be the evaluator's own doing.

If the agency evaluator, alone or with a contractor, attempts to carry out an evaluation of a program where these flaws exist, our experience indicates that there are two highly likely outcomes. First, the evaluator's attempt to define the program in measurable and logical terms will flounder. No available methodology can bridge the gap between the program as implemented in the field and the program as suggested by program goal statements. Thus the results of his evaluation are likely to be labeled "inconclusive," "abstract," or "an effort to develop methodology." Second, his findings will not be responsive to the information needs of those in charge of the program. He may produce the wrong information or information that is too imprecise or too sparse. Even if the evaluation is technically unimpeachable, those in charge of the program may find it irrelevant to their decision context, seeing no way to act upon the information.

We have suggested that the definition of measurable program design and of testable assumptions about how the program works is a major policy issue which should be resolved by policy makers and program managers within the discretionary boundaries of program legislation. Program policy making is not the job of the agency evaluator, and he should not undertake the task even if it is disguised as a "technical" choice of the proper program measures needed to conduct an evaluation.

Some Sources of Leverage

Is there a strategy that evaluators can adopt to return the jobs of policy making and program management to policy makers and evaluators—and improve the utility and yield of evaluation (and program) dollars? Fortunately, some factors in the present federal environment may supply the leverage needed to force attention to the three conditions (lack of definition, lack of clear logic, and lack of management) that have proven costly to program effectiveness and evaluation.

First, there is less naivete about federal social programs today. More awareness exists that attacking a vague problem with an unproven social, behavioral, or economic theory is not likely to bring success. Raising issues about program definitions and assumptions is now more likely to strike a responsive chord in this climate. Secondly, the federal budget is not expanding rapidly, and the present administration and the Congress are placing more emphasis on accountability. Third, both the Congress and citizens are pushing for more effective delivery of public services, and more evidence of effectiveness.

The evaluator, with some help from high level policy makers and program managers, may be able to take advantage of these potential sources of leverage and use them to force the definition that makes evaluation possible. At least he may assure that his efforts are expended in areas where there is the best chance of success. The tool that we recommend he employ is a "preassessment of evaluability" for every program that is a candidate for evaluation.

Preassessment of Evaluability"

We recommend a process of pre-evaluation design.[4] If conducted in proper detail, this process can provide what might be called a "rapid feedback evaluation" of the present status of a program and its information base, and can make clear whether a major evaluation effort is or is not warranted. In essence, the three root causes of problems in program evaluation can be transformed into a set of criteria for determining the evaluability of a public program. These criteria are expressed in the following questions:

- Are the problems, intended program interventions, anticipated outcomes, and the expected impact sufficiently well defined as to be measurable?
- In the assumptions linking expenditure to implementation of intervention, intervention to the outcome anticipated, and immediate outcome to the expected impact on the problem, is the logic laid out clearly enough to be tested?
- Is there anyone clearly in charge of the program? Who? What are the constraints on his ability to act? What range of actions might he reasonably take or consider as a result of various possible evaluation findings about the measures and assumptions discussed above?

In a sense the criteria are sequential. Measurable definitions form a basis for the testable assumptions. Then both serve as a basis for the consideration of the range of decisions that those in charge of the program might make as a result of information about actual costs, interventions, outcomes, and impact.

In practice the evaluator will have to judge the degree to which the three criteria are satisfied for particular programs. The evaluator generally has several programs in his agency that can be evaluated at any one time. In initial planning, the evaluator should focus on testing each program against these three criteria, using the best information available from the programs themselves to assess how valuable each program may be. This assessment should be discussed directly with policy makers and program officials. The interaction between evaluator and program officials may assist policy makers and program officials to define the measures and specify the logic of assumptions that need to be tested.

The next task is to decide which programs meet all three criteria. Then programs that meet some criteria, or almost meet all criteria, may be sorted out. Finally, in most agencies, a third group of programs will emerge which satisfy few—if any—of the three criteria.

At this point the evaluator will have completed his own preassessment of the "evaluability" of the programs of his agency. It is almost useless to explore questions of use and methodology for programs that clearly do not meet the criteria. The next and final step is both a possible source of leverage for the evaluator and a somewhat risky business in many agencies.

Clearly Naming the Problem for Others

The evaluator has now created three lists of programs: "evaluable," "potentially evaluable with further program or management definition," and "not evaluable." Since these problems are now understood to involve policy and management questions, as well as evaluation design questions, the list has two uses.

First, the evaluator should evaluate only the programs that are evaluable. He should agree to help with the definitional problems of potentially evaluable programs. But he should not hesitate to name the nature of the problem. The evaluator should tell policy makers and program managers whether their programs are or are not evaluable, and why. Second, the evaluator should bring the serious problems on the list to the attention of the top level of the agency hierarchy so they will know which programs are or are not evaluable, and why.

These actions may be very risky things to do in many agencies, but it can prevent a lot of useless evaluation attempts and later recrimination. We believe that they would force improvements in program performance as well.

Notes

1. Joseph S. Wholey, et al., *Federal Evaluation Policy* (Washington, D.C.: The Urban Institute, 1970).
2. Garth N. Buchanan and Joseph S. Wholey, "Federal Level Evaluation," *Evaluation,* Vol. 1, No. 1 (Fall 1972), pp. 17-22.
3. For a concise overview of the literature in which these criticisms have been put forward see Francis G. Caro (ed.), *Readings in Evaluation Research,* Russell Sage Foundation, 1971, pp. 9-15. In our own work we have had access to unpublished internal assessments of evaluation efforts by several federal agencies; the majority of these note agency dissatisfaction with their evaluation product and identify many of these apparent causes as major influences.
4. See John D. Waller and John W. Scanlon, *Urban Institute Plan for the Design of an Evaluation* (Washington, D.C.: The Urban Institute, March 1973).

1974 (300-308)

DONALD R. WEIDMAN

Writing a Better RFP:
Ten Hints for Obtaining More
Successful Evaluation Studies

Every year, a great many program evaluation studies are performed under contracts from government agencies. Many of these studies turn out to be low in quality, misleading, irrelevant, and generally unusable.

The existence of this problem has been noted many times, and numerous efforts to understand its causes and improve the situation have been attempted.[1] While these various analyses have a good deal of insight and experience to offer, their recommendations for the most part are of little help to the typical government official responsible for an evaluation study. Such a person usually has relatively little expertise in performing evaluation studies, does not have the authority or influence to change the program design or management system, and has a fairly short time in which to get the study effort underway. Frequently, in fact, he or she does not even have the option of deciding not to go ahead with the study effort.

The aim of this article is to offer some helpful hints which experience has shown can greatly improve the chance of success of a contracted evaluation study. The focus is on the RFP (request for proposals)—the formal invitation to prospective contractors to submit bids for performing a study.

The reason for this focus is simple. The RFP has a strong and enduring influence on the entire course of an evaluation study effort. The winning bidder prepares his/her study plan and assembles a staff specifically to accomplish what the RFP requests. The contractor has only a small amount of flexibility in deviating from the work schedule initially set forth, since he or she has budgeted for a tight schedule, using lower level professionals as much as possible, in order to obtain a low bid. The work statement in the contract is substantially the same as the "scope of work" in the RFP—since the losing bidders would, quite properly, protest any major changes. Indeed,

it is often possible to predict the ultimate success of an evaluation study simply by reading the RFP—before the contractor is selected and without any other knowledge of the program.

190

The characteristics of a good RFP for an evaluation study are not necessarily those of a good RFP for some other purpose. It is only through extensive experience that we are beginning to recognize how a good evaluation study RFP should look. The ten suggestions that follow are an attempt to distill much of this experience in a form that will be directly useful to the government official who must prepare an evaluation study RFP.

1. Be explicit about important constraints.

If you expect to be able to compare program effects in urban vs. rural areas, you must say so explicitly. It may be obvious to everyone in your agency that such a comparison is important, but it won't be obvious to the contractor. He or she may believe poverty vs. non-poverty areas to be the crucial test; and a sample chosen to perform one comparison may not work for another. Another example: if you can't allow clients to be interviewed without their prior consent, say so. In general, it is fair to expect the contractor to be (or quickly become) familiar with the program structure and operations, but you cannot expect him or her to know all of the many program experiences and unwritten policies which are common knowledge within your agency—at least, not during the crucial design stage.

2. Avoid placing unnecessary constraints.

It is equally important not to state any constraints unless they are genuinely needed. Detecting program effects is often a difficult task, even with the most sophisticated evaluation methods. Even the smallest procedural constraint can mean the difference between success and failure; what seems innocuous to the RFP writer may be disastrous to the evaluator. A favorite offense of this type is specifying sample size or composition before output measures are determined or required confidence levels are agreed upon—and yet these are essential to determining the proper sample composition. A predetermined sample is nearly always either inadequate or wasteful (or both). Other commonly specified items, which unnecessarily restrict the study, are milestones for intermediate steps in the study and composition of site visit teams. Such premature specifications of study procedures seem to be written in as indirect attempts to obtain some (usually unmentioned) essential feature. Sample size specification, for example, may be intended to achieve a desired (but unspecified) degree of confidence. Far better to specify what you want to get out of the study, and let the technical experts determine the best way of accomplishing it. A suggested rule of thumb: don't make any specifications concerning study procedures unless they are required or prohibited by law.

3. Ask for the use of standard evaluation procedures as much as possible.

An extensive amount is known about evaluation methodology by now. Using standard methods increases the probability of meeting deadlines, gives predictable levels of confidence in the results, decreases the chance of vast cost overruns, makes the findings more readily comparable to those from other studies, and generally increases the likelihood of success. Yet some RFPs go out of their way to lose these advantages by asking for the use of untested methods, giving points for "creativity," and so on. There is no benefit to such an approach. The bidders should be allowed to propose new methods and you should select them if they can prove their methods are better; but the points should be for quality, not innovation. You are seeking valid evaluation information, not an award for the most far-out evaluation study of the year.

4. Adjust your expectations to known data reliability and availability.

You often know enough about your program to know that many project records are missing, incomplete, or just plain untruthful. Perhaps data definitions have been interpreted differently in different localities. Whatever the problem, you must face up to the fact that no amount of "analysis" can get facts out of data if the facts aren't there to begin with. The RFP should not ask the evaluator to perform historical analyses and impact assessments, or any other task which can only be done using data from the past, if such data are unreliable. Sometimes government officials with considerable experience in contracting for evaluation studies make a mistake in this area. They have previously asked for analyses of this sort and the contractors have supplied them. What these officials don't realize is that they have been sold garbage. It is possible to compute lots of things from any collection of data—and even throw in some statistical tests showing internal consistency. Some contractors will calculate whatever they are asked for. But none of the "answers" have any meaning unless the data are reliable to begin with. No final impact data can be any more accurate than the baseline data. If you must have impact information, then you simply have to reconcile yourself to collecting baseline data first, waiting for some additional program effects, and collecting more data.

5. Use opinions as measures only if the program is intended to change opinions.

In other words, opinions are very poor *proxy* measures for anything. Unsystematic observations are not accurate measures of changes that have taken place. Most people, in fact, are usually extensively uninformed even about current situations. They tend to judge circumstances against their (often subconscious) expectations, rather than to observe objectively. Moreover, this sort of bias cannot be expected to "average out" by surveying large numbers of people; on the contrary, a large population sample is likely to be quite poorly informed on most questions. The only valid use of opinion surveys is to measure opinions. Unless the program had as a primary objective to change opinions, don't bother with them.

6. Require a clear separation between the results of the data collection and analysis, on the one hand, and the evaluator's judgments and intuition on the other.

There is no such thing in program evaluation as "objective opinion." An opinion may be more or less disinterested, more or less biased, but any opinion is intrinsically *subjective*, not "objective." An evaluation study must present more than just opinion, no matter whose opinion is involved. Don't forget that there will be determined efforts to discredit the evaluation findings, however they come out—and subjective opinions are rarely convincing to those who are predisposed to disagree with them. The only non-rejectable information is that which is scientifically obtained from careful measurement. This is not to say that the informed opinions of the evaluator are not important—they are. But they should be presented in a separate section clearly labeled "opinion." The RFP should make clear that the main purpose of the study is to produce unimpeachable, objectively verifiable facts.

7. Specify at least one acceptable measure of accomplishment.

More evaluation studies are rejected for being irrelevant than for any other reason: "That wasn't what the program was trying to accomplish." The problem is that official statements of program objectives are inevitably ambiguous. But evaluators must collect specific data items and produce specific output measures. Most "irrelevant" studies were honest and sensible attempts to measure ambiguous objectives—and the evaluator guessed wrong. The agency got nothing of value from the effort. If the RFP specifies at least one measure for each objective, the agency will get at least one set of usable data. There is a mistaken notion that the definition of performance measures is a technical task that the contractor ought to do. The truth is, the definition of measures is a definitional task, and ultimately a policy-setting task—since it defines what the program is trying to achieve—and the contractor cannot and should not be setting policy. One helpful rule of thumb: the evaluation questions posed in the RFP must be more precise than the official statements of program objectives.

8. Keep the questions few in number, and establish priorities.

Information is not free. Obtaining even the most sketchy and incomplete answer to a question requires adding items to a questionnaire, recording additional data in the field, performing calculations—in short, spending time and money. In addition, it is a fact that answering different questions often requires different methods. A sample that is representative for the purposes of one measure of success may not be representative for another. Someone is going to have to decide what questions are the most important to answer—with partial answers to the others falling out as time and luck permit. As a rule, you can't expect to get really good answers to more than one or two questions, no matter how expensive and lengthy the evaluation study. If they aren't the questions of most importance to the agency, the whole effort will be wasted.

9. If you want several different kinds of studies done, write several RFPs.

Management auditing, measurement of efficiency, determination of program impact, long-range policy analyses, public opinion polling, and controlled experimentations all use different techniques and require different skills. Few can put together a study team which is strong in more than one or two of these methodologies. If an RFP asks that several different kinds of studies be done in a single package, the result will be delays, poor quality work on at least part of the effort, and inefficiencies. Many government officials believe that what a contractor learns about a program from one kind of effort will somehow improve the quality of his work on another kind of effort; but experience refutes this belief. Few government officials believe that selecting and monitoring contractors for several sharply focused studies is just as quick and easy—and more satisfying—than doing one omnibus contract for a multi-pronged study; but experience shows that it is.

10. Require few formal reports from the contractor; depend on frequent informal contacts.

The more formal, written reports required from the contractor, the more the study effort will be spent on composing, typing, editing, and reproducing reports—and the less chance the contractor will have to make up for delays in data availability, to adapt procedures to take advantage of lessons learned along the way, or simply to think about the information being developed. Furthermore, written reports are nearly useless vehicles for monitoring a project's progress; if the technical monitor doesn't know what's going on through frequent informal contracts, he or she is not going to find out through contractor-prepared status reports. Ideally, each agency should have clear procedures on how contract studies are to be monitored. A rule of thumb: the RFP should ask for formal reports only if they will be needed as separate final products when the study effort is over.

These ten suggestions are not ivory tower speculations; they stem from the "real world" of evaluation contracting. Following them will not require any increase in time, manpower, or resources than an agency is already spending—although admittedly it may require challenging some deeply entrenched misconceptions. But others have done it. The rewards in improved quality and utility of evaluation findings will be worth the effort.

Note

1. See, for example, Pamela Horst et al., "Program Management and the Federal Evaluator," *Public Administration Review,* Vol. 34, No. 4 (July/August 1974), pp. 300-308; Carol H. Weiss, "Utilization of Evaluation: Toward Comparative Study," in Francis G. Caro (ed.), *Readings in Evaluation Research* (New York: Russell Sage Foundation, 1971), pp. 136-142; Joseph S. Wholey et al., "If You Don't Care Where You Get To, Then It Doesn't Matter Which Way You Go," in Gene M. Lyons (ed.), *Social Research and Public Policies* (Hanover, N.H.: Dartmouth College, 1975), pp. 175-197; and James G. Abert, "Bridging Some Gaps Between Policy-Related Research and Its Generation and Use by the Public Sector," *The Bureaucrat,* Vol. 5 (October 1976), p. 273.

ROBERT F. CLARK

The Proverbs of Evaluation:
Perspectives from CSA's Experience

In 1946, Herbert Simon published an article in *Public Administration Review* entitled "The Proverbs of Administration."[1] He noted that proverbs almost always can be arrayed in mutually contradictory pairs. One example was "Look before you leap!" as contrasted with "He who hesitates is lost."

Similar examples spring readily to mind. "Absence makes the heart grow fonder" is contradicted by "out of sight, out of mind." Similarly, "Money is the root of all evil" is offset by "A heavy purse makes a light heart." Finally, "A good conscience is a continual feast" confronts the more cynical view that "Conscience is that small voice which warns us that someone may be looking."

Simon then pointed out that the field of administration is dominated by certain principles or "proverbs." For each of these, however, one can conjure up a set of circumstances which either undermine or at least constrain severely the application of the principle.

Let us take just two of these principles. One asserts that administrative efficiency depends on unity of command. Simon describes a situation in which an accountant in a school department is subordinate to an educator. If unity of command is observed slavishly, the accountant cannot take technical direction from the finance department. Evidently some "duality of command" is called for. Where two authoritative commands conflict, a subordinate should know which individual in the hierarchy he or she is expected to follow. However, on a day to day basis, employees in an organization must themselves reconcile conflicting commands from many different authoritative sources.[2]

The second principle is that greater efficiency is achieved with a more limited span of control. Sometimes a ratio of six or seven subordinates per supervisor is given as an outer limit. Unfortunately, this principle is offset by the notion that organizations should seek to reduce the number of levels through which individuals must report. In large organizations or highly scientific enterprises, it may be advisable to widen the span of control in order to reduce the number of reporting levels. In short, depending on their mission, organizations face a choice between structuring a broad-based, relatively flat pyramid and a tall, narrow pyramid. Span of control emerges as a highly relative proposition.[3]

Just as with administration, there have grown up in recent years what we might call the proverbs of evaluation. For a field which relies so heavily on empirical verification, it is surprising how many of these proverbs have found their way into the conventional wisdom with little to recommend them beyond a surface plausibility.

I would like to cite three such proverbs. I would then propose to examine each of them in the light of recent experience in the U.S. Community Services Administration and other available evidence.

By way of background, the Community Services Administration is a small independent federal agency whose primary mission is to help "eliminate the paradox of poverty in the midst of plenty." The agency carries out this mission through a number of programs which are designed to attack the causes and conditions of poverty at the local level and promote greater self-sufficiency among low-income groups.

The programs administered by CSA include community food and nutrition, energy conservation, housing, senior opportunities and services, summer youth and recreation, community economic development, and a variety of research and demonstration programs. By far, the largest is the local initiative program, under which communities enjoy considerable flexibility in planning and carrying out local anti-poverty activities. CSA provides grant-in-aid assistance to a national network of some 870 community action agencies and 41 community development corporations, as well as a number of limited purpose agencies. The agency has approximately 1,000 employees divided among its headquarters and 10 regional offices. The total agency budget for fiscal year 1979 was $545 million.

The evaluation function in CSA is centralized in the Evaluation Research Division, which is located in the Office of Policy, Planning and Evaluation. In the regional offices, there are personnel who combine evaluation with other duties. While they report to the regional director, they receive planning guidance, technical direction and resources for their evaluation activities from headquarters.

First Proverb: The Experimental Design

The first proverb of evaluation is that methodologically the standard of excellence is represented by the experimental design. Essentially, this means the random assignment of the eligible target population to treatment and control groups and the selection, measurement, and comparison of key variables over time. In the roster of evaluation methods, experimental designs invariably take precedence over quasi-experimental and non-experimental designs.[4]

The issue of which evaluation method is most appropriate is often treated as a technical problem alone, whereas it entails administrative and budgetary considerations as well. In the most obvious case, an experimental design may be desirable, but resource constraints are prohibitive. Under other circumstances, a time series design with or without controls may be preferred in order to detect the shape and direction of program trends. Unless there are unimpeachable bodies of historical records, a new data base will have to be constructed. A multiple time series design could conceivably extend the total time line of an evaluation beyond the point where the findings will prove useful to anyone but outside researchers. Consistent with acceptable standards of validity and reliability, there are advantages to reducing to the extent possible the amount of original field data collection and focusing scarce evaluation resources heavily on the policy analytic and utilization aspects of program evaluation.

In CSA, we employ multiple methods and multiple measures in the conduct of program evaluations. We are probably too eclectic (and therefore non-scientific) in the eyes of the social science community, but we have found such flexibility to be necessary. Our "clients," the agency program managers, usually want the answers to a large number of questions about program effects; we endeavor to accommodate their interests consistent with a credible analytical framework. At the national level, we have undertaken what might be called descriptive assessments of certain programs. While they employ standard data collection protocols, they in effect yield comparative case studies across a sample of project sites. The objective is to make heuristic judgments about overall program effects within a limited time period and develop recommendations about program policy, management, regulations, funding criteria, and technical support. At the same time they provide a basis for designing a more rigorous impact evaluation subsequently.

Where the program data base is amenable, we conduct more experimentally-based evaluations aimed at determining the national impact of programs. A pre-test, post-test design with controls is most feasible when evaluation is built in at an early stage in the development of a demonstration program. Even in such cases, field data collection can extend over one or two years, a fact which bears on the potential utility of the findings. In the current study of a rural home repair demonstration program, which is serving as a pilot for a potentially larger operational program, the final results will not be available until after the legislative reauthorization cycle is well underway. Consequently, we will have to rely extensively on interim reports in providing information and policy advice to senior agency officials. While it is not likely that the final results will differ significantly from the interim, there is an undeniable element of risk.

It is tempting to say that, all things being equal, the experimental design is preferable. The difficulty is that, in administrative settings, things are rarely "equal," in the sense that rigorous experimental evaluation corresponds neatly with the content and timing of policymaker needs. Nor can one argue that the solution is to approximate the experimental design as nearly as possible. The selection of methods and measures tends to be much more situational, depending on the questions to be addressed and the schedule of decisions to be influenced.

These considerations suggest that there is a counterpart to the first evaluation proverb. While the experimental design may be preferred in theory, multiple methods and multiple measures often yield more usable results.[5]

Second Proverb: Program Manager Involvement

The second evaluation proverb is that greater credibility is assured when program managers are intimately involved in the design, conduct, and interpretation of an evaluation. This proverb has great appeal, since it promises to help reduce the legendary tension between researchers and action personnel. Beyond its potential incompatibility with the first proverb, this one, applied uncritically, can generate counterproductive effects.

In the first instance, program managers and other users of evaluation findings are not passive. They will act to project their needs into the evaluation whether or not they fit tidily with the proposed methodology. The positive aspect is that the evaluation gains a more precise sense of direction. The latent negative consequence is that it can begin to lose its analytical focus. Program managers who are not cognizant of the limitations of evaluation may expect from it the answers to most of their problems. In an effort to be accommodating, evaluators can continue incorporating issues and questions for study to the point that their reach exceeds their grasp.

Under OMB Circular A-40, *Management of Federal Reporting Requirements* (May 3, 1973, revised), the Office of Management and Budget reserves the right to review and approve data collection instruments which are sponsored by a federal agency and which are administered to 10 or more human subjects. In designing the survey instruments for one particular evaluation, the evaluation contractor with our encouragement drew heavily on the concerns and experiences of the program manager. As a result, the survey instruments contained a large number of open-ended questions. When the package of instruments was submitted to OMB, it was rejected on the grounds that open-ended questions would place too great a burden on respondents and would yield answers of questionable analytical value.

This experience indicates that the interaction between evaluation and program personnel should emphasize a narrowing rather than a broadening of the analytical perspective. In the final analysis, the professional judgment of the evaluator should prevail. Further, one ignores at one's peril the presence of the "silent partner" at these deliberations, namely the Office of Management and Budget. It is not enough for evaluation and program personnel to agree on the focus of a study. They must also endeavor to anticipate the reaction of OMB on the question of public burden.

It is also true that involving program managers in all phases of an evaluation takes time. The consequence of this appears rarely to be taken into account in the literature. The net effect of such involvement is to extend the total time line of an evaluation. Involvement requires the coordination of schedules, the exploration of issues, the building of consensus, agreements on course of action, and follow through on commitments. From the standpoint of the evaluator, involvement is repaid by the enhanced willingness of program managers to cooperate in the data collection phases and to use the results in program policy making. If involvement contributes to a delay in the generation of results, however, it may diminish their value for those same program managers who must make decisions within certain time frames in response to other outside pressures and demands.

These caveats aside, there are several clear advantages to involving program offices and, where feasible, local project operators in the establishment of evaluation parameters. For example, CSA has undertaken an evaluation of 51 State Economic Opportunity Offices (SEOO); at our request, the national SEOO association set up an evaluation committee with which we communicate on various phases of the evaluation. This arrangement yields two benefits, one from their standpoint, one from ours. From CSA's standpoint, the existence of a formal committee means that there is a designated entity with which to interact on evaluation issues; this reduces the incidence of random comment or isolated complaint. From the SEOO standpoint, there is greater confidence in the intent and soundness of the evaluation design and more incentive to use the results constructively.

Scriven has proposed the notion of meta-evaluation, which means simply the evaluation of evaluation.[6] It appears to be true that no involvement of action personnel in the evaluation process diminishes an appreciation for the findings and undermines their utility. On the other hand, total involvement can delay the production of findings in a timely fashion and again adversely affect their utilization. A question for meta-evaluation might then be: What type and degree of involvement by program managers is most consistent with the timely production and effective use of evaluation findings? In addition to problems of design and method, more attention must be paid to the administrative and budgetary context within which evaluation planning occurs.

The second proverb, therefore, cannot be applied injudiciously. It too has its counterpart. The involvement of non-evaluators is desirable; however, carried to extremes, it can adversely affect the quality and timeliness of evaluation findings.

Third Proverb: Focus on Decision Making

The third and final evaluation proverb is that evaluation results should affect specific and discrete program decisions.[7] It is not often that evaluation planners begin with the proposition that Evaluation X should yield findings by such-and-such a date for Program Manager Y in order to influence his Decision Z concerning Matters A, B, and C. Whether they do or not, there is a widespread belief that evaluation findings are not being used by those for whom they are intended. The test which is applied either explicitly or implicitly is whether or not the evaluation led to program decisions concerning authorization, design, appropriations, regulations, funding criteria, administrative practices or technical support.

In CSA's experience, evaluation exerts an influence on decision making, though perhaps in ways not always anticipated. In one case, the agency requested comments on an evaluation in progress from an outside consultant. These comments included data on the population at risk and therefore eligible for program benefits. At the request of the director of the agency, the comments accompanied by the population data were transmitted. These data were drawn upon by the director in her discussions with the Office of Management and Budget in support of a new program authority. This along with other factors was helpful in securing approval for the program, which was included as part of the president's budget for fiscal year 1980. Meanwhile the evaluation itself is proceeding; in its final form it may or may not exert an equivalent effect on agency program decisions.

In another case, a regional office withdrew funding from a large urban CAA which on most counts was in compliance with agency regulations and which delivered services in a reasonably efficient manner. The evaluation had concluded that the CAA was administratively sound but programmatically deficient. While delivering services efficiently, it was falling short in its more vital mission—to advocate for low income persons, to mobilize community resources, to involve low income groups in its programming and to foster community-based planning around poverty issues. This evaluation demonstrated that an organization could function well administratively, yet fail to act as a true community action agency.

The question of the utility of evaluation findings is emerging as a field for empirical inquiry. As a form of meta-evaluation, it contrasts with the speculative, often pessimistic tone of observers like Weiss,[8] Wholey,[9] and Davis and Salasin.[10] For instance, Weeks distinguishes between conceptual utilization and instrumental utilization.[11] The latter refers to the direct application of findings to specific program decisions; the former pertains to the cumulative influence of findings from several studies in shaping the thinking in a problem area.

Based on a survey of 57 local projects in California, Weeks finds a high degree of instrumental utilization. He is also led to expect that at the federal level utilization would be more conceptual than instrumental. Weeks underscores the unintended beneficial side effects of evaluation, which include, at least at the local level, the clarification of program goals and a greater curiosity about what works and what does not.[12]

Summary: Proverbs and Their Counterparts

It is perhaps timely to recapitulate. The proverbs of evaluation, like other proverbs, appear to serve us better when they come in contrasting pairs. For each of the three proverbs we have been examining, there exists a counterpart.

Proverb Number 1. Methodologically, the standard of excellence is the experimental design. On the other hand: Multiple methods and multiple measures often produce more usable findings.

Proverb Number 2. The greater the involvement of program personnel in evaluation, the higher the credibility of the results. On the other hand: The involvement of non-evaluators in the research process can compromise the quality and timeliness of results.

Proverb Number 3. The test of good evaluation is its effect on specific program decisions. On the other hand: The cumulative influence of evaluation research, including side benefits, is real and significant, even if not easily traceable.

CSA's experience suggests that while the first in each pair of evaluation proverbs reflects a sound academic orientation, the second is better attuned to operational realities. There is little doubt that governmental agencies suffer from a dearth of trained social scientists capable of performing first-rate evaluation research. It is equally the case that even trained evaluators cannot carry out their function effectively, unless they are prepared to adapt their methods to contextual, structural, and programmatic conditions. Additionally, governmental agencies need to devise systems which not only lead to the production of evaluative information, but which facilitate its flow from those who produce it to those who can best use it.

At both the academic and practitioner levels, evaluation needs to be examined as a subsystem, which acts interdependently with other public agency subsystems. In addition to research, attention must be focused on research administration. Evaluation will continue to be regarded in many quarters as an expensive frill unless and until appropriate linkages can be forged between it and other governmental functions. Every step in the evaluation cycle needs to be analyzed in order to eliminate those which unnecessarily create delay in the timely communication of useful findings, analyses and recommendations.

In an era of fiscal conservatism, evaluators must concentrate on realistic evaluation planning within a socio-political context. They must be prepared to account for the expenditure of public funds on evaluation research rather than direct program services. By endeavoring to reconcile the proverbs of evaluation within the constraints imposed by governmental structures, they are more likely to generate valid, timely, and useful information. The result in turn will be better-designed, better-managed, most cost-effective policies and programs. Such a result would reinforce evaluation as an intellectually challenging enterprise as well as a fiscally sound investment.

Notes

1. Herbert Simon, "The Proverbs of Administration," *Public Administration Review*, Vol. 6 (Winter, 1946), pp. 53-67.
2. Op. cit.
3. Op. cit.
4. Peter H. Rossi and S.R. Wright, "Evaluation Research: An Assessment of Theory, Practice and Politics," *Evaluation Quarterly*, Vol. 1, No. 1, p. 13.
5. Francis G. Caro, "Approaches to Evaluative Research: A Review," *Human Organization*, Vol. 28, No. 2, pp. 87-99.
6. Michael Scriven, "An Introduction to Meta-Evaluation," *Educational Product Report*, Vol. 2, No. 5, 1969, pp. 36-38.
7. Michael Q. Patton, *Utilization-Focused Evaluation*, Beverly Hills, Calif.: Sage, 1978, p. 28.
8. Carol Weiss, *Evaluation Research*, Englewood Cliffs, New Jersey: Prentice-Hall, 1972, p. 3.
9. Joseph Wholey, "Contributions of Social Intervention Research to Government Practices," in Irvin A. Kraft, ed. *Critical Human Behavioral Issues in Social Intervention Programs, Annals of the New York Academy of Sciences*, Vol. 218, June 22, 1973, p. 37.
10. Howard R. Davis and Susan E. Salasin, "The Utilization of Evaluation," in Elmer E. Struening and Marcia Guttentag, eds., *Handbook of Evaluation Research*, Beverly Hills, Calif.: Sage, 1975, Vol. 1, p. 625.
11. Edward C. Weeks, "The Managerial Use of Evaluation Findings at the Local Level," paper presented at the Annual Meeting of the American Society for Public Administration, Baltimore, Maryland, April 1-4, 1979.
12. Op. cit.

1979 (562-566)

CAROL H. WEISS

The Many Meanings of Research Utilization

This is a time when more and more social scientists are becoming concerned about making their research useful for public policy makers, and policy makers are displaying spurts of well publicized concern about the usefulness of the social science research that government funds support. There is mutual interest in whether social science research intended to influence policy is actually "used," but before that important issue can profitably be addressed it is essential to understand what "using research" actually means.

A review of the literature reveals that a diverse array of meanings is attached to the term. Much of the ambiguity in the discussion of "research utilization"—and conflicting interpretations of its prevalence and the routes by which it occurs—derives from conceptual confusion. If we are to gain a better understanding of the extent to which social science research has affected public policy in the past, and learn how to make its contribution more effective in the future, we need to clarify the concept.

Upon examination, the use of social science research in the sphere of public policy is an extraordinarily complex phenomenon. Authors who have addressed the subject have evoked diverse images of the processes and purposes of utilization. Here I will try to extract seven different meanings that have been associated with the concept.

The Knowledge-Driven Model

The first image of research utilization is probably the most venerable in the literature and derives from the natural sciences. It assumes the following sequence of events: basic research → applied research → development → application. The notion is that basic research discloses some opportunity that may have relevance for public policy; applied research is conducted to define and test the findings of basic research for practical action; if all goes

203

well, appropriate technologies are developed to implement the findings; whereupon application occurs.[1]

Examples of this model of research utilization generally come from the physical sciences: biochemical research makes available oral contraceptive pills, research in electronics enables television to multiply the number of broadcast channels. Because of the fruits of basic research, new applications are developed and new policies emerge.[2]

The assumption is that the sheer fact that knowledge exists presses it toward development and use. However well or poorly this model describes events in the natural sciences,[3] in the social sciences few examples can be found. The reasons appear to be several. Social science knowledge is not apt to be so compelling or authoritative as to drive inevitably toward implementation. Social science knowledge does not readily lend itself to conversion into replicable technologies, either material or social. Perhaps most important, unless a social condition has been consensually defined as a pressing social problem, and unless the condition has become fully politicized and debated, and the parameters of potential action agreed upon, there is little likelihood that policy-making bodies will be receptive to the results of social science research.

I do not mean to imply that basic research in the social sciences is not useful for policy making. Certainly many social policies and programs of government are based, explicitly or implicitly, on basic psychological, sociological, economic, anthropological, and political scientific understandings. When they surface to affect government decisions, however, it is not likely to be through the sequence of events posited in this model.

Problem-Solving Model

The most common concept of research utilization involves the direct application of the results of a specific social science study to a pending decision. The expectation is that research provides empirical evidence and conclusions that help to solve a policy problem. The model is again a linear one, but the steps are different from those in the knowledge-driven model. Here the decision drives the application of research. A problem exists and a decision has to be made, information or understanding is lacking either to generate a solution to the problem or to select among alternative solutions, research provides the missing knowledge. With the gap filled, a decision is reached.

Implicit in this model is a sense that there is a consensus on goals. It is assumed that policy makers and researchers tend to agree on what the desired end state shall be. The main contribution of social science research is to help identify and select appropriate means to reach the goal.

The evidence that social science research provides for the decision-making process can be of several orders. It can be qualitative and descriptive, e.g., rich observational accounts of social conditions or of program processes. It can be quantitative data, either on relatively soft indicators, e.g., public attitudes, or on hard factual matters, e.g., number of hospital beds. It can be statistical relationships between variables, generalized conclusions about the associations among factors, even relatively abstract (middle-range) theories about cause and effect. Whatever the nature of the empirical evidence that social science research supplies, the expectation is that it clarifies the situation and reduces uncertainty, and therefore, it influences the decision that policy makers make.

In this formulation of research utilization, there are two general ways in which social science research can enter the policy-making arena. First, the research antedates the policy problem and is drawn in on need. Policy makers faced with a decision may go out and search for information from pre-existent research to delimit the scope of the question or identify a promising policy response. Or the information can be called to their attention by aides, staff analysts, colleagues, consultants, or social science researchers. Or thay may happen upon it in professional journals, agency newsletters, newspapers and magazines, or at conferences. There is an element of chance in this route from problem to research to decision. Available research may not directly fit the problem. The location of appropriate research, even with sophisticated and computerized information systems, may be difficult. Inside experts and outside consultants may fail to come up with relevant sources. The located information may appear to be out-of-date or not generalizable to the immediate context. Whether or not the best and most relevant research reaches the person with the problem depends on the efficiency of the communications links. Therefore, when this imagery of reseach utilization prevails, the usual prescription for improving the use of research is to improve the means of communication to policy makers.

A second route to problem-solving use is the purposeful commissioning of social science research and analysis to fill the knowledge gap. The assumptions, as with the search route, are that decision makers have a clear idea of their goals and a map of acceptable alternatives and that they have identified some specific informational needs to clarify their choice. This time they engage social scientists to provide the data, analytic generalizations, and possibly the interpretations of these generalizations to the case in hand by way of recommendations. The process follows this sequence: definition of pending decision → identification of missing knowledge → acquisition of social science research → interpretation of the research for the decision context → policy choice.

The expectation is that research generated in this type of sequence, even more than research located through search procedures, will have direct and immediate applicability and will be used for decision making. In fact, it is usually assumed that the specific study commissioned by the responsible government office will have an impact and that its recommendations will affect ensuing choices. Particularly the large-scale government-contracted policy study, tailored to the specifications set by government staff, is expected to make a difference in plans, programs, and policies. If the research goes unused, the prescription to improve utilization that arises from this imagery is to increase government control over both the specification of requested research and its conduct in the field. If the research had actually met decision makers' information needs, it is assumed, it would have been used.

Even a cursory review of the fate of social science research, including policy research on government-defined issues, suggests that these kinds of expectations are wildly optimistic. Occasional studies have direct effect on decisions, but usually on relatively low-level, narrow-gauge decisions. Most studies appear to come and go without leaving any discernible mark on the direction or substance of policy. It probably takes an extraordinary concatenation of circumstances for research to influence policy decisions directly: a well defined decision situation, a set of policy actors who have responsibility and jurisdiction for making the decision, an issue whose resolution depends at least to some extent on *information,* identification of the requisite informational need, research that provides the information in terms that match the circumstances within which choices will be made, research findings that are clear-cut, unambiguous, firmly supported, and powerful, that reach decision makers at the time they are wrestling with the issues, that are comprehensible and understood, and that do not run counter to strong political interests. Because chances are small that all these conditions will fall into line around any one issue, the problem-solving model of research use probably describes a relatively small number of cases.

However, the problem-solving model remains the prevailing imagery of research utilization. Its prevalence probably accounts for much of the disillusionment about the contribution of social science research to social policy. Because people expect research use to occur through the sequence of stages posited by this model, they become discouraged when events do not take the expected course. However, there are other ways in which social science research can be "used" in policy making.

Interactive Model

Another way that social science research can enter the decision arena is as part of an interactive search for knowledge. Those engaged in developing policy seek information not only from social scientists but from a variety of sources—administrators, practitioners, politicians, planners, journalists, clients, interest groups, aides, friends, and social scientists, too. The process is not one of linear order from research to decision but a disorderly set of interconnections and back-and-forthness that defies neat diagrams.

All kinds of people involved in an issue area pool their talents, beliefs, and understandings in an effort to make sense of a problem. Social scientists are one set of participants among many. Seldom do they have conclusions available that bear directly and explicitly on the issue at hand. More rarely still do they have a body of convergent evidence. Nevertheless, they can engage in mutual consultations that progressively move closer to potential policy responses.

Donnison describes this interactive model of research use in the development of two pieces of legislation in Great Britain. He notes that decisions could not wait upon completion of research but had to be made when political circumstances compelled.

> Research workers could not present authoritative findings for others to apply; neither could others commission them to find the "correct" solution to policy problems: they were not that kind of problem. Those in the four fields from which experience had to be brought to bear [politics, technology, practice, and research] contributed on equal terms. Each was expert in a few things, ignorant about most things, offered what he could, and generally learnt more than he could teach.[4]

In this model, the use of research is only one part of a complicated process that also uses experience, political insight, pressure, social technologies, and judgment. It has applicability not only to face-to-face settings but also to the multiple ways in which intelligence is gathered through intermediaries and brought to bear. It describes a familiar process by which decision makers inform themselves of the range of knowledge and opinion in a policy area.

Political Model

Often the constellation of interests around a policy issue predetermines the positions that decision makers take. Or debate has gone on over a period of years and opinions have hardened. At this point, decision makers are not likely to be receptive to new evidence from social science research. For reasons of interest, ideology, or intellect, they have taken a stand that research is not likely to shake.

In such cases, research can still be used. It becomes ammunition for the side that finds its conclusions congenial and supportive. Partisans flourish the evidence in an attempt to neutralize opponents, convince waverers, and bolster supporters. Even if conclusions have to be ripped out of context (with suppression of qualifications and of evidence "on the other hand"), research becomes grist to the mill.

Social scientists tend to look askance at the impressment of research results into service for a position that decision makers have taken on other grounds. They generally see it as an illegitimate attempt to "use" research (in the pejorative sense) for self-serving purposes of agency justification and personal aggrandizement. Using research to support a predetermined position is, however, research utilization, too, in a form which would seem to be neither an unimportant nor improper use. Only distortion and misinterpretation of findings are illegitimate. To the extent that the research, accurately interpreted, supports the position of one group, it gives the advocates of that position confidence, reduces their uncertainties, and provides them an edge in the continuing debate. Since the research finds ready-made partisans who will fight for its implementation, it stands a better chance of making a difference in the outcome.[5]

One of the appropriate conditions for this model of research use is that all parties to the issue have access to the evidence. If, for example, bureaucrats monopolize research that would support the position of clients, then equity is not served, but when research is available to all participants in the policy process, research as political ammunition can be a worthy model of utilization.

Tactical Model

There are occasions when social science research is used for purposes that have little relation to the substance of the research. It is not the content of the findings that is invoked but the sheet fact that research is being done. For example, government agencies confronted with demands for action may respond by saying, "Yes, we know that's an important need. We're doing research on it right now." Research becomes proof of their responsiveness. Faced with unwelcome demands, they may use research as a tactic for delaying action ("We are waiting until the research is completed . . .").

Sometimes government agencies use research to deflect criticism. By claiming that their actions were based on the implications and recommendations of social science research studies, they may try to avoid responsibility for unpopular policy outcomes. Or support for a research program can become a tactic for enhancing the prestige of the agency by allying it with social scientists of high repute. Some agencies support substantial amounts of research and in so doing, build a constituency of academic supporters who rally to their defense when appropriations are under congressional review. These are illustrations of uses of research, irrespective of its conclusions, as a tactic in bureaucratic politics.

Enlightenment Model

Perhaps the way in which social science research most frequently enters the policy arena is through the process that has come to be called "enlightenment."[6] Here it is not the findings of a single study nor even of a body of related studies that directly affect policy. Rather it is the concepts and theoretical perspectives that social science research has engendered that permeate the policy-making process.

There is no assumption in this model that decision makers seek out social science research when faced with a policy issue or even that they are receptive to, or aware of, specific research conclusions. The imagery is that of social science generalizations and orientations percolating through informed publics and coming to shape the way in which people think about social issues. Social science research diffuses circuitously through manifold channels—professional journals, the mass media, conversations with colleagues—and over time the variables it deals with and the generalizations it offers provide decision makers with ways of making sense out of a complex world.

Rarely will policy makers be able to cite the findings of a specific study that influenced their decisions, but they have a sense that social science research has given them a backdrop of ideas and orientations that has had important consequences.[7] Research sensitizes decision makers to new issues and helps turn what were non-problems into policy problems. A recent example is child abuse.[8] Conversely, research may convert existing problems into non-problems, e.g., marijuana use. Research can drastically revise the way that policy makers define issues, e.g., acceptable rates of unemployment, the facets of the issue they view as susceptible to alteration, and the alternative measures they consider. It helps to change the parameters within which policy solutions are sought. In the long run, along with other influences, it often redefines the policy agenda.

Unlike the problem-solving model, this model of research use does not assume that, in order to be useful, research results must be compatible with decision makers' values and goals. Research that challenges current verities may work its way into official consciousness[9] and, with support from dissident undergrounds, overturn accustomed values and patterns of thought.

The notion of research utilization in the enlightenment mode has a comforting quality. It seems to promise that, without any special effort, truth will triumph; but the enlightenment process has its full share of deficiencies. When research diffuses to the policy sphere through indirect and unguided channels, it dispenses invalid as well as valid generalizations. Many of the social science understandings that gain currency are partial, oversimplified, inadequate, or wrong. There are no procedures for screening out the shoddy and obsolete. Sometimes unexpected or sensational research results, however incomplete or inadequately supported by data, take the limelight. As an environmental researcher has noted, "Bad science, being more newsworthy, will tend to be publicized and seized on by some to support their convictions."[10] The indirect diffusion process is vulnerable to over-simplification and distortion, and it may come to resemble "endarkenment" as much as enlightenment.

Moreover, the enlightenment model is an inefficient means for reaching policy audiences. Many vital results of social science research never penetrate to decision-making centers. Some results take so long to come into currency that they are out-of-date by the time they arrive, their conclusions having been modified, or even contradicted, by later and more comprehensive analysis.

Finally, recent reviews of research on poverty, incomes, unemployment, and education suggest that social science research has not led to convergent conclusions.[11] As more studies are done, they often elaborate rather than simplify. They generate complex, varied, and even contradictory views of the social phenomena under study, rather than cumulating into sharper and more coherent explanation. The effect may be to widen and enrich our understanding of the multiple facets of reality, but the implications for policy are *less* simple and clear-cut. When the diverse research conclusions enter the policy arena, the direction they provide for policy is confused. Advocates of almost any policy prescription are likely to find some research generalizations in circulation to support their points of view.

Research as Part of the Intellectual Enterprise of the Society

A final view of research utilization looks upon social science research as one of the intellectual pursuits of a society. It is not so much an independent variable whose effects on policy remain to be determined as it is another of the dependent variables, collateral with policy—and with philosophy, journalism, history, law, and criticism. Like policy, social science research responds to the currents of thought, the fads and fancies, of the period. Social science and policy interact, influencing each other and being influenced by the larger fashions of social thought.

It is often emerging policy interest in a social issue that leads to the appropriation of funds for social science research in the first place, and only with the availability of funds are social scientists attracted to study of the issue. Early studies may accept the parameters set by the policy discussion, limiting investigation to those aspects of the issue that have engaged official attention. Later, as social science research widens its horizons, it may contribute to reconceptualization of the issue by policy makers. Meanwhile, both the policy and research colloquies may respond, consciously or unconsciously, to concerns sweeping through intellectual and popular thought ("citizen participation," "local control," spiraling inflation, individual privacy). In this view, research is one part of the interconnected intellectual enterprise.

These, then, are some of the meanings that "the use of social science research" can carry. Probably all of them are applicable in some situations. Certainly none of them represents a fully satisfactory answer to the question of how a polity best mobilizes its research resources to inform public action.

An understanding of the diversity of perspectives on research utilization may serve many purposes. For one, it may help to overcome the disenchantment with the usefulness of social science research that has afflicted those who search for use only in problem-solving contexts. For another, it may enable us to engage in empirical study of the policy uses of research with better awareness of its diverse and often subtle manifestations; if immediate impact of a specific study on a specific decision is only one indicator of use, we will have to devise more complex but more appropriate modes of study.

Finally, we may need to think more deeply about the proper role of social science in public-policy making. There has been much glib rhetoric about the vast benefits that social science can offer if only policy makers paid attention. Perhaps it is time for social scientists to pay attention to the imperatives of policy-making systems and to consider soberly what they can do, not necessarily to increase the use of research, but to improve the contribution that research makes to the wisdom of social policy.

Notes

1. An example of R.G. Havelock, *Planning for Innovation through Dissemination and Utilization of Knowledge,* Ann Arbor, Mich.: Institute for Social Research, 1969, Chapter 1.

2. See Julius H. Comroe, Jr. and Robert D. Dripps, "Scientific Basis for the Support of Biomedical Science," *Science* (April 9, 1976), Vol. 192, pp. 105-111 for a review of basic research that led to important clinical advances in treatment of cardiovascular and pulmonary diseases.

3. There is some evidence that even in areas of need in the natural sciences, basic research does not necessarily push toward application. For example, Project Hindsight indicated faster, and probably greater, use of basic science when it was *directed* toward filling a recognized need in weapons technology. C.W. Sherwin et al., *First Interim Report on Project Hindsight* (Summary), Defense Documentation Center, June 1966. Also C.W. Sherwin and Raymond S. Isenson, "Project Hindsight," *Science,* Vol. CLVI (June 23, 1967).

4. David Donnison, "Research for Policy," *Minerva,* Vol. 10, No. 4 (1972), pp. 519-536, citation p. 527.

5. Carol H. Weiss, "Where Politics and Evaluation Research Meet," *Evaluation,* Vol. 1, No. 3 (1973), pp. 37-45.

6. Morris Janowitz, "Professionalization of Sociology," *American Journal of Sociology,* Vol. 78 (1972), pp. 105-135; Elisabeth T. Crawford and Albert D. Biderman, "The Func-

tions of Policy-Oriented Social Science," in Crawford and Biderman (eds.), *Social Scientists and International Affairs* (New York: Wiley, 1969), pp. 233-243.

7. See, for example, Nathan Caplan, Andrea Morrison, and R. Stambaugh, *The Use of Social Science Knowledge in Policy Decisions at the National Level,* Ann Arbor, Mich.: Institute for Social Research, 1975.

8. Janet Weiss, "Using Social Science for Social Policy," *Policy Studies Journal,* Vol. 4, No. 3 (Spring 1976), p. 236.

9. Henry Aaron, *Politics and the Professors,* Washington, D.C.: Brookings, 1978.

10. Cyril Comar, "Bad Science and Social Penalties," *Science* (June 16, 1978), Vol. 200, p. 1225.

11. Aaron, *op. cit.* Also David K. Cohen and Janet A. Weiss, "Social Science and Social Policy: Schools and Race," in C.H. Weiss (ed.), *Using Social Research in Public Policy Making,* Lexington, Mass.: Lexington/Heath, 1977, pp. 67-83.

1979 (426-431)

GERALD L. BARKDOLL

Type III Evaluations:
Consultation and Consensus

The fantasy of program evaluation involves three imaginary characters:
(1) a top executive who supports and uses the results of evaluations to make
important decisions, (2) a program manager who encourages and supports
the evaluation of his/her program, and (3) a program analyst whose insightful recommendations produce "slam bang" changes in the efficiency
and effectiveness of the program.

The reality of program evaluation frequently contrasts markedly with the
fantasy. It includes: (1) a top executive who distrusts or ignores any evaluation done by anyone else, (2) a program manager who uses guerrilla or
subversive tactics to thwart, mislead, and discredit evaluations and
evaluators, and (3) program analysts whose efforts are equally divided between survival and the advocacy of personal agendas with little time left for
clinical, unbiased, independent assessment.

This case study describes one agency's (the Food and Drug Administration[1]) efforts to improve the quality, acceptance, and use of evaluation, i.e.,
to more closely approximate the evaluation fantasy. The evolution of
evaluation at FDA has proceeded through three distinct phases, each
distinguished by a different type of evaluation activity. Each of these types
of evaluation is described in terms of the characterizing dimensions such as
analytical techniques, participants' roles and activities, and acceptance. The
first two types of evaluations (Type I and Type II) practiced in FDA are
widely used by other organizations; however, the Type III evaluations are
unique or, at least, rarely practiced.[2] The success of the Type III evaluations
in FDA may suggest solutions to the problems encountered by practitioners
of Type I and II evaluations.

Type I Evaluation

Type I evaluation was practiced in FDA until the early 1970s. It is called
(in retrospect) "investigative reporting" and "critical parent." It was large-

ly an internal extension of one of the basic functions of a regulatory agency—surveillance and compliance. The FDA constantly monitors the manufacturing and quality control functions of the industries it regulates, and initiates corrective actions such as seizures, injunctions, and prosecutions against firms whose performance or products fall outside prescribed standards. Type I evaluation was simply this surveillance/compliance model applied to the performance and behavior of FDA managers and programs.

Program analysts (like inspectors) were rewarded when they found something wrong. In fact, many of the program analysts were former inspectors who had turned their attention from products and manufacturers to management. Their motto was: "You've got to find the problem before you can fix it." Type I evaluations almost always focused on problem identification and frequently extended to the assignment of responsibility (or guilt).

The attitude of the program analyst was one of the distinguishing characteristics of Type I evaluation. In many respects the analyst's attitude and approach was that of a "parent" as defined by transactional analysis. If the analyst was sufficiently aggressive and confident, he or she presumed the role of parent. The less confident analyst assumed the role of parent perceived in the commissioner. The program manager's response as another parent, or a child, or an adult virtually assured a confrontation or other dysfunctional activity.

In one sense, Type I evaluation was spectacularly successful since even the least experienced analyst could find some problems. This is not surprising since the problems that were identified usually involved the shortfall or underachievement of a program's performance measured against a standard chosen by the analyst. The analyst looking for a problem simply had to select different standards of performance until he or she found one beyond the program's present level of achievement. L.W. Green[3] has described the various standards available for evaluation efforts. These have been paraphrased below to show the ease of demonstrating program shortfalls by providing a moving target for the program manager to shoot at:

(1) historical standards: e.g., this year's performance versus last year's performance.
(2) normative standards: e.g., a program's performance versus the performance of similar or comparable program or versus regional, national, or international standards.
(3) theoretical standards: the design or "if everything went right" standard, given the existing resource limitations.
(4) absolute standards: e.g., the zero defect standard independent of resource limitations.

(5) negotiated or compromised standards: based on a standard-setting process such as managing by objectives.

Type I evaluations produced one of three results: (1) a quick fix of the problem, (2) a heated debate resulting from unrealistic expectations, or (3) random and unexpected reactions from program managers. The quick-fix solutions were the characteristic that made this an attractive technique. The technique was particularly attractive to the impatient, frustrated, and short-term executive. Unrealistic expectations frequently developed from the concept that "every problem has a solution" without consideration of the constraints of limited resources, the existing scientific state of the art, or the legislative mandate. Some old problems were resurrected, debated, and laid back to rest without substantive progress being made; this unproductive "cycling" added to both manager and analyst frustrations.

The program managers' random and unexpected reactions from Type I evaluations ranged from stone-walling to aggressive counter-attacks. In retrospect these random reactions are understandable and predictable given the primary (and primal) motivational force of Type I evaluations—pain avoidance. If the program manager being evaluated cannot tolerate the humiliation of publicly exposed faults, flaws, and shortfalls, he or she may deny their existence by attacking the validity of the standard, asserting that the measurement techniques are inaccurate or inappropriate, and questioning the motives and motivations of the analysts.

A decision was made to change the form and content of evaluations in the FDA. This decision was made as a result of management dissatisfaction with the relative benefits and "costs" of Type I evaluation. Some analysts were hired (with different skills) and the managers of the evaluation function were replaced.

Type II Evaluations

Type II evaluations became the predominant style of evaluation practices in FDA from the early 1970s to 1977. It is described as "technical," "scientific," and "analytical" by its supporters and as "abstract," "aloof," and "theoretical" by its critics. Just as Type I evaluations resembled the regulatory functions of FDA, Type II evaluations resembled scientific and research functions of the agency.

Type II evaluation was frequently described as "analysis" since it focused on the collection and manipulation of analytical data. The following project is representative of the scope, focus, and acceptance of Type II evaluation.

The Compliance Curve Model: A model of the food industry was constructed using the data from 17,000 food plant inspections. The model described the relationship between the compliance rate of the industry (the status of industry's manufacturing practices compared with FDA standards) and the frequency of FDA inspections.

The model demonstrated what had long been suspected but never demonstrated mathematically:

• Individual firms frequently "drift" out of compliance if they are not inspected.

• An inspection often serves as a one-time "shock" that moves the inspected firm back into compliance or reverses the "drift" before the firm reaches an out-of-compliance state.

The model was computer-based, responded quickly to "what if" questions, and was highly touted as an effective management tool. It did provide new macro level insights for the top management of the agency. Its usefulness, however, was quite limited to the program manager and front line supervisors who made the day-to-day operating decisions. Although the model was technically sophisticated and was built on an unusually large data base, it only dealt with two variables. The supervisor's scheduling of inspections dealt with many variables—e.g., inspector qualification, plant location, and consumer complaints.

Dozens of other Type II evaluations were designed to answer questions such as: (1) If some firms in a particular industry are inspected, will the entire industry improve its manufacturing practices? (2) Can more violators be "caught" with abbreviated inspections than with fewer in-depth inspections? and (3) Are warning letters an effective mechanism for increasing industry compliance? It is apparent that Type II evaluations focused largely on operational and quantitative agency functions.

Type II evaluations were rigorous and exhaustive. They were designed to withstand aggressive peer review. A substantial number of evaluations involved "state-of-the-art" mathematical, statistical, and computer techniques and resulted in papers for technical journals and conventions. Type II evaluations were frequently done as "investment" projects, i.e., they were designed and completed without a specific request from the commissioner or other line manager. These investment projects were successful when the results were surprising or uniquely insightful, and a line manager "client" was interested in the results.

In reality, the typical program manager was frequently unaware or not interested in Type II evaluations since they were by design clinical and impersonal, were frequently too abstract to impact on his/her decision agenda, and often focused on analytical technique rather than program content.

There were, however, a number of achievements and advantages of the Type II evaluations:

(1) They frequently presented a new macro level and/or analytical perspective on project activities which complemented the executive and line manager's macro perspective based on day-to-day activity.
(2) They reestablished the credibility of the analysts since they were technically sound and clinically neutral rather than judgmental and polemical.
(3) They provided "state-of-the-art" application of skills and opportunities for publications which, in turn, attracted technically competent analysts to the evaluation staff.

A change in the evaluation staff philosophy was precipitated by a change in agency management, i.e., a new commissioner. The new commissioner requested that independent, unbiased evaluations be done of *agency programs.* This request came at an opportune time since the lack of program impact was producing a growing frustration among analysts, and data for analytical manipulation was becoming more difficult and costly to obtain. Type II evaluations were not abandoned since some decisions and problems are very amenable to model building, statistical analysis, and other analytical tools; however, the number of Type II evaluations was reduced and the remaining ones were integrated with the Type III evaluations.

Type III Evaluations: Consultative/Consensus

The new commissioner's request for useful, independent evaluation that would fit his "decision agenda" produced ambivalent feelings in analysts and program managers. The analysts welcomed the commissioner's interest and support but were anxious to avoid the dysfunctional characteristics of Type I evaluations. Program managers saw the evaluations both as an opportunity to engage the commissioner's attention on their program and perhaps get some free analytical support while simultaneously running the risk of public humiliation.

An evaluation process was designed to provide the desired in-depth analytical analysis while simultaneously avoiding the obvious pitfalls. The mechanics of the new process were designed to assure a positive, problem-solving atmosphere and to involve all participants (analysts, commissioner, program managers, and others) in a joint, cooperative effort. The characteristics of the evaluation process include:

(1) *Cooperation:* The evaluations were conducted by two to four-member teams including representatives from the commissioner's evaluation staff, the program managers' staff, and one or two other interested groups, e.g., commissioner's staffs. This team approach not only fostered a cooperative attitude and atmosphere but assured the appropriate mixture of skills and program knowledge.

(2) *Openness:* The evaluation plan, activity and progress reports, and draft and final findings, conclusions and recommendations were shared on a "real time basis" with all participants. This open process was to assure that none of the participants received any surprises (pleasant or otherwise) and to demonstrate the analysts' supportive, problem-solving orientation. The final evaluation report was distributed to all interested parties and subsequently discussed (and sometimes debated) in a meeting between the commissioner, the program manager, the evaluation team, and other line and staff people involved and interested in the program. Twenty to 40 people participated in these meetings.

(3) *Timeliness:* Evaluations were completed in three months and reported in written and oral form. This obviously tight time frame always encouraged, and sometimes dictated, a concentration on a few important issues. This limited, but intense, focus was designed to keep interest high and to improve the efficiency of the evaluations and avoid prolonged, counter-productive, inquisition-type efforts.

Type III evaluations, by design, involve a number of different people in the agency. Although each of these people play a different role in the agency, each contributes to an effective evaluation and implementation of the evaluation results. The perceptions of three of these people are presented below:[4]

The Commissioner—Donald Kennedy, Ph.D., became commissioner of FDA in 1977 and subsequently requested that independent assessments be made of each of the agency's programs. He made the following comments shortly after leaving the FDA (June 1979) to become provost of Stanford University.

Question: What did you have in mind when you requested evaluations of FDA programs?

Dr. Kennedy: As a new commissioner, I needed some important information about the way programs were operating. The daily newspaper identified the agency's "crisis of the day," but it didn't tell me about program strategies and management capabilities—the precursors of "crises of the future."

Question: Was the purpose of the evaluations to avoid future problems?

Dr. Kennedy: Yes, but they were to do other, equally important things. For example, the FDA's resources are meager in comparison to our responsibility and our impact. I had to ensure that program managers had implemented the most cost-effective strategies and operations. Equally important, the program evaluations gave program managers, and the support staffs they depend on, an opportunity to consider new options and alternatives in an atmosphere of cooperation and support. This was a positive stimulus for all of us.

Question: What aspect of the evaluations did you find most useful to your own management needs?

Dr. Kennedy: There is no single answer to that question since the evaluation techniques and tools were eclectic—selected to fit the characteristic and needs of the specific project. In some instances, it was important for us all to gain the same understanding of the program's issues and goals. In other cases, it was important to understand how the program was like other private and government activities, and how these similar activities were successfully or unsuccessfully managed. In some instances, the evaluations discovered impediments to the program's success that I was able to resolve by redirecting the activities of support staffs or other line organizations.

Question: Do you think Type III evaluations are applicable to other management situations?

Dr. Kennedy: Certainly the combination of a positive, supportive attitude combined with hard work by sensitive, talented analysts is likely to be helpful in any organization. We went out of our way to avoid confrontation. I would advise others not to turn the process into a contest between evaluators and performers.

A Program Manager—Daniel L. Michels, drug quality assurance project manager and deputy associate director for compliance, Bureau of Drugs.

Question: How does it feel to have your program evaluated?

Mr. Michels: The first reaction is always defensive, particularly when you don't know the rules or the players. In general, evaluations are viewed as "no win" situations by managers. This evaluation was no different at the outset, but it turned out to be relatively painless and, in retrospect, positive.

Question: Isn't it embarrassing to have your program's problems presented to the commissioner?

Mr. Michels: Not in this case. I had an opportunity to participate in the process and present my views before the evaluation was completed. Most importantly, I had "equal time" with the analysts before the commissioner in a supportive and non-acrimonious environment.

Question: Did you agree with all of the evaluation team's recommendations?

Mr. Michels: Of course not. I suspect that the evaluation would not have been very useful if I had. But the criteria for evaluation were well described by the evaluation team as well as the logic leading to recommendations. Consequently, we were able to focus on the program and its problems, rather than on searching for a particular "villain."

Analyst—Tim Hegarty is a senior program analyst and has conducted three program evaluations as well as directing and advising program analysts who have performed a number of other program evaluations.

Question: Why are the Type III evaluations successful?

Mr. Hegarty: Lots of reasons. Certainly the commissioner's interest and involvement is critical.

Question: Management support?

Mr. Hegarty: Yes, but that alone won't do it. You need the trust and cooperation of the program people. After all, they know a lot more about the program than we do . . . at least at the beginning of the evaluation they do.

Question: How do you get this trust?

Mr. Hegarty: It isn't easy. You've got to demonstrate you're not out to get them. You tell them what you're interested in, ideas you have, and so forth.

In summary, Type III evaluations contrasted to Type I and Type II evaluations in a number of ways. The following table displays some of the most important and obvious contrasts.

Five evaluation techniques have been developed during the first 18 months of Type III evaluations. Each of these techniques has contributed to the completion of the evaluations and the acceptance and implementation of the evaluation recommendations. The techniques include:

(1) A hierarchical sequence of evaluation. The evaluation teams have focused sequentially on the project's overall strategy, operational and tactical activities, and management's systems. The efficiency, effectiveness, and impact of each is examined and described in the final report. If major issues are developed at the strategy or tactical level, the evaluation is focused at that level.

(2) Reality testing. The current estimates of workload, completion dates, processing rates, available resources, and required resources are challenged and tested to determine if they are reasonable (or even possible). This type of analysis has produced a number of conclusions that began: "Let's stop kidding ourselves. . . ."

(3) Extending the planning horizon. The question, What happens if we continue our present (or planned) direction and level of activity? has produced some surprising answers. These, in turn, have produced changes in program strategy and operations.

(4) Learning from similar activities. Project managers have frequently

Comparison of Three Types of Evaluation

	Type I Investigative Reporting	Type II Technical State of the Art	Type III Consultative Consensus
Purpose	Identify and correct problems	• Analyze data to gain new insights • Apply sophisticated techniques	Support and facilitate improved management and decision making
Focus	Problem programs and responsible individuals (guilty person)	Available data and new techniques	All programs
Communication of Findings and Conclusions	To individuals supervisor or public announcement (closely held until release)	Technical papers	Iterative discussion with all parties
Openness	Controlled/closed until end	Passively open (open if anybody is interested)	Actively open throughout evaluation process
Change Mechanism (What Precipitated Change)	• Fear of public embarrassment • Avoidance of punishment	The inherent power of new insights and data	Program managers' desire to improve program management
Constraints and Limitations	Counteractivities of person or program being evaluated	• Available data • Analytical techniques	• Number of capable analysts • Time and effort to assure openness and participation
Immediate Response of Program manager	Anxiety and counterattack	Impressed by technical sophistication	Initially anxious then neutral to constructive to open
Longer-Term Response of Program Manager	• Establish defensive staffs to neutralize evaluation staff, or • "yes, sergeant" program manager who agrees to all recommendations but does not actively implement	Results are interesting but usually not useful	Use results of the evaluation to improve program management and get additional agency support
Analysts Were Perceived as:	Critical parents or advocates of predetermined position	Clinical technicians (honest and without ulterior motives but not very relevant)	Supportive problem solvers

believed their project is unique. The Type III evaluations have frequently learned of and described similar activities (in industry and government) that provide comparative performance measures, solutions to problems, and ideas for new initiatives.

(5) Getting agreement on basic goals. Most projects involve two or more organizational units. The Type III evaluations have sometimes uncovered the fact that the participants have different or conflicting goals which must be resolved in order to develop a common program strategy.

Twelve Type III evaluations were completed in the first 18 months. The FDA programs which have been evaluated account for approximately 50 percent of the agency's resources.

The Type III evaluations have rarely produced the "slam bang" change that analysts dream of. They have, however, had dramatic impacts on the agency. The 12 Type III evaluations have produced 58 recommendations. Each of these recommendations has been considered and discussed by the affected parties. Fifty-two of the recommendations have been accepted basically unchanged, however, the impact of the evaluations has extended well beyond the recommendations. This extended impact has been substantial in three ways:

(1) The program manager has frequently made changes in program activities *before* the evaluation is completed since he or she is kept informed on new data and insights developed during the evaluation. Special care must be taken to ensure that the program analyst receives adequate recognition for these pre-recommendation changes to keep his/her ego intact.

(2) The Type III evaluations are educational to members in staffs that must support the program manager. This increased awareness, sensitivity, and understanding provide an improved atmosphere for program performance and success.

(3) Interest of the commissioner, program manager, and analysts extend beyond the accomplishment of the "quick fix" improvements. Positive cooperation is maintained to continue work on problems much beyond the impact life of Type I and II evaluations.

Using Type III Evaluations in Other Agencies

The success of Type III evaluation in FDA was based in part on the previous partial success of Type I and Type II evaluations, and from the evolving recognition of the shortcomings of Type I and Type II evaluations. A review of the recent literature and other forums suggests that there is an increasing expectation that evaluation is and should be an integral part of managing public programs, and current practice and theory is similar to

Type I and II evaluations previously practiced in FDA. The application of Type III techniques to another organization, however, would neither be obvious nor easy.

A number of factors would determine the applicability of Type III evaluation. These include:

Trust: Program managers, analysts, and agency officials must trust each other and must be convinced that all the participants' efforts are for the purpose of improving the organization, not for personal (or hidden agenda) purposes. Typically, this trust must be established in the day-to-day operations of the organization and carried over to the evaluation activities.

Talented Analysts: Type III analysts must not only have the technical skills expected of all good analysts but must have, and aggressively exhibit, a service orientation toward all parties. Analysts with "critical parent" personalities are very injurious to the atmosphere needed for Type III evaluations.

Cooperative Management: A cooperative, consensus-building management style provides a receptive setting for Type III evaluation. Combative, autocratic, or dictatorial management styles do not.

Notes

1. FDA is responsible for assuring the safety of human food, animal feeds, cosmetics, and for assuring the safety and efficacy of human drugs, medical devices, electronic radiological products, biologics, and animal drugs.
2. Type I, II, and III are the author's designations for the three forms of evaluation activities observed at FDA and in other government agencies.
3. Green, L.W. "Towards Cost-Benefit Evaluations of Health Education: Some Concepts, Methods, and Examples." *Health Education Monographs,* 1974, 2: 34.
4. Each of the quoted participants was asked to respond to a series of questions about Type III evaluation. The questions focused on expectation, experience, and perceived impact. Each of the responses are literal (but edited) quotes.

1980 (174-179)

Organization of the
Evaluation Function

The *PAR* articles selected for Part III of this volume describe (1) various aspects of the problems associated with organizing executive branch agencies to integrate the evaluation function, and (2) various strategies for coping with those problems. Some of these problems involve tensions between public performance and attitudes of administrators, between organizational imperatives and managerial abilities to respond, between the viewpoints of evaluators and those of bureaucrats, between the technical function and the managerial role, between the competition for power and the advancement of knowledge. Coping strategies include new evaluation methods and procedures to overcome organizational hurdles, as well as mixed-model and centralized organizational structures for the evaluation function (see the last section of the introductory essay).

The first article, "The Deadly Sins in Public Administration" by Peter F. Drucker (*PAR,* Vol. 40, No. 2, March/April 1980, pages 103-106), covers six of the modern bureaucratic routines and rituals which demonstrate clearly both why evaluation is needed and why there are obstacles to its success and use. The author is not especially sympathetic to public administrators and their problems, gives short shrift to organizational imperatives, charges public managers with "cowardice" and inattention to performance, expects public programs to be conducted in contemplation of their own mortality, and wonders why the excellent performance of public service institutions used to be taken for granted, whereas now it is malperformance that is taken for granted. While the word "evaluation" is never mentioned in the article, Drucker's thesis implies that if evaluation is now needed to address the six deadly sins he describes, it is the fault of public administrators that this is so. He identifies the sins as:

(1) setting "lofty," undefined objectives (Horst, *et al.,* call them "vaporous"; see their article in Part II of this volume);

224

(2) trying to do too many things at once without establishing priorities among them;

(3) believing that "fat is beautiful" and acting on that belief;

(4) failing to develop empirical evidence before implementing programs nationwide;

(5) ensuring that feedback on program results will *not* be available; and

(6) refusing to abandon programs when the time comes to do so.

The author points out that although these sins may well be merely symptoms of deeper problems in modern government, at least "we know how to avoid them." This point, however, is in conflict with the Siu, Wildavsky, and Hargrove articles of Part III which instill some doubt in the reader about current abilities to solve performance problems or conciliate evaluation/organization conflicts with any abiding success.

The second article, "Chinese Baseball and Public Administration," by Ralph G. H. Siu (*PAR,* Vol. 35, No. 6, November/December 1975, pages 636-640), takes a profoundly different view from Drucker of public administration's problems. He ascribes these largely to exogenous factors, like constant change in the modern world, ever-increasing complexity (which makes it difficult to get a handle on "the total problem"), and the growing importance of perception versus reality. Siu implies that modern administrators are not really at fault because they face a tough world which judges them less on their performance than on their image, and makes it hard for them to function because of complexity and change combined. In the author's words,

> The singular art that most characterizes the great public administrator is Chinese baseball. Chinese baseball is played almost exactly like American baseball—same players, same field, same bats and balls, same method of scoring, and so on. The batter stands in the batter's box, as usual. The pitcher stands on the pitcher's mound, as usual. He winds up, as usual, and zips the ball down the alley. There is one and only one difference: after the ball leaves the pitcher's hand and as long as the ball is in the air, anyone can move any of the bases anywhere. In other words, everything is continually changing—not only the events themselves, but the very rules governing the judgment of those events and the criteria of values as well. . . . In the ballgame of public administration, everything is in flux and all systems are open.

The author is as scornful of the uses of scientific objectivity, analysis, and efforts to establish cause-and-effect relationships as Drucker is scornful of public administrators' fear and trembling. Yet, in a certain sense, Siu asks for forgiveness for public administrators' performance on the basis of the deeper causes of their problems which he sees as outside their control. But this is having one's cake and eating it, by arguing against the soundness of scientific demonstrations of cause-and-effect relationships while asking readers to accept one's own reasoning from cause to effect. This contradiction, however, in no way detracts from the power of the author's overall insights into the personal goals of the public administrator and the reader's increased understanding of the consequent difficulties for evaluation to play a role in the achievement of those goals.

The third article, "The Self-Evaluating Organization" by Aaron Wildavsky (*PAR*, Vol. 32, No. 5, September/October 1972, pages 509-520), probes deeply into the basic tensions between an evaluative outlook and an organizational one and describes the problems these pose for evaluators in an agency:

> Evaluation and organization may be contradictory terms. Organizational structure implies stability while the process of evaluation suggests change. Organization generates commitment while evaluation inculcates skepticism. Evaluation speaks to the relationship between action and objectives while organization relates its activities to programs and clientele.

These contradictions, of course, necessarily place evaluators in a precarious position within agencies, no matter what structure is preferred or how it is implemented. As Wildavsky points out,

> Prepared to impose change on others, evaluators must have sufficient stability to carry out their own work. They must maintain their own organization while simultaneously preparing to abandon it. They must obtain the support of existing bureaucracies while perusing anti-bureaucratic policies. They must combine political feasibility with analytical purity.

This, of course, raises the question of whether changes in the evaluation process, product or organization can do much to improve the success and usefulness of the evaluation function without similar changes in the orientations and incentives of organizations. If, as Wildavsky states, it is inevitable that "the needs of the members displace the goals of the organization," and that "the public purposes that the organization was supposed to serve give way to its private acts," then the malperformance Drucker describes is also inevitable and, by the same token, it is *not* clear that "we know to avoid" the deadly sins of public administration which stem from the substitution of agency agendas for public goals.

The fourth article is "The Bureaucratic Politics of Evaluation: A Case Study of the Department of Labor" by Erwin C. Hargrove (*PAR*, Vol. 40, No. 2, March/April 1980, pages 150-159). This is a very remarkable and useful record of a relationship among three offices, of which two were evaluation units (one centralized and the other decentralized) and the third was the program office (for CETA). The case study points up eight types of organizational evaluation problems:

(1) relationships within agencies between "academics" and other evaluators;
(2) relationships between both types of evaluators and program managers;
(3) state-of-the-art uncertainties in program evaluation (in particular, how to do a process evaluation—the year was 1974—and whether or how effectiveness and process evaluations of the same program should be related to each other (see the introductory essay);
(4) preference for three different evaluation approaches rooted in different types of information need (i.e., the need of program managers for implementation information, and the need of the centralized evaluation unit for accountability information to pass on to the Secretary of Labor, OMB, and the Congress);
(5) decentralized unit illusions and uncertainties (despite the fact that OPER was within the Manpower Administration—now the Employment and Training Administration—"OPER evaluators had àlways seen themselves as working for the assistant secretary, *not for program managers,*" emphasis added);
(6) centralized evaluation unit powerlessness because it was not authorized to perform evaluations;
(7) difficulties for top-level managers to make technical decisions; and
(8) dependence of "less competent" evaluation staff on "friendly contractors."

The paper, thus, has some important implications for the structure of an agency's evaluation function, in particular, for four of the points raised in the introductory essay with regard to the mixed model of evaluation organization (i.e., including centralized and decentralized units as in the Department of Labor): first, the uncertain feasibility of Units as in the the model; second, the need for a higher-locus office outside the agency; third, the usefulness of having a technically competent "honest broker" at the Assistant Secretary level to resolve evaluation problems; and fourth, the likelihood of major delays and increased costs for the planning and performance of evaluations.

The fifth article is "The Role of Evaluation and the Evaluator in Improving Public Programs: The Bad News, the Good News, and a Bicentennial Challenge" by Joseph S. Wholey (*PAR,* Vol. 36, No. 6, November/December 1976, pages 679-683). This is the first paper in Part III to outline some coping strategies for the administrative problems evaluation can be expected to address. Although Wholey's paper preceded Drucker's by about four years, it, nonetheless, lays out some evaluative methods that could deal effectively with two out of six of the deadly sins. In this sense, there is agreement between the two authors at least that two of the sins can be avoided. Wholey proposes ways to devise measurable program objectives (Drucker's sin #1), and to assure feedback on program results (Drucker's sin #5). Because of the systematic approach he takes, it might well be argued that he has also addressed the issue of priority setting (Drucker's sin #2). However, it is important to note that Wholey is essentially concerned with what evaluators alone can do. In this article, the burden is clearly on them to strengthen the role of evaluation: by creating a market for their services, by doing some research on consumer attitudes toward evaluation, by coming closer to user requirements for evaluation products.

The sixth article, "Program Evaluation and the Policy Process in State Government" by Larry Polivka and Laurey T. Stryker (*PAR,* Vol. 43, No. 3, May/June 1983, pages 255-259), focuses on the importance of organizational position along with the efforts of evaluators, for the success and usefulness of the evaluation function. Although the authors' paper recounts an experience at the state rather than the federal level, the problems posed and inferences drawn appear germane to the organization of the evaluation function generally. A strong case is made in this paper for centralized organization of the evaluation function. The advantages (see the introductory essay) are quite clear:

(1) protected visibility of the unit;
(2) access by the unit to all users;
(3) immunity from "self-serving interests";
(4) certitude that evaluations selected are of high priority to users;
(5) ability to promote use via direct communications (persuasion) as well as via other mechanisms;
(6) efficiency of the unit; and
(7) evident feasibility of the organizational structure.

No disadvantages are noted. However, some implied—although apparently quite treatable—problems can be discerned in a few of the criteria for transfer noted by the authors (for example, the evaluators must be prepared to play an assertive role, and should not be demoralized when decision makers pay attention to factors other than the evaluative findings). This article, like those of Wholey and Drucker, recognizes that there are problems but believes whole-heartedly and straightforwardly that the self-evaluating organization is perfectly possible.

The last article is "Evolution of a Research Program on Weed Control" by Roy L. Lovvorn and Marguerite Gilstrap (*PAR,* Vol. 13, No. 1, Winter 1953, pages 33-37). It is included here partly out of nostalgia—it shows how much simpler organizations used to be (or seemed to be) than they are (and do) now (see the articles by Siu, Wildavsky, and Hargrove)—and partly to show how settings for the evaluation function do differ (see the introductory essay). In their paper, the authors report on the factors that led to the creation of a new research division in a bureau already possessing thirteen other research divisions and four divisions devoted to agricultural engineering. In other words, from the viewpoint of evaluation organization, this bureau is different from the other agencies discussed heretofore in this volume, because *all* of the divisions are involved in evaluation and because those evaluations do *not* involve the bureau's own programs. (This kind of setting can be found in many other agencies: for example, the Congressional Research Service, the General Accounting Office, the Office of Technology Assessment, the Congressional Budget Office, the National Science Foundation, the National Institutes of Health, and so forth.) The authors report that the decision to organize the new research units as an additional bureau division, rather than in some other form, came about for the following six reasons:

(1) A discovery had been made in 1947 that a compound (a new herbicide: 2,4-D) had been placed on the market "while researchers in the weed project were still making tests to determine the extent of its value." This unfortunate event was interpreted as showing that the new research needed a broader structure and a lot more power.
(2) A grass-roots movement, specifically targeting a division of weed research, ended up with the introduction of a bill in Congress (in 1947) promoting just such a division.
(3) The researchers working on weed control had to divide their time between weed study and other duties, yet a larger amount of research, and a critical mass of researchers were needed.
(4) There was a requirement "for several lines of scattered research" to be brought together under one roof and for weed research to be given "the recognition its importance warranted."
(5) For the work in weed control to receive "proper emphasis," it was necessary that it be represented by a leader "on a par with the division heads."
(6) Intimate coordination was required between crop and weed specialists, among plant physiologists, ecologists, and chemists, across agencies (especially, with the Department of Interior) and with the states.

From the viewpoint of Drucker's six deadly sins, it is interesting to note that the fashion of spreading untested innovations across the nation is not a new one. However, in 1947 this was cause for alarm and for action, whereas in the 1960s, for the programs Drucker evokes, the spreading was done by the administrators themselves. It is also interesting that the six reasons given above seem to have been the essential criteria for determining the organization of the new research unit. It does not appear from the article that any organizational structure other than the divisional one was ever considered. Further, concerns of bureau or divisional territoriality, of organizational imperatives, or of private agendas being substituted for public goals are absent from the article. Is this because the concerns were not there, or because it was not the fashion to write about them in 1947? In any case, there emerges from this article the sense of a very different agency climate from today's, one in which decision making processes were a great deal simpler. The reader can only speculate whether this is so because the constant change and complexity of modern public administration evoked by Siu were not yet advanced; or whether, as Drucker surmises, it is because public trust in adequate performance by government organizations, in those days, was a matter of course, and agencies simply did not concern themselves overly with satisfying anyone's perception that they had, in their decision making, covered all the bases.

PETER F. DRUCKER

The Deadly Sins in Public Administration

No one can guarantee the performance of a public service program, but we know how to ensure non-performance with absolute certainty. Commit any two of the following common sins of public administration, and non-performance will inevitably follow. Indeed, to commit all six, as many public service agencies do, is quite unnecessary and an exercise in overkill.

(1) The first thing to do to make sure that a program will not have results is to have a lofty objective—"health care," for instance, or "to aid the disadvantaged." Such sentiments belong in the preamble. They explain why a specific program or agency is being initiated rather than what the program or agency is meant to accomplish.[1] To use such statements as "objectives" thus makes sure that no effective work will be done. For work is always specific, always mundane, always focused. Yet without work there is non-performance.

To have a chance at performance, a program needs clear targets, the attainment of which can be measured, appraised, or at least judged. "Health care" is not even a pious intention. Indeed it is, at best, a vague slogan. Even "the best medical care for the sick," the objective of many hospitals in the British National Health Service, is not operational. Rather, it is meaningful to say: "It is our aim to make sure that no patient coming into emergency will go for more than three minutes without being seen by a qualified triage nurse." It is a proper goal to say: "Within three years, our maternity ward is going to be run on a 'zero defects' basis, which means that there will be no 'surprises' in the delivery room and there will not be one case of post-partum puerperal fever on maternity." Similarly, "Promoting the welfare of the American farmer" is electioneering, while "Installing electricity in at least 25 percent of America's farms within the next three years"—the first goal of the New Deal's Rural Electrification Administration, which was, perhaps, the most successful public service agency in all our administrative history—was an objective that was specific,

231

measurable, attainable—and attained. It immediately was converted into work, and very shortly thereafter, into performance.

(2) The second strategy guaranteed to produce non-performance is to try to do several things at once. It is to refuse to establish priorities and to stick to them. Splintering of efforts guarantees non-results. Yet without concentration on a priority, efforts will be splintered, and the more massive the program, the more the splintering effects will produce non-performance. By contrast, even poorly conceived programs might have results if priorities are set and efforts concentrated.

It is popular nowadays to blame the failure of so many of the programs of Lyndon Johnson's "War on Poverty" on shaky theoretical foundations. Whether poorly conceived or not, quite a few of the Headstart schools had significant results; every one of them, without exception, was a school that decided on one overriding priority—having the children learn to read letters and numbers—despite heavy criticism from Washington and from all kinds of dogmatists.

An even more impressive example is the Tennessee Valley Authority (TVA) in the thirties. Despite tremendous opposition, the bill establishing the TVA only passed Congress because its backers promised a dozen different and mutually antagonistic constituencies: cheap power, cheap fertilizer, flood control, irrigation, navigation, community development, and whatnot. TVA's first administrator, Arthur Morgan, a great engineer, then attempted to live up to these promises and to satisfy every one of his constituencies. The only result was an uncontrollably growing bureaucracy, uncontrollably growing expenditures, and a total lack of any performance. Indeed, the TVA in its early years resembled nothing as much as one of those "messes" which we now attack in Washington. Then President Roosevelt removed Morgan and put in a totally unknown young Wisconsin utilities lawyer, David Lilienthal, who immediately—against all advice from all the "pros"—announced his priority: power production. Within a year, the TVA produced results. Lilienthal, by the way, met no opposition, but was universally acclaimed as a saviour.

(3) The third deadly sin of the public administrator is to believe that "fat is beautiful," despite the obvious fact that mass does not do work; brains and muscles do. In fact, overweight inhibits work, and gross overweight totally immobilizes.

One hears a great deal today about the fallacy of "throwing money at problems," but this is not really what we have been doing. We have been throwing manpower at problems, with Vietnam, perhaps, being the worst example, and it is even worse to overstaff than to overfund. Today's administrators, whether civilian or military, tend to believe that the best way to tackle a problem is to deploy more and more people against it. The one certain result of having more bodies is greater difficulties in logistics, in personnel management, and in communications. Mass increases weight, but not necessarily competence. Competence requires direction, decision, and strategy rather than manpower.

Overstaffing is not only much harder to correct than understaffing, it makes non-performance practically certain. For overstaffing always focuses energies on the inside, on "administration" rather than on "results," on the machinery rather than its purpose. It always leads to meetings and memoranda becoming ends in themselves. It immobilizes behind a facade of furious busyness. Harold Ickes, FDR's Secretary of the Interior and one of the New Deal's most accomplished administrators, always asked: "What is the fewest number of people we need to accomplish this purpose?" It is a long time since anyone in Washington (or in the state government) has asked that question.

(4) "Don't experiment, be dogmatic" is the next—and the next most common—of the administrator's deadly sins. "Whatever you do, do it on a grand scale at the first try. Otherwise, God forbid, you might learn how to do it differently." In technical or product innovation, we sometimes skip the pilot-plant stage, usually to our sorrow. But at least we build a model and put it through wind tunnel tests. In public service, increasingly we start out with a "position"—that is, with a totally untested theory—and go from it immediately to national, if not international, application. The most blatant example may have been the ultra-scholastic dogmatism with which we rushed into national programs in the "War on Poverty" that were based on totally speculative, totally untried social science theories, and backed by not one shred of empirical evidence.

However, even if the theories on which a program is based are themselves sound, successful application still demands adaptation, cutting, fitting, trying, balancing. It always demands testing against reality before there is final total commitment. Above all, any new program, no matter how well conceived, will run into the unexpected, whether unexpected "problems" or unexpected "successes." At that point, people are needed who have been through a similar program on a smaller scale, who know whether the unexpected problem is relevant or not, or whether the unexpected success is a fluke or genuine achievement.

Surely one of the main reasons for the success of so many of the New Deal programs was that there had been "small scale" experiments in states and cities earlier—in Wisconsin, for instance, in New York State or in New York City, or in one of the reform administrations in Chicago. The outstanding administrators of the New Deal programs—Frances Perkins at Labor, Harold Ickes at Interior, or Arthur Altmeyer at Social Security—were all alumnae of such earlier small-scale experiments. Similarly, the true unsuccessful New Deal programs, the WPA for instance, were, without exception, programs that had not first been developed in small-scale experimentation in state or local governments but were initiated as comprehensive, national panaceas.

(5) "Make sure that you cannot learn from experience" is the next prescription for non-performance in public administration. "Do not think through in advance what you expect; do not then feed back from results to expectations so as to find out not only what you can do well, but also to find out what your weaknesses, your limitations, and your blind spots are."

Every organization, like every individual, does certain things well. They are the things that "come easy to one's hand." Nevertheless, every organization, like every individual, is also prone to typical mistakes, has typical limitations, and has its own blind spots. Unless the organization shapes its own expectations to reflect the accuracy of results, it will not find out what it does well and, thus, not learn to apply its strengths. Moreover, it will not find out what it does poorly and will, thus, have no opportunity to improve or to compensate for its weaknesses or its blind spots. Typically, for instance, certain institutions expect results much too fast and throw in the towel much too soon. A good many of the "War on Poverty" agencies did just that. Also, there are many organizations which wait much too long before they face up to the fact that a program or a policy is unsuccessful—our Vietnam policies, both civilian and military, probably belong here. One can only learn by feedback, and we know that feedback from results always improves performance capacity and effectiveness. Without it, however, the weaknesses, the limitations, the blind spots increasingly dominate. Without learning from results through feedback, any organization, like any individual, must inevitably deteriorate in its capacity to perform. Yet, in most public service institutions such feedback functions are either non-existent or viewed with casual skepticism. If the results do not conform to expectations, they are all too frequently dismissed as irrelevant, as indications of the obtuseness of clients, as the reactionary obscurantism of the public, or, worst of all, as evidence of the need to "make another study." Most public service institutions, governmental ones as well as non-governmental ones, are budget-focused, but the budgets measure efforts rather than results. For performance, the budget needs to be paralleled with a statement of expected results—and with systematic feedback from results—on expenditures and on efforts. Otherwise, the agency will, almost immediately, channel more and more of its efforts toward non-results and will become the prisoner of its own limitations, its weaknesses, and its blind spots rather than the beneficiary of its own strengths.

(6) The last of the administrator's deadly sins is the most damning and the most common: the inability to abandon. It alone guarantees non-performance, and within a fairly short time.

Traditional political theory, the theory inherited from Aristotle, holds that the tasks of government are grounded in the nature of civil society and, thus, are immutable: defense, justice, law and order. However, very few of the tasks of modern public administration, whether governmental or non-governmental public service institutions, such as the hospital, the Red Cross, the university, or the Boy Scouts, are of that nature. Almost all of them are manmade rather than grounded in the basic essentials of society, and most of them are of very recent origin to boot. They all, therefore, share a common fate: they must become pointless at some juncture in time. They may become pointless because the need to which they address themselves no longer exists or is no longer urgent. They may become pointless because the old need appears in such a new guise as to make obsolete present design, shape, concerns, and policies. The great environmental problem of 1910, for instance—and it was a very real danger—was the horrendous pollution by the horse, with its stench and its liquid and solid wastes, which threatened to bury the cities of that time. If we had been as environmentally conscious then as we are now, we would have saddled ourselves with agencies which only ten years later would have become totally pointless and yet, predictably, ten years later they would have redoubled their efforts, since they would have totally lost sight of their objectives. Moreover, a program may become pointless when it fails to produce results despite all efforts, as do our present American welfare programs. Finally—and most dangerous of all—a program becomes pointless when it achieves its objectives. That we have a "welfare mess" today is, in large measure, a result of our having maintained the welfare programs of the New Deal after they had achieved their objectives around 1940 or 1941. These programs were designed to tackle the problems caused by the temporary unemployment of experienced (and almost entirely white) male heads of families—no wonder that they then malperformed when applied to the totally different problems caused in large measure by the mass movement of black females into the cities 10 or 15 years later.

The basic assumption of public service institutions, governmental or non-governmental ones alike, is immortality. It is a foolish assumption. It dooms the organization and its programs to non-performance and non-results. The only rational assumption is that every public service program will sooner or later—and usually sooner—outlive its usefulness, at least insofar as its present form, its present objectives, and its present policies are concerned. A public service program that does not conduct itself in contemplation of its own mortality will very soon become incapable of performance. In its original guise it cannot produce results any longer; the objectives have either ceased to matter, have proven unobtainable, or have been attained. Indeed, the more successful a public service agency is, the sooner will it work itself out of the job; then it can only become an impediment to performance, if not an embarrassment.

The public service administrator who wants results and performance will, thus, have to build into his own organization an organized process for abandonment. He will have to learn to ask every few years: "If we did not do this already, would we now, knowing what we know now, go into this?" And if the answer is "no," he better not say "let's make another study" or "let's ask for a bigger budget." He better ask: "How can we get out of this?" or at least: "How can we stop pouring more effort, more resources, more people into this?"

II

Avoidance of these six "deadly sins" does not, perhaps, guarantee performance and results in the public service organization, but avoiding these six deadly sins is the prerequisite for performance and results. To be sure, there is nothing very recondite about these "do's and don'ts." They are simple, elementary, indeed, obvious. Yet, as everyone in public administration knows, most administrators commit most of these "sins" all the time and, indeed, all of them most of the time.

One reason is plain cowardice. It is "risky" to spell out attainable, concrete, measurable goals—or so the popular wisdom goes. It is also mundane, pedestrian and likely to "turn off" backers or donors. "The world's best medical care" is so much more "sexy" than "every emergency patient will be seen by a qualified triage nurse within three minutes." Furthermore, to set priorities seems even more dangerous—one risks the wrath of the people who do not really care for electric power or fertilizer, but want to protect the little snail darter or the spotted lousewort. Finally, of course, you do not "rank" in the bureaucracy unless you spend a billion dollars and employ an army of clerks—"fat is beautiful."

Perhaps so, but experience does not bear out the common wisdom. The public service administrators who face up to goal-setting, to ordered priorities, and to concentrating their resources (the public service administrators who are willing to ask: "What is the smallest number of people we need to attain our objectives?") may not always be popular, but they are respected, and they rarely have any trouble at all. They may not get as far in their political careers as the ones who put popularity above performance, but, in the end, they are the ones we remember.

III

But perhaps even more important than cowardice as an explanation for the tendency of so much of public administration today to commit itself to policies that can only result in non-performance is the lack of concern with performance in public administration theory.

For a century from the Civil War to 1960 or so, the performance of public service institutions and programs was taken for granted in the United States. It could be taken for granted because earlier administrators somehow knew not to commit the "deadly sins" I have outlined here. As a result, the discipline of public administration—a peculiarly American discipline, by the way—saw no reason to concern itself with performance. It was not a problem. It focused instead on the political process, on how programs come into being. *Who Gets What, When, How?,* the title of Harold Lasswell's 1936 classic on politics, neatly sums up one specific focus of American public administration, with its challenge to traditional political theory. The other focus was procedural: "The orderly conduct of the business of government" an earlier generation called it. It was a necessary concern in an America that had little or no administrative tradition and experience and was suddenly projected into very large public service programs, first in World War I, then in the New Deal, and finally in World War II. We needed work on all phases of what we now call "management": personnel, budgeting, organization, and so on. But these are inside concerns. Now we need hard, systematic work on making public service institutions perform.

As I noted, for a century, from the Civil War until 1960 or so, performance of public service institutions was taken for granted. For the last 20 years, however, malperformance is increasingly being taken for granted. Great programs are still being proposed, are still being debated, and, in some instances, are even still being enacted, but few people expect them to produce results. All we really expect now, whether from a new Department of Education in Washington or from a reorganization of the state government by a new governor who preaches that "small is beautiful," is more expenditure, a bigger budget, and a more ineffectual bureaucracy.

The malperformance of public service institutions may well be a symptom only. The cause may be far more basic: a crisis in the very foundations and assumptions on which rests that proudest achievement of the Modern Age, national administrative government.[2]

But surely the malperformance of the public service institution is in itself a contributing factor to the sickness of government, and a pretty big one. Avoiding the "deadly sins" of public administration may only give symptomatic relief for whatever ails modern government, but at least we know how to do it.

Notes

1. On this, see my article, "What Results Should You Expect? A User's Guide to MPO," *Public Administration Review,* Vol. 36, pp. 12-19.
2. I hope eventually to finish a book on this subject, tentatively entitled "Can Government Be Saved?," on which I have been working for ten years or more.

1980 (103-106)

R. G. H. SIU

Chinese Baseball and Public Administration

Let me attempt to present one man's shirt-sleeve opinion as to what it takes to be a great administrator.

When we speak of a great public administrator, we immediately sense a person with a strong philosophical base. Such a person reminds me of a deep placid pool on the surface of which the winds may churn up violent waves or a rock may cause ripples to appear. But these disturbances all eventually disappear back into the deep placid pool. The great public administrator combines the wisdom of the sage with the instruments of the executive. We may call him the philosopher-administrator.

Philosopher-Administrator

I shall now advance a series of hints about the indescribable manner in which the philosopher-administrator goes his way, makes his decision, and gets things done in today's bureaucratic setting.

In order to get our bearings, let me describe an example of the kinds of scenarios so characteristic of the Washington scene. It involves the long debate of not too many years ago over whether the United States should have gone ahead with the installation of our antiballistic missile or ABM system.

Just before President Johnson left office he obtained congressional approval for research and development on the Sentinel ABM system, but not for deployment. The purpose of the Sentinel system, so he said, was to provide a thin area defense for cities against small-scale nuclear attack of the type that could be launched by China.

The congressional and scientific opponents began to shore up their arguments against actual deployment, as President Nixon took office. As anticipated, the new President soon asked for authority to deploy the ABM. In the midst of the debate, however, the President shifted the premises. He

238

stated that the intended deployment was not to protect American cities against small-scale nuclear threat. That was impractical, so he said. It was to protect our own intercontinental ballistic missiles against the Soviet's attacking missiles, so that we can retaliate in case they struck first. The Sentinel's name was changed to Safeguard to confirm the modified mission. This switch in justification unbalanced the anti-ABM forces and the President won the inning in the Senate by one vote. It was agreed to deploy two ABM Safeguard sites to protect our intercontinental ballistic missiles instead of our cities.

The anti-ABM forces then regrouped and prepared another plan of debate against the expected next request of the President for further deployment of the Safeguard system to protect more American intercontinental ballistic silos. They began to line up their analyses of cost-effectiveness and so on.

But the President again surprised his opposition. He suddenly announced in a news conference that he intended to expand the ABM system not to protect our own intercontinental ballistic missiles, as he had said the previous year, but to provide an area defense for the entire United States against small-scale nuclear threat, which he had said was impractical. Now, he said, the system would be "virtually infallible" against this kind of threat and was "absolutely essential" if we were to have a "credible" foreign policy in the Far East. The name Safeguard was retained but the mission was changed back to what the Sentinel's used to be. The carefully revised arguments on the part of the anti-ABM cadre were again caught off base at the time and point of action.

This illustration is sufficient to suggest that the public administrator embroiled in complex issues must maintain a readiness posture of omnidirectional vision, resilience, and saliency. We shall examine such a stance in four parts, namely:

1. Can we identify a singularly important art that characterizes all great public administrators?
2. Can we frame some basic management principles underlying this administrative artistry?
3. Can we describe the main pitfalls that the great public administrator intuitively avoids?
4. Can we encapsulate his style of leadership in some simple guidelines?

The Essential Art

Let us take up the first question straightaway.

The answer is yes. The singular art that most characterizes the great public administrator is Chinese baseball.

Chinese baseball is played almost exactly like American baseball—same players, same field, same bats and balls, same method of scoring, and so on. The batter stands in the batter's box, as usual. The pitcher stands on the pitcher's mound, as usual. He winds up, as usual, and zips the ball down the alley. There is one and only one difference: after the ball leaves the pitcher's hand and as long as the ball is in the air, anyone can move any of the bases anywhere.

In other words, everything is continually changing—not only the events themselves, but the very rules governing the judgment of those events and the criteria of values as well. The secret of Chinese baseball then is not keeping your eye on the ball, but on the bases, as well.

This kind of situation is alien to the technological tradition of fixed boundary conditions, clearly defined variables, nonsubjective assessments, and rational consistency within a closed system. In the ball game of public administration, everything is flux and all systems are open. There is no such a thing as a social problem like a mathematical problem that can be solved for all times, such as "two plus two equals four." Take the so-called "environmental problem." There is no such thing. There are only environmental issues—never fully delineated, never solved, always changing, always in need of alert adjustments.

Basic Management Principles

So much for the primary art of Chinese baseball. We will now address ourselves to the second question and discuss the three basic management principles derived from the artistry of Chinese baseball.

The first management principle pertains to the mark of a wise man, which is: Act from an instantaneous apprehension of the totality.

Like knocking on a table—the sound does not wait for the completion of the knock before issuing forth. Knock and sound, cause and effect, plans and operations, means and end—all merge in the instant.

I would like to call your attention to the key word "apprehending," which stands in contrast to the word "understanding." It is important, of course, to understand things with the mind. But that is not enough. Even though persons can give a logical and learned dissertation on many items, they will never be great public administrators unless they develop an unerring gut-feeling about the psychosocial forces that move people. Only then will they be able to reach into a mass of conflicting data and opinions and pull out the right thing to do and do it at the right moment.

The second key word in this first management principle is "totality." One must apprehend the totality. There is no need for us to belabor the common sense admonition about seeing the big picture or getting the full story. But you might be interested in some preliminary experiments on the comparative effectiveness of the so-called wholist strategy and the so-called partist strategy in solving problems.

The wholist strategy begins with the totality, so that all factors are included within the net of consideration. The unnecessary and less relevant components are then successively eliminated, until the desired equilibrium is reached. In this case the tentative decision is always correct but imprecise, due to the varying degrees of extraneous chaff and noise, until the final answer is found.

In contrast, the partist strategy begins with a small group of factors assumed to be necessary and sufficient to solve the problem. Different combinations and permutations are then successively tested and discarded until the desired equilibrium is reached. The modeling approach is, of course, the most fashionable of today's partist strategies. In this case, the tentative decision is always precise but wrong until the correct one is found.

Experiments show that given infinite time to complete the task, either strategy delivers the correct answer. When only limited time is available, however, the results show that the wholist strategy is superior. When we take the game of Chinese baseball into consideration, the odds become overwhelmingly in favor of the wholist strategy for the resolution of social issues. In other words, instantaneously apprehend the totality.

The second management principle pertains to the social meaning of one's own operations. Just as it is impossible to demonstrate the rigor of a closed mathematical system from within, so must one go beyond his or her own operations to give it meaning. This is accomplished by the second management principle, which is: Subsume yourself but resonate.

In applying the technique of subsuming and resonating, public administrators will first have to be clear as to the level of their own operational concern and the level of the context in which their operations are imbedded. They then impart social significance and value to their operations by subsuming them in the larger context and looking at them from the interest and viewpoint of the larger context alone. Yet since they remain operationally responsible for their contributing component, executives must still retain the identity of their operational entity. To give their operational component broader-based relevance from the larger context and at the same time to give the larger context the full benefit of their operational interactions, public administrators must continually keep resonating one against the other.

An example of awareness in subsuming and resonating involves the justification of programs before budget officers. Accomplished public administrators appreciate the fact that the decisive factor in the allotment of money to their particular programs is not the need for support nor their contributions per se, but the relative need of their particular programs as compared to others from the viewpoint of the overall subsuming context.

Being sensitive to the feelings of the individuals within the subsuming context, administrators then present their arguments in such a form that there are implicit answers to the issue in their favor.

The third management principle pertains to the nature of leadership, which is: Pay due respect to the virtual presences.

Human beings behave like animals in many respects. Both are driven by many similar instincts, such as sex, hunger, and territoriality. But there is one thing which is unique to human kind. I have called this the creation of the response to virtual presences.

A virtual presence is something which is not present in a real sense, yet exerts a practical effect as if it were. The products of our imagination are virtual presences. A good example is the square root of minus one. In commonsensical respects, there can't be such a thing in reality. It cannot be plus one, since plus one times plus one equals plus one, not minus one. Nor can it be minus one, since minus one times minus one equals plus one, not minus one. Yet this purely imaginary number is used very effectively in calculations involving real events, producing very worthwhile and practical answers that cannot be obtained in any other way. There would not have been any modern physics in the sense we know it today had not the virtual presence of the square root of minus one been invented.

Many of our social activities are driven by virtual presences. There would not have been such rapid cultural progress of the kind we know today, had not the virtual presence of fame been blandished before the young by their elders. There would not have been such massively destructive wars had not the virtual presence of patriotism been drummed into the citizenry by its leaders.

Having assumed the role of influencing others, the great public administrator thoroughly appreciates the ramifications of what I consider to be the basic axiom of social dynamics. And that is: The fashioning and controlling of virtual presences in the leverage of power. The real effects of the virtual presences of the great administrator are always, on balance, socially beneficent.

Common Pitfalls

Given the art of Chinese baseball and an intuitive grasp of the three basic management principles we have just described, the great public administrator automatically avoids the pitfalls that entrap the mediocre.

Let me briefly describe three typical pitfalls to give you some feel of what we are driving at.

The first and foremost of these pitfalls is poor timing. There is no need to remind a sophisticated group like you about timing. But there have been relatively few among the large number of public administrators with whom

I have had personal contact who possessed a really keen sense of timing. They simply do not know how to use the instrument of time. They are unable to allow precisely for lead time, lag time, incubation time, time to build up a head of steam, time to forget, time to get bored, and so on. They do not have the feeling for matching the duration of different acts to come into fruition against their respective times of need. They fail to lay the basis for the resolution of conflicts before their actual onset. As a result they only have the fortitude of facing crisis after crisis. They only know how to solve problems. They never develop the art of de-existing them.

For example, many junior public administrators and quite a few senior ones as well are too impatient. They want to come to an answer as soon as possible, instead of when the answer is needed. They keep insisting on making tentative fixes as they go along, instead of making only the final decision when all of the data and the moment for action are at hand. The net effect is that their chain of decisions becomes a continuous revision of preconceptions.

Premature closure is another feature of inexperience and impatience. The mediocre leader launches into the final campaign before the situation has been conducively prepared psychologically. The favorable resolution, if attained under such circumstances, is always extra costly. And the leader may even fail.

The second managerial pitfall that the great public administrator intuitively avoids is the lack of alternative viable tactical objectives.

The Roman slave, Publilius Syrus, had said, "Bad is the plan which is not susceptible of change." In other words, be sure that your strategy is sufficiently flexible. This is accepted by managers. The trouble is that many of them mistake flexibility for a lack of specificity of objectives. This is not flexibility, but fuzziness.

The kind of flexibility we are talking about is the freedom of tactical movement within a given strategic thrust. In other words, do not be committed to a single fixed tactical target from the very beginning. This would lock you into a rigid course of advance, which would be much more readily frustrated by the circumstantial changes in the interim.

General Sherman's march through the South in the Civil War illustrates the point on the battlefield. The Confederates never did know which of several towns he was going to attack until he turned at the last minute from his general direction of march, when it was too late for the Confederates to respond effectively.

The AMK Company's take-over of United Fruit not too many years ago illustrates the principle of alternative tactical opportunities in business. Up to the last minute, AMK could have either moved forward to clinch control of United Fruit by acquiring more shares, or it could have made money by selling the shares it had acquired. AMK chose to gain control.

A third illustration is provided by the story of a prisoner of the Sultan of Persia. The Sultan had sentenced two men to jail. One of them, knowing how well the Sultan loved his stallion, offered to teach the horse to fly within a year in return for his life. The Sultan, fancying himself as the master of the only flying horse in the world, agreed to the offer.

The other prisoner looked at his friend in disbelief. "You know horses don't fly. What made you come up with a crazy idea like that? You're only postponing the inevitable."

"Not so," said the clever tactician. "I have actually given myself four chances for freedom. First, the Sultan might die during the year. Second, I might die. Third, the horse might die. And fourth, you know, I might just teach that horse to fly!"

The third and last pitfall which we have time to discuss is being overly scientific. One of the chief weaknesses of young forceful executives brought up in the modern techniques of systems analysis, operational research, and the like and suddenly catapulted into positions of considerable social complexity is their entrancement with rationality and the so-called scientific management. They have yet to fully appreciate the forte and the limitations of science and logic. They fail to use scientific approaches when they should be used and fail to disregard them when they should be disregarded.

Let me relate two simple stories to caution against the fundamental uncertainties surrounding the scientific method when inappropriately used.

The first story concerns the law of cause and effect. It lies at the root of scientific work and has served science well. Actually the law itself has never been proven rigorously. This is shown by the story of the little chicken which ran away in fright at its first sight of a man. After the man left, the chicken came out of its hiding place only to find some corn on the ground, which the chicken then enjoyed eating. This sequence was repeated over and over again—999 times. In terms of the law of cause and effect, this would mean that whenever the man appears, the corn must also appear. So when the man came out the thousandth time, the scientific chicken ran forward to thank him for the delicious corn—only to have its neck wrung for supper that night. Obviously the assumed law of cause and effect failed the chicken miserably on that last go-round.

The second story concerns the fundamental issue of objectivity itself. Scientists pride themselves on being objective. There are many situations, however, when objectivity simply cannot be invoked. This is shown by the story of the Mormon student who wrote a critical graduate thesis on Mormon history. On the day of the oral examination, one of the professors asked the student: "Do you think that you, who are a Mormon, can be objective enough to write a fair critique on Mormon history?" Whereupon the student replied: "Yes, if you, who are not a Mormon, consider yourself objective enough to judge it."

These stories partly explain why seasoned public administrators are reluctant about using mathematical modeling and purely scientific techniques as the final arbiters of their decisions. They recognize that science provides critical inputs to only one of the three basic questions they have to answer before making the final decision. These are: Does it add up? Does it sound okay? Does it feel right?

Science contributes primarily to the first question, does it add up? It contributes little to the second, does it sound okay? and even less to the third, does it feel right? The great public administrator always ensures that the final decision answers all three questions affirmatively.

Day-to-Day Guidelines

So much for examples of the major pitfalls that the philosopher-administrator intuitively avoids. Let us now take the opposite tack and come up with some time-proven, self-explanatory, day-to-day guidelines that the philosopher-administrator subconsciously follows. As a concluding offering therefore here are ten proverbs for public administration—five for planning and five for operations:

The five proverbs for planning are:
1. The shrike hunting the locust is unaware of the hawk hunting him.
2. The mouse with but one hole is easily taken.
3. In shallow waters, shrimps make fools of dragons.
4. Do not try to catch two frogs with one hand.
5. Give the bird room to fly.

The five proverbs for operations are:

1. Do not insult the crocodile until you have crossed the river.
2. It is better to struggle with a sick jackass than carry the wood yourself.
3. Do not throw stone at mouse and break precious vase.
4. It is not the final blow of the ax that fells the tree.
5. The great public administrator not only brings home the bacon but also the applesauce.

1975 (636-640)

AARON WILDAVSKY

The Self-Evaluating Organization

Why don't organizations evaluate their own activities? Why do they not appear to manifest rudimentary self-awareness? How long can people work in organizations without discovering their objectives or determining the extent to which they have been carried out? I started out thinking it was bad for organizations not to evaluate, and I ended up wondering why they ever do it. Evaluation and organization, it turns out, are to some extent contradictory terms. Failing to understand that evaluation is sometimes incompatible with organization, we are tempted to believe in absurdities much in the manner of mindless bureaucrats who never wonder whether they are doing useful work. If we asked more intelligent questions instead, we would neither look so foolish nor be so surprised.

Who will evaluate and who will administer? How will power be divided among these functionaries? Which ones will bear the costs of change? Can evaluators create sufficient stability to carry on their own work in the midst of a turbulent environment? Can authority be allocated to evaluators and blame apportioned among administrators? How to convince administrators to collect information that might help others but can only harm them? How can support be obtained on behalf of recommendations that anger sponsors? Would the political problem be solved by creating a special organization—Evaluation Incorporated—devoted wholly to performing the analytic function? Could it obtain necessary support without abandoning its analytic mission? Can knowledge and power be joined?

Evaluation

The ideal organization would be self-evaluating. It would continuously monitor its own activities so as to determine whether it was meeting its goals or even whether these goals should continue to prevail. When evaluation suggested that a change in goals or programs to achieve them was desirable,

246

these proposals would be taken seriously by top decision makers. They would institute the necessary changes; they would have no vested interest in continuation of current activities. Instead they would steadily pursue new alternatives to better serve the latest desired outcomes.

The ideal member of the self-evaluating organization is best conceived as a person committed to certain modes of problem solving. He believes in clarifying goals, relating them to different mechanisms of achievement, creating models (sometimes quantitative) of the relationships between inputs and outputs, seeking the best available combination. His concern is not that the organization should survive or that any specific objective be enthroned or that any particular clientele be served. Evaluative man cares that interesting problems are selected and that maximum intelligence be applied toward their solution.

To evaluative man the organization doesn't matter unless it meets social needs. Procedures don't matter unless they facilitate the accomplishment of objectives encompassing these needs. Efficiency is beside the point if the objective being achieved at lowest cost is inappropriate. Getting political support doesn't mean that the programs devised to fulfill objectives are good; it just means they had more votes than the others. Both objectives and resources, say evaluative man, must be continuously modified to achieve the optimal response to social need.

Evaluation should not only lead to the discovery of better policy programs to accomplish existing objectives but to alteration of the objectives themselves. Analysis of the effectiveness of existing policies leads to consideration of alternatives that juxtapose means and ends embodied in alternative policies. The objectives as well as the means for attaining them may be deemed inappropriate. But men who have become socialized to accept certain objectives may be reluctant to change. Resistance to innovation then takes the form of preserving social objectives. The difficulties are magnified once we realize that objectives may be attached to the clientele—the poor, outdoor men, lumbermen—with whom organizational members identify. The objectives of the organization may have attracted them precisely because they see it as a means of service to people they value. They may view changes in objectives, therefore, as proposals for "selling out" the clients they wish to serve. In their eyes evaluation becomes an enemy of the people.

Evaluative man must learn to live with contradictions. He must reduce his commitments to the organizations in which he works, the programs he carries out, and the clientele he serves. Evaluators must become agents of change acting in favor of programs as yet unborn and clienteles that are unknown. Prepared to impose change on others, evaluators must have sufficient stability to carry out their own work. They must maintain their own organization while simultaneously preparing to abandon it. They must obtain the support of existing bureaucracies while pursuing antibureaucratic policies. They must combine political feasibility with analytical purity. Only a brave man would predict that these combinations of qualities can be found in one and the same person and organization.

Evaluation and organization may be contradictory terms. Organizational structure implies stability while the process of evaluation suggests change. Organization generates commitment while evaluation inculcates skepticism. Evaluation speaks to the relationship between action and objectives while organization relates it activities to programs and clientele. No one can say for certain that self-evaluating organizations can exist, let alone become the prevailing form of administration. We can learn a good deal about the production and use of evaluation in government, nonetheless, by considering the requirements of obtaining so extraordinary a state of affairs—a self-evaluating organization.

The Policy-Administration Dichotomy Revisited

Organization requires the division of labor. Not everyone can do everything. Who, then, will carry out the evaluative activity and who will administer the programs for which the organization is responsible?

Practically every organization has a program staff, by whatever name called, that advises top officials about policy problems. They are small in numbers and conduct whatever formal evaluation goes on in the organization. They may exert considerable power in the organization through their persuasiveness and access to the top men, or they may be merely a benign growth that can be seen but has little effect on the body of the organization. Insofar as one is interested in furthering analytical activities, one must be concerned with strengthening them in regard to other elements. The idea of the self-evaluating organization, however, must mean more than this: a few men trying to force evaluation on an organization hundreds or thousands of times larger than they are. The spirit of the self-evaluating organization suggests that, in some meaningful way, the entire organization is infused with the evaluative ethic.

Immediately we are faced with the chain of command. How far down must the spirit of evaluation go in order to ensure the responsiveness of the organization as a whole? If all personnel are involved there would appear to be insuperable difficulties in finding messengers, mail clerks, and secretaries to meet the criteria. If we move up one step to those who deal with the public and carry out the more complex kind of activity, the numbers involved may still be staggering. These tens of thousands of people certainly do not have the qualifications necessary to conduct evaluative activities, and it would be idle to pretend that they would. The forest ranger and the national park officer may be splendid people, but they are not trained in evaluation and they are not likely to be. Yet evaluational activity appropriate to each level must be found if evaluation is to permeate the organization.

There has long been talk in the management circles of combining accountability with decentralization. Organizational subunits are given autonomy within circumscribed limits for which they are held strictly accountable to their hierarchical superiors. Central power is masked but it is still there. Dividing the task so that each subunit has genuine autonomy would mean giving them a share in central decisions affecting the entire organization. Decentralization is known to exist only to the extent that field units follow inconsistent and contradictory policies. One can expect the usual headquarters—field rivalries to develop—the one stressing appreciation of local problems and interests, the other fearing dissolution as the mere sum of its clashing units. Presumably the tension will be manifested in terms of rival analyses. The center should win out because of its greater expertise, but the local units will always be the specialists on their own problems. They will have to be put in their place. We are back, it seems, to hierarchy. How can the center get what it wants out of the periphery without over-formalizing their relationship?

One model, the internalized gyroscope, is recorded in Herbert Kaufman's classic on *The Forest Ranger.* By recruitment and training, the forest rangers are socialized into central values that they carry with them wherever they go and apply to specific circumstances. Central control is achieved without apparent effort or innumerable detailed instructions, because the rangers have internalized the major premises from which appropriate actions may generally be deduced. The problem of the self-evaluating organization is more difficult because it demands problem solving divorced from commitments to specific policies and organizational structures. The level of skill required is considerably higher and the locus of identification much more diffuse. The Israeli Army has had considerable success in inculcating problem-solving skills (rather than carrying out predetermined instructions) among its officers.[1] But their organizational identification is far more intense than can be expected elsewhere.

Suppose that most organizational personnel are too unskilled to permit them to engage in evaluation. Suppose it is too costly to move around hundreds of thousands of government officials who carry out most of the work of government. The next alternative is to make the entire central administration into an evaluative unit that directs the self-evaluating organization. Several real-world models are available. What used to be called the administration class in Great Britain illustrates one type of central direction. They move frequently among the great departments and seek (with the political ministers involved) to direct the activities of the vast bureaucracy around them. They are chosen for qualities of intellect that enable them to understand policy and for qualities of behavior that enable them to get along with their fellows. At the apex stands the Treasury, an organization with few operating commitments, whose task it is to monitor the activities of the bureaucracy and to introduce changes when necessary. Economic policy, which is the special preserve of the Treasury, is supposed to undergo rapid movement, and its personnel are used to changing tasks and objectives at short notice. Though divorced in a way from the organizations in which they share responsibility with the political ministers, top civil servants are also part of them by virtue of their direct administrative concerns. Complaints are increasingly heard that these men are too conservative in defense of departmental interests, too preoccupied with immediate matters, or too bound by organizational tradition to conduct serious evaluation. Hence, the Fulton Report claimed, they adapt too slowly, if at all, to changing circumstances. Tentative steps have been taken, therefore, to establish a Central Policy Review Staff to do policy analysis for the cabinet and to otherwise encourage evaluative activity.

Germany and Sweden have proceeded considerably further in the same direction. Departments in Sweden are relatively small groups of men concerned with policy questions, while administration is delegated to large public corporations set up for the purpose.[2] The state governments in Germany (the *Lander*) do over 90 percent of the administrative work, with the central government departments presumably engaged with larger questions of policy. The student of public administration in America will at once realize where he is at. The policy-administration dichotomy, so beloved of early American administrative theorists, which was thoroughly demolished, it seemed, in the decades of the '40's and '50's, has suddenly reappeared with new vitality.

The policy-administration dichotomy originated with Frank Goodnow and others in their effort to legitimate the rise of the civil service and with it the norm of neutral-competence in government. They sought to save good government from the evils of the spoils system by insulating it from partisan politics. Congress made policy, and the task of the administrative apparatus was to find the appropriate technical means to carry it out. Administrative actions were thought to be less general and more technical so that well-motivated administrators would be able to enact the will of the people as received from Congress or the President. Civil servants could then be chosen on the basis of their technical merits rather than their partisan or policy politics. An avalanche of criticism, begun in earnest by Paul Appleby's *Policy and Administration,* overwhelmed these arguments on every side. Observation of congressional statutes showed that they were often vague, ambiguous, and contradictory. There simply were not clear objectives to which the administrators could subordinate themselves. Observation of administrative behavior showed that conflicts over the policy to be adopted continued unabated in the bureaus and departments. Important decisions were made by administrators that vitally affected the lives of people. Choice abounded and administrators seized on it. Indeed, they were often themselves divided on how to interpret statutes or how generally to frame policies under them. Interest groups were observed to make strenuous efforts to get favorable administrative enactments. Moreover, sufficiently precise knowledge did not exist to determine the best way to carry out a general objective in many areas. Given the large areas of uncertainty and ignorance, the values and choices of administrators counted a great deal. Taken at this level there was not too much that could be said for maintaining the distinction between policy and administration. Nevertheless, nagging doubts remained.

Were politics and administration identical? If they were, then it was difficult to understand how we were able to talk about them separately. Or was politics simply a cover term for all the things that different organs of the government did? If politics and administration could be separated in some way, then a division of labor might be based on them. No doubt the legislative will, if there was one, could be undermined by a series of administrative enactments. But were not these administrative decisions of a smaller and less encompassing kind than those usually made by Congress? Were there not ways in which the enactments of Congress were (or could be) made more authoritative than the acts of administrators? Overwhelming administrative discretion did violence to democratic theory.

As the world moves into the 1970's, we will undoubtedly see significant efforts to rehabilitate the policy-administration dichotomy. The dissatisfactions of modern industrial life are being poured on the bureaucracy. It seems to grow larger daily while human satisfaction does not increase commensurately. It has become identified with red tape and resistance to change. Yet no one can quite imagine doing away with it in view of the ever-increasing demand for services. So politicians who feel that the bureaucracy has become a liability,[3] clientele who think they might be better served under other arrangements, taxpayers who resent the sheer costs, policy analysts who regard existing organizations as barriers to the application of intelligence, will join together in seeking ways to make bureaucracy more responsive. How better do this than by isolating its innovative functions from the mass of officialdom? Instead of preventing administration from being contaminated by politics, however, the purpose of the new dichotomy will be to insulate policy from the stultifying influences of the bureaucracy.

Who Will Pay the Costs of Change?

While most organizations evaluate some of their policies periodically, the self-evaluating organization would do so continuously. These evaluative activities would be inefficient, that is, they would cost more than they are worth, unless they led to change. Indeed the self-evaluating organization is purposefully set up to encourage change.

The self-evaluating organization will have to convince its own members to live with constant change. They may think they love constant upset when they first join the organization, but experience is likely to teach them otherwise. Man's appetite for rapid change is strictly limited. People cannot bear to have their cherished beliefs challenged or their lives altered on a continuing basis. The routines of yesterday are swept away, to be replaced by new ones. Anxiety is induced because they cannot get their bearings. They have trouble knowing exactly what they should be doing. The ensuing confusion may lead to inefficiencies in the form of hesitation or random behavior designed to cover as many bases as possible. Cynicism may grow as the wisdom of the day before yesterday gives way to new truth, which is in turn replaced by a still more radiant one. The leaders of the self-evaluating organization will have to counter this criticism.

Building support for policies within an organization requires internal selling. Leaders must convince the members of the organization that what they are doing is worthwhile. Within the self-evaluating organization the task may initially be more difficult than in more traditional bureaucracies. Its personnel are accustomed to question policy proposals and to demand persuasive arguments in their support. Once the initial campaign is proven successful, however, enthusiasm can be expected to reach a high pitch after all existing policies have been evaluated, new alternatives have been analyzed, and evidence has been induced in favor of a particular alternative. The danger here is overselling. Convinced that "science" is in their favor, persuaded that their paper calculations are in tune with the world, the evaluators believe a little too much in their own ideas. They are set up for more disappointment from those who expect less. How much greater the difficulty, then, when continuous evaluation suggests the need for another change in policy. Now two internal campaigns are necessary: the first involves unselling the old policy and the second involves selling the new one. All virtues become unsuspected vices and last year's goods are now seen to be hopelessly shoddy. Perpetual change has its costs.

Maintenance of higher rates of change depend critically on the ability of those who produce it to make others pay the associated costs. If the change makers are themselves forced to bear the brunt of their actions, they will predictably seek to stabilize their environment. That is the burden of virtually the entire sociological literature on organizations from Weber to Crozier. The needs of the members displace the goals of the organization. The public purposes that the organization was supposed to serve give way to its private acts. Its own hidden agendas dominate the organization.

Rather than succumb to the diseases of bureaucracy, the self-evaluating organization will be tempted to pass them on to others. The self-evaluating organization can split itself off into "evaluating" and "administering" parts, thus making lower levels pay the costs of change, or it can seek to impose them on other organizations in its environment. We shall deal first with difficulties encountered in trying to stabilize the evaluative top of the organization while the bottom is in a continuous state of flux.

Let us suppose that an organization separates its evaluative head from its administrative body. The people at the top do not have operating functions. They are, in administrative jargon, all staff rather than line. Their task is to appraise the consequences of existing policies, work out better alternatives, and have the new policies they recommend carried out by the administrative unit.

Who would bear the cost of change? One can imagine evaluators running around merrily suggesting changes to and fro without having to implement them. The anxiety would be absorbed by the administrators. They would have to be the ones to change gears and to smooth out the difficulties. But they will not stand still for this. Their belief about what is administratively feasible and organizationally attainable must be part of the policy that is adopted. So the administrators will bargain with the evaluators.

Administrators have significant resources to bring to this struggle. They deal with the public. They collect the basic information that is sent upward in one form or another. They can drag their feet, mobilize clientele, hold back information, or otherwise make cooperation difficult. The evaluators have their own advantages. They have greater authority to issue rules and regulations. They are experts in manipulating data and models to justify existing policies or denigrate them.

Held responsible for policy but prohibited from administering it directly, the evaluators have an incentive to seek antibureaucratic delivery systems. They will, for example, prefer an income to a service strategy.[4] The evaluators can be pretty certain that clients will receive checks mailed from the central computer, whereas they cannot be sure that the services they envisage will be delivered by hordes of bureaucrats in the manner they would like. Providing people with income to buy better living quarters has the great advantage of not requiring a corps of officials to supervise public housing. Evaluators do not have the field personnel to supervise innumerable small undertakings; they, therefore, will prefer large investment projects over small ones. They can also make better use of their small number of people on projects that are expensive and justify devotion of large amounts of analytical time. Contrarywise, administrators will emphasize far-flung operations providing services requiring large numbers of people that only they can perform. In a house of many mansions they will be the masters.

There are circumstances, of course, in which administrators and evaluators will reverse their normal roles. If the evaluators feel that there is not enough government employment, for example, they may seek labor-intensive operations. Should the administrators feel they are already over-burdened, they may welcome policies that are easily centralized and directed by machines performing rote operations. The more likely tendency, however, is for administrators and evaluators to expand into each other's domain. Each one can reduce the bargaining powers of the other by taking unto himself some of his competitors' advantages. Thus the administrators may recruit their own policy analysts to compete with the evaluators who, in turn, will seek their own contacts within the administrative apparatus in order to ensure a steady and reliable flow of information. If this feuding goes far enough, the result will be two organizations acting in much the same way as the single one they replaced but with additional problems of coordination.

Evaluation Incorporated

It is but a short step from separating evaluation from administration to the idea of rival teams of evaluators. A rough equivalent of a competitive market can be introduced by allowing teams of evaluators to compete for direction of policy in a given area. The competition would take place in terms of price (we can accomplish a specified objective at a lower cost), quality (better policies for the same money), quantity (we can produce more at the same cost), maintenance (we can fix things when they go wrong), experience (we have a proven record), values (our policies will embody your preferences) and talent (when it comes down to it, you are buying our cleverness and we are superior). The team that won the competition would be placed in charge until it left to go elsewhere or another team challenged it. The government might raise its price to keep a talented team or it might lower it to get rid of an incompetent one. The incentives for evaluation would be enormous, restrained, of course, by ability to perform lest the evaluators go bankrupt when they run out of funds or lose business to competitors.

The first task of the new enterprise would be to establish its own form of organization. What organizational arrangements are necessary to make competition among evaluators feasible?

Evaluators must either be assured to employment somewhere or engage in other dispensible occupations from which they can be recruited at short notice. A handful of evaluators could always be recruited by ad hoc methods from wherever they are found. But teams of evaluators sufficient to direct major areas of policy would be difficult to assemble at short notice. They would all be doing different things instead of working together, which is part of the experience they need to be successful. Nor can they form a team unless they can all promise to be on the job at a certain time if their bid is successful, yet at the same time have other jobs to fall back on if they are turned down.

In the previous model, where the evaluators generate new policies and the administrators carry them out, these bureaucrats carried the major burden of uncertainty. Under the new model this imbalance is redressed because the evaluators have to worry about security of employment. Few people like to shift jobs all the time; even fewer like the idea of periodic unemployment alternating with the anxiety of bidding to get jobs and performing to keep them. Mechanisms will be found, we can be certain, to reduce their level of uncertainty to tolerable dimensions.

Evaluators may choose to work within existing administrative organizations, accepting a lower status, learning to live with disappointment, in return for job stability. This is one pattern that already exists. Evaluators may go to private industry and universities on the understanding they will be able to make occasional forays into government as part of a tiny group of advisors to leading officials. This is also done now. Both alternatives do away with the idea of competition; they merely graft a small element of evaluation onto existing organizations on a catch-as-catch-can basis.

In order to preserve evaluators who are in a position to compete for the direction of policy, it will be necessary for them to form stable organizations of their own. Like the existing firms of management consultants they resemble, these evaluators would bid on numerous projects; the difference would be that they would do the actual policy work as part of the public apparatus rather than making recommendations and then disappearing. Evaluation, Incorporated, as we shall call it, would contain numerous possible teams, some of whom would be working and others who would be preparing to go to work. The firm would have to demand considerable overhead to provide services for the evaluators, to draw up proposals, and to compensate those of its members who are (hopefully) temporarily out of work. Keeping Evaluation, Incorporated, solvent by maintaining a high level of employment will become a major organizational goal.

Evaluation, Incorporated, is an organization. It has managers who are concerned with survival. It has members who must be induced to remain. It has clients who must be served. So it will constitute itself a lobby for evaluation. When the demand for its services is high, it will be able to insist on the evaluative ethic; it will take its services to those who are prepared to appreciate (by paying for) them. But when demands are low, Evaluation, Incorporated, must trim its sails. It has a payroll to meet. Rather than leave a job when nonanalytical criteria prevail, it may have to swallow its pride and stay on. Its managers can easily convince themselves that survival is not only good for them but for society, which will benefit from the good they will be able to do in better times.

If their defects stem from their insecurities, the remedy will be apparent; increase the stability of evaluators by guaranteeing them tenure of employment. Too close identification with party or policy proved, in any event, to be a mixed blessing. They feasted while they were in favor and famished when they were out. Apparently they require civil service status, a government corporation, say, devoted to evaluation.

Perhaps the General Accounting Office (GAO), which is beginning to do analytic studies, will provide a model of an independent governmental organization devoted to evaluation. Since it has a steady source of income from its auditing work, so to speak, it can afford to form, break up, and recreate teams of evaluators. Its independence from the Executive Branch (the Accountant General is responsible to Congress and serves a 15-year term) might facilitate objective analysis. But the independence of GAO has been maintained because it eschews involvement in controversial matters. If the new General Evaluation Office (GEO) were to issue reports that increased conflict, there would undoubtedly be a strong impulse to bring it under regular political control. The old auditing function might be compromised because objectivity is difficult to maintain about a program one has sponsored, or because public disputes lower confidence in its operations. Opponents of its policy positions might begin to questions its impartiality in determining the legality of government expenditures. Yet protection would be difficult to arrange because the new GEO did not have a political client.

By attending to the problems of an organization that supplies evaluation to others, we hope to illuminate the dilemmas of any organization that wishes to seriously engage in continuous analyses of its own activities.

Evaluation, which criticizes certain programs and proposes to replace them with others, is manifestly a political activity. If evaluation is not political in the sense of party partisanship, it is political in the sense of policy advocacy. Without a steady source of political support, without that essential manifestation of affection from somebody out there in society, it will suffer the fate of abandoned children: the self-evaluating organization is unlikely to prosper in an orphanage.

Adjusting to the Environment

The self-evaluating organization is one that uses its own analysis of its own programs in order to alter or abolish them. Its ability to make changes when its analysis suggests they are desirable is an essential part of its capacity to make self-evaluation a living reality. Yet the ability of any single organization to make self-generated changes is limited by the necessity of receiving support from its environment.

The leaders of a self-evaluating organization cannot afford to leave the results of their labors up to the fates. If their "batting average" goes way down, they will be in trouble. Members of the organization will lose faith in evaluation because it does not lead to changes in actual policy. Those who are attracted to the organization by the prospect of being powerful as well as analytical will leave to join more promising ventures, or old clients will become dissatisfied without new ones to take their place. As the true believers depart, personnel who are least motivated by the evaluative ethic will move into higher positions. Revitalization of the organization via the promotion and recruitment of professing evaluators will become impossible.

In order to avoid the deadly cycle—failure, hopelessness, abandonment—leaders of the self-evaluating organization must seek some proportion of success. They must select the organization's activities, not only with an eye toward their analytical justification, but with a view toward receiving essential support from their environment. Hence they become selective evaluators. They must prohibit the massive use of organizational resources in areas where they see little chance of success. They must seek out problems that are easy to solve and changes that are easy to make because they do not involve radical departures from the past. They must be prepared to hold back the results of evaluation when they believe the times are not propitious; they must be ready to seize the time for change whether or not the evaluations are fully prepared or wholly justified. Little by little, it seems, the behavior of the leaders will become similar to those of other organization officials who also seek to adapt to their environment.

The growing conservatism of the self-evaluating organization is bound to cause internal strains. There are certain to be disagreements about whether the organization is being too cautious. No one can say for sure whether the leaders have correctly appraised the opportunities in a rapidly shifting environment. If they try to do too much, they risk failure in the political world. If they try to do too little, they risk abandoning their own beliefs and losing the support of their most dedicated members. Maintaining a balance between efficacy and commitment is not easy.

Now the self-evaluating organization need not be a passive bystander negotiating its environment. It can seek to mobilize interests in favor of the programs it wishes to adopt. It can attempt to neutralize opposition. It can try to persuade its present clientele that they will be better off, or instill a wish to be served on behalf of new beneficiaries. One fears that its reputation among clientele groups may not be the best, however, because, as a self-evaluating organization, it must be prepared to abandon (or drastically modify) programs and with them the clientele they serve. The clients will know that theirs is only a marriage of convenience, that the self-evaluating organization is eager to consider more advantageous alliances, and that they must always be careful to measure their affection according to the exact degree of services rendered. The self-evaluating organization cannot expect to receive more love than it gives. In fact, it must receive less.

Evaluation can never be fully rewarded. There must, in the nature of things, be other considerations that prevail over evaluation, even where the powers that be would like to follow its dictates. The policies preferred by the self-evaluating organization are never the only ones being contemplated by the government, there are always multitudes of policies in being or about to be born. Some of these are bound to be inconsistent with following the dictates of evaluation. Consider the impact of fiscal policy upon analysis. Suppose the time has come for financial stringency; the government has decided that expenditures must be reduced. Proposals for increases may not be allowed no matter how good the justification. Reductions may be made whether indicated by analysis or not. Conversely, a political decision may be made to increase expenditure. The substantive merits of various policies have clearly been subordinated to their immediate financial implications.

Evaluation may be wielded as a weapon in the political wars. It may be used by one faction or party versus another. Of particular concern to the self-evaluating organization is a one-sided approach to evaluation that creates internal problems. It is not unusual, as was recently the case in Great Britain when the Conservative Party returned to office, for a government to view evaluation as a means of putting down the bureaucracy. A two-step decision rule may be followed: the recommendations of evaluation may be accepted when they lead to reduction and rejected when they suggest increases in expenditure. Before long the members of the organization become reluctant to provide information that will only be used in a biased way. The evaluative enterprise depends on common recognition that the activity is being carried out somehow in order to secure better policies, whatever these may be, and not in support of a predetermined position. If this understanding is violated, people down the line will refuse to cooperate. They will withhold their contribution by hiding information or by simply not volunteering to find it. The morale of the self-evaluating organization will be threatened because its members are being asked to pervert the essence of their calling.

It's the same the whole world over: the analytically virtuous are not necessarily rewarded nor are the wicked (who do not evaluate) punished. The leaders of the self-evaluating organization, therefore, must redouble their effort to obtain political help.

Joining Knowledge with Power

To consider the requirements necessary for a self-evaluating organization is to understand why they are rarely met. The self-evaluating organization, it turns out, would be susceptible to much the same kinds of anti-evaluative tendencies as are existing organizations. It, too, must stabilize its environment. It, too, must secure internal loyalty and outside support. Evaluation must, at best, remain but one element in administrative organizations. Yet no one can say today that it is overemphasized. Flights of fancy should not lead anyone to believe that inordinate attention to evaluation is an imminent possibility. We have simply come back to asking how a little more rather than a little less might become part of public organizations. How might analytic integrity be combined with political efficacy?

Evaluative man seeks knowledge, but he also seeks power. His desire to do good is joined with his will to act powerfully. One is no good without the other. A critical incentive for pursuing evaluation is that the results become governmental policy. There is little point in making prescriptions for public policy for one's own private amusement. Without knowledge it would be wrong to seek power. But without power it becomes more difficult to obtain knowledge. Why should anyone supply valuable information to someone who can neither help nor harm him? Access to information may be given only on condition programmatic goals are altered. Evaluative man is well off when he can pyramid resources so that greater knowledge leads to enhanced power, which in turn increases his access to information. He is badly off when the pursuit of power leads to the sacrifice of evaluation. His own policy problem is how to do enough of both (and not too much of either) so that knowledge and power reinforce rather than undermine one another.

The political process generates a conflict of interest within the evaluative enterprise. The evaluators view analysis as a means of deciding on better policies and selling them to others. Clients (elected officials, group leaders, top administrators) view analysis as a means of better understanding the available choices so they can control them. Talk of "better policies," as if it did not matter who determined them, only clouds the issues.

The evaluative group within an organization would hope that it could show political men the worth of its activities. The politicians, in turn, hope to learn about the desirability of the programs that are being evaluated. But their idea of desirability manifestly includes the support which programs generate for them and the organizations of which they are a part. Hence evaluation must be geared to producing programs that connect the interests of political leaders to the outcomes of governmental actions, otherwise, they will reject evaluation and with it the men who do it.

A proposed policy is partly a determinant of its own success; the support it gathers or loses in clientele is fed back into its future prospects. By its impact on the future environment of the organization, the proposed policy affects the kinds of work the organization is able to do. Pure evaluative man, however single-minded his concentration on the intrinsic merits of programs, must also consider their interaction effects on his future ability to pursue his craft. Just as he would insist on including the impact of one element in a system on another in his policy analysis, so must he consider how his present recommendations affect future ones. A proper evaluation includes the impact of a policy on the organizations responsible for it.

Consider in this organizational context the much-discussed problem of diverse governmental programs that may contribute to the same ends without anyone being able to control them. There may be unnecessary redundancy, where some programs overlap, side by side with large areas of inattention to which no programs are directed. More services of one kind and less of another are provided than might be strictly warranted. Without evaluation no one can really say whether there are too many or too few programs or whether their contents are appropriate. But an evaluation that did all this would get nowhere unless it resulted in different institutional processes for handling the same set of problems.

Even on its own terms, then, evaluation should not remain apart from the organizations on which it is dependent for implementation. Organizational design and policy analysis are part of the same governmental process. If an organization wishes to reduce its identification with programs (and the clients who support them), for example, so that it can afford to examine different types of policy, it must adopt a political strategy geared to that end.

The self-evaluating organization would be well advised not to depend too much on a single type of clientele. Diversification is its strategy. The more diverse its services, the more varied its clientele, the less the self-evaluating organization has to depend on any one of them, the more able it is to shift the basis of its support. Diversity creates political flexibility.

Any organization that produces a single product, so to speak, that engages in a limited range of activities is unlikely to abandon them willingly. Its survival, after all, is bound up in its program. If the program goes, the organization dies. One implication drawn from these considerations is that the traditional wisdom concerning governmental organization badly needs revision.[5] If the basic principle of organization is that similar programs should be grouped together, as is now believed to be the case, these organizations will refuse to change. On the contrary, agencies should be encouraged to differentiate their products and diversify their outputs. If they are not faced with declining demand for all their programs, they will be more willing to abandon or modify a single one. The more varied its programs, the less dependent the organization is on a single one, the greater its willingness to change.

No matter how good its internal analysis, or how persuasively an organization justifies its programs to itself, there is something unsatisfying about allowing it to judge its own case. The ability of organizations to please themselves must ultimately (at least in a democratic society) give way to judgment by outsiders. Critics of organizations must, therefore, recognize that their role is an essential one. Opposition is part and parcel of the evaluative process. The goal would be to secure a more intelligent and analytically sophisticated level of advocacy on all sides. Diverse analyses might become, as Harry Rowen has suggested, part of the mutual partisan adjustment through which creative use is made of conflicts among organized interests.

Competition, per se, however, need not lead to fundamental change. Organizations may go on the offensive by growing bigger instead of better, that is, by doing more of the same. The change in which they are interested is a change in magnitude. We are all familiar with the salesmanship involved in moving to new technologies or larger structures where internal dynamism and grandiose conceptions are mistaken for new ideas. Motion may be a protection against change.

Competition, if it is to lead to desirable consequences, must take place under appropriate rules specifying who can make what kind of transaction. No one would advocate unrestrained competition among economic units in the absence of a market that makes it socially advantageous for participants to pursue their private interests in expectation of mutual gain. Where parties are affected who are not directly represented in the market, for instance, the rules may be changed to accommodate a wider range of interests. Competition among rival policies and their proponents also takes place in an arena that specifies rules for exercising power in respect to particular decisions. Evaluators must, therefore, consider how their preferred criteria for decision will be affected by the rules for decision in political arenas within which they must operate.

We have, it appears, returned to politics. Unless building support for policies is an integral part of designing them, their proponents are setting themselves up for disappointment. To say that one will first think of a great idea and then worry about how it might be implemented is a formula for failure.[6] A good evaluation not only specifies desirable outcomes but suggests institutional mechanisms for achieving them.

If you don't know how to make an evaluation, it may be a problem for you but not for anyone else. If you do know how to evaluate, it becomes a problem for others. Evaluation is an organizational problem. While the occasional lone rider may be able to fire off an analysis now and then, he must eventually institutionalize his efforts if he is to produce a steady output. The overwhelming bulk of evaluation takes place within organizations. The rejection of evaluation is done largely by the organizations that ask for it. To create an organization that evaluates its own activities evidently requires an organizational response. If evaluation is not done at all, if it is done but not used, if used but twisted out of shape, the place to look first is not the technical apparatus but the organization.

Organization is first but not last. Always it is part of a larger society that conditions what it can do. Evaluation is also a social problem. So long as organizational opposition to evaluation is in the foreground, we are not likely to become aware of the social background. Should this initial resistance be overcome, and individual organizations get to like evaluation, however, it would still face multiple defenses thrown up by social forces.

Evaluation as Trust

For the self-evaluating organization all knowledge must be contingent. Improvement is always possible, change for the better is always in view though not necessarily yet attained. It is the organization *par excellence* that seeks knowledge. The ways in which it seeks to obtain knowledge, therefore, uniquely defines its character.

The self-evaluating organization would be skeptical rather than committed. It would continuously be challenging its own assumptions. Not dogma but scientific doubt would be its distinguishing feature. It would seek new truth instead of defending old errors. Testing hypotheses would be its main work.

Like the model community of scholars, the self-evaluating organization would be open, truthful, and explicit. It would state its conclusions in public, show how they were determined, and give others the opportunity to refute them. The costs and benefits of alternative programs for various groups in society would be indicated as precisely as available knowledge would permit. Everything would be above board. Nothing would be hidden.

Are there ways of securing the required information? Can the necessary knowledge be created? Will the truth make men free? Attempting to answer these profound queries would take me far beyond the confines of this exploratory article. But I would like to suggest by illustration that the answers to each of them depend critically on the existence of trust among social groups and within organizations. The acceptance of evaluation requires a community of men who share values.

An advantage of formal analysis, in which the self-evaluating organization specializes, is that it does not depend entirely on learning from experience. That can be done by ordinary organizations. By creating models abstracting relationships from the areas of the universe they wish to control, evaluators seek to substitute manipulation of their models for events in the world. By rejecting alternatives their models tell them will work out badly (or not as well as others), these analysts save scarce resources and protect the public against less worthy actions. Ultimately, however, there must be an appeal to the world of experience. No one, not even the evaluators themselves, are willing to try their theoretical notions on large populations without more tangible reasons to believe that the recommended alternatives prove efficacious.[7]

Since the defect of ordinary organizations is that they do not learn well from experience, the self-evaluating organization seeks to order that experience so that knowledge will be gained from it. The proof that a policy is good is that it works when it is tried. But not everything can be tried everywhere. Hence experiments lie at the heart of evaluation. They are essential for connecting alleged causes with desired effects in the context of limited resources.

The ability of the self-evaluating organization to perform its functions depends critically upon a climate of opinion that favors experimentation. If resources are severely constrained, for example, leading to reluctance to try new ventures, the self-evaluating organization cannot function as advertised. Should there exist strong feeling that everyone must be treated alike, to choose another instance, experimentation would be ruled out. Take the case of the "More Effective Schools" movement in New York City. The idea was to run an experiment to determine whether putting more resources into schools would improve the performance of deprived children. In order to qualify as a proper experiment, More Effective Schools had to be established in some places but not in others, so that there would be control groups. The demand for equality of treatment was so intense, however, that mass picketing took place at the school sites. Favored treatment for these schools was taken as *prima facie* evidence of discrimination. It became apparent that More Effective Schools would have to be tried everywhere or nowhere. Clearly the social requisites of experimentation would have to exist for self-evaluating organizations to be effective. Unless groups trust each other, they will neither allow experiments to be conducted nor accept the results.

Although ways of learning without experimentation may be found, no evaluation is possible without adequate information. But how much is enough? Hierarchies in organizations exist in order to reduce information. If the men at the top were to consider all the bits of data available in the far-flung reaches of the organization, they would be overwhelmed.

As information is weeded and compressed on its way through the hierarchy, however, important bits may be eliminated or distorted. One of the most frequently voiced criticisms of organizations is that the men at the top do not know what is going on. Information is being withheld from them or is inaccurate so that they make decisions on the basis of mistaken impressions. The desire to pass on only good news results in the elimination of information that might place the conveyer in a bad light. Top officials may, therefore, resort to such devices as securing overlapping sources of information or planting agents at lower levels. There are limits to these efforts, however, because the men at the top have only so much time to digest what they have been told. So they vacillate between fear of information loss and being unable to struggle out from under masses of data.

How might the self-evaluating organization deal with information bias? Organization members would have to be rewarded for passing on bad news. Those who are responsible for the flow of information must, at the least, not be punished for telling the truth. If they are also the ones in charge of administering the policy, it will not be possible to remove them for bad performance because once that is done their successors will be motivated to suppress such information. The top men must themselves be willing to accept the blame though they may not feel this is their responsibility and though their standing may be compromised. The very idea of a hierarchy may have to give way to shifting roles in which superior and subordinate positions are exchanged so that each member knows he will soon be in the other's position. The self-evaluating organization clearly requires an extraordinary degree of mutual trust.

The spread of self-evaluating organizations could enhance social trust by widening the area of agreement concerning the consequences of existing policies and the likely effects of change. Calculations concerning who benefited and to what degree would presumably aid in political cost-benefit analyses. The legitimacy of public institutions would be enhanced because they resulted from a more self-consciously analytical process that was increasingly recognized as such. Evaluation would be informative, meliorative, and stabilizing in the midst of change. It sounds idyllic.

More information, per se, need not lead to greater agreement, however, if the society is wracked by fundamental cleavages. As technology makes information more widely available, the need for interpretation will grow. Deluged by data, distrustful of others, citizens may actually grow apart as group leaders collect more information about how badly off they are compared to what they ought to be. The more citizens trust group leaders rather than governmental officials, the greater the chance their differences will be magnified rather than reconciled. The clarification of objectives may make it easier to see the social conflicts implicit in the distribution of income or cultural preferences concerning the environment or the differing styles of life attached to opposing views of the ideal society. Evaluation need not create agreement; evaluation may presuppose agreement.

Notes

1. Dan Horowitz, "Flexible Responsiveness and Military Strategy: The Case of the Israeli Army," *Policy Sciences,* Vol. 1, No. 2 (Summer 1970), pp. 191-205.
2. Hans Thorelli, "Overall Planning and Management in Sweden," *International Social Science Bulletin,* Vol. VIII, No. 2 (1956).
3. The most dramatic and visible change can be found in the American presidency. Presidents have increasingly bureaucratized their operations. Within the Executive Office there now exist sizeable subunits, characterized by specialization and the division of labor, for dealing with the media of information and communication, Congress, foreign

and domestic policy, and more. At the same time, Presidents seek the right to intervene at any level within the Executive Branch on a sporadic basis. The administrators are being prodded to change while the President stabilizes his environment. Thus we find President Nixon saying that he wants something done about that awful Bureau of Indian Affairs, as if it did not belong to him, or asking citizens to elect him again so he can save them from the compulsory busing fostered by his own bureaucracy. He wants to escape blame for bureaucratic errors but keep the credit for inspiring changes.

4. See Robert A. Levine, "Rethinking our Social Strategies," *The Public Interest,* No. 10 (Winter 1968).
5. William A. Niskanen, *Bureaucracy and Representative Government* (Chicago: Aldine-Atherton, 1971).
6. For further discussion along these lines see Jeffrey L. Pressman and Aaron Wildavsky, *Implementation: The Economic Development Administration in Oakland* (Berkeley and Los Angeles: University of California Press, forthcoming).
7. An exception of a kind is found in the area of defense policy where the purpose of the analytical exercises is to avoid testing critical hypotheses. Once the hypotheses concerning a nuclear war are tested, the evaluators may not be around to revise their analyses. See Aaron Wildavsky, "Practical Consequences of the Theoretical Study of Defense Policy," *Public Administration Review,* Vol. XXV, No. 1 (March 1965), pp. 90-103.

1972 (509-520)

ERWIN C. HARGROVE

The Bureaucratic Politics of Evaluation:
A Case Study of the Department of Labor

According to Miles' Law, "Where you stand depends upon where you sit."[1] We have all had the experience of suddenly understanding the point of view of previous antagonists when we find ourselves in their shoes. Advocacy inhibits empathy. Space and task thus have psychological properties that can become a basis for bureaucratic politics even if no external non-governmental interests are involved. This story is an illustration of that truth.

It is the story of the inability of three units of government within the same department to develop a common plan for the evaluation of the Comprehensive Employment and Training Act (CETA). The Under Secretary of Labor, the Assistant Secretary for Manpower, the Assistant Secretary for Policy, Evaluation and Research, and the Office of Management and Budget all wished such a plan to be developed. The Department of Labor units devoted much effort to collaboration, but in the end, the effort fell short. An explanation may throw light on the difficulty of linking evaluation research to the administration of programs. Too often evaluation research is a program in itself which proceeds quite apart from the implementation of policy.

The thesis of this paper is that attitudes toward knowledge influence bureaucratic behavior. These attitudes, in turn, are derived in part from bureaucratic positions and in part from the professional modes of thought which reside in different governmental roles. Since knowledge is always incomplete and since organization necessarily has a division of labor, a bureaucratic politics of knowledge is inevitable.

The Setting

Congress passed CETA in December 1973, and the program was set in place in the country during the following summer. CETA was intended primarily as a manpower training program. Since that time, a public employment title has been added as an anti-recession device, but the controversies over CETA described here revolve around how best to assess the efficacy of programs which train people for employment.[2]

The law was the first of three modified "special revenue sharing" measures which were enacted by the Republican administration and Democratic Congress. The law gathered a number of categorical training programs which had been developed in the previous decade into one broad category. This category, Title I, was bounded by federal maxims that training was to be given to the unemployed, lower income groups, the technologically displaced, and those whose increased skills might improve the functioning of labor markets. Training was to be planned and supervised by state, county, and city governments acting as prime sponsors. Each prime sponsor organization was to be composed of manpower professionals who would develop annual plans of service for their labor market area and provide these services themselves or through contractors. Federal regional office officials were to approve the plans and provide continuous technical assistance.

The federal role under CETA was to be loosely supervisory and evaluative rather than tightly administrative. Administrators in Washington and the regional offices were to allocate funds, assess results, sponsor research, and carry such knowledge to the prime sponsors through demonstrations and technical assistance.

The pre-CETA categorical program structure had required much closer federal supervision of field administration. Regional office staffs planned services for given areas and wrote contracts with quite diverse training organizations. Great attention had to be given to financial probity and administrative accountability. Questions about the efficacy of training had to take a back seat in the turmoil of day-to-day administration.

Evaluation research in this earlier time reflected the fragmentation of categorical programs. The studies were of specific programs by different contractors at different times. Comparability was missing. The programs themselves were continually being amended by Congress so that studies were often obsolete upon completion. Program managers seldom found specific evaluations helpful because time and management changes had usually made the research obsolete.[3]

The passage of CETA created a more orderly framework for evaluation. It became possible to think of a long-term study of a national sample of prime sponsors which might capture the effects of training on the future earnings of trainees and assess the relative effectiveness of different treatment strategies.

Two kinds of evaluation research have dominated the field. The first studies the effects of a national program in order to assess how benefits balance costs. Thus, one asks if participation in manpower training programs increases the subsequent earnings of trainees to a degree greater than if they had not participated. These gains can be compared to the costs of the program. This research also seeks to compare the effectiveness of different treatments. For example, how do classroom study and on-the-job training compare in their effects?

This research has usually looked at national programs as a whole by focusing on the recipients of services and control groups rather than the local units which deliver services. The findings have been of most value to policy officials who must decide how results should affect future budgets.

The managers of federal programs have not found such evaluation research helpful because it does not tell whether service delivery might be improved through administrative action. Therefore, program managers have relied upon a second kind of evaluation research. They commission short-term studies of administrative problems in specific programs, and they rely on management information reports from local deliverers of service to assess whether such units are delivering services efficiently. These kinds of information are seldom joined to data about the effects of a program on recipients. The focus is on short-term management problems.

It is desirable to join these two evaluation strategies. They are best linked by joining reports on costs, enrollments, and treatments in a sample of local units to a study of the impact of such training on the subsequent experience of recipients. It was difficult to do this with the crazy quilt structure of categorical manpower programs, but the uniform structure of the CETA program is congenial to joining the two kinds of evaluation research.

There is a third dimension to the evaluation problem which is broader than the question of efficient management. The delivery institutions may vary in their capacities to manage treatment strategies for desired outcomes effectively. Research on the implementation of federal social programs suggests that the capacities of local institutions to learn and assimilate treatment strategies devised elsewhere is crucial for implementation. It is also suggested that these strategies are necessarily altered to fit the character of local institutions as the price of implementation.[4] The federal role in CETA, as in the other special revenue sharing programs, is one of providing technical assistance to local units to increase their institutional capacities. Knowledge of these capacities is required for the new federal role.

The structure of the CETA program afforded an opportunity for these three kinds of knowledge to be joined in a common, overall research strategy. The fact that this was not done is the story to be told.

Organizational Division of Labor

Three units within the Department of Labor shared the responsibility for developing CETA evaluation plans. These were the office of the Assistant

Secretary for Policy Evaluation and Research (ASPER) and two units within the Manpower Administration.[5] The first of these was the CETA program itself, which was responsible for the administration of the law. The second was a small office of evaluation research within the Office of Policy, Evaluation and Research of the Manpower Administration (OPER). That office within OPER had the responsibility of developing all plans and instruments for the evaluation of CETA with assistance and advice from ASPER and the program divisions in the Manpower Administration. Each of these units had a particular orientation to knowledge that would become crucial to the performance of the new task. The Assistant Secretary for Policy, Evaluation and Research (ASPER) and his staff were located within the Office of the Secretary of Labor and had the secretary and undersecretary as their principal clients. The professional staff in this office were primarily career civil servants, but the directors of each of the divisions were academic economists on leave from universities. The dominant mode of thought was that of the economist. Whether the work was program-budget analysis or the planning of evaluation or other research, the emphasis was upon assessing and comparing programs by the economic calculus of benefits and costs. An adversarial stance was assumed in regard to the program divisions as the best way to serve the need of policy makers for an unbiased view of department programs.

The small evaluation division in ASPER was headed during fiscal year 1974 by George Johnson, an economist on leave from the University of Michigan. Johnson had succeeded Orley Ashenfelter, who had served for a year and then returned to Princeton. Both economists had been brought into government by James Blum, the acting deputy assistant secretary, who directed the program-budget analysis and evaluation efforts. Blum was convinced that evaluation research was essential for program-budget analysis of the kind carried out by his analysts in the annual budget cycle. It was seen as the best way to assess the merits of programs.

The principal commitment of Ashenfelter and Johnson, who had been collaborators in academic research, was to the development of the state of the evaluation art. In the manpower area this centered on the difficult task of assessing the contribution of training to the subsequent earnings of trainees through the use of social security data, control groups, and analysis of changing wage levels. ASPER itself was not to study programs but to develop the methods and means by which the program agencies might carry out evaluation.

In 1973, Johnson wrote a paper postulating that local governments were likely to use federal public employment funds as a substitute for local expenditures without much net increase in the number of people employed. Program managers in the Manpower Administration, which administered the public employment programs, were not satisfied with Johnson's paper. There were complaints that the paper had been circulated throughout government without having been shown to Manpower Administration officials in advance. Moreover, it was seen as an academic paper which only advanced hypotheses and which could be used to discredit existing programs.

These contrasting viewpoints were firmly anchored in organizational missions. They might be reduced or increased according to the temperaments of individuals at any given time, but the divisions were fundamental. It was assumed from the ASPER side that they were functional. The secretary would benefit from the advice of a disinterested adversary about programs. Program officials would accept the argument in the abstract but they did not like the reality. This was to be expected, but perhaps, more importantly, the ASPER adversarial stance weakened the technical assistance role. The implied sense of ASPER methodological superiority was reinforced by the latent challenge to the validity of programs.

For the most part program managers were not interested in the ASPER evaluation approach because the actual or expected findings were either inconclusive or remote in time. As one experienced civil servant put it:

> You get very bright people applying econometric techniques to limited data and, over and over, they come up with the conclusion that we can't say whether the programs are doing good or not. . . . The situation now is that the evaluator says "we can't tell" and the program people say "fine" and go on with the program.[6]

Program officials wanted evaluation research which would speak to their responsibilities for management. This was seen in a positive form by the respect accorded a small team within the OPER evaluation office which did studies of particular projects at the request of program managers. For example, the unit had written a report on the nine Comprehensive Manpower Projects—the demonstration prototypes for CETA prime sponsors. The report dealt with the political, bureaucratic, and operational problems involved in setting up such bodies. It provided the kind of knowledge an official in Washington could use if he were charged with writing guidelines and regulations for prime sponsors.

Charles Green, the head of this unit, believed that his success was due to his ability to answer the questions that managers asked. He withheld nothing critical but did not challenge the assumption of programs. His reports were never published and did not have wide circulation. Program managers had learned that he would explore a problem quickly and accurately.

Aside from the respect shown for Green's unit, the general attitude among managers toward most evaluation research sponsored by the Manpower Administration was also very critical. This research was developed by the evaluation unit within the Office of Policy Evaluation and Research

(OPER). The unit included the small, in-house, research staff directed by Green, but its main work was to write Requests for Proposals and arrange for evaluation studies to be done by external contractors.

Pierce Quinlan, the director of the CETA program, was very skeptical about the value of such evaluation work:

> . . . if the evaluators are left to their own devices they will revert. They have to be shown the importance of field, policy and budget concerns. . . . OE (evaluation unit) has become less a part of the operation of the organization and more a group of people who are dealing only with contractors. . . .[7]

These attitudes reflected the *ad hoc*, fragmented manner in which evaluation had been conducted before 1973. Many separate studies of programs were carried out under general guidance from the evaluation division of the Manpower Administration, but that unit was, itself, separated in psychological space from the program divisions. The evaluation unit in OPER was a small unit of eight to ten professionals. With the exception of one economist, their people were former program operators rather than specialists in evaluation. Their primary assignment was to write RFPs, fund studies, and disseminate the findings to the program divisions. They were one of the three units in OPER, the others being the policy analysis and research and development divisions. OPER was characterized as being quite separate from the program divisions in a study of the Manpower Administration done at this time by the National Academy of Sciences.[8]

In 1971, an Urban Institute team was brought in to analyze the evaluation systems of the department. The Urban Institute report concluded that the links between OPER's evaluation research and the work of program officials were weak.[9] Policy makers, such as the Assistant Secretary for Manpower, seemed to pay little attention to setting evaluation goals. OPER staff reported that they could not get such officials to think continuously or systematically about such questions. Program managers were reported to want answers to operational and management questions. All of this meant that the OPER evaluation group was more or less left to its own devices in developing a research program. The result was what might have been expected. A set of bureaucratic routines developed which became identified by the staff of the unit as the best way to thrive and keep their autonomy within the department. These routines revolved around the writing and funding of proposals to study categorical programs.

This was a rational response to the structure of the situation. Four factors were particularly important. First, the OPER evaluation staffs were not specialists; therefore, the research had to be done outside government. Second, the programs were numerous, varied, and continually changing so that there was sure to be discontinuity in research studies and findings. Third, the concerns of program managers reflected this discontinuity. That is, they were more interested in management than in evaluation. Finally, the contractors who did the research were necessarily given considerable autonomy because neither OPER nor the program divisions were organized separately or jointly to provide guidance. The resulting conjunction of these factors was that most evaluation studies were simply conducted for their own sake with little thought given to how they might reflect policy goals or be used to improve programs.

The studies conducted over a period of several years ranged from cost-benefit analyses, institutional descriptions, management analyses, and combinations of all three approaches. OPER staff lacked the kind of conceptual and methodological commitment which characterized ASPER. Each person had his own beliefs about good and bad evaluation, but the agenda of the unit was set more by the fragmentation of the situation than by any theory. The desire for bureaucratic autonomy in this situation thus became a defense of business as usual.

These background sketches of ASPER, OPER and the program managers are important for the story which follows. The general orientations toward knowledge and organization which have been described can be seen in the actions of the members of each group as they dealt with the others.

The Search for a Plan

During the spring of 1974, the ASPER and OPER evaluation staffs debated the design of the CETA evaluation. ASPER wanted to limit what was studied and the methods used to that which could be reliably measured. They were prepared to define the programs as having one goal—increase in the earnings of participants. In addition, they were ready to rely primarily upon social security data for that evidence despite obvious problems of the lack of such data for many women and youths before training. Their energies went into safeguarding the methodological correctness of the plan for a longitudinal evaluation of the impact of training on earnings. It was hoped that treatment and impact data would be joined in this longitudinal study through surveys of the prime sponsors. The OPER staff, by contrast, were skeptical that earnings data would be valid and believed, furthermore, that there were many goals of the program other than earnings. They were sure that this plurality of purposes was shared by the actual deliverers of service at the grass roots. The OPER staff were not methodologically sophisticated and, therefore, their efforts seemed awkward to ASPER staff with their academic orientation.

In January, 1974, OPER had prepared and advertised bids for a longitudinal evaluation of CETA which was to be a follow-up study of

CETA participants. This was a particular point of contention because ASPER thought it was a mistake to plan elaborate interviews and re-interviews with program participants while only data from social security records would be available for the control group. Eventually, the plan was killed by the Assistant Secretary for Manpower under OMB pressure, prodded by ASPER. OPER had autonomy in designing the process evaluation and in April released a draft which was to be a request for proposal (RFP) on administrative process to complement a future longitudinal impact study. The RFP called upon the contractors to analyze the ways prime sponsors were using their authority in terms of the distribution of services and to focus upon specific questions such as institutional change, degree of decategorization, role of community groups and advisory councils in the planning process, use of CETA funds to displace the costs of previously locally funded services, the client groups served, and analysis of training costs. Sample surveys of prime sponsors were to be conducted in four regional projects. The purpose was to gather broad impressions about the changes in institutions and delivery of services caused by CETA, and to gather baseline data on effectiveness for use by the Manpower Administration in administering technical assistance to prime sponsors. There was no explicit link with the impact data to be eventually gathered, although the document stated that the link would occur in the future. This vagueness made ASPER uneasy.

In March, the OMB desk officer who was responsible for CETA evaluation questions surveyed the plans for evaluation of the program which were to go into effect in the new fiscal year.[10] He was in regular contact with the ASPER evaluation unit and shared their belief in the fullest possible integration of treatment and impact data. As he watched the conflict and inconclusive scuffling between ASPER and OPER over the two RFPs, he concluded that an integrated system was not going to emerge and that a great deal of money might be wasted. He also observed that no links were planned between the management information system intended for CETA, to be operated by the prime sponsors, and the administrative process evaluation plans. Therefore, he wrote a memo to the directors of CETA and OPER and the Associate Manpower Administrator for budget and management information and threatened to stop funding of any plans until something was done to get the information networks meshed in complementary ways. It was not clear to him that he would prevail, but he intended to fight it all the way up to the top of OMB and at least make a record of an OMB position. It should be added that he was a former close associate of Pierce Quinlan, the head of CETA, having once worked for him in the Manpower Administration. He described his thinking about the issue:

> The evaluation and field management systems are free-floating, non-interlocking systems. I thought it important that we decide what we want to

know from management information and evaluation. I talked to everybody. . . . (The OPER people) suffer from historical paralysis. . . . Do things the way they did in the past, i.e., evaluate with contracts. Decide what to do, call academics in and set objectives and put out RFP's. They let the management group draw up an information system. . . .[11]

He said that he had written a memo to the head of OPER which called for an integrated management information and evaluation system. Then, the process evaluation came to him and it incorporated none of the meshing he wanted:

I blew my stack—wrote the memo. Then said I would stop the money. That got them. It's big bucks. The lack of interrelationships was evident. People started looking more seriously.[12]

The RFP to study CETA implementation was suspended by William Kolberg, the Assistant Secretary for Manpower, after a meeting of the CETA Policy Committee in the Manpower Administration. OPER fought for their plan but they had a new antagonist, Pierce Quinlan, the director of CETA, who had, up to that time, shown very little interest in the design of the evaluation for CETA. He was now concerned about two things. First, he wanted to have the MIS funded. Second, he saw an opportunity to find a use for some of his surplus staff who were left over from old categorical programs. This was in connection with Kolberg's idea to dispense with the use of contractors for the process evaluation and to rely upon newly-trained department staff instead. Kolberg decided that an internal staff would be built to design and carry out a new administrative process evaluation which would be integrated with an impact survey to be developed in cooperation with ASPER and the Census Bureau.

The OMB examiner who had triggered these actions commented: "I was late on this because I didn't reckon with the strength of the bureaucratic walls that divide these people." He was not sure what the final product would be and was sure that he could not design an integrated system, but he wanted the department to try. He reported that his superiors in OMB were very much behind him and would be talking to the under secretary about the issues.

Kolberg had been the head of OPER and knew the history of separation between evaluation and program administration. It was his hope that the development of a full-time departmental research staff would reduce that gap. He saw these events as an opportunity to transform the Manpower Administration as a bureaucracy to meet the functional demands of the new federal role in CETA.

The Steering Committee

A steering committee was created by Kolberg which was to develop the process evaluation design. There were three men from the program side on it, representing CETA, field operations, and administration and budget, respectively. They sat with representatives from OPER. ASPER was not involved in the work of the administrative process evaluation.

As a result of this development, the OPER evaluation division was forced to fight a war on two fronts. The steering committee worked over the summer and fall to develop process evaluation plans. ASPER continued to provide design guidance to OPER on the impact plan. The responsibility to develop a CETA evaluation plan lay with the Manpower Administration, and the ASPER role was solely that of technical assistance. One result was that the ASPER staff never met the representatives from the program divisions who sat on the steering committee. OPER dealt with each group separately.

The CETA steering committee was chaired by Seymour Brandwein, the head of OPER evaluation. A working group of technical staff was to draw up the actual evaluation plans according to guidelines set by the steering committee. Final authority was lodged in the CETA policy committee, composed of division directors, which had been the parent group for the initial implementation of the Act and which was chaired by the assistant secretary. In his memo to the steering committee, Kolberg said that the change from contract research to the use of Manpower Administration staff to design and run evaluations was intended:

> to integrate the policy, management and evaluation of CETA into a comprehensive whole and to ensure that federal staff are the direct beneficiaries of evaluation information. The direct involvement of MA staff in the evaluation will enable the Manpower Administration to be more responsive to policy and management changes required as a result of operating experiences.[13]

The first meeting of the steering committee saw a disagreement over the interpretation of their assignment. The chairman assumed that the committee would advise him on how to improve the canceled RFPs and rewrite them. The program staff insisted on beginning the design over again. They wanted answers to questions which would permit them to fulfill CETA administrative responsibilities. They had been the key members of the group which had written the regulations for CETA in the spring of 1974. They wanted evaluation knowledge which would permit them to assess how well the regulations were working in securing compliance with the law.

Bob Jones of the CETA staff was the informal leader of this group. He explained what kind of knowledge program people wanted by saying that:

> Program people want to hang their hats on specific, hard data items. They don't want to be able to say, "you could do it better." Want to say, yes or no and hang their hats on compliance activities. The dream is to have a three-month study of CETA which will say that, "these things worked out for these reasons," so that I can go in and change the regulations to make it work. The evaluation is unable to assess the importance of things because of the squishiness of factors. Can't make hard conclusions. So the evaluation guy, like any researcher, is unwilling to lay himself on the line. He comes up with generalities. Let the program guy make the decision.[14]

He admitted that this was a limited viewpoint on the part of program staff and he expressed a concern that the national direction of CETA could turn into a new exercise in federal monitoring and enforcing. However, he added:

> All I'm trying to do is raise questions. I'm trying to ensure that evaluation tests the assumptions we put in the regs. That's a pedestrian viewpoint but that's all I can demand at this point. To the extent that we find information on earnings and placements I think they will be lost. They will be late in coming and will be ignored. There will be new programs and knowledge won't affect them.[15]

The program representatives insisted that a new beginning be made on the design of the process evaluation and that the old RFP plan be scrapped. The continuing disagreement between evaluation and program staff on the steering committee, and between Brandwein and Jones, was over the degree to which the process evaluation should ask questions that would contribute to the national management of the program. Brandwein and his staff were less interested in management than in developing broad descriptive pictures of delivery systems. They saw the program people as focusing too narrowly and the program people saw them as failing to link inquiry to the needs of management.

ASPER and OPER

In July 1974, Ernst Stromsdorfer, an economist on leave from Indiana University, became head of the ASPER Evaluation Unit. The assistant secretary had been particularly keen to have Stromsdorfer because he wanted ASPER to emphasize technical assistance to the agencies. This was in keeping with the trend toward institutionalizing evaluation capability within the agencies. Stromsdorfer saw his role as an educative one and was determined to deal with OPER with an attitude of respect and forbearance even in the face of lack of cooperation.

However, his basic values were academic, and he had the economists' skepticism of government bureaucracies because they did not pass market tests in the services they offered. He also had strong negative views about the "Connecticut Avenue" contractors who did much evaluation research because he thought that they did poor work and were 20 years behind academia in their methodology. His chief responsibility in regard to the CETA evaluation plans was to help design the longitudinal study (CLMS). His chief recourse, if he disagreed with the plans, was to persuade OMB of his view.

His first experiences with OPER were discouraging. The talks dealt with the design of the longitudinal study of CETA. He wanted agreement on a model of CETA as a delivery system in which there would be a link between different strategies of service delivery, such as classroom instruction or on-the-job training, and the subsequent experience of clients. He thought of this as a formal production function model and was quick to dismiss the kind of knowledge which program officers wanted as "management information." He had no direct perception of their views, but as the expressed desire for short-run information about institutional change came to him through the reports of the Steering Committee and the working group, he could see the trend and did not like it.

There were several difficult meetings between ASPER and OPER staff about questions of sample size and whether the process and impact studies could be explicitly joined. Seymour Brandwein, the head of evaluation in OPER, was skeptical of the latter possibility. He continued to talk of the process evaluation as a two-year experimental pilot study. Such findings might be able to be built into the impact study in time, he felt.

The Plan

However, on July 17, OPER produced a document which laid out a comprehensive evaluation plan for CETA embodying both process and impact information. Neither the steering committee nor ASPER liked it. It fell between stools and did not satisfy the priorities of either group. The CETA program people saw it as far too loose and impressionistic and directed that it be rewritten and focused on federal responsibilities for implementation of the law. ASPER saw it as simply another variation on a process evaluation—"something their contractors would write"—which was seeking short-run information for management decisions but which was not joined to the long-run need to know about the impacts of programs. Nor did they see a link between the study of delivery and impact.

The paper began with an emphasis upon the importance of increased earnings as the chief "long-term" criterion for evaluating manpower programs. It then asserted that such knowledge was several years off in the future and that information about the achievement of short-term criteria was required. The legislation was said to point to some of these, such as the assumption that the shift of authority to state and local government "will result in a constructive and effective approach to program formulation" with community participation in goal setting, efficient consolidation of programs, and the matching of training programs to local area employment needs. There was also a need to know about program operations. Were the administrative support systems of the prime sponsors adequate? Was there fruitful intergovernmental cooperation?

The bulk of the paper dealt with the plans for the short-term "implementation" survey of a sample of 60 prime sponsors by Manpower Administration staff which was to begin soon thereafter. The short-term criteria were said to be derived from the "CETA concept" of institutional change, i.e., decentralization, decategorization, and consolidation. These criteria were drawn from the goals which were explicit or implicit in the legislation about the advantages of prime sponsorship for matching delivery of services to the needs of local populations and employment situations. There were also criteria for assessing how efficiently the sponsors organized, planned, and actually delivered services. When these two kinds of information were combined with the regular quarterly reports on the disposition of trainees in programs and eventual job placement which were to be sent by sponsors to the regional offices and Washington, a knowledgeable basis for technical assistance and program revision would exist.

The "long-term" survey was focused upon the subsequent earnings of trainees when compared to a control group and the relative effectiveness of different service delivery strategies in that regard. The intention was expressed that the long-term and short-term studies could somehow be linked. The 60 prime sponsors of the first study were to be included within the 150 studies of the long-term effort. An effort would be made to relate program formulation factors, such as the role of planning councils, and program operations, such as classroom training, to increases in long-term earnings. The study was described as one continuous effort parceled out in three phases. The first period would be a mapping of institutional changes. The second focus would be on changes within and across programs in strategies and priorities of services. These two phases comprised the short-term effort. The long-term survey would draw on the first two and have its findings in place by 1978. Toward the end of this four-year period, it might be possible to see the interplay between institutional changes, program changes, and effects on earnings.

The document did not provide a formal, production function model of CETA as a delivery system in which delivery strategies were linked to outcomes. Possible relationships between the two dimensions were discussed in the most general terms. Nor were the institutional change variables dealt with in a systematic way in terms of the kinds of evidence that would be required to assess change. Rather, they were discussed in general, impressionistic terms. The general tone of the paper was that of an exploratory effort in which it was going to be determined if certain things had happened and if those phenomena could be related to a number of possible consequences.

The document was too broad and diffuse for the CETA staff on the Steering Committee and for ASPER, but each wanted something different from it. The program managers wanted greater specification given to measuring institutional changes. ASPER wanted a more rigorous production function model of CETA with clear causal linkages stipulated. Each was critical of undue emphasis upon the demands of the other.

It was not so much that the program people and ASPER each denied the legitimacy of the viewpoint of the other but that there was little mutual interest. OPER, of course, was caught in between while each protagonist sought to bend OPER to its will. A bureau such as OPER resists adopting the agenda of an external group because then it will have to adapt its staffing, repertoire, and routines to carry out the new agenda. Often this cannot be done without disrupting the stable patterns of the bureau and the implicitly accepted notion of the health of the unit. So one should not have expected perfect cooperation between ASPER and OPER, or between OPER and the rest of the Manpower Administration. ASPER was making demands for methodological understanding which may have been beyond the ken of most of the OPER staff. They were being asked to develop new internal professional capabilities without additional staff. These demands were not only a threat to individuals in the evaluation unit but to the identity of the unit as a whole. ASPER efforts at persuasion about matters of sample size and the functions of a control group did not really get to the heart of the problems. The office of evaluation had to find its own way to design the CETA plan in order to keep internal stability and health. On the other hand, the demands of the CETA members of the steering committee ran against the grain of a long practice of maintaining autonomy in the setting of evaluation targets and planning projects. Except for the small consulting unit described earlier, OPER evaluators had always seen themselves as working for the assistant secretary, not for program managers. The document of July 17 very much reflected these competing demands and tensions, and it would be most surprising if it had not done so.

Denouement

In September, ASPER and OPER reached an agreement that OPER would go ahead with plans for the administrative process evaluation and for the Comprehensive Longitudinal Manpower Survey. There was a compromise that the process plan would be labeled a management oversight study which would lack links to the eventual impact work and that the CLMS would be regarded as a pilot which would prepare the way in 18 months or so for the full impact survey by exploring methodological problems. This study would embody both treatment and impact data collection so that the two might be joined. ASPER had compromised on the initial process of management oversight work because of a greater concern for the CLMS and what would follow. Rather than fight against a management overview, they would leave that to the program people and work on OPER to make sure that the CLMS was properly done. The sample size had to be increased, the questionnaire was to have minimal qualitative inquiries, and it would be susceptible to machine scanning. The sample of prime sponsors would be paid to provide reports on program inputs beyond those required by the regular MIS.

At the same time, the program staff members of the Steering Committee asked that the process evaluation be revised to make it even more directly answerable to the needs of program managers. In September, a responsive memo was written by OPER for the CETA policy committee which set out the general scope of the inquiry. The first phase of the study was to begin immediately and produce findings by the spring of 1975. Subsequent work would be blended with longer-range, process-impact studies in ways not explicitly set out. Clearly, the emphasis was upon meeting the short-run needs of CETA program staff in order to report to Congress during the appropriations process and revise regulations and guidelines, if necessary. The underlying theme was the necessity to test the assumptions in the act to see if the institutional changes called for were taking place.

Answers to these questions were to be obtained from site visits to a sample of 66 prime sponsors by teams of Manpower Administration staff drawn from Washington and the regional offices. The methods of data collection were to be impressionistic. The interviewers were to talk with representative staff and other citizens conversant with CETA in the field and then write descriptive reports under categorical headings. No particular concern for scientific exactitude was expressed. This was not a survey which specified and measured changes in variables in order to link such changes to outcomes.

During October, the time of the program managers on the steering committee was absorbed in preparation of the administration plan for public employment in the face of the growing recession; they did not pay attention to the actual development of the instruments of inquiry. In October, OPER sent the process evaluation and CLMS plans to OMB for approval. It subsequently became clear that departmental clearance to do so had not been given. The normal chain of events was for the Manpower Administration, ASPER, and the Assistant Secretary for Administration to approve evaluation plans. However, OPER staff were concerned that time was passing and there were no evaluators in the field to capture the first months of the new program.

The program examiner in OMB who received the plan for review was the same person who had triggered the creation of the steering committee in the spring with his memo. Now, in November, he was confronted with the fruits of that work and did not like them. His first objection to the field research plan was that it was a very loose series of questions through which interviewers were to record their impressions. It was a device for reporting, not survey research. His second objection was that it was not related to the CLMS. He found that OPER staff could not answer the question of how the questions were to be related to a model of CETA. Rather, they saw themselves as seeking discrete answers to specific questions:

> . . . the process and impact studies got separated to serve separate offices. ASPER would do their mathematical thing on impact and OPER would do process. There is no linkage . . . the god damn thing will produce an enormous volume of bits. It will never get pulled together. There is plenty of provision for impressionistic studies. We want hard data linked to models that can tell us how the program is operating in terms of certain assumptions. . . .[16]

He placed the blame on the failure to create a research capability in OPER. The OPER staff were being asked to perform beyond their capacities. This OMB perspective was clear enough. It was congruent with the ASPER view and influenced by it.

In the next weeks of the Christmas season, there was continuous wrangling in long meetings about what to do about evaluation. OPER argued strongly to Kolberg that he fight for departmental approval of the process evaluation as it had been designed. Quinlan announced plans to conduct his own short-run evaluation of CETA development and said that he would hire the OPER consulting unit headed by Green to do the study. OPER petitioned ASPER to write an analytical foreword to the existing CLMS so that it, too, might win OMB approval. Stromsdorfer replied that he would be glad to help but that all the questions in the instrument had to be logically related to the model of the delivery system.

After several weeks of negotiations, three separate studies finally emerged. CETA was to conduct its own short-run descriptive study of what was happening in the program. OPER would go ahead with its process evaluation.[17] The under-secretary asked OMB to agree to this but told ASPER to impose future design constraints on what was done. Finally, ASPER and OPER were able to agree on a CLMS design as a pilot for the ultimate impact evaluation. The Steering Committee was abolished by

TABLE 1

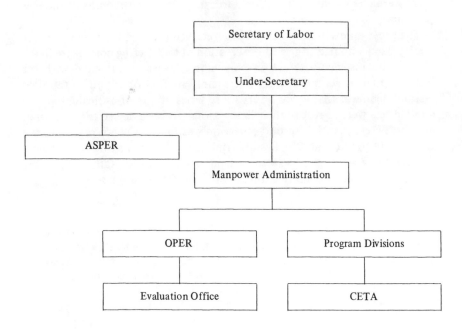

Kolberg as quickly as he had created it. He concluded that it was a terribly divisive force and something of a laughingstock.

There had been an institutional splintering of the CETA evaluation effort into three original tendencies, each of which was rooted in a different part of the department. Institutional missions were stronger than ideas. Kolberg and Quinlan were worried about going before congressional committees in a recession in the spring of 1975 with no data about program performance. Therefore, when OMB broke the whole thing apart, the strongest incentive was to accept the disagreements and get the evaluation moving as quickly as possible lest they be naked in the spring. The under-secretary seemed to have been much less concerned with the merits of the different plans than with the necessity to reach agreement and get a CETA plan evaluation going. When the fragile bonds of unity symbolized in the Steering Committee were broken, there was no incentive on anyone's part to put them back together.

Conclusion

Three incomplete approaches to knowledge emerged:

1. ASPER analysts wished a comprehensive evaluation research plan based on a production function modeling of the delivery system and its consequences.

2. CETA program managers wished to use evaluation to assess the degree to which prime sponsors conformed to the regulations.

They expected to use the data from the Management Information System to evaluate the efficiency of individual prime sponsors. They did not place much value on the ASPER plan for a production function modeling of services and outcomes.

3. The OPER evaluation staff were not competent to develop a research design based on a production function model. They also sought independence of CETA program managers as best they could. They were without the help of friendly contractors and, therefore, floundered.

One might ask whether anything was lost by the splintering of efforts. Perhaps separate kinds of knowledge should be sought in different places. This is a realistic conclusion. Each part of the department would get the information it needed to do its job. It is undesirable to try to force a holistic approach to knowledge in the absence of agreement about what is needed. It is also the case that no one knew how to combine the diverse modes of thought into one research plan. Much was lost in the process nonetheless:

1. It would have been useful for ASPER analysts and CETA managers to join forces in production function studies. Federal managers could have used knowledge of effective delivery strategies as the basis for federal technical assistance to prime sponsors.

2. It is not clear that the OPER evaluation unit had a useful role. It lacked professional competence and looked to contractors who were not integrated into the work of the department.

3. Production function knowledge is important but not sufficient. One also needs knowledge of institutional processes. Program managers knew this because of their responsibilities. ASPER was not sensitive to this need.

4. Research strategies are needed which provide both knowledge of production functions, as in the CLMS, and studies of the prime sponsors as institutions. In fact, the Employment and Training Administration is moving in that direction. The CLMS is underway, and the Office of Research and Development in OPER is sponsoring research on institutional change and service capabilities of the prime sponsors.[18]

But ASPER and CETA program managers have not collaborated in developing or utilizing this knowledge. The work of creating organizational unity is even more difficult than that of creating conceptual and methodological unity.[19]

The structure of the CETA programs provides possible remedies for these deficiencies of method and organization. Research strategies which tie together inquiry about impact, treatment, and institutional processes could be developed over time. If the decentralized structure of the program continues, Washington officials may see their responsibilities in a more foresighted way. They will look beyond the monitoring of prime sponsors and ask how they might encourage and strengthen prime sponsors to so organize themselves that effective service delivery strategies are implemented. All kinds of evaluation knowledge would be necessary. They must self-consciously broaden their understanding of their roles in this way. If this happened, the incentives for collaboration on evaluation within the department might be increased.

Notes

1. Rufus E. Miles, "The Origin and Meaning of Miles' Law," *Public Administration Review*, No. 5, September/October 1978, pp. 399-403.
2. Erwin C. Hargrove and Gillian Dean, "The Search for Accountability: Changing Manpower Service Delivery under CETA," prepared for the National Commission for Manpower Policy, forthcoming in *Policy Analysis*. Carl E. Van Horn, "Implementing CETA: The Federal Role," *Policy Analysis*, Spring, 1978, pp. 159-184.
3. Jon H. Goldstein, *The Effectiveness of Manpower Training Programs: A Review of Research on the Impact on the Poor*, Paper No. 3.
   Studies in Public Welfare, Subcommittee on Fiscal Policy of the Joint Economic Committee, Congress of the United States, November 20, 1972, Washington, D.C.: U.S. Government Printing Office, 1972.
4. Paul Berman and Milbrey W. McLaughlin, *Federal Programs Supporting Educational Change: Volume IV, The Findings in Review*, Santa Monica, California: The Rand Corporation, 1975.
5. In 1975 the name of the agency was changed to the Employment and Training Administration.
6. Interview with Seymour Brandwein, Department of Labor, 1974.
7. Interview with Pierce Quinlan, Department of Labor, 1974.
8. National Academy of Sciences, *Knowledge and Policy in Manpower: A Study of the Manpower Research and Development Program in the Department of Labor*, Washington, D.C.: 1975, Chapter 9.
9. Memos and interviews, 1970-71. Evaluation Program Files, The Urban Institute, Washington, D.C.
10. This person preferred not to be identified by name. He took the characteristic OMB view that he was not acting as an individual but serving an institution. In fact, the director of his unit and the associate director of OMB for Human Resources supported his actions.
11. Interview with DOL program examiner, Office of Management and Budget, 1974.
12. *Ibid.*
13. Memo of Assistant Secretary William Kolberg to CETA Evaluation Steering Committee, Department of Labor, 1974.

14. Interview with Robert Jones, Department of Labor, 1974.
15. *Ibid.*
16. Interview with DOL program examiner, Office of Management and Budget, 1974.
17. After the first wave of field interviews, OPER cancelled the process evaluation because of the unreliability of the data.
18. Two continuing research projects which illustrate the direction OPER should take are: William Mirengoff and Lester Rindler, *The Comprehensive Employment and Training Act: Impact on People, Places and Programs,* Washington, D.C.: National Academy of Sciences, 1976; and Randall B. Ripley, *The Implementation of CETA in Ohio,* R. and D. Monograph 44, Washington, D.C.: U.S. Government Printing Office, 1977.
19. The result is that very little is known about how well a program which costs $9 billion a year is working.

1980 (150-159)

JOSEPH S. WHOLEY

The Role of Evaluation and the Evaluator in Improving Public Programs: The Bad News, the Good News, and a Bicentennial Challenge

Editor's note: The following is adapted from speeches given at the 1975 Conference on Evaluation sponsored by the National Conference of State Criminal Justice Planning Administrators and at the Management Science Workshop held in conjunction with 1976 ASPA National Conference.

A number of people have asked me to talk and write on "The Role of Evaluation and the Evaluator." I have real trouble doing that.

One problem is that the word "evaluation" seems to cover everything from multi-million-dollar social experiments to one-day site visits.

Second, many people think that evaluation can help others; few think that evaluation will help them do their own job better.

Finally, to many people, evaluation is an activity that produces long, inconclusive reports that are never used for anything. In fact, the most frequent complaint about evaluation, both from evaluators and from their intended audience, is that evaluations aren't useful or aren't used.

What, then, is evaluation—and what is its role?

We define *evaluation* as systematic measures and comparisons to provide specific information on program results for use in policy or management decisions.[1]

By definition, then, the role of evaluation is to provide feedback on program results for use by policy makers and program managers. But policy makers and managers *already* get plenty of informal feedback on program results. Evaluation may be too costly or too time-consuming to help the busy policy maker or manager enough to be worth his time and attention.

In point of fact, evaluation is seldom sufficiently timely, relevant, and conclusive to provide useful feedback to decision makers.

A number of observers have noted that unrealistic expectations have often been raised about the results that can be achieved by evaluation because:

• Many programs are operated without a clear and agreed-upon statement of the objectives of the program, expressed in measurable terms. (In such cases, one cannot expect evaluation studies to answer the crucial question as to whether the program is meeting its objectives.)

• Many programs operate on a very limited scale, providing resources to meet only a small fraction of the need. Frequently, evaluation studies seem to be inconclusive regarding the impact of the program. (In such cases, it is not the evaluation study that is inconclusive; it is the program impact that is inconclusive.)[2]

The *good news* for today is that some evaluation processes are available that:

• are relatively simple and inexpensive.

• promote fruitful interaction and communication between evaluator and intended user of evaluation information, and

• provide information useful for policy formulation and program management.

We have found at least two ways in which evaluators can help policy makers and program managers who are willing and able to direct their programs to some specific objectives; I'd like to share these with you today.

A Role for Evaluation in Policy Formulation and Communication

It is often very difficult to get agreement on policy directions, either within large organizations or between organizations.

Evaluators can help identify, document, and clarify the most important objectives of a project, a program, or an agency, documenting or helping develop agreed-on measures of success which can then be used in communicating policy directions and managing for results.

In many programs, of course, just spending the money is the objective. In a good many other cases, however, the program is intended to produce certain activities, outcomes, or impacts beyond the spending of money—and evaluators can help those in charge to agree on what is to be accomplished.

The best example I have seen of this evaluation role was in the planning for Cincinnati's Community Sector Team Policing Program, where evaluators helped police department planning personnel to specify measures of process and outcome corresponding to department objectives. Some of those measures were then used from time to time in managing the program.[3]

We have been excited to find that evaluators can communicate with decision makers. One useful technique is to contrast the decision makers' broadly stated program goals with the absence of measurable objectives and plausible links between program activities and objectives.[4] Through close interaction with policy makers and program managers, evaluators can then help decision makers to focus on achievable objectives and to specify their needs for information on the results of program activities.

By getting reactions to suggested measures and comparisons, evaluators can help secure and document agreement (or disagreement) on measurable program objectives and can clarify the feasibility and costs of measuring progress toward objectives and of testing hypotheses relating program activities to program objectives.

Documenting the extent to which there exist (a) agreed-on measurable objectives, (b) plausible, testable hypotheses linking program activities to objectives, and (c) intended uses for evaluators' feedback and helping policy makers and managers to define program objectives in measurable terms (processes we have called "evaluability assessment" and "program design") are among the most valuable services that evaluators can provide. Like evaluation itself, these pre-evaluation efforts are justified to the extent that policy makers and managers desire the direction and accountability that exist in an evaluable measurable program.

These types of interaction can be useful whether or not an evaluation of the program is carried out. Many programs would profit from participation by an evaluation specialist during the early planning and implementation stages.

Interaction among management, evaluators, and subordinate organizational units will be required to ensure that measurable objectives and specific measures and data collection procedures are defined appropriately. Such definitions of objectives and measures of progress can be important in ensuring that a public agency is in a position to properly manage implementation of its most important programs.

A Role for Evaluation in Program Management

Evaluators can provide managers with current information on resources expended, activities implemented, and results achieved, comparing actual program performance with some fixed or relative standard while the program is in progress. When program performance is judged inadequate, management can take corrective action; e.g., in funding or refunding decisions or redirection of program activities.

A number of potentially useful tools for monitoring federal, state, and local programs have been developed and tested:

• Relatively inexpensive, systematic *telephone surveys of* random samples of relevant federal/state/local program staffs and recipients of program services, from which one can obtain statistically reliable objective and subjective data on what services are actually being delivered by the program (to what extent are process objectives being met?) and what are staff members' and recipients' attitudes toward and experiences with those services (to what extent are output objectives being achieved?);

• *Signaling systems* that present information on which local projects are performing "extremely well" or "extremely poorly," displaying the relative performance of projects that are comparable from the managers' perspective;

• Comparisons of *actual project performance with expected project performance,* using information obtained from site visits, from project reporting systems, or from anonymous surveys.

The results have shown the power and potential utility of relatively inexpensive performance monitoring systems:

• In the Cincinnati Police Division, surveys of police officers', citizens' and aides' attitudes and experiences reversed a tentative decision to kill the Community Service Aide (police paraprofessional) Program.[5]

• In the Cincinnati Police Division, anonymous surveys of patrolmen and first-level supervisors were used to determine whether planned delegation of authority was actually in effect; *telephone surveys* of businessmen and households were used to determine whether hoped-for changes in police behavior, citizen attitudes, and crime rates had occurred.[6]

• In a health education demonstration program, *telephone surveys* of federal regional office staff members, state agency staff members, local Community Action Program staff members, and Head Start project directors and Head Start teachers were used to determine whether the planned program had been implemented and to learn the attitudes, opinions, and experiences of those involved in the program.[7]

• For the national Legal Services Program, a highly structured *site visit* data-collection schedule and site visit reporting format were developed to obtain observers' *subjective appraisals* of the quality of services delivered by each Legal Services project and effectiveness of those services in meeting national program goals.[8]

• In the District of Columbia, *observers' ratings* of the cleanliness of streets and alleys (based on comparisons with reference photographs) were used to monitor the effectiveness of the Sanitation Department.[9]

• In a child health care demonstration program, *quarterly progress reports* on health services required by each child and health services delivered to each child were used to monitor individual projects.[10]

• In the Atlanta Public Schools, the *relative achievement levels* of children in schools serving children from similar socioeconomic backgrounds were compared in monitoring the overall effectiveness of individual schools.[11]

If you haven't read John Waller's *Monitoring for Government Agencies*[12] (in fact, if you haven't read it in the last week or so), I strongly urge you to spend some time on it.

How Evaluators Can Play a Stronger Role

Since evaluation has so seldom been useful (not sufficiently conclusive, relevant, and timely to be used), the prudent evaluator will *interact with and involve potential users* of the information in order to estimate which evaluations are worth the cost of implementation.

In our experience, the evaluations that can be done in a non-experimental program are usually quite simple. Talking to potential users about how and whether they would use the evaluation information that can be provided helps focus limited evaluation resources on important, answerable questions.

Frequently, the evaluator has to *create a market* by showing himself or herself useful in small, simple ways early in the game. (If an evaluator can't produce *something* useful in the first six months, he or she's not going at his job right!)

Evaluation is a relatively new product—experience tells us that this particular product hasn't been used very much to date. Just as with other new products, evaluation programs need *market research* to determine consumer attitudes toward and experiences with their products in particular, the uses made or not made of their products, the reasons for use or non-use, and consumer views on how the products could be made more useful.[13]

We have found it extremely helpful to go back to customers to measure their satisfaction with, and use of, evaluation products after they have had opportunity to review and react to the evaluations. By formally or informally monitoring his own success, the evaluator can pick up clues as to how he can enhance the values of his services.

In 1973, The Urban Institute's Program Evaluation Group went back to our customers to get their appraisal of the utility of our past products. We identified demands for evaluations that more closely fit the short time constraints faced by policy makers—and demands for inclusion of narrative/anecdotal data as a part of, or companion to, quantitative evaluations.[14] By interacting with their customers, other evaluation groups can get their own clues as to what types of information are needed, wanted, and likely to be used in their own environment.

Conclusion

For many years evaluators and administrators have been meeting in conferences and workshops.

Sometime in this, the Bicentennial Year (or very soon thereafter!), I'd like to see an evaluation conference in which all the papers have the same title: "How Evaluation Was Used in Improving the Programs in Our Agency."

This could be a three-day conference, two-day conference, or a one-day conference. In my judgment, the specific focus on *use* would do a lot for evaluators—and for citizens and taxpayers throughout the country.

Notes

1. The word "we" is used more than editorially. Many of the thoughts expressed here result from interaction with colleagues at The Urban Institute over the last several years, including, in particular, Peter Bloch, Garth Buchanan, Sumner Clarren, Pamela Horst, Dona Kemp, Joe Nay, John Scanlon, Richard Schmidt, Alfred Schwartz, Leona Vogt, John Waller, Donald Weidman, Bayla White, Thomas White, and Richard Zamoff.
2. Joseph S. Wholey, et al., "Evaluation: When Is It Really Needed?" *Evaluation Magazine,* Vol. 2, No. 2 (1975), pp. 89-93.
3. See the series of reports by Alfred Schwartz and Sumner Clarren on evaluation of Cincinnati's Community Sector Team Policing Program (Washington, D.C.: The Urban Institute, 1974-76).
4. See Pamela Horst, et al., "Program Management and the Federal Evaluator," *Public Administration Review,* Vol. 34, No. 4 (July/August 1974), pp. 300-308; and Joseph S. Wholey, et al.
5. Alfred Schwartz and Sumner Clarren, *Evaluation of Cincinnati's Community Sector Team Policing Program* (Washington, D.C.: The Urban Institute, final report, in draft).
6. Alfred Schwartz and Sumner Clarren, *Evaluation of Cincinnati's Community Sector Team Policing Program: A Progress Report* (Washington, D.C.: The Urban Institute, March 1975).
7. Richard Zamoff, et al., *Evaluation of Head Start Experience with "Health That's Me" in the Second Year* (Washington, D.C.: The Urban Institute, September 1973).
8. Hugh Duffy, et al., *Design of an On-Site Evaluation System for the Office of Legal Services* (Washington, D.C.: The Urban Institute, 1973).
9. Louis Blair and Alfred Schwartz, *How Clean Is Our City?* (Washington, D.C.: The Urban Institute, October 1972).
10. Leona Vogt, et al., *Health Start: Final Report of the Evaluation of the Second Year Program* (Washington, D.C.: The Urban Institute, December 1973).
11. Bayla White, et al., *The Atlanta Project: How One Large School System Responded to Performance Information* (Washington, D.C.: The Urban Institute, March 1974).
12. John Waller, et al., *Monitoring for Criminal Justice Planning Agencies* (Washington, D.C.: The Urban Institute, August 1974, and U.S. Government Printing Office, March 1975), revised and reprinted as *Monitoring for Government Agencies* (Washington, D.C.: The Urban Institute, February 1976).
13. See Richard Schmidt, et al., *The Market for Evaluation Services in the Department of Health, Education, and Welfare* (Washington, D.C.: The Urban Institute, May 1974).
14. John W. Scanlon, *Urban Institute Program Evaluation Staff Self Assessment,* Urban Institute working paper, June 1973 (unpublished manuscript, in draft).

1976 (679-683)

LARRY POLIVKA
LAUREY T. STRYKER

Program Evaluation and the Policy Process in State Government: An Effective Linkage

During the last 20 years, government at all levels has experienced enormous growth. At the state level, expenditures have grown more than 200 percent and the number of programs has increased several fold since 1970. This growth and complexity in the public sector has made the relationship between program evaluation and public policy a major concern of evaluators, policy analysts, and public officials.[1]

The nature of this relationship will become an even more pressing issue if revenue shortages continue or worsen and some federal programs are shifted to the states with reduced funding. State executives and legislators will need to make hard decisions concerning the expansion, continuation, or reduction of programs. The need to justify these decisions in terms of objective, rational criteria drawn from data-oriented policy analyses and program evaluations is likely to increase as policy makers attempt to limit the ability of interest group lobbies to set the policy agenda and the terms of debate concerning uses of state resources.

If evaluation results are to be used consistently in the public sector, some means must be found to move program evaluation from the periphery to the center of the policy and budget-making processes so it can play a role more equal to that of other sources of information (financial, political, etc.) in the development of public policy. In fact, if this does not occur, program evaluation may fall victim to the budget reductions required by the fiscal retrenchment in the public sector.

The following questions must be addressed in any effort to improve the effectiveness of program evaluation by making greater use of evaluation results:

1. Where should the evaluation function be located?
2. How should evaluation topics and questions be chosen?
3. What mechanisms exist or should be created to relate evaluation find-

ings to the principal decision-making processes of state government (policy development, program planning/monitoring, and budgeting) and to increase the probability that policy recommendations will be implemented?

4. How should evaluations be conducted and presented in order to maximize their use by decision makers?

5. What should be the evaluator's role in stimulating the use of his/her studies?

In this article, we attempt to address these questions through an assessment of one state's (Florida's) effort to develop an effective program evaluation capacity by integrating it with part of the state policy process. The Florida experience cannot provide definitive answers, but it does suggest steps that can be taken by other states interested in making their evaluation activities more effective.

Organization of the Evaluation Unit

In 1979, Governor Bob Graham created an evaluation and program review unit (PRE) in his Office of Planning and Budgeting (OPB). The Office of Planning and Budgeting consists of six policy units covering broad program areas (education, natural resources, general government, human services, public safety, and economic development) which are responsible for guiding the development of the governor's policy priorities and formulating the governor's budget recommendations for submission to the legislature.

The principal purposes of the evaluation unit are to:

1. Bring a rigorous analytical perspective to bear on agency budget requests;

2. Assess agency effectiveness in meeting program objectives established by the legislature and the governor;

3. Develop program performance outcome measures that serve as the basis for performance agreements between the governor and agency secretaries.

The unit consists of eight professional positions supported through general revenue and federal grant funding. An average of 20 studies are conducted annually, ranging from the very broad in scope *(The Effectiveness of Community Alternatives to Institutions)* to the relatively narrow *(An Assessment of the State Dredge and Fill Control Program)*.

The studies cover a wide spectrum of methodological approaches, including simple, short-term policy analyses based on investigative reporting techniques, systematic program assessments based on a secondary analysis of available quantitative data, and more elaborate outcome evaluation designs based on extensive data collection and statistical analysis. The PRE unit has also encouraged and assisted agencies in establishing program monitoring systems designed to make evaluation a routine activity.

Regardless of methodology, all of the studies are policy oriented and culminate in a series of recommendations prepared in collaboration with agency and governor's office staff. The final recommendations are sent to the governor for his review and approval.

Research conducted or sponsored by the unit has been used to influence major budget allocation decisions, formulate executive policies, develop legislation, and provide feedback on the implementation status of the governor's goals.

Effectiveness of the Evaluation Unit

In the following section, we discuss the major questions concerning the issue of evaluation effectiveness (i.e., impact on policy and budget) in terms of our experiences in the PRE unit over the past three years.

Location of Evaluation

The unit's ability to conduct studies that influence decisions is partially a function of the protected visibility and accessibility to agencies, the legislature, the governor's chief policy advisors, and the budget development process provided by the unit's location in the governor's Planning and Budgeting Office.

Florida's experience indicates that the state budget office, particularly if it is in the governor's office and has a formal policy-planning role, is one of the best places to develop an evaluation/critical analysis capability. This conclusion is true both in terms of what the unit can do itself and what it can do to support evaluation efforts throughout state government by being relatively immune to the self-serving interests of agencies and the political crosswinds and constantly shifting priorities of the legislature.

The foregoing does not mean that evaluation work cannot be effectively conducted in agencies or by legislative staff. Agency research staff are frequently in the best position to conduct studies that are sensitive to the concrete realities and organizational nuances of these programs, and legislative staff are frequently in the best position to conduct studies with greatest likelihood of having a direct policy impact. These activities, however, are no substitutes for the presence of an evaluation capacity at the heart of the executive branch.

Leviton and Hughes note that:

> Communications within bureaucracies tend to be obstructed. . . . "Communication through the bureaucratic hierarchy can adversely affect utility, because the evaluator may fail to gain a complete, unbiased idea of the user's needs."[2]

The location of the PRE unit in the governor's Planning and Budgeting Office and the process used to select projects remove some of the bureaucratic obstructions to clear communication. They insure that the projects selected and issues addressed have a high priority with key decision makers, and that the results of studies are communicated directly to them. Direct access to the policy and budget development mechanisms also reduces the possibility of distortion.

Leviton and Hughes also point out that one of the main threats to the credibility of evaluations is the "suspicion that the researchers have been coopted or have suppressed information."[3] The location of the PRE unit outside the agency whose programs are evaluated reduces this actual or perceived credibility threat. The principal PRE evaluation clients do not have the same vested interests in programs as agency staff. As a result, negative findings are less likely to be glossed-over, and positive findings are more likely to be accepted as valid by external audiences.

Selection Process

Each year the unit solicits high priority research topics from the agencies, governor's office staff, and the legislature. A background report is prepared on each recommended topic that describes the major policy question and probable research strategy required to complete the study. A package containing the research topics and background reports is sent to the governor, who reviews and sets priorities for the topics. As a rule, his top 15 topics constitute the main annual research agenda for the unit.

The active participation of key decision makers in the selection process is an important step in the effort to influence policy through evaluation, although it is no guarantee that they will use the results. Their lack of involvement, however, would substantially reduce any chance of effectively using the results in the policy process, and also would increase the risk that the results will not be relevant to the resolution of major issues.

Implementation of Recommendations

All of the policy recommendations contained in studies conducted by PRE are developed through negotiations with agency and legislative staff after review and approval by policy experts in the governor's office. The final recommendations are approved by the governor's planning and budgeting director and submitted to the governor. Implementation occurs through incorporation of evaluation results into the following policy development, budgeting, and program monitoring mechanisms.

• *The Governor's High Priority Policies Statement.* Each year the governor's policy specialists and the agencies prepare a set of rank-ordered policy positions for the governor's review and approval. During the past three years many of the evaluation-based recommendations have been selected as policy priorities and used in the development of the agency policy guides and the state budget. The governor's statement is also used by the policy specialists as a major criterion for the annual selection of evaluation topics.

• *Agency Policy Guides.* The policy guides contain an extensive analysis of the major issues confronting each state agency, followed by a discussion of the chosen policies, including detailed justification for each choice. Evaluation findings and recommendations often surface as chosen policies.

• *The Budget Development Process.* PRE staff review each budget request submitted by the agencies in a program area where an evaluation has been conducted to determine the extent to which the request reflects the recommendations generated by the evaluation. PRE staff give their review comments to the policy and budget specialists to use as a source of information in deciding whether to support, modify, or reject agency budget requests.

• *Performance Agreement Monitoring.* Each of the executive agencies prepares an annual performance agreement with the governor's Planning and Budgeting Office. The agreement contains a number of quantitative performance measures that indicate how much progress the agency intends to make in achieving the governor's policies related to their agency's mission. Many of the evaluation-generated recommendations are incorporated into the measures. Agencies provide quarterly status reports on the measures.

• *Program Budget Measures.* Process (efficiency) and outcome (effectiveness) variables either used in the conduct of evaluations or developed from evaluation findings are included in the biennial budget recommendations the governor submits to the legislature. This approach represents an effort to develop fairly precise cost-effectiveness estimates tied to narrowly defined programs. The number of programs affected, however, is limited given the large number of programs defined as budget entities (more than

200) and the relatively small evaluation capacity that is limited to studies in high priority areas.

• *Legislation.* Several PRE evaluations have produced recommendations that require new legislation or changes in current law in order to be implemented. Many of these recommendations become a part of the governor's annual legislative agenda.

The evaluator should be prepared to exploit every opportunity to use evaluation results in the policy and budget decision processes. This is particularly true of opportunities to routinize the use of evaluation results by integrating them into the more formal kinds of mechanisms described above. If evaluation results are not systematically included in formal decision-making processes, their use will depend on the sponsorship of individual decision makers or the exigencies of the moment. The support of key public officials and propitious timing are important, but they are not sufficient if the goal is to move beyond the episodic, haphazard use of results toward a more consistent and comprehensive method of evaluation utilization.

Participation in the policy and budget development mechanisms permits continuous verbal communication of evaluation results, which can be a more effective means of ensuring utilization than the reading of written reports. Participation in these mechanisms also allows the evaluator to "broker knowledge" from sources other than PRE conducted or sponsored studies (e.g., journals and research from other states).

Formal policy and budget development mechanisms support a relatively rational approach to the assessment of issues and programs, and are far more open than less formal policy development procedures to evaluation information. The governor's political priorities, the bureaucratic turf-guarding concerns of agencies, the intuitive knowledge of dedicated and experienced agency staff, the interests of legislators and their staff, the lobbying of interest groups, and the availability of objective information including evaluation results interact in frequently unpredictable ways to generate the policy framework for government activities. Within this context, the credibility of evaluation and policy analysis research is largely a function of the balance that is maintained among the goals of being responsive to the political agenda of the clients of the research, adhering to sound methodological and data interpretation procedures, and taking full advantage of opportunities to participate actively in the policy and budget development processes.

Evaluation Strategies

PRE staff have been flexible in selecting research methods. This approach assumes an advanced level of technical training and practical competence on the part of the evaluation staff. Practical competence means that an evaluator can create innovative combinations of standard evaluation research techniques under conditions of uncertainty and in a political environment of competing and frequently contradictory interests. Consequently, it is important that the evaluator have substantive knowledge of the program to be studied and the political factors influencing the key policy issues.

PRE staff make a systematic effort to prevent evaluation studies from carrying more methodological baggage than personnel resources, time, the scope of concern (What is it that is important to know?), and the assurance of a reasonable level of validity permits or requires. Thus, PRE studies have covered a wide range of methodological refinement, from simple assessments and formative evaluations based on a few interviews with key informants and reviews of documents to elaborate studies involving many variables and complex statistical procedures.

PRE staff have addressed several policy issues through a series of studies conducted over a period of two to three years. For example, policy issues concerning the relative cost/effectiveness of community alternatives to mental hospitals, training schools for delinquents and prisons have been the focus of eight studies since 1979. These issues have major budgetary and ideological implications and need to be thoroughly researched as the community programs expand. PRE and agency staff will continue the collection of evaluation data on community and institutional programs for the next several years and amend policy recommendations as more information becomes available.

Role of Evaluator in Implementation of Recommendations

Because of the PRE unit's autonomy from the agencies and the legislature, the presence of evaluators and policy budget specialists within the same organizational unit, and the several implementation mechanisms described above, the evaluator/analyst is in a position to play a relatively active role in the implementation of policy recommendations based on evaluation findings. Through direct, daily contact the evaluator has an opportunity to inform or remind the policy and budget specialists of the findings and recommendations of studies. In most cases, the specialists have been involved in the development of the study design and the policy recommendations and thus have at least a general acquaintance with the content of a particular study.

The development of the governor's Priorities and Policies Statement, the Policy Guides, the Agency Performance Agreement, and the Program Budget Measures depend on the generation and use of an expanding body of objective information generally and evaluation findings in particular. Consequently, PRE staff have been provided an array of opportunities to use evaluation results in the formulation of policies, program plans, monitoring procedures, and the budget.

One or both sides to a policy or budget dispute frequently use evaluation results as ammunition. Partisanship in the use of evaluation results increases the chance that the results will have a significant impact on policy. It also increases the chance that the findings will be distorted and manipulated. Direct, continuous contact with policy and budget specialists, and agency and legislative staff and participation in the formal policy development mechanisms have provided PRE staff with numerous opportunities not only to bring evaluation results into the policy-making arena, but also to limit the possibility that they will be distorted in debate.

Evaluation results can help frame the domain of debate. Weiss has pointed out that:

> Research evidence does sometimes serve to reduce conflict by narrowing the zone of uncertainty. It establishes which variables are implicated in outcomes, something about their relative importance, and the inter-relationships among them. It keeps people from arguing about what actually is, and saves them time to deal with the issue of values—with what ought to be. Although it does not resolve the policy issue, it focuses debate more sharply on its problematical and value-related facts.[4]

PBS, ZBB, MBO, and other policy planning and budgeting innovations of the last 20 years have contributed to efforts to clarify and rationalize the development of public policy. Evaluation, however, has made a more direct contribution to the substance as opposed to the form of policy decision making by often focusing on the fundamental value choices that are inherent in the decision to initiate or terminate a policy or to increase or reduce funding for a program.

PRE staff attempt to maintain a balance between the need to actively pursue the use of evaluation results and the requirement that the evaluator not infringe on the role of the policy and budget specialist. In short, the evaluator must be sensitive to the political and psychological nuances of the volatile environment in which she/he works.

Conclusions

The location of the PRE unit, the procedures used to select projects, and the participation in formal policy development and budgeting processes have substantially broadened the domain in which evaluation can function as part of the policy process in Florida state government. Evaluation results have been used to build a body of objective information that is essential to the effective operation of a formalized policy process. The use of evaluation results has also influenced the cognitive style of the emerging policy process by helping rationalize the discussion of what is (by "narrowing the zone of uncertainty") and sharpening the focus of value issues (what ought to be). The use of results from a series of correctional studies may illustrate these conclusions.[5]

The findings from these studies have shown that several stereotypes about the inmate and probation populations and assumptions about program effectiveness are either inaccurate or incomplete. A near majority of inmates have relatively minor crime records (two prior arrests or less) and were never arrested for a violent crime. A majority were not armed (70 percent) when committing the crime for which they were sent to prison, and more than 70 percent of the population 24 and under were never placed on probation prior to their incarceration. In short, many inmates do not appear to be a serious threat to the safety of the community. This information has been used to inform the debate over how much to spend for new prisons and to encourage the search for community alternatives to prisons.

The same studies have also shown that participation in prison programs (e.g., vocational training) can have a positive influence on an inmate's ability to adjust (avoid reconviction and unemployment) in the community after release. This information has provided an alternative to the pervasive notion that "nothing works" in corrections and that funding for programs should be cut or kept at a low level.

Through the use of the policy and budget development mechanisms, these findings have contributed to the emerging debate over what to do about rising crime and prison overcrowding. They have helped to broaden the debate to include such policy issues as sentencing strategies, crime and employment, community alternatives, and expedited releases from prison. By illuminating "what is" (who goes to prison and what happens when they leave?) the evaluations have helped to broaden and deepen the debate over what ought to be (who should go to prison and what should prison do?).

More specifically, the findings and recommendations from these studies have been used to formulate policies which call for the incarceration of violent and repetitive property offenders and a few other categories of offenders who represent a clear and continuing threat to the safety of the public and the development of specific types of community sanctions (restitution, community services, fines, house arrest, etc.) for many non-violent, first-time offenders who now go to prison. These policies and others concerning the direction of prison programs (more vocational training and job placement activities) are reflected in the agency policy guides, the budget, performance agreements, and the other policy implementation mechanisms described above. They are also reflected in the final recommendations of the Florida Task Force on Prison Overcrowding, which was composed of the governor, attorney general, and several legislators.

In summary, our experience indicates that program evaluation can play a consistently influential role in the policy and budget development processes of state government if the following conditions are met:

1. Evaluations are done by a unit organizationally close to key decision makers, rather than buried in the bureaucracy;

2. Key decision makers are actively involved in the selection of evaluation topics and the formulation of research designs;

3. The policy budget development processes have a formal structure with relatively rational decision making procedures that are heavily dependent on information, including evaluation data;

4. Evaluations are clearly designed to address a significant policy issue(s) and are neither any more or less methodologically sophisticated than is required to make a reasonably valid, relevant, and timely contribution to the resolution of the policy issues;

5. The evaluator is prepared to play an assertive role in the policy and budgeting processes by clearly articulating and actively defending policy positions most compatible with the findings of her/his study;

6. Evaluators are not demoralized by the fact that decision makers will frequently make policy choices that are responsive to factors other than evaluation findings. Political and fiscal conditions, change and evaluation findings and recommendations which are initially rejected may later be used in the generation of new or amended policies.

Finally, evaluation does not necessarily contribute to the technocratic domination of public policy—to increasing the power of "experts" over elected officials. Evaluation can produce information and provide an analytical perspective that are essential to breaking policy deadlocks, to the emergence of policy issues that have been long suppressed, and to a general opening-up of the policy process that broadens participation and facilitates debate concerning questions of value. Evaluation may be a product of technocratic inventiveness, but its use can be a means of advancing politics by illuminating what is, defining alternatives, and providing part of the framework for a greatly expanded discussion of policy choices.

Notes

1. Carol Weiss, "Where Politics and Evaluation Meet," in *Evaluation 1*, Vol. 3, pp. 37-45; H.R. Davis and S.E. Salasin, "The Utilization of Evaluation," in E.K. Struening and M. Gutlentag (eds.), *Handbook of Evaluation Research*, Vol. 1, Sage; M. Rein and S.H. White, "Can Policy Research Help Policy," *The Public Interest*, Vol. 49 (Fall), pp. 119-136; V.G. Neilsen, "Why Evaluation Does Not Improve Program Effectiveness," *Policy Studies Journal*, Vol. 3, No. 4 (Summer), pp. 385-389; R. Agarwala-Rogers, "Why Is Evaluation Research Not Utilized?" in M. Gutlentag (ed.), *Evaluation Studies Review Annual*, Vol. 2, Sage; G.B. Cox, "Managerial Style: Implications for the Utilization of Program Evaluation Information," *Evaluation Quarterly*, Vol. 1, No. 4 (December), pp. 499-508; Carol Weiss and M.J. Bucuvalas, "The Challenge of Social Research to Decision-Making," in C. H. Weiss (ed.), *Using Social Research in Public Policy Making*, Lexington Books; L.E. Lynn, Jr. (ed.), "Knowledge and Policy: The Uncertain Connection," *National Academy of Sciences*, M.C. Alkin, R. Daillak and P. White, *Using Evaluations: Does Evaluation Make a Difference?*, Sage; Laura Leviton and Edward F.X. Hughes, "Research on the Utilization of Evaluation: A Review and Syntheses," *Evaluation Review*, Vol. 5, No. 4 (August), pp. 525-548.
2. Leviton and Hughes, *op. cit.*
3. Carol Weiss, "Improving the Linkage Between Social Research and Public Policy," in L.E. Lynn, Jr. (ed.), *Knowledge and Policy: The Uncertain Connection*, National Academy of Sciences, p. 76.
4. Leviton and Hughes, *op. cit.*
5. "The Adult Corrections Issue Paper," Office of Planning and Budgeting, Office of the Governor, Florida, 1982.

1983 (255-259)

ROY L. LOVVORN
MARGUERITE GILSTRAP

Evolution of a Research Program
on Weed Control

Agricultural losses from weeds, which have now reached an estimated five billion dollars annually, are equal to those from both insects and plant diseases.

This article reviews the factors that led to a recent expansion in federal-state weed research, the thinking behind the choice of a division in a research bureau as the proper administrative level for the work, and some of the concepts of the present program. It also examines certain administrative problems that are arising as the program moves forward.

Background

Crop losses from weeds first began to show up strikingly during World War I. They were especially alarming in the Grain Region and the Cotton Belt where big farm holdings were being increasingly mechanized and where persistent species of noxious annual and herbaceous perennial weeds had become established.

Many of these weed species were brought to this country during the nineteenth century by immigrants who carried their own crop seed for planting the new land. By 1900 the major weeds of Europe and many from Asia and other continents had gained a foothold in areas favorable for their growth. During the same period exploitative farming had paved the way for aggressive native species to invade millions of acres of cropland.

An infestation of bindweed brought the problem to a head in the thirties. As often is the case the first solution attempted was through legislation. Several states in the Grain Belt passed laws requiring individual farmers to control the bindweed on their land and assessing penalties on those who failed to do so. Unfortunately, farmers did not know how to control the weed, and officials soon found the regulations could not be enforced. Their recognition of the seriousness of the problem led them to ask for research assistance.

A federal-state research program to find measures for the control of bindweed was initiated in 1935. The project, for which there was an appropriation of $40,000, was placed under the direction of an agronomist in the Division of Cereal Crops and Diseases in the Bureau of Plant Industry of the United States Department of Agriculture. The small amount of weed research previously carried on in the Bureau had been in connection with studies in the Office of Botany designed to improve the grazing areas of public lands. In moving weed investigations to the Division of Cereal Crops and Diseases, Bureau officials were influenced by the fact that bindweed was most serious on land formerly planted to grains and that methods of control must be tied in with grain production. Possibly another factor was the effective pattern of cooperative work with the state agricultural experiment stations pioneered by leaders in the Division.

Eight states—California, Colorado, Idaho, Iowa, Kansas, Minnesota, Nebraska, and Washington—joined with the USDA in organizing regional research to tackle bindweed. Preliminary conferences considered the work already in progress and mapped plans for strengthening it and initiating new investigations.

Cooperative arrangements between the USDA and the states followed a well-established pattern. Each cooperator agreed to a memorandum of understanding which defined objectives of the study and responsibilities of the participants. Specific operating procedures and lines of supervision were set up for the various work units.

There is no set pattern for the separate work units of a project. Each is designed to fit in with the facilities and personnel of the cooperating experiment station. In some cases they are manned by USDA scientists for whom the state provides office and laboratory space, land for field plots, and machinery for working them. The state's responsibility may also include professional, clerical, laboratory, and field assistants or the USDA may pay for part or all of the personnel in the unit. In some states, the USDA pays a part of the salary of a scientist on the station staff assigned to the cooperative work.

The administrative framework of a project was adequate for the combined studies on bindweed, and within five years the researchers had some satisfactory control methods for it. By that time, however, other weeds had gained headway and in some areas were responsible for greater crop losses than bindweed.

Increasingly aware of the weed problem and of the need to discuss it and endeavors of common interest, state regulatory officials took the leadership in setting up the first weed control conference organized in the United States. Federal-state scientists, representatives of chemical and farm machinery companies, and farmers assisting in the regulatory programs were asked to join the Western Weed Control Conference inaugurated in 1939. Annual meetings enabled workers to get a clearer picture of the size and complexity of weed problems in the region, to enlist public interest in them, and to compare techniques and jointly plan cooperative projects in federal-state research to overcome weed infestations. In 1944 a similar conference was formed in the North Central States. The Northeastern Conference was organized in 1947 and the Southern Conference got under way the following year.

The first increase in funds came in 1947 when the USDA appropriation of $46,000 was boosted to a little more than $90,000. An important factor in the expansion was a dramatic new herbicide—2,4-D. Scientists working on fundamental studies of plant physiology at the Plant Industry Station, Beltsville, Maryland, during the war had first suggested its use. While researchers in the weed project were still making tests to determine the extent of its value the compound was placed on the market. Farmers did not wait for the tests to be completed. Thousands of them bought the powerful compound, and some suffered losses because research had not developed principles for its use.

The immediate task facing the researchers was to work out safe and effective methods for using potent compounds on a wide scale. Beyond that, the discovery that growth regulators could be used to control weeds opened up a wide avenue of study. The need for a broader structure of research was apparent.

Establishment of the Division of Weed Investigations

In addition to the original bindweed project—gradually expanded over the years to include studies on other weeds in grains and on the new herbicides—a number of smaller research investigations had been initiated in the Bureau. These were concerned with the control of certain weeds in other crops—for example, alligator weeds in sugar cane, and grassy weeds in cotton. The studies were limited in scope in most cases, claiming the attention of a researcher who divided his time between the weed study and other duties. Neither he nor the division head who supervised him was interested in weeds primarily. The work was incidental to other crop research. There was no formal arrangement by which the men giving part time to weed studies could discuss their common experiences and compare their findings with those of others working on related weed problems.

The situation called for a new administrative framework for weed investigations, in which several lines of scattered research could be brought together and weed research could be given the recognition its importance warranted. It should be a part of the Bureau of Plant Industry, Soils, and

Agricultural Engineering since the study of weeds is essentially a plant subject. To dovetail into the organization, the expanded structure should be a division, since 1934 the Bureau's major administrative unit. At the time the decision on weed investigations was in the making there were ten plant divisions set up for the most part on commodity lines, three divisions of soils, and four of agricultural engineering. Plans for combined research are worked out by heads of the divisions. For the work in weeds to receive proper emphasis, it was necessary that it be represented by a leader on a par with the division heads. He must be in a position to view the whole function of weed research, to recognize problems in the order of their importance, and to give priority to the more serious ones.

Interested agricultural groups in the Grain Belt and the West made the first move to obtain a division of research. At their request a bill proposing the establishment of a weed division in the Bureau of Plant Industry, Soils, and Agricultural Engineering was introduced in Congress in June, 1947. The measure was opposed by Department officials on the grounds that the necessary authorization was already available, that this would be the only division in the Bureau established by specific legislation, and that the action might cause administrative difficulties in the future. They said the division would be organized as plans could be worked out and funds were available.

Beginning in 1948, additional funds for weed studies were included in appropriations under the Research and Marketing Act of 1946. In that year an RMA sum of $60,500 was added to the regular appropriation of $93,490. The following year an RMA appropriation of $76,500 was added to the regular appropriation of $98,930; and in 1950 RMA funds totaling $116,700 were made available in addition to the regular appropriation of $91,310.

The Division of Weed Investigations was inaugurated in January, 1950. In announcing the administrative decision to establish the Division, Dr. R.M. Salter, then chief of the Bureau said, "Reorganization does not mean any immediate marked expansion in resources. It does emphasize, however, that the importance and scope of weed research has progressed to a point where the interests of the program can now be handled most satisfactorily through a responsible organization on a par in all respects with other units handling functions similar in degree of importance."

Administration of the Program

Today we know that control of many of the persistent noxious weeds encroaching on our land is too big a job for individual farmers. Even so, the research program is based on the concept that good farming is the first step toward weed control, that it is cheaper to prevent weeds than to control them, and that much can be done to prevent weeds through seed certification, crop rotation, and other well-established practices.

Research on weeds can be done most effectively by pooling resources of the Division with those of other agencies in the USDA, with other federal agencies, with the state agricultural experiment stations, and with industry. A large body of fundamental studies in plant physiology, ecology, and chemistry must be carried on continuously if scientists are to come up with long-term answers to the weed problem.

Work in the Division is set up in seven projects. They are concerned with research on (1) weeds in field crops; (2) weeds in horticultural crops; (3) weeds on grasslands and range; (4) weeds associated with irrigated farming; (5) perennial weeds; (6) physiological characteristics of weeds; and (7) the evaluation of chemical herbicides.

Weed researchers work closely with the crop specialists. In approaching a number of problems the crop specialist has selected the varieties to be grown and the methods of culture, the weed man has chosen the chemicals or other controls to be evaluated. Experience has shown that these relations must be developed cooperatively in man-to-man encounter and that they must be based on mutual confidence.

In addition to conducting basic research on plany physiology and the ecology of weeds, the Division works closely with the Bureau researchers who carry on fundamental studies of plant growth regulators and related compounds and with farm machinery specialists who are concerned with the design principles of new tools for applying herbicides and for other methods of weed control.

Departmentwise, weed research is coordinated through a departmental committee in which a representative of the Division meets with men from the Soil Conservation Service, the Forest Service, and the Bureau of Entomology and Plant Quarantine. The Division is responsible for reviewing all manuscripts prepared by USDA researchers on brush control. It cooperates in an advisory way with the Production and Marketing Administration, which is responsible for issuing labels when products have been thoroughly tested for approval under the pesticide regulatory act.

Cooperation with the Department of the Interior on research to control weeds in irrigation waters dates back to 1947 and provides an excellent example of harmonious working relationships between government agencies. An interdepartmental committee on weeds serves as a clearinghouse on subject matter and legislative proposals.

In evaluating new chemicals for herbicidal purposes, the Division obtains compounds from other agencies in the USDA and from the National Research Council, the Department of Defense, and many industries. Out of the screening studies are coming suggestions for synthesizing new compounds that may be of even greater value than those under study. Even more important may be the better understanding of the relationship between chemical structure and plant toxicity in families of compounds. The Division conducts these studies in cooperation with industry.

Following a long tradition of federal-state research, the Division has cooperative work in progress with eighteen state experiment stations. Although the work of the states must be directed primarily toward the solution of weed problems within their geographic boundaries, findings may be applicable in other states. The Division assists the states in planning and coordinating research and in defining regional and national limitations of results. It helps in assembling annual data accumulated by all cooperators, summarizing the findings, and making them available to everyone concerned.

Several states are cooperating with the Division and with the Department of the Interior in the search for methods of controlling halogeton, a poisonous weed now infesting 2 million acres of range land in the Inter-Mountain States.

To keep up with the rapidly growing literature on weeds and related subjects, the Division compiles a quarterly bibliography covering publications in this country and other parts of the world to which it has access. The compilation issued in July, 1952, listed 335 articles. The greatest number—69—dealt with physiological investigations. The bibliography is published in the new magazine *Weeds,* initiated in 1951 by members of the regional weed control conferences and others interested in weed research.

Problems and Achievements

As one would expect, the more serious difficulties in administering weed research arise out of the size and scope of the weed problem itself. As the public becomes more aware of present losses and potential threats, great pressure is brought to bear for research to find immediate solutions. The fact that chemical herbicides are being developed at a phenomenal rate and that new ones are continually coming into the picture has intensified this pressure. On the surface it appears that we have wonderfully effective tools. All that is needed are practical measures for using them.

One of the major tasks is to get the time, manpower, and money to build up a reservoir of fundamental research, out of which may come the practical applications. The time element must be stressed. Basic studies cannot be hurried.

As L.M. Stahler pointed out at the 1951 North Central Weed Conference, "We have had neither time nor manpower to inquire into and to establish the underlying or basic reactions, causes, and principles associated with the discovery or development of new materials or new practices that we have fitted to practical field use. This is a real weakness in our research."

There is now considerable evidence that the chemical approach to weed control will require continuous research. As research gets the upper hand over one noxious pest, another moves in to dominate the scene. This has been strikingly demonstrated in the Ohio River Valley where wild cucumber, somewhat resistant to 2,4-D, replaced giant ragweed as the number one pest at the end of a two-year spraying program.

As in many other areas today, the big problem is getting and keeping trained personnel. The Division must compete with a rapidly expanding industry that wants men with the same broad training in agronomy, horticulture, botany, and chemistry.

The size of the job already calls for more travel—and more funds for travel—than are provided at this time. Mounting costs for research make it necessary continually to revise plans to cope with them.

On the credit side of the ledger, weed research is now well established in the federal-state pattern. It is supported by a large group of well-informed men—regulatory officials, crop specialists, farm leaders, and people in the chemical and farm machinery industries. An example of the broad cooperative approach to the problem may be found in the remarkably uniform recommendations for field applications of herbicides prepared by research extension and regulatory agencies in the North Central Conference and used in some twenty states and Canadian provinces. This uniformity is particularly impressive in view of the fact that none of the compounds now most widely used were known to the weed specialists ten years ago. Today they help to control the weeds on more than 20 million acres of rich cropland.

1953 (33-37)